THE MORALITY OF ADOPTION

RELIGION, MARRIAGE, AND FAMILY

Series Editors

Don S. Browning
John Witte, Jr.

THE MORALITY OF ADOPTION

Social-Psychological, Theological, and Legal Perspectives

Edited by

Timothy P. Jackson

William B. Eerdmans Publishing Company
Grand Rapids, Michigan / Cambridge, U.K.

© 2005 Wm. B. Eerdmans Publishing Co.

Wm. B. Eerdmans Publishing Co.
255 Jefferson Ave. S.E., Grand Rapids, Michigan 49503 /
P.O. Box 163, Cambridge CB3 9PU U.K.

Printed in the United States of America

10 09 08 07 06 05   7 6 5 4 3 2 1

ISBN-10: 0-8028-2979-1
ISBN-13: 978-0-8028-2979-5

www.eerdmans.com

Contents

Series Foreword

The Religion, Marriage, and Family series has a complex history. It is also the product of some synergism. The books in the first phase evolved from a research project located at the University of Chicago and supported by a generous grant from the Division of Religion of the Lilly Endowment. The books in this new phase of the series will come from more recent research projects located in the Center for the Study of Law and Religion in the School of Law of Emory University.

This second phase of the series will include books from two of this Center's projects, both supported by generous grants from The Pew Charitable Trusts and Emory University. The first project was called Sex, Marriage, and Family in the Religions of the Book and began with an Emory University faculty seminar in 2001. The second project was called The Child in Law, Religion, and Society and also was initiated by a semester-long Emory faculty seminar that met during the autumn of 2003.

Although the first phase of the Religion, Marriage, and Family series primarily examined Christian perspectives on the family, it also included books on theological views of children. In this second phase, family in the broad sense is still in the picture but an even greater emphasis on children will be evident. The Chicago projects and the Emory projects have enjoyed a profitable synergistic relationship. Legal historian John Witte, director of the two Emory projects, worked with practical theologian Don Browning on the Chicago initiatives. Later, Browning worked with Witte on the research at Emory. Historian Martin Marty joined Witte and Browning to lead the 2003 seminar on childhood.

Some of the coming books in the Religion, Marriage, and Family series will be written or edited by Emory faculty members who participated in the two seminars of 2001 and 2003. But authors in this new phase also will come from other universities and academic settings. They will be scholars, however, who have been in conversation with the Emory projects.

This series intends to go beyond the sentimentality, political manipulation, and ungrounded assertions that characterize so much of the contemporary debate over marriage, family, and children. In all cases, they will be books probing the depth of resources in Christianity and the other Abrahamic religions for understanding, renewing, and in some respects redefining current views of marriage, family, and children. The series will continue its investigation of parenthood and children, work and family, responsible fatherhood and motherhood, and equality in the family. It will study the responsibility of the major professions such as law, medicine, and education in promoting and protecting sound families and healthy children. It will analyze the respective roles of church, market, state, legislature, and court in supporting marriages, families, children, and parents.

The editors of this series hope to develop a thoughtful and accessible new literature for colleges, seminaries, churches, other religious institutions, and probing laypersons. In this post-9/11 era, we are all learning that issues pertaining to families, marriage, and children are not just idiosyncratic preoccupations of the United States; they have become worldwide concerns as modernization, globalization, changing values, emerging poverty, changing gender roles, and colliding religious traditions are disrupting families and challenging us to think anew about what it means to be husbands, wives, parents, and children.

In *The Morality of Adoption: Social-Psychological, Theological, and Legal Perspectives,* editor Timothy Jackson has assembled and introduced a state-of-the-art discussion on the theology and ethics of adoption. At first glance, adoption is a wonderful thing. Christians have rightly considered themselves as a people adopted by God, and adoption has been a central Christian practice for many branches of Christianity.

But the practice of adoption also raises many profound questions that are illuminated by the chapters in this book. What are the proper motivations for adoption? Should it be done to fulfill parental desires or to meet the needs of an abandoned child? Who should adopt? Should adoption be restricted to married couples? Should singles be allowed to adopt? Should gays and lesbians have the right? Should we be able to adopt children from different racial and ethnic groups? What about the ethics of adopting children from other countries? Should adopted children have a right to know their natural parents? The questions go on and on.

The answers to these questions are not simple. Yet the questions themselves are seldom discussed from an explicitly Christian theological and ethical perspective — at least not carefully. But the outstanding group of scholars in this volume do discuss and throw much light on these questions. At a time when more and more children over the world are seeking adoption and a time when foster care seems in a state of crisis, it is time for society and religious institutions to address this neglected topic.

DON S. BROWNING *and* JOHN WITTE, JR., *editors*

Acknowledgments

This book grew out of a project on "Sex, Marriage, and the Family" funded by The Pew Charitable Trusts and administered by The Center for the Interdisciplinary Study of Religion at Emory University. I would like to thank Pew and the Center for their generous support, especially the Center's director, John Witte Jr. Professor Witte it was who first suggested that I translate my growing interest in adoption into a collection of essays.

I would also like to thank The Institute for Research on Unlimited Love and its president, Stephen G. Post, for a related grant. The opinions expressed in these pages are those of the authors and do not necessarily reflect the views of The Pew Charitable Trusts, the CISR, or the Institute.

Third, I greatly appreciate two permissions to reprint material in this book: the *Christian Century* graciously allowed me to reprint three "Letters to Derek" by Gilbert Meilaender, and New York University Press similarly let me reprint Sandra Patton-Imani's "Navigating Racial Routes."

My debt to the individual contributors to this volume is deep and obvious, but I would like before closing to express my gratitude to two extraordinary editors: Gina Weiser, of Emory, and Hannah Timmermans, of Eerdmans.

All of the above made this book both possible and necessary.

General Introduction

TIMOTHY P. JACKSON

Demographics and Definitions

"Separated At Birth In Mexico, United At Campuses On Long Island" —
so reads the full-page headline of the *New York Times'* "New York Report"
for Monday, March 3, 2003.[1] The remarkable story beneath the banner
tells of how Tamara Rabi and Adriana Scott, twin girls from Guadalajara
adopted by different families at birth, ended up meeting each other as college students in New York twenty years later. Tamara had been raised Jewish in an apartment in Manhattan, while Adriana had been brought up
Roman Catholic in a house on Long Island; Tamara was attending
Hofstra, while Adriana was enrolled at Adelphi. Neither woman knew that
her twin sister existed until a mutual friend noted the striking physical
and biographical resemblances and made the connection. The twins' first
contact was by e-mail, and their first meeting in person was in a McDon-
ald's parking lot. Though different in interesting ways, they immediately
hit it off.

The social and ethical complexities of this story make it a ready emblem for contemporary American adoption. Indeed, the unpredictable
"happy ending" for all concerned makes it a very positive emblem, a show-
case for religious and ethnic goodwill within the diverse (yet apparently
small) American melting pot. But there are, of course, more straightforward and less satisfying adoption (and nonadoption) outcomes.

"Agency Admits Errors in Fatal Case of Abused Boy" — so reads the

---

1. "Separated at Birth in Mexico, United at Campuses on Long Island," *New York
Times*, 3 Mar. 2003, Sec. A, p. 25.

nearly full-page headline of the *Atlanta Journal Constitution* for Wednesday, August 20, 2003.[2] In this case, Kyshawn Punter, age two, was beaten to death by his stepfather,[3] Shaun Stewart, age twenty-five. Investigators found that the child welfare workers for Georgia's Division of Family and Child Services "repeatedly made mistakes and violated policies" in this instance.[4] The boy had twice been removed from his Atlanta-area home because of suspected abuse, only to be returned by county DFCS agents and a juvenile court. At the time of the beating, the child's mother, Shanderi Punter Stewart, a soldier, was stationed at an army base in South Carolina. Thus the stepfather, the suspected abuser, was the sole parental custodian. Ms. Stewart denies having any prior awareness of her son's being harmed or in danger, but one wonders why Kyshawn, palpably bruised and battered, was not kept in state custody or moved into foster care.

The bureaucratic mismanagement and altogether too predictable "unhappy ending" of this story have made Kyshawn Punter almost literally a poster boy for the overhaul of the state DFCS in Fulton and Dekalb counties. Just two days after reporting the boy's violent death, the *AJC* ran a story detailing a class-action lawsuit that "charges that Georgia's current social services system fails at both ends of child protection."[5] Kyshawn's sad fate was again rehearsed to drive home the question of whether state workers act appropriately to reunite children safely with their parents or, alternatively, to move them into foster care or adoption "within a reasonable period of time."[6]

This book collects a number of essays on the social-psychological, theological, and legal dimensions of American adoption practices, both positive and negative. As a preliminary to the essays, some data, definitions, and a typology may prove helpful: There are between five and six million adoptees in the United States today, and in 1998 approximately ten thousand adoptions overseen by the federal Department of Health and Human Services crossed racial or cultural lines.[7] Some additional adoption statistics for the United States:

---

2. "Agency Admits Errors in Fatal Case of Abused Boy," *Atlanta Journal Constitution*, 20 Aug. 2003, Sec. A, p. 1.

3. It is not clear whether the stepfather legally adopted the son.

4. "Agency Admits Errors."

5. "Foster Care Suit Expanded," *Atlanta Journal Constitution*, 22 Aug. 2003, sec. C, p. 5.

6. "Foster Care Suit Expanded."

7. Adam Pertman, *Adoption Nation: How the Adoption Revolution is Transforming America* (New York: Basic, 2000), pp. 9 and 211.

- According to the most recent estimates, which include international adoptions, 8 percent of adoptions are transracial.[8]
- International adoptions have increased dramatically over the last decade. According to the U.S. State Department, in 1992, 6,472 children were adopted from abroad. In 1999, the number had increased to 16,396.
- According to the U.S. Department of Health and Human Services, in 1999, 33 percent of children adopted from foster care were adopted by single parents, the overwhelming majority of whom were single women (31 percent).
- It is estimated that about one million children in the United States live with adoptive parents, and that between 2 percent and 4 percent of American families include an adopted child.[9]

The increasing number and legitimacy of various kinds of adoption constitute an ongoing revolution in how families are formed today, especially in the United States. Not only is the American family both changing and being changed by adoption practices, the very definition of adoption is also evolving. "Adoption" can be defined either actively, as taking on a (usually legal) parental role in relation to someone not one's own biological progeny, or passively, as *being taken in* as a (usually legal) son or daughter by someone not one's own biological parent. The first construal focuses on the older, stronger party to the transaction and is no doubt the more common understanding of the term. The second construal, in which accent falls on the younger, weaker party, comes less readily to mind.

Types of Active Adoption

Even when "adoption" is defined actively, as taking on a (usually legal) parental role in relation to someone not one's (legally recognized) biological progeny, there are many general types and subtypes. Some of these types and subtypes are metaphorical rather than literal, or theoretical possibili-

---

8. See, for example, Kathy S. Stolley, "Statistics on Adoption in the United States," *Future of Children: ADOPTION* 3, no. 1 (spring 1993): 34.

9. National Adoption Information Clearinghouse website, www.calib.com/naic/. Accessed August 15, 2003; The Office of Children's Issues, U.S. State Department website, http://travel.state.gov/children's_issues.html. Accessed August 15, 2003; U.S. Dept. of Health and Human Services, Administration for Children and Families, Children's Bureau website, http://www.acf.dhhs.gov/programs/cb/. Accessed August 15, 2003.

ties rather than actual practices, but they are worth listing in some detail if we want to appreciate the moral complexity of the current scene. Below are twenty-one broad divisions and fifty subdivisions. They are not exhaustive or mutually exclusive. Those that are typically judged to be positive or readily acceptable are followed by a plus sign (+); those typically judged to be negative or highly problematic are followed by a minus sign (-); those typically judged to be odd, ambiguous, or even paradoxical, but not quite wrong, are followed by a question mark (?); and those that may be seen as any or all of the above, depending on circumstances, are marked with multiple symbols. I do not always share the judgments indicated — in fact, I will argue against several of them in the pages that follow — but they are evidently widely held.[10]

A. **Self-adoption (? + -)**
   (1) "inner child" therapy wherein one parents one's (former) self (? +)
   (2) cloning wherein one duplicates one's (genetic) self without sexual reproduction (-)

B. **Relative adoption (+)**
   (1) biological relatives — such as aunts, uncles, or grandparents — do the adopting (+)
   (2) stepparents do the adopting (+)

C. **Nonrelative adoption (+ ?)**
   (1) friends adopt (+)
   (2) strangers adopt (+ ?)

D. **Single-parent adoption, when the parent is homosexual (- ?)**
   (1) male adopts male (-)
   (2) male adopts female (?)
   (3) female adopts female (?)
   (4) female adopts male (-)

10. These distinctions are meant to be suggestive, even provocative. My impressions of how American society generally evaluates the various adoptions listed are largely intuitive and anecdotal, but I believe them to be plausible. They are informed by considerable reading, conversation, and experience, yet I have made no effort to poll individuals or groups in a statistically rigorous way. If the reader disagrees with my choice of symbols, she should simply substitute her own and consider her reasons why. I emphasize, again, that A through U are meant to be descriptive of the way Americans commonly judge adoptions; my own normative views will be laid out, with supporting arguments, in Chapter 9.

E. **Single-parent adoption, when the parent is heterosexual (+ ?)**
   (1) male adopts male (+)
   (2) male adopts female (?)
   (3) female adopts female (+)
   (4) female adopts male (?)

F. **Homosexual couple adoption (- ?)**
   (1) gay male couple adopts male (-)
   (2) gay male couple adopts female (?)
   (3) lesbian couple adopts female (-)
   (4) lesbian couple adopts male (?)

G. **Heterosexual couple adoption (+)**
   (1) straight couple adopts male (+)
   (2) straight couple adopts female (+)

H. **Same-age adoption (? -)**
   (1) minor adopts minor (? -)
   (2) adult adopts adult (?)

I. **Trans-age adoption (? +)**
   (1) minor adopts adult (?)
   (2) adult adopts minor (+)

J. **Same-race adoption (+)**
   (1) dark adopts dark (+)
   (2) light adopts light (+)

K. **Trans-race adoption (- ?)**
   (1) dark adopts light (-)
   (2) light adopts dark (?)

L. **Same-religion adoption (+ ?)**
   (1) Roman Catholic and Protestant Christianity (+)
   (2) Judaism (?)[11]

M. **Trans-religion adoption, involving conversion or re-education of the adoptee (+ -)**
   (1) when "one of us" adopts "one of them" (+)
   (2) when "one of them" adopts "one of us" (-)

11. Michael Broyde points out, in Chapter 6 of this volume, that Judaism does not acknowledge the possibility of changing another's identity so as to adopt him or her as a legal heir. One may take on parental responsibilities toward another, but there is no altering or annulling the blood relationship.

N. **Same-nationality adoption (+)**
   (1) democratic adopts democratic (+)
   (2) nondemocratic adopts nondemocratic (+)
O. **Trans-nationality adoption (+ -)**
   (1) democratic adopts nondemocratic (+)
   (2) nondemocratic adopts democratic (-)
P. **Same-class adoption (+ ?)**
   (1) rich adopts rich (+)
   (2) poor adopts poor (?)
Q. **Trans-class adoption (+ ?)**
   (1) rich adopts poor (+)
   (2) poor adopts rich (?)
R. **Same-ability adoption (+ ?)**
   (1) able-bodied adopts able-bodied (+)
   (2) disabled adopts disabled (-?)
S. **Trans-ability adoption (+ -)**
   (1) able-bodied adopts disabled (+)
   (2) disabled adopts able-bodied (-)
T. **Same-species adoption (+ ?)**
   (1) human adopts human (+)
   (2) nonhuman adopts nonhuman, e.g., Zeus adopts Athena (?)
U. **Trans-species adoption (? +)**
   (1) human adopts "higher" nonhuman, e.g., Joseph adopts the Christ (?)
   (2) human adopts "lower" nonhuman, e.g., a pet-lover adopts a dog or a cat (+)
   (3) nonhuman adopts "higher" human, e.g., Mr. Peabody, of cartoons, adopts Sherman (?)
   (4) nonhuman adopts "lower" human, e.g., Zeus adopts a hero as his son (+) or the Christian God adopts the man Jesus (?)

The pattern that emerges across these graded types is that, in most cases, we tend to approve adoptions in which like adopts like, especially when this involves folks *like us* adopting other folks *like us*. When the similarity is of family, race, religion, ethnicity, or class, there are few objections. In some cases, proximity makes for hostility or at least confusion — as when adopters and adoptees are close in age or when they are of the same sex while the parent(s) are homosexual — but these cases are rare. (Apparently, same-sex attraction or seduction is feared in homosexual adoption, even as opposite-sex attraction or seduction may be feared in single-parent adoption, especially if the single parent is a male.) When unlike adopts unlike, however, negative judgments are much more prevalent. What I have called "trans-race," "trans-religion," and "trans-nationality" adoptions often join those that cross (presumed) sexual orientation to elicit objection. When someone alien wishes to adopt "one of us," the misgivings are especially strong.

We also tend to approve adoptions in which a more powerful or better-off party adopts one that is vulnerable or worse-off, of course, and this fact can cut against my affinity hypothesis. We traditionally approve of adults adopting minors, the healthy adopting the sick, and the rich adopting the poor, for example, at least among heterosexual couples. In ancient Rome, citizens were frequently applauded for adopting slaves. In cases like these, however, the approval seems to turn on the anticipation that the "less fortunate" party will eventually *become* like the "more fortunate" (by, for example, growing into maturity, regaining health, inheriting wealth, or acquiring civil status). When the "less fortunate" is thought to be *forever* unlike the "more fortunate," on the other hand, there can be difficulties. As a result of racial prejudice, it is still true in America that some people look askance at the adoption of a black child by white parents, for instance, not to mention of a white child by black parents. As a result of disability prejudice, some also doubt the wisdom of able-bodied parents taking in a permanently handicapped child, and vice versa. Moreover, the profoundly weak and powerless, such as embryos and fetuses, are often not allowed to become the subjects of adoption at all (see John Mayoue's essay herein).[12]

Some criticize mixed-ethnicity, mixed-religion, mixed-race, and mixed-ability adoption not out of prejudice but in an attempt to affirm

---

12. To punctuate his opposition to stem cell research that destroys human embryos, President Bush recently appeared at the White House with babies born from eggs fertilized in vitro and then transferred to the wombs of unrelated women willing to carry them to term and raise them. These embryos were "spare" — i.e., unwanted by their biological parents and the fertility clinics involved — and so would likely have been discarded. "Early adoptions" by mothers (and fathers) not the biological parents seem preferable to Mr. Bush to the discarding by clinics or the destruction by researchers that is the fate of many artificially generated embryos (sometimes called "pre-embryos"). Many people do not agree, of course. See "House Approves a Stem Cell Bill Opposed by Bush," *New York Times,* 25 May, 2005, Sec. A, p. 1.

TIMOTHY P. JACKSON

the distinctive needs and traditions of historically marginalized people. Can Occidental parents really enable an adopted Asian child to discover her roots? Can Christians properly raise an adopted Jew, as such? Will they want to? In America, only blacks can appreciate and affirm the identity of other blacks, and only the disabled can appreciate and affirm the identity of others who are disabled, the argument runs. I recognize some force to this line of reasoning, but it often serves to reinforce old divisions. The challenge is the familiar democratic one of honoring particularizing differences without degenerating into factionalism.

Let me dwell for a moment on transracial adoption. In *Black Boy* (1945), Richard Wright recalls how "having been thrust out of the world because of my race, I had accepted my destiny by not being curious about what shaped it."[13] From childhood, Wright felt like an orphan in his native country, cut off by color prejudice from both himself and the American dream. Paradoxically, something similar can happen when transracial adoption provides a too-protected enclave *within* the world. In her contribution to this volume (Chapter 4), Sandra Patton-Imani documents how being welcomed into a family, independently of race, can preclude a black girl from learning about her racial identity and thus cause her to lose part of her cultural heritage. Patton-Imani relates the poignant testimony of Kristin, a black daughter of white adoptive parents, who likes the story of "Little Black Sambo" but has little sense of its danger and offensiveness. Her parents failed to teach her to recognize and reject racist stereotypes, thus depriving her of still-important survival skills. In Wright's case, alienation from society pushed him toward complacency, even fatalism, in the face of social injustice. In Kristin's case, naive assimilation into society had a similar effect. She was not curious about her racial status and history and thus was overly accepting of the ongoing racism of her wider society.

Exponents of liberal democracy, black and white, often sing the praises of legal nondiscrimination and community integration. And there is surely something profoundly right about this affirmation of human equality and solidarity. As Patton-Imani and others have illustrated, however, colorblindness also has its drawbacks, including in adoption contexts. A black child raised by white parents, like Kristin, may not acquire the defense mechanisms necessary to combat the racism in her own life and in the lives of others. She may even deny her concrete makeup and identify primarily with white persons and their common attitudes and

13. Richard Wright, *Black Boy (American Hunger): A Record of Childhood and Youth* (New York: Harper Perennial Classics, 1998), p. 288.

xviii

practices. This can lead to a tragic lack of self-understanding, a failure to cultivate a positive sense of racial identity or even a tendency to internalize a debilitating self-hatred.

How do we respect individuating differences of race, traditional creed, national origin, sexual orientation, and so on, while simultaneously affirming shared human needs, capacities, and obligations? We want to avoid a flat-footed identity politics that assumes that all black, white, yellow, or red people, say, are the same and must be reared the same by the same. But a too-abstract universalism blinds us to differences that really do make a difference. There are two, largely empirical, questions here: (1) How do children adopted across racial, ethnic, and/or sexual-orientation boundaries actually fare over time? And (2) What beliefs and behaviors tend to optimize their moral and material well being? The evidence, including the cases of Tamara Rabi and Adriana Scott described earlier, suggests that such children often do quite well — at least as well as their counterparts adopted by parents of the same race, ethnicity, or sexual orientation.[14] Nonetheless, there are typical challenges for transracial, trans-ethnic, and trans-sexual-orientation adoptees, and these challenges can and should be met with openness and intentionality. Some such adoptees end up feeling marginalized and ill-treated, even spiritually and physically disinherited, even though their adoptive parents are personally loving. Crucial remedies, and preventatives, for this are education and conversation. Hawley Fogg-Davis is persuasive when she endorses transracial adoption, but only with the proviso that adoption agencies be sensitive to race factors and that prospective parents agree to school their child in his or her racial identity. The cost of not doing this is too frequently public homelessness and private resentment, the inability to execute what Fogg-Davis, echoing Patton-Imani, calls the "racial navigation" necessary for a healthy sense of self in dialogue with others.[15]

---

14. See Rita J. Simon, Howard Altstein, and Marygold S. Melli, *The Case for Transracial Adoption* (Washington, D.C.: American University Press, 1994). See also my essay, "Suffering the Suffering Children," in this volume; Frederick W. Bozett and Marvin B. Sussman, eds., *Homosexuality and Family Relations* (New York: Haworth, 1990); Ann Sullivan, ed., *Issues in Gay and Lesbian Adoption* (Washington, D.C.: Child Welfare League of America, 1995); and Stephen Hicks and Janet McDermott, eds., *Lesbian and Gay Fostering and Adoption: Extraordinary Yet Ordinary* (London: Jessica Kingsley, 2000).

15. Hawley Fogg-Davis, *The Ethics of Transracial Adoption* (Ithaca, N.Y.: Cornell University Press, 2002), esp. chap. 1. Fogg-Davis helpfully proposes a middle way for adoption policy between simple colorblindness and what she calls "racial solidity," the view that only blacks should adopt blacks (and only whites should adopt whites).

Racial, ethnic, and sexual identity matters, in short, but, again, too much identity politics may move us to neglect those in psychic and material want, merely because those who would help are unlike them. I too believe that parents who adopt across social boundaries should school their children in the children's native legacy, but it is worth noting that such schooling may be the richer for being provided by loving adults with different bodies, bents, and backgrounds. If we are now disinclined to thwart interracial *eros* by prohibiting miscegenation, for example, how can we frustrate interracial *agape* by forbidding mixed adoption? Both loves rightly presume a common humanity that binds us, even with all our idiosyncrasies.

The Tasks of This Volume

I have laid out some selected statistics on adoption in America, as well as some broad types of adoption and their frequent evaluation, but I hasten to add that the perceived morality is in flux today, as are the sociological and legal particulars. A narrowness of affection, an apparently genetic tribalism, at times moves us to draw invidious contrasts between "us" and "them," even as a broad altruism, an equally powerful if not innate solidarity with all life, urges us to give of ourselves to others, including suffering children. Reactions to the stories of Tamara, Adriana, Kyshawn, and Kristin remain contested. Is there any way to decipher why some forms of adoption are or ought to be morally and legally permissible, while others are not or ought not to be? It is a central task of this volume to help the reader answer that question. The chapters are far from monolithic, in either academic discipline or political ideology, and no doubt many disagreements and uncertainties will remain. But essential social-psychological, theological, and legal resources are provided by a number of contemporary experts. The theology section includes Jewish, Roman Catholic, and Protestant perspectives, for example, without pretending that these are seamless.

I have chosen a brief reflection by my niece and a series of letters written by a friend as a "Literary Overture" to these chapters. Marcie Jackson speaks of a foster baby who lived with her family for several months, while Gilbert Meilaender addresses his adoptive son in six missives, later published in "The Christian Century," from which I have selected three. These pages are included not only as an aid to intellectual clarity and emotional engagement but also as a spur to practical action. Spurring moral action with respect to adoption is the key task of the entire book.

Literary Overture

Destiny Marie

MARCIE JACKSON

She had skin the color of Hershey's syrup and bright hazel eyes that knew how to smile before her mouth learned. I had a cold when my parents brought her home from the hospital so I couldn't hold her for a week. I spent that time marveling at her round face, afloat in a sea of blankets. She wore that serene expression that only babies can. When I finally got to hold her, I felt her tiny warm body conform to my arms beneath layers of soft cotton as I thought, "This is my sister."

Her mother had named her Destiny Marie before she had been given up for adoption. Technically, she was not my sister in the biological sense, but she was a member of my family in every other way. We fattened her up on milk and kisses. I helped my mother dress her on Sunday mornings in the same lacy outfits that my mother and I had worn as infants. I watched my father dance with her and sing her to sleep, just as he had with my brothers and me. We loved her as we loved each other.

— MARCIE JACKSON
beloved niece of the
editor of this volume

Letters to Derek

GILBERT MEILAENDER

Gifts and Achievements

Dear Derek:

I have not forgotten the day we learned that you would be coming to live with us. I was sitting in my office at Oberlin and Mom called. She said that Children Services had a three-month-old boy who was due to come out of the hospital but could not be sent home to his biological parents. They needed to place him in a foster home and wanted to know if we'd take him.

At the time, we were doing foster care only for preadoptive infants, and you were not one. Still, though you didn't fit the profile, there you were. Ready to leave the hospital, needing a home. And the question was: Would we take you? Mom and I talked it over, and I can still remember saying to her, just as casually as I might comment on the weather, "Well, if you want to, it's OK with me."

Here we are, 18 years later, and it's still OK with me. But I have often thought about that moment, about how casually I made what turned out to be a lifelong commitment, and about how such moments shape our lives. I'll want to say more about that. For today, though, I want to write words about both the debt of thanks you owe to others and the pride you should take in where you've come.

You were, you know, born very prematurely, and you had a rough start in life that left you behind in lots of ways. For a long time I wasn't sure you could ever catch up. Clearly, you have, but you didn't accomplish it on your own. I'm not sure any little child ever got more attention from older brothers and sisters than you got from Peter, Ellen, and Hannah. Peter throwing the ball to you time after time and then chasing it down when you threw it who-knows-where. Ellen and Hannah playing games with you for hours on end. But for all the thanks you owe them, you owe still more to Mom. It would be impossible to count the hours she devoted to you — driving you to therapists, reading up on your problems, giving you attention in the countless ways that you needed to catch up and, then, to flourish.

In short, you owe a considerable debt of gratitude to others for where you've come today. You couldn't have done it without them, but it's also true that you've done it. We're proud of the person you've become — and you should be too. You have accomplished a great deal through sheer force of will and perseverance. You can picture it a little like those moving belts in the airport. Because the belt moves as you walk along it, your rate of progress depends on help. But still, if you want to move along quickly, you yourself have to walk.

I hope over the years you'll keep both of these truths in mind: that you owe much to others, and that we give you credit for what you've achieved. And really, you know, even though your case is special because you were adopted, both of these lessons are true for all of us. We're all indebted from the start, before we are even able to form the words "thank you." There's really no repaying such debts. All we can do is be grateful.

One way we show that gratitude is precisely by applying ourselves — as you have done. We don't waste all the help we've received. We're most likely not to do that when we learn to recognize even our greatest achievements as, finally, gifts from others and from God. It's not that there are some things you received from others for which you must be thankful — and other things that you've accomplished on your own. No. The very things you accomplish are also the gifts of others. And the point of those gifts is precisely that you should live and flourish. I trust that you will.

Love, Dad

Being Adopted

Dear Derek:

I've written you four letters already, and it occurs to me that, although I've talked about how we adopted you, I haven't said all that much about what being adopted actually means. We should think together about this before I finish these letters.

It's natural, I think, that you should wonder about that — about why you're adopted, whether it makes any difference, and whether it makes you a different sort of person. Obviously, we don't plan or intend that children should be adopted. We expect that children can be cared for by their biological parents, and usually they are. That's a good thing. Those biological ties are important, because human beings are bodies. We're connected to each other by bonds of kinship and descent, in which a child is a kind of bodily image of the marriage of a man and woman. If we pretended this was not important, we'd be thinking of ourselves as more like angels — bodiless spirits. But we're not made like that.

Children are a gift God gives parents, and usually this gift turns out to help both parents and children. Parents begin to learn what it means really to love and care for someone else. They learn that their own plans and desires must often be interrupted or even set aside because of the needs of their children. And children learn what it means to have someone love them unconditionally — not because they have certain abilities or talents, but just because parents love their children.

Sometimes this doesn't work out, though. Then we have to remember that we are not just bodies who have to accept whatever happens, but we are also free to step in and try to help when things go wrong. That's what adoption is for, and that's why you are adopted. Your parents just couldn't take care of you, and so you needed to be taken into another home where you could have a mother and a father. You needed to have parents who could and would love you unconditionally, for without that kind of love no child can flourish (as, indeed, you have flourished).

So the "natural" connection of children and parents is important, but human beings are not only "natural" but also "historical" beings. I was not your biological father, but after you'd been living with us for a few

---

years — after we'd shared that much history — I had nevertheless become your true father.

How long does that take? Who can say? Probably it only dawns on us gradually that it is happening or has happened. But at some point it became clear to Mom and me that — without any biological connection at all — you had nevertheless become our son, and we had become your parents. This too is a gift God gives, even if it's not given in the natural, biological way. So adoption goes beyond biology — but also mimics it. When you were adopted you were given not just two people who would care for you, but a new mother and father, from whom you yourself could gradually learn what it means to be part of a family.

Does it make any difference that you're adopted? Well, of course it does. How could it not? It means you have a special history that's a little different from that of many other people. It means, I hope, that as you grow older you will appreciate just how important is the bond of parents with their children and will be able to help others appreciate it as well. And certainly I hope you'll know — with an absolute certainty — that you have received love without condition and are therefore now able to give such love as well.

This is finally a theological point, and I think I'll need one more letter to do it justice. That'll give you something to look forward to!

Love, Dad

Adoptees One and All

Dear Derek:

I wrote last time that being adopted makes you different, and so, of course, in an obvious way it does. But I also hinted that we still had one more thing to think about in order to get the proper theological perspective on adoption.

Has it occurred to you that every Christian is adopted? That's what St. Paul says in Galatians chapter 4. God sent his son Jesus, Paul writes, "so that we might receive adoption as sons." And because we have become God's children by adoption, he has "sent the Spirit of his Son into our hearts, crying, 'Abba! Father!'" Each one of us has been rescued from our natural state; each has experienced the love of a new and better father; each has become part of a new and better family. So you might think of your own experience of being adopted as an image — inadequate and hazy, to be sure — of what each of us can and must experience if we are really to flourish as human beings made to know the love of God. By God's grace, we're all adoptees.

Once we see this, we should realize that there's a sense in which every Christian father or mother is, in some respects, an adoptive parent — even of their own biological children. Think, for instance, of what we believe happens in baptism. Parents hand their child over to God in baptism, and the child becomes part of a new family, the body of Christ. In other words, parents acknowledge that, important and dear to us as our families are, it is even more important to be taken by adoption into that new family in which we learn to name as our Father the One whom Jesus called his Father. So we relinquish our children and then receive them back — not as our possession but as those God gives us to care for.

This, by the way, is why it's such a mistake when — as sometimes happens — Christians begin to think of baptism as primarily a family event. It's only natural, of course, that family members take special interest in the occasion. But if we begin to think of it as an event primarily for them, it's almost as if we're missing what baptism is really about for Christian faith. We're treating as essential what baptism itself teaches us is not the most important thing.

I think, in fact, that having you for a son has taught me this more clearly than years of theological study. If someone had asked me twenty years ago whether I could love a child who was not my biological child as much as one who was, I would have said that I doubted it. The biological tie seemed so important — and is so important — that I just couldn't imagine that the lack of it could be overcome. You have taught me that I was wrong, for I know that I love you every bit as much as I love Peter, Ellen, or Hannah. So, thanks to you, I've learned something about myself.

But more important, I've learned a crucial theological lesson. We might say that biological parents are, in a way, obligated to love their children, while adoptive parents do not act from obligation. There's something to that, and — precisely because there is — we should remember that God is under no obligation to love us and does not love us because he must. Why, then, does he love us? Well, how can I answer that question except with another? Why do I love you? Just because I do. And, likewise, just because God does. We have no claims on God. We cannot plead the importance of biological kinship. We can only learn to be grateful that, for his own mysterious reasons, he has adopted us as his children.

I like to think that this is a lesson you will not forget. It will, I think, make you yourself a better father some day. I hope I'm around to see that day, because I have every confidence that you'll be a good one.

Love, Dad

I. Social-Psychological Perspectives

1. The Moral Psychology of Adoption and Family Ties

MARY STEWART VAN LEEUWEN AND
GRETCHEN MILLER WROBEL

This chapter, co-authored by a social psychologist and a developmental psychologist, each with an academic base in a Christian liberal arts institution, is divided into two sections. The first will consider the theoretical approaches to biological and adoptive parenting embraced by adherents of two influential and competing paradigms in psychology, behaviorism and evolutionary psychology, and then will consider the limitations of both in light of a Christian theology of hospitality. The second section will document, with more specific reference to current empirical literature, some of the characteristics of hospitable adoptive families. These include structuring an adoptive family narrative that recognizes but does not dwell on its differences from families formed by birth; engaging in optimal processes of attachment; and responding to the unique needs of adoptive children at different developmental stages (including the need for a progressively nuanced telling of the adoption story). Finally, we will consider how the current trend toward openness in adoption has influenced kin relationships in adoptive families.

Before we launch into the substance of our chapter, however, a few comments may be helpful regarding the origins of our interest in the topic of adoption. One of us (Mary Stewart Van Leeuwen) has memories of a childhood friend who was one of five children adopted by a Christian couple in the Plymouth Brethren tradition. Some of the children were adopted as infants, others after varying periods of foster care. Although the course of these children's lives — in terms of both material and psychological success — was quite varied, the adoptive parents stayed strongly connected and concerned with all of them, right up until the parents' own deaths. As an academic psychologist, I myself occasionally have been asked to write reference letters for would-be adoptive parents, and at present, within about sixty paces of my office at a Christian university, I have no fewer than half a dozen colleagues who are either adoptive parents or are themselves adopted. Finally, my location in the Reformed theological tradition has given me a strong sense of the ultimate priority of covenant family over biological family, even while respecting natural-theological (and even some evolutionary) accounts that are more apt to stress the power of intergenerational genetic ties.

In fact, it does not usually take anyone long to think of someone they know whose life has been touched by adoption. The other of us (Gretchen Miller Wrobel) has friends and a family member who are adopted, and friends who are adoptive parents. These relationships have given me the opportunity to hear how adoption has influenced lives. While not an adopted person or an adoptive parent myself, I have had a career-long interest in adoption beginning with my doctoral thesis, which was related to transracial adoption. Specifically, I have been interested in the lives of adopted children and the unique perspective they bring to the discussion of adoption. One of my goals has been to raise the level of discourse in the empirical literature to include the direct voice of adopted children. This voice has been traditionally lacking, as the literature has focused on the experiences of adopted adults, adoptive parents, and birth parents.

Psychological Paradigms and the Theory of Hospitality

Reductionistic Views of Adoption: Behaviorism and Evolutionary Psychology

In an era flush with accounts of the human genome project, the genetic cloning of organs and even organisms, and a stream of books on evolutionary psychology, it is easy to forget how recently the psychology of child rearing was characterized by an environmentalist zeal with scant use for anything smacking of innate biological "instincts" either in children or their parents. Behaviorist pioneer John Broadus Watson, whose 1928 best-selling *Psychological Care of the Infant and Child* [1] was probably the "Dr. Spock" of its era, did concede that there were genetically heritable differ-

1. John Broadus Watson and Rosalie Raynor Watson, *The Psychological Care of the Infant and Child* (New York: Norton, 1928).

ences in bodily structure. "But," he added, "do not let these undoubted facts of inheritance lead you astray as they have some of the biologists. The mere presence of these structures tells us not one thing about function. . . . Our hereditary structure lies ready to be shaped in a thousand different ways depending on the way in which the child is brought up."[2]

Watson's radical environmentalism, based on Pavlov's earlier research in respondent conditioning, in the end may have contributed to a burden of maternal guilt that eventually rebounded into the second wave of feminism, for if children are almost entirely the sum of their upbringing, then their primary caretakers necessarily bear a huge responsibility for the results. But in an era also captivated by eugenics — to the point of having laws, enforced in some states until the 1970s, for the compulsory sterilization of the "unfit" — Watson's behaviorist pronouncements were welcome news to adoptive parents inasmuch as his assertions downplayed the significance of biological inheritance for children's skills and character. "[T]housands of sons and daughters of the wicked," Watson sarcastically wrote against the mystique of the bloodline, "grow up to be wicked because they couldn't grow up any other way in such surroundings. But let one adopted child who had a bad ancestry go wrong and it is used as incontestable evidence for the inheritance of moral turpitude and criminal tendencies."[3]

So convinced was Watson of the irrelevance of genetic ties for successful child rearing that he even considered Plato's argument (from *The Republic*) that it might be best for biological parents and children not to know each other, and for children to be reared largely in state-financed settings by unrelated caretakers.[4] His Pavlovian reasoning was that a child reaching for its parent simply reflected a conditioned association between the parent and food, and that catering to that connection by cuddling children too much would produce a race of dependent and underachieving (read: un-American) adults.

Watson further insisted that apart from a biological heritage of reflexes and bodily structures, children were born with only the primitive emotions he labeled fear, rage, and love, which could be generalized and/or redirected with indefinite plasticity according to the principles of re-

2. John Broadus Watson, "What the Nursery Has to Say about Instincts," in *Psychologies of 1925*, ed. Carl Murchison (Worcester, Mass.: Clark University Press, 1926), p. 4.

3. Watson, "What the Nursery Has to Say," p. 9.

4. David Cohen, *J. B. Watson: The Founder of Behaviorism* (London: Routledge and Kegan Paul, 1979). No less a figure than Bertrand Russell endorsed this Platonic aspect of Watson's theory in his review of Watson's 1928 child-rearing manual.

spondent conditioning. Thus in 1926 he threw down his famous child-rearing gauntlet: "Give me a dozen healthy infants, well-formed, and my own specified world to bring them up in and I'll guarantee to take any one at random and train him to become any type of specialist I might select — a doctor, lawyer, artist, merchant-chief and yes, even beggarman or thief, regardless of his talents, penchants, tendencies, abilities, vocations and race of his ancestors."[5] To Watson, in sum, adoption was no huge moral or psychological challenge either for parents or children, since "instinctive" bonds between kin were minimal, anything beyond minimal emotional attachment was unhealthy, and heredity counted for next to nothing in terms of child-rearing outcomes.

From the late 1940s until his death in 1990 — and despite other basic theoretical differences between them — B. F. Skinner continued Watson's emphasis on minimal attachment between parents and children, and on the primacy of environment over genetic legacy and blood ties in child-rearing outcomes. Skinner's 1948 novel *Walden Two*[6] is his version of a behaviorist-cum-socialist utopia where child-rearing practices seem to represent a cross between Plato's *Republic* and the emerging practices of the Israeli *kibbutzim*. The children of Walden Two do know their biological parents, but they are housed away from them from birth on, call them by their first names, and get equal care and attention from a range of adults who may or may not have children of their own. Biological parenting thus becomes a more avuncular relationship, and all adults become something like quasi-adoptive parents to all of the community's children, without playing favorites. Needless to say (since anything can happen in a fictitious utopia),[7] the children raised in Walden Two grow up with no sense of competition, jealousy, or unresolved Oedipal feelings and easily weather parental losses caused by death or divorce, since the children's attachments to adults are so deliberately diffused from birth on.

As a behaviorist evangelistic tract, *Walden Two* did not really catch on until the 1970s, when a new wave of anti-establishment sentiment inspired at least two groups of people to set up small communities — one in Mexico, one in Virginia — using Skinner's novel as a serious blueprint. But although both communities still exist, neither has retained more than a superficial resemblance to the fictitious Walden Two, and espe-

5. Watson, "What the Nursery Has to Say," p. 10.
6. B. F. Skinner, *Walden Two* (New York: MacMillan, 1948).
7. See Daniel W. Bjork, *B. F. Skinner: A Life* (Washington, D.C.: American Psychological Association, 1997).

cially not in their child-rearing practices, which are now centered around biological nuclear families and whose children are no doubt just as charming and just as perverse as anywhere else in North America.[8] Moreover, the work of comparative psychologist Harry Harlow in the 1950s and 1960s showed, in his famous infant monkey experiments, that the need for comfort and body contact is in fact independent of the need for food, and that its chronic absence can produce devastating consequences in the social and emotional development of children.[9]

An older and larger experiment in the weakening of ties between parents and their biological children can be seen in the religious and secular *kibbutz* movement in Israel. Committed to an ideology of both economic and gender equality, this movement structured its rural communities over half a century ago to have infants and children sleep and eat separately from parents and be nurtured as a group by trained child-care workers, in order to free up mothers as well as fathers for full participation in the economic and political life of the *kibbutzim*. But as in the would-be Walden Two communities, most *kibbutzim* have gradually moved back to nuclear family living arrangements, although communal meals, communal child care, and a common purse remain normative.[10]

None of this would surprise contemporary evolutionary psychologists, who began arguing in the 1960s that humans are on a much tighter genetic leash than behaviorists were willing to concede. Adherents of this new form of nativism appeal to studies done by behavior geneticists to argue that the variance in children's intelligence, temperament, and even religious proclivities is at least as dependent on heredity as on environment.[11] More fundamentally, evolutionary psychologists hold that many

8. See Kathleen Kinkade, *A Walden Two Experiment: The First Five Years of Twin Oaks Community* (New York: Wm. Morrow, 1973), and *Is It Utopia Yet? An Insider's View of Twin Oaks Community in Its Twenty-Sixth Year* (Louisa, Va.: Twin Oaks, 1994).

9. See Deborah Blum, *The Monkey Wars* (New York: Oxford University Press, 1994), and *Love At Goon Park: Harry Harlow and the Science of Affection* (Cambridge, Mass.: Perseus, 2002).

10. See Ofra Anson, Arieh Levenson, and Dan Y. Bonneh, "Gender and Health on the Kibbutz," *Sex Roles* 22 (1990): 213-33, and Aryei Fishman, *Judaism and the Collective Life: Self and Community in the Religious Kibbutz* (New York: Routledge, 2002).

11. For example, Thomas J. Bouchard Jr., "Longitudinal Studies of Personality and Intelligence: A Behavior Genetic and Evolutionary Psychology Perspective," in *International Handbook of Personality and Intelligence*, ed. D. H. Saklofske and M. Zeidner (New York: Plenum, 1995), pp. 81-106. For a critique of the misuse of the concept of heritability by behavior geneticists, however, see David Moore, *The Dependent Gene: The Fallacy of "Nature vs. Nurture"* (New York: W. H. Freeman, 2001), especially ch. 2.

behaviors previously thought to be culturally malleable have genetically based survival relevance, especially for the propagation of one's genes in future generations. Thus, according to the theory of kin selection, an adult is likely to invest resources in members of the next generation in proportion to the percentage of genes shared with them. That percentage is obviously highest in the case of biological children, less in the case of nieces or nephews, still less in the case of distant cousins, and least in the case of non-kin.[12]

Why, then, would anyone ever adopt unrelated children? (For that matter, why wouldn't we all be wildly enthusiastic about the possibility of cloning ourselves?) Well, apparently in the long run of human history people haven't much adopted outside of kin ties — or at least not in areas other than the West. On a worldwide basis, according to the work of anthropologist Joan Silk, most adoptions involve blood relatives.[13] Where they don't (as is more commonly the case in the United States), evolutionary psychologists theorize that it is because we are hardwired not just to enjoy sex but to take some pleasure in child rearing, since both are normally correlated with the propagation of our genes.

Thus evolutionary psychologists predict that most non-kin adoptions will be by people who have tried but failed to have their own biological children, which apparently is the case.[14] In addition, evolutionary psychologists invoke the theory of reciprocal altruism. Ordinarily, our putative altruistic genes are weeded out by natural selection: the indiscriminately good-hearted are less likely to get their genes reproduced because they don't watch out sufficiently for their own and/or their own close kin's interests. Even generosity to unrelated people can be adaptive, however, if the costs are small compared to the benefits and if the altruist

12. William D. Hamilton, "The Genetical Evolution of Social Behavior," parts I and II, *Journal of Theoretical Biology* 7 (1964): 1-16 and 17-52. See also Steven J. C. Gaulin and Donald H. McBurney, *Psychology: An Evolutionary Approach* (Upper Saddle River, N.J.: Prentice-Hall, 2001). To complicate matters, evolutionary psychologists argue that men are less likely than women to invest even in the long-term care of their own biological offspring, since by being promiscuous ("cads" rather than "dads") they can get as many, if not more, of their genes reproduced as by forming monogamous pair-bonds and helping to raise the children of one woman.

13. Joan Silk, "Human Adoption in Evolutionary Perspective," *Human Nature* 1 (1990): 25-52. See also John Boswell, *The Kindness of Strangers: The Abandonment of Children in Western Europe from Late Antiquity to the Renaissance* (New York: Pantheon, 1988), and also Stephen G. Post, *More Lasting Unions: Christianity, the Family, and Society* (Grand Rapids: Eerdmans, 2000), especially ch. 5.

14. Gaulin and McBurney, *Psychology*, p. 225.

and the recipient regularly exchange these two roles, thus minimizing the risk that one member of the pair will freeload on the other's generosity. This is seen as one reason (in addition to the attractions of regular sex and security about the paternity of one's offspring) that men and women pair-bond: they in effect scratch each other's backs by engaging in a division of labor in which the benefits to both normally outweigh the costs. And the same is said to be true of adoption, at least in the long run: the children that you raise are likely to support you in your old age, even if they aren't vehicles for the propagation of your genes.[15]

Beyond Reductionism: Adoption and the Theology of Hospitality

From the perspective of a Christian worldview that emphasizes the transformation of created yet fallen cultural tendencies, there may be something to be learned about the moral psychology of adoption from both the behavioral and the evolutionary psychological perspectives, though both are reductionistic in quite opposite ways. Inasmuch as "ought" implies "can" and inasmuch as a robust creation theology holds that we are embodied creatures (not quasi-Cartesian angels driving around in irrelevant fleshly automobiles),[16] we need to take seriously the constraints of both nature and nurture when discussing ethical expectations for any sphere of life. On the other hand, neither Skinner's nor Watson's theory about the Platonic plasticity of parenting bonds was ever affirmed empirically: the longitudinal *kibbutz* experiment, if anything, seems to challenge it. But the "selfish gene" theory of some evolutionary psychologists also raises certain questions. For example, why only in the West has the tendency to indulge the pleasure-in-child-rearing gene at one remove (by adopting unrelated children) come to the fore? Why are most people more attached to their grandchildren than to their nieces and nephews, who share the same percentage of their genes? And if altruism, whether kin-related or reciprocal, is really just disguised self-interest, why do we award Nobel Peace Prizes to the likes of Mother Teresa?

Kin selection and reciprocal altruism have been the explanations of choice among evolutionary psychologists since about the 1960s, and both

15. Robert Trivers, "The Evolution of Reciprocal Altruism," *Quarterly Review of Biology* 46 (1971): 35-57.

16. The metaphor comes from Lewis Smedes, *Sex for Christians* (Grand Rapids: Eerdmans, 1976).

assume that behind every apparently altruistic act lies a self-serving urge to get as many copies as possible of one's own genes into the next generation. But Darwin himself also presented the idea of "group selection" to explain the evolution of human altruism, and his explanation is now enjoying something of a revival among both biologists and social scientists.[17] On this account, although non-kin-based altruism may yield little or no advantage to *individuals* and their offspring, it does confer survival advantages on entire *groups* (such as tribes or villages) and thus will be selected for over the long haul — not as a replacement for the forces of kin-based genetic chauvinism but as an evolutionary force that runs alongside and sometimes trumps the latter.[18]

Ethicist Stephen Post has further argued that, within the Christian tradition, "the successful practice of adoption is proof that parents can transcend the 'selfish gene' of [some] evolutionary psychologists, and that children can prosper without the narrative of a biological lineage."[19] He acknowledges that the historical record of the church is fragmentary with regard to adoption practices, and that behavior has not always been consistent with theological ideals. Nevertheless, he cites several biblical texts used by the early church to provide a "sacred canopy"[20] for adoption, even as the church appealed to natural-theological principles to defend the normal connection between biological procreation and child nurture. These texts included the Deuteronomic injunction to care for widows and orphans, Jesus' placing kingdom membership above family ties, the several Pauline texts that use an adoption metaphor to explain the nature of salvation, the adoption of Jesus by Mary's husband Joseph, and the agapic relinquishment by God of God's Son for the benefit of humankind. Historian John Boswell has also noted that the early church appealed to the adoption metaphor to challenge the traditional Jewish emphasis on biological lineage.[21]

17. See, for example, Elliott Sober and David Sloane Wilson, *Unto Others: The Evolution and Psychology of Unselfish Behavior* (Cambridge, Mass.: Harvard University Press, 1998), and Matt Ridley, *The Origins of Virtue: Human Instincts and the Evolution of Cooperation* (Harmondsworth, U.K.: Penguin, 1996).

18. B. F. Skinner was a clear proponent of such group selection in his novel *Walden Two* — to the extent of assuming that it trumped almost completely what would later be called kin selection or altruism.

19. Post, *More Lasting Unions*, p. 121.

20. The phrase originates with sociologist Peter Berger, *The Sacred Canopy: Elements of a Sociological Theory of Religion* (Garden City, N.Y.: Doubleday, 1967).

21. Boswell, *Kindness of Strangers*, ch. 3.

With the exception of the first, however, these texts are overwhelmingly from the Christian rather than the Hebrew Scriptures. Using them as the main tent poles for adoption's sacred canopy risks falling into Marcionite thinking (the heresy that with the advent of Christ the Hebrew Scriptures were rendered theologically irrelevant). Moreover, appealing to adoption language as a polemic against the Jewish preoccupation with genealogy may produce a theology of adoption that is at least covertly anti-Semitic.[22] This, however, is not inevitable: there is, for example, a medieval artistic tradition that specifically links the story of Moses' adoption by Pharaoh's daughter with the adoption of Jesus by his mother's husband Joseph — both considered to be events in which divine sovereignty, mediated by human altruism, overcomes what might otherwise be a human tragedy.[23]

We would also like to argue for the recovery and extension of a theology of *hospitality,* to help unite the Hebrew and Christian Scriptures and to broaden the sacred canopy under which adoption becomes one way in which God's people welcome "strangers" of many kinds. This they do both in gratitude for the divine hospitality shown by God to them, individually and corporately, and in anticipation of the new heaven and earth in which people from "all the nations" will live in peace.[24] Behaviorist and evolutionary psychological accounts of adoption are materialist and causal, and hence cannot tell the whole story, either singly or together. The biblical drama locates actors in a continuing cosmic narrative — both historical and eschatological — in which the mercy and sovereignty of God empower persons to be open-handed rather than purely instrumental in the way they view relationships. Adoption is one of many manifestations of that trust. Indeed, it is not uncommon for Christians to state that children — by whatever means they come into a family — are simply "on loan" from God.

Ethicist Christine Pohl, though not concentrating on adoption per se, traces biblical and church-historical practices of hospitality while analyzing eight contemporary Christian communities of hospitality.[25] She cites accounts of hospitality to "angels unaware" (cf. Heb. 13:2) in the patriarchal narratives, as well as frequent reminders to the Israelites to see

22. For a contemporary Jewish theological analysis, see Michael Gold, "Adoption: The Jewish View," *Adoption Quarterly* 3, no. 1 (1999): 3-13.

23. Boswell, *Kindness of Strangers,* pp. 145-49, 185-86, and fig. 5.

24. Cf. Isa. 2:1-4 and Mic. 4:1-5 NRSV.

25. Christine Pohl, *Making Room: Recovering Hospitality As a Christian Tradition* (Grand Rapids: Eerdmans, 1999).

themselves as stewards and sojourners in a land ultimately owned by God. As captives delivered from the alien power of Egypt, they were to be strangers welcoming strangers, extending hospitality not only to the poor, widowed, and fatherless of clan and tribe but also to vulnerable resident aliens who lived among them. Indeed, though hospitality to travelers was routine in the Ancient Near East, the legal mandate to love the alien as oneself seems to have been unique to Israel.[26] New Testament discussions of hospitality continue and extend these themes. Believers are to welcome one another as Christ has welcomed them; thus "hospitality is important symbolically in its reflection and reenactment of God's hospitality, and important practically in meeting human needs and forging human connections."[27] Nor was this practice limited to the household of faith, for "the believer's responsibility moved outward from fellow Christians to the world."[28]

Reformation theologians brought together biblical, classical, patristic, and Renaissance-humanistic understandings about hospitality. To Calvin, recalling the parable of the Good Samaritan, strangers deserve consideration both because everyone bears the image of God and because everyone shares the human experience of vulnerability and dependency. As urbanization gathered momentum, Calvin also stressed "the dangers of social disconnection and the harm that comes from the absence of relationships that give people a place in the community."[29] In the eighteenth century John Wesley appealed to the parable of Dives and Lazarus to argue for "holding together the qualities of universal love and particular, personal care. Lofty statements about loving every person as one's neighbor had to be accompanied by acts which brought the Christian face-to-face with those persons most commonly excluded from 'the neighborhood.'"[30] Thus, at the turn of the third millennium, Christian communities of hospitality — such as L'Abri, the Catholic Worker, L'Arche, Jubilee Partners, and St. John's and St. Benedict's monasteries — cater to groups as diverse as the urban poor, the adult mentally handicapped, university students, and persons seeking spiritual renewal and direction.

26. Pohl, *Making Room*, ch. 2.

27. Pohl, *Making Room*, pp. 29-30 (Pohl's summary of Calvin's reasoning).

28. Pohl, *Making Room*, p. 31.

29. Pohl, *Making Room*, p. 66. She notes that Luther's co-optation of the language of hospitality to exclude "ungrateful" Jewish "guests" in Germany is a sad exception to this tradition and contrasts with his sacrificial hospitality to other needy people.

30. Pohl, *Making Room*, p. 77.

Adoption is continuous with all of these practices — to which we might add godparenting, the practice of including entire church congregations in baptismal vows, and the mentoring and teaching of young persons in the many ways these have historically been done by "people of the Book." Adoption arguably requires an unusual commitment, in terms of enduring uncertain waiting periods and often forfeiting a great deal of money for legal and adoption agency fees. But, as Rodney Clapp has trenchantly observed, having children by *any* means fits badly with our present culture's habits of serial polygamy, material acquisitiveness, resentment of limitations, and all-demanding career tracks. Nor, he adds (as a biological parent himself), can we assume that our flesh-and-blood children "are automatically friends, never strangers":

> For all our scientific understanding, for all our child psychology, children — even modern children — remain mysterious. . . . And every child, from the first midnight it bawls for a feeding to the first bizarre teenage hairstyle, often acts in ways that surprise and even distress parents. Who do not sometimes, even in the happiest families, feel their children as intruders in their lives? Of course we know our children intimately. But we also know them as strangers. One evidence that we find our children strange is the enduring popularity of self-help books about children. . . . If any of them 'worked' as effectively as they are all touted to work, there wouldn't be so many of them on the market. So why do we continue to buy such books? I think this vast literature reassures us in the face of the strangeness, the alien qualities, of our children.[31]

Clapp, writing as a Protestant evangelical, thus concludes that "Christians have children so [that they] can become the kind of people who welcome strangers."[32] Lisa Sowle Cahill, writing as a Jesuit-trained Catholic (and the parent of both biological and internationally adopted children), agrees. "[T]he Christian family is not the nuclear family focused inward on the welfare of its own members but the socially-transformative family that seeks to make the Christian moral ideal of love of neighbor part of the common good. . . . [I]f the socially radical meaning of Christianity is taken seriously, Christian families can become vehicles of social justice, even as they strengthen and build upon their bonds of kinship, af-

---

31. Rodney Clapp, *Families At the Crossroads: Beyond Traditional and Modern Options* (Downers Grove, Ill.: InterVarsity, 1993), pp. 142-43.
32. Clapp, *Families At the Crossroads,* p. 148.

fection, and faithfulness."[33] If these writers are correct, our primary ethical challenge has less to do with adoption per se than with creating and rediscovering ways to transcend the rhetoric of both the selfish gene and the culture of narcissism so that adoption, as part of the continuum of biblical hospitality, becomes a natural expression of kingdom theology.

Yet each form of hospitality, adoption included, has its own peculiar and historically nuanced challenges, and in the following sections we turn to the recent empirical and theoretical literature on adoption to see what these are.

The Psychology of Adoption and Family Ties

Welcoming, hospitable families are those that are sensitive to the needs of their adopted children, and families that provide warm and caring environments for growth and development give attention to their children's emotional, cognitive, social, spiritual, and physical needs. In nurturing the whole child, the family provides a foundation on which the ups and downs of growth and change can take place. But for the adoptive family such nurturance includes additional adoption-related tasks (for example, telling the adoption story, supporting the development of adoptive identity). Moreover, the development of the adopted child is influenced by communication styles used to incorporate adoption into the family system.

How family members communicate with one another has always been of interest to social scientists. David Kirk was among the first to write about the unique communication needs of adoptive families in his pioneering work *Shared Fate,* in which he described the mutual need and aid shared by members of adoptive families.[34] In order to describe styles of coping with the unique demands of adoptive parenting, Kirk identified two important concepts related to communication about adoption: "Acknowledgement-of-Difference" and "Rejection-of-Difference."[35] Acknowledgement-of-difference reflects an open communication style that recognizes but does not dwell on the differences between biological and adoptive family formation and parenting. Rejection-of-difference is the

33. Lisa Sowle Cahill, *Family: A Christian Social Perspective* (Minneapolis: Fortress, 2000), p. xii.

34. H. David Kirk, *Shared Fate: A Theory of Adoption and Mental Health* (New York: Free Press, 1964).

35. Kirk, *Shared Fate,* ch. 4.

opposite: denial of, or withdrawal from, acknowledgement of any difference between the two types of families. These two concepts anchor a continuum of styles for coping with the particular tasks of adoptive parenting. Kirk acknowledged that these two approaches were not mutually exclusive but in practice were mixed together by parents.[36] Kirk also concluded that adoptive parents who leaned toward the acknowledgement-of-difference end of the continuum in their interactions would more readily develop an open style of communication about adoption and empathy for their adopted children. Kirk related acknowledgement-of-difference and its associated empathy with the adopted child to greater satisfaction on the part of adoptive parents with adoption as a means of family formation. Thus acknowledgement-of-difference is conducive to good communication and stability in adoptive families, while rejection-of-difference is associated with poor communication and family outcomes.[37]

David Brodzinsky expanded on the work of Kirk by suggesting a curvilinear relationship between acknowledgement and rejection of differences and family functioning.[38] He emphasized that an overemphasis on adoption-related difference as well as a strong denial of difference could be detrimental to adoptive families. Mediating the two extremes by acknowledging difference without dwelling on it is assumed to facilitate optimal adjustment.[39]

Adoptive Parenting and Family Formation

While an open but not insistent communication style about adoption is associated with positive adoption adjustment,[40] communication about adoption must respond to the developmental needs of the adopted child

36. Kirk, *Shared Fate*, p. 68.

37. Kirk, *Shared Fate*, p. 99.

38. David M. Brodzinsky, "Adjustment to Adoption: A Psychosocial Perspective," *Clinical Psychology Review* 7 (1987): 25-47.

39. David M. Brodzinsky, Daniel W. Smith, and Anne B. Brodzinsky, *Children's Adjustment to Adoption: Developmental and Clinical Issues* (Thousand Oaks, Calif.: Sage, 1998).

40. See David M. Brodzinsky and Ellen Pinderhughes, "Parenting and Child Development in Adoptive Families," in vol. 1 of *Handbook of Parenting*, ed. Marc Bornstein (Hillsdale, N.J.: Erlbaum, 2002), pp. 279-311; Harold D. Grotevant, Gretchen Miller Wrobel, Manfred H. Van Dulman, and Ruth G. McRoy, "The Emergence of Psychosocial Engagement in Adopted Adolescents: The Family As Context Over Time," *Journal of Adolescent Research* 16 (2001): 469-90; Kirk, *Shared Fate*.

and family. Adoptive families share the same basic parenting tasks as families formed by birth, but progress through stages of family formation and parenting with unique, developmentally related adoption tasks.

The first of these tasks has to do with loss. Adoption is valuable for forming families, yet it encompasses loss.[41] Members of the adoption triad[42] — adoptive parents, adopted children, and birth parents — are influenced by the loss inherent in adoption. Birth parents lose a child born to them and experience associated grief,[43] possibly a lost sense of control over their lives, and loss of self-esteem from a sense of failure as parents.[44] Adoptive parents may have sensed a loss of fertility, of control over their lives, or of status in their families of origin.[45] Adopted children experience the loss of birth parents and an associated personal history that may later prompt some to learn more about their birth parents.[46] Issues of loss present themselves throughout an adopted person's lifetime: some will seek assistance in dealing with the issues as they arise, while others will possess the problem-solving skills and insight to deal effectively with these issues on their own.[47]

The second task concerns the process of becoming an adoptive parent. For many adoptive parents it is the challenge of infertility that leads them to consider adoption as an alternate means of forming a family. Recognizing and working through the loss associated with the inability to have birth children are fundamental to adoptive family formation.[48]

41. Miriam Reitz and Kenneth W. Watson, *Adoption and the Family System* (New York: Guilford, 1992).

42. The adoption triad is part of the adoption kinship network, which includes the adoption triad and extended adoptive and birth family members. See Harold D. Grotevant and Ruth G. McRoy, *Openness in Adoption: Exploring Family Connections* (Thousand Oaks, Calif.: Sage, 1998).

43. Cinda Christian, Ruth G. McRoy, Harold D. Grotevant, and Chalandra Bryant, "Grief Resolution of Birthmothers in Confidential, Time-Limited Mediated, Ongoing Mediated, and Fully Disclosed Adoptions," *Adoption Quarterly* 1, no. 2 (1997): 35-58.

44. Reitz and Watson, *Adoption and the Family System*, p. 131; Robin C. Winkler, Dirck W. Brown, Margaret van Keppel, and Amy Blanchard, *Clinical Practice in Adoption* (New York: Pergamon, 1988), ch. 4.

45. Reitz and Watson, *Adoption and the Family System*, p. 131; Winkler et al., *Clinical Practice*, ch. 5.

46. Gretchen Miller Wrobel, Harold D. Grotevant, and Ruth G. McRoy, "Adolescent Search for Birthparents: Who Moves Forward?" *Journal of Adolescent Research* 19 (2004): 132-51.

47. Gretchen Miller Wrobel and Harold D. Grotevant, "Adoption," in *Children's Needs II: Development, Problems, and Alternatives,* ed. George G. Bear, Kathleen M. Minke, and Alex Thomas (Bethesda, Md.: National Association of School Psychologists, 1997), pp. 287-98.

48. Brodzinsky and Pinderhughes, "Parenting and Child Development," p. 288; Kirk,

When issues of infertility are well thought out, with an honest recognition of the associated grief process, movement to acceptance of adoption as a viable alternative for family formation becomes possible.[49] Though full grief resolution is not viewed as necessary for movement to adoptive parenthood,[50] understanding the issues associated with the loss of an anticipated birth child is important. As with any loss, infertility cannot be totally removed from a person's experience. Adoption solves childlessness, not infertility.[51] Elinor Rosenberg points out that by acknowledging the missing biological link between generations, couples can accept that "the continuous link will be the psychological relationship that will carry on the family history."[52]

Brodzinsky and Pinderhughes delineated five additional tasks associated with becoming an adoptive parent, ones that also apply to prospective parents for whom infertility is not part of the motivation for adoption.[53] First, there is the approval process. The home study process requires prospective adoptive parents to open themselves to the scrutiny of social work professionals as to their adequacy for parenting. Despite the educational and supportive intent of the home study, it can feel evaluative in nature, producing anxiety beforehand and relief upon approval. Second, there is the period during which consent for the adoption is given, parental rights are terminated, and adoption finalization occurs. This waiting period may delay the feeling of entitlement that forms when parents "claim" the child as their own.[54] Third, unlike pregnancy, adoption is characterized by an uncertain, often long, timeline for achieving parenthood. The process can take from a few months to one or more years. The uncertainty about when a placement will be made can be frustrating. Fourth, adoption is still characterized by social stigma. Adoptive parents have identified several negative societal attitudes, including the idea that the biological tie is important for bonding and love (implying that emotional ties formed in adoptive families are inferior), that adopted

---

Shared Fate, ch. 1; Reitz and Watson, *Adoption and the Family System*, ch. 6; Elinor B. Rosenberg, *The Adoption Life Cycle: The Children and Their Families through the Years* (New York: Free Press, 1992), ch. 3.

49. Reitz and Watson, *Adoption and the Family System*, ch. 6; Rosenberg, *Adoption Life Cycle*, ch. 3.

50. Brodzinsky and Pinderhughes, "Parenting and Child Development," pp. 286-87.

51. Reitz and Watson, *Adoption and the Family System*, p. 108.

52. Rosenberg, *Adoption Life Cycle*, p. 59.

53. Brodznisky and Pinderhughes, "Parenting and Child Development," pp. 287-88.

54. Reitz and Watson, *Adoption and the Family System*, pp. 125-26.

children are second-rate because of an unknown genetic past, and that adoptive parents are not the child's "real" parents.[55] Even when adoptive parents are satisfied with their decision to adopt, they and their children must cope with negative attitudes in the larger society that they personally do not hold. Families formed across racial or national lines may encounter additional prejudices. Finally, adoptive parents have fewer readily (5) available role models to turn to for advice, especially advice related to the unique challenges of adoption.

Becoming an Adoptive Family

The placement of a child with adoptive parents begins the process of developing a mutual understanding that allows the fundamental task of parent-child attachment to occur.[56] An attachment is an affectional tie that binds persons together, endures over time, and provides a context of security within which the child grows. First attachments develop with primary caregivers over the first six to eight months of life and are held to be essential for positive development.[57] Attachment theory has important implications for adopted children, especially for those adopted after the age of six months, since a first attachment may have been broken, developed without a full sense of security, or not developed at all due to neglect.

Although early attachments are important, they are not rigid determinants of the future development of the child.[58] It is often assumed that because a child's first attachment may not be to the adoptive mother, mother-infant attachments in adoptive families are less secure than in

55. Charlene Miall, "The Stigma of Adoptive Parent Status: Perceptions of Community Attitudes Toward Adoption and the Experience of Informal Social Sanctioning," *Family Relations* 36 (1987): 34-39.

56. "Bonding" and "attachment" are two terms used to describe the affection parents and children feel for each other. Confusion between the terms and the processes they represent is prevalent in discussions of the social-emotional development of children. Attachment is a learned skill while bonding is not. The two terms are not interchangeable and the emotional intensity of the two cannot be compared because of qualitative difference between the processes. The present focus will be on the learned behavior of attachment. See Kenneth W. Watson, "Bonding and Attachment in Adoption: Towards Better Understanding and Useful Definitions," *Marriage and Family Review* 24 (1997): 159-73, for a complete discussion of the issues.

57. John Bowlby, *Attachment and Loss,* vol. 1 (New York: Basic, 1969).

58. Ross A. Thompson, "Sensitive Periods in Attachment?" in *Critical Thinking about Critical Periods,* ed. Donald Bail (Baltimore: Paul H. Brooks, 2001), pp. 83-106.

nonadoptive families. Empirical support for this assumption is equivo-cal.[59] Current attachment theory views affectional ties as developing throughout childhood, with no one critical period dominating the pro-cess. Johnson and Fein describe attachment as a developmental process that allows relationships to stabilize, as well as change, over time.[60] Thus the ability to maintain multiple attachments and behavioral expectations of others is viewed as adaptive, allowing for remediation. For children who have had difficult attachment histories, it is possible to learn how to form attachments later in life,[61] though early disruptions can prolong the initial adoptive-mother/infant attachment process.[62]

Development of attachments is strengthened in a nurturing, care-giving environment characterized by parents who are sensitive to their child's needs, and is enhanced when there is a match between parental expectations and the child's personality and behavior. This type of envi-ronment provides a secure home where trust and emotional ties can de-velop between parent and child. Viewing attachment in a broader, dy-namic context, not tied to critical periods of development with only good or bad outcomes, allows for families and professionals to intervene, if necessary, in developmentally appropriate ways.[63] This broader view is especially helpful when "unmatched expectations"[64] occur between adoptive parents and children who are older at the time of placement. All parties enter into adoption with excitement and notions of what it will be like to be an adoptive family. When these expectations are realistic about the work and time it takes to become a family, there is adequate room for the attachment process to take place. Understanding that at-tachment is a dynamic developmental process rightly challenges the no-tion that the lack of a very early mother-infant "bond" will dictate poor childhood adjustment.

In addition to providing a warm and secure home that facilitates

59. See Jacqueline Portello, "The Mother-Infant Attachment Process in Adoptive Families," *Canadian Journal of Counseling* 27 (1993): 177-90, for a review of empirical findings.

60. Daniel Johnson and Edith Fein, "The Concept of Attachment: Applications to Adoption," *Children and Youth Services Review* 13 (1991): 397-412.

61. K. Watson, "Bonding and Attachment," p. 170.

62. Portello, "Mother-Infant Attachment Process," p. 182, and Carollee Howes, "At-tachment Relationships in the Context of Multiple Caregivers," in *Handbook of Attachment: Theory, Research, and Clinical Applications*, ed. J. Cassidy and P. Shaver (New York: Guilford, 1999), p. 678.

63. Portello, "Mother-Infant Attachment Process," p. 185; Thompson, "Sensitive Pe-riods in Attachment?" p. 101.

64. Reitz and Watson, *Adoption and the Family System*, pp. 129-30.

positive attachments, adoptive parents need to provide space for the exploration of their child's adoptive status. This exploration can include dealing with adoption-related loss, satisfying curiosity about the adoption history, and forming an adoptive identity. Adoptive parents bring unique strengths that can enhance their ability to handle the additional tasks associated with parenting an adopted child. Brodzinsky and Pinderhughes point out that, when compared to nonadoptive parents, adoptive parents bring stability to parenthood because they are generally older at first time parenthood, more settled in careers, more financially secure, and married longer.[65] Those adoptive parents who have dealt with infertility issues feel a "powerful sense of fulfillment with the arrival of a child."[66] In addition, adoptive parents have been socialized to adoptive parenthood through working with adoption agencies. All these factors provide strengths and resources to the adoptive parents at the time of family formation and beyond, supporting positive outcomes.[67]

The Young Child in the Adoptive Family

As children grow in their understanding of the world and use their developing language skills to describe their experience, adoption-related parenting focuses on adoption revelation. The telling of the adoption story is the initial task of adoption-related communication. When relayed early in the preschool years, it ensures that the adoptive parents are the first to reveal to their child his or her adoptive status. The telling of the adoption story shifts the emphasis from integrating the child into the family and forming secure ties to the task of family differentiation, which acknowledges that the adopted child is connected to both birth and adoptive families and identifies the roles of each in the life of the adopted child.[68]

The adoption story typically contains a discussion of adoption in general, information surrounding the circumstance of the child's birth, and how the child came to his or her family. Adoptive parents need to help their child come to terms with the loss of birth parents as parents and to reassure their child that despite relinquishment by the birth family, he or

65. Brodzinsky and Pinderhughes, "Parenting and Child Development," p. 288.
66. Brodzinsky and Pinderhughes, "Parenting and Child Development," p. 288.
67. David M. Brodzinsky and Loreen Huffman, "Transition to Adoptive Parenthood," *Marriage and Family Review* 12 (1988): 267-86.
68. Brodzinsky, Smith, and Brodzinsky, *Children's Adjustment to Adoption*, p. 27.

[handwritten annotations in top margin: "assumption! ?? What would cause a child to feel unwanted by their birth parents?? Was Moses unwanted?"]

she will always belong to the adoptive family.[69] Clinicians encourage parents to acknowledge their child's loss[70] and help reframe the relinquishment from being unwanted to being wanted.[71] Many families celebrate their child's adoption with rituals that mark the coming of the child to the family.[72] Such rituals can help communicate acceptance of adoptive family formation and influence the child's perceptions of the role birth parents and other birth family members have in the family system. How the story is told is important because it sets the tone for present and future parent-child communication about adoption.[73]

For children, comprehension of the adoption story is related to their developmental stage. Understanding the concept of adoption influences understanding of their own circumstances. Based upon their research, Brodzinsky and his colleagues have identified a continuum of understanding of adoption that parallels cognitive development.[74] Young children can relay their adoption story to others but do not differentiate between adoption and birth as alternative pathways to family formation until they are of school age. For the very young child the concepts of adoption and birth are fused together, and joining the adoptive family is seen as a singular process involving both adoption and birth. Children often retrospectively report that they were told of their adoption around the age of four or five, when in actuality their parents told them as toddlers. This difference may be due to young children's lack of cognitive sophistication for meaningful understanding.[75] Brodzinsky describes the six-year-old child as capable of differentiating clearly between adoption and birth as alternative pathways to family formation and of accepting the adoptive family relationship as permanent without understanding why. At the next

---

69. Paul M. Brinich, "Adoption from the Inside Out: A Psychoanalytic Perspective," in *The Psychology of Adoption,* ed. David M. Brodzinsky and Marshall D. Schechter (New York: Oxford University Press, 1990), pp. 42-61.

70. Reitz and Watson, *Adoption and the Family System,* p. 132.

71. Winkler et al., *Clinical Practice in Adoption,* ch. 5.

72. See Mary M. Mason, *Designing Rituals of Adoption for the Religious and Secular Community* (Minneapolis: Resources for Adoptive Parents, 1995).

73. Gretchen Miller Wrobel, Julie K. Kohler, Harold D. Grotevant, and Ruth G. McRoy, "The Family Adoption Communication Model (FAC): Identifying Pathways of Adoption-Related Communication," *Adoption Quarterly* 7, no. 2 (2003): 53-84.

74. David M. Brodzinsky, Leslie Singer, and Anne Braff, "Children's Understanding of Adoption," *Child Development* 55 (1984): 869-78.

75. Ruth G. McRoy, Harold D. Grotevant, Susan Ayers-Lopez, and A. Furuta, "Adoption Revelation and Communication Issues: Implications for Practice," *Families in Society: The Journal of Contemporary Human Services* 50 (1990): 550-57.

level (eight to eleven years of age), children understand adoption permanence in a quasi-legal sense. They can articulate that an authority figure,
such as a judge or social worker, in some vaguely described way makes the
relationship permanent. Finally, in adolescence there is a full understanding of adoption as a permanent family relationship based on the legal
transfer of rights from birth to adoptive parents. The stages in understanding adoption underscore the importance of parents and children engaging in adoption-related communication throughout childhood, even
as they remember that it is important to acknowledge but not dwell on
the differences between adoptive and nonadoptive families.

Middle Childhood and the Adoptive Family

Middle childhood brings a time of heightened questioning by children
about their adoptive status. This is a time for exploring what it means to
be adopted and to have a birth family. Questions about the birth family
arise as adopted children more fully comprehend what it means to lose a
birth family while gaining an adoptive one. Regardless of how much information they have about their birth parents and birth families, all children are curious about both.[76] A growing sense of ambivalence about
adoption may take place in middle childhood as the adopted child deals
with the loss of his or her birth family. These feelings are common, and
adoptive parents should not regard them as the result of psychopathology
in the child or a parenting deficit in themselves. The child's ambivalence
is a typical part of a normal grief reaction.[77]

Parents who affirm their child's curiosity allow exploration of the
child's questions and emotions to take place openly.[78] At the same time,
parents need effectively to match communication about adoption with
what their child is seeking to understand. Parents who are not able to support their child's curiosity in a nurturing manner can create barriers to
information, increasing the possibility for future adjustment problems.[79]
When confronted with questions about birth parents and birth family
members, adoptive parents must make a decision about what information

76. Gretchen Miller Wrobel, Susan Ayers-Lopez, Harold D. Grotevant, Ruth G.
McRoy, and Meredith Friedrick, "Openness in Adoption and the Level of Child Participation," *Child Development* 67 (1996): 2358-74.

77. Brodzinsky, Smith, and Brodzinsky, *Children's Adjustment to Adoption*, p. 30.

78. Portello, "Mother-Infant Attachment Process," p. 187.

79. Brodzinsky and Pinderhughes, "Parenting and Child Development," p. 291.

they will share with their children. The amount of information parents have, the changing pressure of their child's curiosity, and their child's developmental level all influence information-sharing decisions. The decision to share or withhold information yields four options: (1) share all available information, (2) share all available information while seeking more, (3) share some information and withhold other information, or (4) withhold all available information.[80] Parents report that the decision to share or withhold information is often based on the age of their child. They may withhold information they feel the child is not yet ready to hear with the full intention of sharing it when the time is right. Withholding information can have important implications for an adopted child, which may vary depending upon the nature of the information and timing of subsequent disclosure.[81] In all, it is important for parents to support their child's curiosity and to realize that the need to know is a normative part of growing up adopted.

Adolescence and the Adoptive Family

Adolescence brings about change: physical change that results in sexual maturity, cognitive change that allows for perspective-taking and hypothetical thinking, and a change in social status from child to adult. It is an important time for understanding the meaning of experiences and circumstances within the context of the family and greater community.[82] For adopted adolescents, meaning-making has an added layer of complexity as they negotiate how being adopted influences their personal views and worldviews. Adopted teens do think about their adoptive status. Benson, Sharma, and Roehlkepartain surveyed 881 adolescents about being adopted. Twenty-seven percent of the teens endorsed the statement "adoption is a big part of how I think about myself," and 41 percent said they thought about adoption at least two to three times per month or as frequently as daily.[83] Girls reported more often than boys that adoption

80. Wrobel et al., "The Family Adoption Communication Model."

81. Wrobel et al., "Openness in Adoption and the Level of Child Participation," pp. 2372-73, and Wrobel et al., "Family Adoption Communication Model."

82. See Harold D. Grotevant, "Adolescent Development in Family Contexts," in *Handbook of Child Psychology*, vol. 3: *Social, Emotional, and Personality Development*, ed. Nancy Eisenberg (New York: John Wiley and Sons, 1996), pp. 1097-1149.

83. Peter Benson, Anu Sharma, and Eugene Roehlkepartain, *Growing Up Adopted: A Portrait of Adolescents and Their Families* (Minneapolis: Search Institute, 1994), p. 22.

influenced how they viewed themselves and said they thought about adoption more frequently (though this finding applied only to same-race adoptions).[84]

Two adolescent tasks are especially influenced by adoption: identity development and the psychological work of exploring birth-family connections. The adoptive family is an important context within which these tasks take place.

The development of a personal identity is a core task for all adolescents. Identity is often associated with domains in which individuals have some degree of control (for example, occupation and values). Yet there are many domains that individuals have no control over — such as race, sex, and adoptive status — that influence self-understanding and identity development.[85] Harold Grotevant states that the unique identity challenges adopted adolescents face "are about the givens in their lives rather than about the choices they are to make."[86] Integration of their adoptive status into their emerging sense of identity is crucial for adolescents and "involves constructing a narrative that somehow includes, explains, accounts for, or justifies their adoptive status."[87] This integration begins the process of constructing an adoptive identity.

An early marker of exploration that leads to an adoptive identity is adolescent preoccupation with adoption. Kohler, Grotevant, and McRoy found in their research that the level of intense, reflective thinking about adoption is related to adolescents' relationships in their adoptive families.[88] Adolescents indicating extremely high levels of preoccupation with adoption reported higher levels of alienation from both adoptive mothers and fathers and lower levels of trust for both, when compared to adolescents reporting extremely low levels of preoccupation. In between these extremes, adolescents with the second-highest level of preoccupation reported the same pattern of alienation, but only from fathers, when compared to those reporting moderate and low levels of preoccupation. Despite differences in perceived alienation and trust, all adolescents reported positive family functioning and communication. These researchers

84. Benson, Sharma, and Roehlkepartain, *Growing Up Adopted,* p. 22.

85. Harold D. Grotevant, "Coming to Terms with Adoption: The Construction of Identity from Adolescence into Adulthood," *Adoption Quarterly* 1, no. 1 (1997): 3-27.

86. Grotevant, "Coming to Terms with Adoption," p. 9.

87. Grotevant, "Coming to Terms with Adoption," pp. 10-11.

88. Julie K. Kohler, Harold D. Grotevant, and Ruth G. McRoy, "Adopted Adolescents' Preoccupation with Adoption: The Impact on Adoptive Family Relationships," *Journal of Marriage and Family* 64 (2002): 93-104.

concluded that adolescents who view their adoptive status as more salient may emotionally withdraw from their parents in order to engage in periods of intense reflection about their adoptive status, while adolescents who view adoptive status as less significant may not. Given the context of positive family functioning and communication reported by the adolescents, the study further concluded that adolescents view such times of withdrawal as normative and not detrimental to overall family functioning.

Grotevant and his colleagues conceptualized adoptive identity as being composed of three aspects: an intrapsychic component, a component involving family relationships, and a component involving the social world beyond the family.[89] How adoption is viewed in these three areas contextualizes adoptive identity development. The intrapsychic component encompasses the cognitive and affective processes of adoptive identity formation. Exploration of adoption for self-meaning is normative and includes incorporating what it means to have both a birth and an adoptive family. While adopted adolescents show a wide range of interest in exploring adoptive identity, they influence the intensity with which such exploration occurs by questioning parents about their adoption, independently learning more about adoption from resources outside the family (such as the internet), and talking with other adopted persons.

Previous communication about adoption sets the relational context of the family within which adoptive identity exploration takes place. While adolescents can become more insistent and independent in their exploration, much specific, personal adoption-related information is still controlled by the adults in the adoption kinship network. Adoptive parents need to decide what known information they will share with their adolescents. Information previously withheld because the parent felt the child was not ready to receive it again becomes the focus of a decision about disclosure.[90] Parental expression of empathy and understanding of their adopted adolescent's desire to know more about his or her background promotes an atmosphere that is accepting of continued adoption-related questioning.

The social world of the adolescent influences identity development when descriptions of the adopted adolescent offered by others are compared and contrasted with a self-constructed identity. Positive or negative

89. Harold D. Grotevant, Nora Dunbar, Julie K. Kohler, and Amy Lash Esau, "Adoptive Identity: How Contexts within and beyond the Family Shape Developmental Pathways," *Family Relations* 49 (2000): 379-87.

90. Wrobel et al., "The Family Adoption Communication Model."

social evaluations of adoption can provoke thought about how adoption should be incorporated into the adolescent's identity. Facing the social stigma associated with adoption intensifies in adolescence as teens independently negotiate broader social worlds. Direct experience with social stigma can influence later decisions to search out more specific personal adoption information at the age of majority,[91] and such information-seeking may take place independently of adoptive parents. Negative societal feedback can lead to feelings of not belonging, while positive messages about adoption can enhance self-esteem and promote a secure adoptive identity.

Using the narratives of adopted adolescents, Dunbar and Grotevant have identified four patterns of adoptive identity: unexamined, limited, unsettled, and integrated.[92] These patterns represent a progression of increasing adoption exploration. Adolescents with unexamined identities have not spent time reflecting on a personal meaning of adoption. Adoption is not considered a salient issue, and little emotion is associated with their view of it. Limited adoption identities are associated with a willingness to discuss and think about adoption while having low levels of curiosity. Differences between adoptive and nonadoptive families are downplayed while adoption is viewed positively for all members of the adoption kinship network. Adolescents with unsettled adoption identities put much energy into thinking about adoption and often hold feelings of rejection and anger. Adolescents in this group are in the process of figuring out their feelings about adoption, especially in relation to their birth parents. Those with integrated adoptive identities have explored in depth both positive and negative aspects of their adoption. Overall, they have developed a coherent, positive view of adoption.

It is important to remember that there is no one approach that adopted adolescents take when exploring their adoptive identity. For some the issues are highly salient, while for others they are not. For example, some adopted adolescents may be serious about searching for birth parents while others are not. Both choices are common and potentially healthy.[93] Adoptive parents can be sensitive to the needs of their adoles-

91. Karen March, "Perception of Adopting as Social Stigma: Motivation for Search and Reunion," *Journal of Marriage and the Family* 57 (1995): 653-60.

92. Nora Dunbar and Harold D. Grotevant, "Adoption Narratives: The Construction of Adoptive Identity During Adolescence," in *Family Stories and the Life Course: Across Time and Generations,* ed. M. W. Pratt and B. H. Fiese (Mahwah, N.J.: Earlbaum, 2004).

93. For a discussion of adopted adolescent search behavior, see Wrobel, Grotevant, and McRoy, "Adolescent Search for Birthparents."

cents by providing an open atmosphere that is accepting of adoption-related communication and by understanding that the intensity with which adolescents explore their adoptive identities has implications for their self-understanding.

Adoptive Openness and Family Relationships

Changing adoption practice has begun to highlight issues related to contact between adopted children and birth parents.[94] Adoption practice has grown to include making adoption plans for children in sibling groups, children with special needs, children from countries outside of the United States, and children from racial groups other than that of the prospective parents.[95] Domestic availability of Caucasian infants has decreased, giving birthmothers of these children greater say in formation of adoption plans. Older children placed for adoption often know or remember their birth parents, and many birthmothers placing infants for adoption request some form of continued contact with the adoptive family. A growing number of internationally adopted adolescents and young adults are visiting the country of their birth to gain information about their birth parents and the culture of that country. These are just some of the factors that have influenced the movement to greater openness in adoption. Today most adoption agencies have responded by incorporating openness into their adoption practice.[96]

Grotevant and McRoy have described openness in adoption as a continuum of contact and communication between members of the adopted child's birth and adoptive families.[97] Confidential adoption is characterized by the absence of communication between adoptive and birth families, with information shared at placement being general and nonidentifying. Fully disclosed adoption is at the opposite end of the continuum from confidential adoption and involves varying amounts of

94. For a discussion of the history of open adoption, see Annette Baran and Ruben Pannor, "Open Adoption," in *The Psychology of Adoption,* ed. David M. Brodzinsky and Marshall D. Schechter (New York: Oxford University Press, 1990), pp. 316-31.

95. Harold D. Grotevant and Julie K. Kohler, "Adoptive Families," in *Parenting and Child Development in Nontraditional Families,* ed. M. E. Lamb (Mahwah, N.J.: Erlbaum, 1999), pp. 161-90.

96. Susan Henney, Steven Onken, Ruth G. McRoy, and Harold D. Grotevant, "Changing Adoption Practices toward Openness," *Adoption Quarterly* 1, no. 3 (1998): 45-76.

97. Grotevant and McRoy, *Openness in Adoption.*

direct contact between birth and adoptive families. Mediated adoption is in the middle of the continuum and involves the exchange of nonidentifying information through an intermediary, typically the adoption agency. A decision to participate in an open adoption implies that the adoptive parents have accepted that the boundaries of their family extend to the birth family.[98]

Even though domestic adoption without some form of contact is no longer the norm, many questions remain about the impact openness has on adopted children and their families. How much contact is desirable, between whom, and at what stage of development? Openness is a dynamic process[99] influenced by the desires of the adopted child or adolescent, by adoptive and birth family dynamics, and by the current level of openness.[100] Adoptive parents across all openness levels generally feel secure in their role as parents, though differences do exist.[101] Parents in fully disclosed adoptions demonstrate greater degrees of empathy about adoption, have open communication with their children about adoption, and are less fearful of the birthmother reclaiming the child than are parents in confidential adoptions.

The dynamic nature of adoption does not allow for a single approach that can be applied to all adoption situations. There are differing needs for information among birthmothers, adoptive parents, and adopted children. The desire for information can change in intensity across time, and requests for communication or contact must be negotiated between birth and adoptive families. Moreover, requests from one side may not be in tune with the ability of the recipient to act upon them.

Collaboration in the Adoptive Kinship Network

Grotevant and McRoy have longitudinally followed a nationwide group of adoptive families and birthmothers as part of the Minnesota/Texas Adop-

98. Grotevant, Dunbar, Kohler, and Esau, "Adoptive Identity," p. 384.

99. Harold D. Grotevant, "Openness in Adoption: Research with the Kinship Network," *Adoption Quarterly* 4, no. 1 (2000): 45-65.

100. Gretchen M. Wrobel, Harold D. Grotevant, Jerica Berge, Tai Mendenhall, and Ruth G. McRoy, "Contact in Adoption: The Experience of American Adoptive Families," *Adoption and Fostering* 27 (2003): 57-67.

101. Harold D. Grotevant, Ruth G. McRoy, Carol Elde, and Deborah Lewis Fravel, "Adoptive Family System Dynamics: Variations by Level of Openness in the Adoption," *Family Process* 33 (1994): 125-46.

tion Research Project.[102] Interviews with adoptive parents, birthmothers, and adopted children have revealed how openness can be negotiated over time, with members of the adoption kinship network sometimes encountering an asymmetry in the need for communication. For example, birthmothers, in the early months after placement, expressed a strong need to know that the children they placed were safe and doing well. At the same time, adoptive parents were less intensely interested in communication with the birthmother as they attended to the tasks of family formation. As the adopted children grew and became more curious about their adoptions, birthmothers were sometimes less able to meet a communication request because of a marriage, career demands, or parenting of subsequent children. Understanding the different communication needs of members in the adoption kinship network can help place requests and responses in a broader context. Thus, for example, a lack of response may not mean rejection of the request, but the inability to respond at a particular time.

Such empathic interpretation is an example of collaboration in the adoption kinship network. Collaboration, the ability of adoptive and birth family members to work together across time on behalf of the child's well-being, is an important protective factor in the development of the child.[103] Collaboration involves empathy with one another's viewpoints and needs, willingness to listen and compromise, and commitment to mutuality of relationships for the child's benefit. In openness situations, collaboration in the adoption kinship network allows for empathic interpretations of the complexities associated with boundary negotiation and communication.

Over time, birth and adoptive families may desire a changed level of openness. Two studies demonstrate how collaboration in relationships can affect such a process. In the Grotevant and McRoy study, mutual agreement by the adoptive parents and birth families of pre-adolescent children allowed a change of openness (for families who desired such a change) from mediated to fully disclosed, regardless of who initiated the change.[104] For adoptive families who were dissatisfied with the amount of openness,

102. See Grotevant and McRoy, *Openness in Adoption,* for a complete description of the Minnesota/Texas Adoption Research Project.

103. Harold D. Grotevant, Nicole Ross, Marianne Marchel, and Ruth G. McRoy, "Adaptive Behavior in Adopted Children: Predictors from Early Risk, Collaboration in Relationships within the Adoptive Kinship Network, and Openness Arrangements," *Journal of Adolescent Research* 14 (1999): 231-47.

104. Tai J. Mendenhall, Harold D. Grotevant, and Ruth G. McRoy, "Adoptive Couples: Communication and Changes Made in Openness Levels," *Family Relations* 45 (1996): 223-29.

the desire was for more, not less, contact, and adoptive parents said that they maintained relationships with the birthmother because they felt it was in the best interests of their child.[105] Elsbeth Neil interviewed birth relatives and adoptive parents of thirty-six children in fully disclosed adoptions approximately 2.5 years after placement.[106] At that time, 45 percent of the openness arrangements had changed, with about half increasing in openness or contact frequency and half decreasing.[107] When the families worked out a change in contact that allowed them move to an arrangement that met their particular needs, contact was generally viewed favorably. Further research, however, is needed to describe the family system dynamics involved with openness change for families with adolescents.

Openness and Adolescent Search Intentions

Curiosity about one's adoption spans childhood, adolescence, and adulthood, and openness in adoption does not eliminate children's curiosity.[108] Even for children in adoptions that are characterized by information exchange and contact, curiosity exists. While children in fully disclosed adoptions may know who they look like (unlike those children who have not had face-to-face contact or seen pictures of their birth parents), they are curious about other pertinent details, such as how their birthmother's new job is going or what may change when she moves farther away. For adolescents who are not in fully disclosed adoptions, curiosity leads to a significant amount of psychological work related to searching. Searching represents one attempt to synthesize the dual identities offered by birth and adoptive families.[109]

In contrast to the search literature that primarily focuses on confidentially adopted adults searching for birth parents, Wrobel, Grotevant, and McRoy examined the search intentions of ninety-three adopted adolescents representing the range of openness arrangements.[110] These ado-

---

105. Grotevant, McRoy, Elde, and Fravel, "Adoptive Family System Dynamics," pp. 141-42.

106. Elsbeth Neil, "Contact after Adoption: The Role of Agencies in Making and Supporting Plans," *Adoption and Fostering* 26 (2002): 25-38.

107. Neil, "Contact after Adoption," p. 31.

108. Wrobel et al., "Openness in Adoption and the Level of Child Participation," p. 2371.

109. Reitz and Watson, *Adoption and the Family System*, p. 237.

110. Wrobel, Grotevant, and McRoy, "Adolescent Search for Birthparents."

lescents' responses revealed that *thinking* about searching is normative in the adolescent experience, regardless of whether the person ultimately decides to search or not. All adolescents in the study were able to express their thoughts about searching and their particular desire for contact. Contrary to the common belief that all adopted persons want increased information or contact, there were adolescents who did not want to seek out further information. Satisfaction with the amount of adoptive openness was negatively associated with intention to search for birth parents: those most satisfied said they had no intention to search further, and those least satisfied were sure they would search. The level of openness in the adolescent's adoption was also associated with search intention. Adolescents who had information about their birth parents more often stated they intended to search further or had actually done so. One of the most important findings of this study was that adolescent intentions to search were not related to poor adoptive family relationships or adolescent maladjustment.

Conclusion

Adoptive families have an added layer of complexity to negotiate as their members construct a life together. At each stage of development, good communication, developmentally sensitive parenting, and willingness to engage in the unique tasks of adoptive parenting are associated with positive outcomes for adopted children. These characteristics of strong adoptive families are founded on the more general and enduring principles that can be found in an ethic of Christian hospitality as outlined earlier in this chapter. At the same time, those principles are given flesh and flexibility as adoptive families form, as their children develop, and as the composition and openness of adoptive families continue to change.

2. Adoption, Parentage, and Procreative Stewardship

BRENT WATERS

In the debates over the morality of assisted reproduction (and it is against the background of the growing technological ability to control procreation that the morality of adoption must be assessed), it is ironic that adoption is often invoked by various disputants to bolster their respective arguments. On the one hand, for instance, proponents of reproductive freedom assert that the varying degrees of genetic relatedness (if any) between a child and one or both parents resulting from the use of reproductive technologies is ethically irrelevant, given the legal and moral status of adoption. On the other hand, opponents counter that if a genetic or biological bond is irrelevant to the parent-child relationship, then assisted reproduction is rendered unnecessary given the large number of orphans and unwanted children that need to be adopted. Within these debates, however, little explicit attention has been devoted to adoption as a uniquely moral act.[1] This lack of attention tends to reduce adoption to a reproductive option or alternative, thereby stripping it of its distinctive moral significance.

The purpose of this chapter is to sketch out the lineaments of a normative account of adoption.[2] This is accomplished by examining procre-

---

1. Notable exceptions include Lisa Sowle Cahill, *Sex, Gender, and Christian Ethics* (Cambridge: Cambridge University Press, 1996), pp. 246-49; Germain Grisez, *Living a Christian Life*, vol. 2 of *The Way of the Lord Jesus* (Quincy, Ill.: Franciscan Press, 1993), pp. 689-90; and Stephen G. Post, *More Lasting Unions: Christianity, the Family, and Society* (Grand Rapids: Eerdmans, 2000), pp. 119-50.

2. This essay draws and expands upon previous work appearing in Brent Waters, *Reproductive Technology: Toward a Theology of Procreative Stewardship* (London: Dartman, Longman and Todd, 2001), pp. 68-75, and "Welcoming Children into Our Homes: A Theological Reflection on Adoption," *Scottish Journal of Theology* 55, no. 4 (2002): 424-37.

ative liberty as the dominant moral framework coming to define the public perception of parentage within so-called secular societies. In response, I employ the alternative framework of procreative stewardship to embed a normative understanding of the parent-child relationship within the institutions of marriage and family as informed by the Christian tradition. The moral significance of adoption is further explicated by focusing on issues involving single parents, same-sex couples, and "spare" embryos. The chapter concludes by exploring what kinds of larger questions of social and political ordering are implied by the preceding examination of parentage and adoption.

A Tale of Two Adoptions

What are people doing when they adopt an infant?[3] This presumably straightforward question may seem to be answerable in an equally straightforward manner. All we need to do is describe how individuals become legally recognized parents of infants with whom they share no biological or genetic bond. Yet as the following two vignettes demonstrate, no singular reply can be offered to this seemingly simple question.

The first vignette takes place in the United Kingdom. A young married couple gives birth to their first child. A few years later they want to have a second child, but rather than attempting natural procreation again they decide to adopt. Their motivation is religious: they believe that God is calling them to adopt an infant whose natural parents are unable to provide adequate care. Their decision to adopt initiates a lengthy and arduous process of inspection and introspection. Various social service agencies conduct background checks, the physical and mental health of the prospective adoptive parents is evaluated, their home is inspected a number of times, and they are interviewed extensively regarding their reasons for adopting. This intense scrutiny forces them to ponder and clarify what being a parent means in terms of their religious and moral convictions. Finally, after nearly a year they are declared to be eligible adoptive parents, and a few months later they adopt their second child.

The second vignette occurs at roughly the same time in the United States. A middle-aged couple has been trying unsuccessfully to have a

3. For the sake of clarity, I concentrate on issues pertaining to adopting newborn infants rather than older children.

baby for a number of years. They desperately want a child to fulfill their marriage. They explore the possibility of assisted reproduction, but reject this option for a variety of personal and financial reasons and opt for adoption. They choose to pursue a private adoption because there are few suitable infants available through domestic agencies, and they have heard horror stories about international adoptions. Their lawyer has an excellent placement record, and after a few initial disappointments he locates a good prospect — a pregnant woman in a neighboring state who wants to find a good home for her baby. This is not the first time the lawyer has worked with this woman, and he is confident that she can be depended upon to surrender the baby following birth. After extensive medical tests of the woman, monitoring of the fetus, and more testing of the newborn baby, the couple initiates the necessary legal procedures and brings their new child home. The lawyer's fees, transportation expenses, and medical costs (including prenatal care, fetal testing and screening, delivery, and postnatal care) add up to approximately half the average cost of a successful birth using assisted reproduction. *Motivation A*

In both instances a married couple is awarded legal custody of an infant, but beyond this cursory resemblance the vignettes disclose two contrasting accounts of adoption. Not only are the two couples motivated by differing purposes, but the procedures they follow also reflect contrasting legal principles and social mores regarding the moral meaning and ordering of parentage. In order to compare and assess these differing accounts of adoption, however, we must first examine the contrasting understandings of parentage in which they are embedded. We begin this exploration by examining what is emerging as the dominant secular framework: procreative liberty.

Procreative Liberty

The principal tenets of procreative liberty may be set forth by examining the influential work of its leading proponent.[4] According to John Robertson, "procreative liberty is the freedom either to have children or to avoid having them. Although often expressed or realized in the context of a cou-

---

4. See John A. Robertson, *Children of Choice: Freedom and the New Reproductive Technologies* (Princeton, N.J.: Princeton University Press, 1994). For critical assessments of Robertson's account of procreative liberty, see Gilbert C. Meilaender, *Body, Soul, and Bioethics* (Notre Dame: University of Notre Dame Press, 1995), pp. 61-88, and Waters, *Reproductive Technology*, pp. 19-31.

ple, it is first and foremost an individual interest."[5] Moreover, this interest
is valued highly "because control over whether one reproduces or not is
central to personal identity, to dignity, and to the meaning of one's life."[6]
Consequently, individuals choosing to reproduce should have few, if any,
restrictions imposed upon them regardless of whether the means employed are natural, technologically assisted, or adoptive. The single proviso is that the interests of other persons may not be harmed in exercising
one's reproductive rights. Individuals, for example, should not be forced
to engage in sexual intercourse, donate gametes, or surrender custody of
their children against their will.

Although reproducing is an individual right, it cannot be exercised individually. Thus Robertson goes to great lengths in formulating what he
calls "collaborative reproduction."[7] Collaborative reproduction denotes an
agreement or contract between "commissioners" and "collaborators." Commissioners are individuals wishing to obtain children whom the commissioners, as parents, intend to raise. Most often commissioners are single
persons, or infertile or same-sex couples. Collaborators are individuals providing services, usually donated gametes or gestation, to commissioners.

Since there is no empirical evidence that children are harmed in separating the biological and social aspects of parentage, the most pressing
issue is to establish procedures protecting the respective interests of commissioners and collaborators. This goal is achieved by assigning commissioners a presumptive status in preconception contracts specifying the
roles and responsibilities of all the parties.[8] If collaborators are excluded
from child rearing, their role is limited to providing the services described
above, while if they are included in child-rearing responsibilities, their duties and limitations should be specified. If a dispute occurs, the contract
trumps "the claims of donors or surrogates who later insist on a different
role than they had agreed upon."[9] Consequently, laws should define parentage in contractual terms rather than codifying a biological, genetic, or
gestational relationship to offspring, thereby in the former case supporting a "fundamental" right to "use non-coital means of forming families."[10] Without these contractual safeguards, infertile couples or individ-

5. Robertson, *Children of Choice,* p. 22.
6. Robertson, *Children of Choice,* p. 24.
7. Robertson, *Children of Choice,* pp. 119-45.
8. The presumption holds only so "long as the welfare of offspring will not be severely damaged by honoring those intentions" (Robertson, *Children of Choice,* p. 125).
9. Robertson, *Children of Choice,* p. 126.
10. Robertson, *Children of Choice,* p. 131.

uals without suitable partners are deprived of their right to reproduce, and collaborators are denied financial or altruistic opportunities to assist others in pursuing their reproductive interests.

Although the principal purpose of Robertson's account of collaborative reproduction is to justify a virtually unrestricted use of reproductive technology, his argument also raises an important implication for parentage in general, because he effectively reduces it to an outcome of the will. A parent is an individual who has commissioned a collaborative process that concludes successfully in obtaining a child. As Robertson asserts, commissioners are the true parents because "they were the prime movers in bringing all the parties together to produce the child," in doing so relying on the promises or contracts with the "gamete providers and gestator" to accomplish their goal.[11] Yet if parentage is essentially an act of will, then any means employed to obtain a child is necessarily a form of collaborative reproduction. The only difference among a fertile couple reproducing naturally, an infertile man obtaining donated gametes and a surrogate, and a couple adopting a child is the extent of collaboration required to achieve the identical goal of obtaining a child. In each instance the commissioners have merely employed a different reproductive option.

The imagery of picking and choosing among reproductive options is, however, misleading. In reducing parentage to an assertive will, the resulting choices are not genuine options but differing guises of what is the essentially common act of commissioning a reproductive project. This reductionistic presumption is seen clearly in Robertson's "loop back to adoption."[12] Although collaborative reproduction usually produces a child genetically related to at least one parent, he admits that the techniques deployed do not depend on any biological relationship, and, as adoption already demonstrates, there is no compelling reason to believe that such a relationship needs to be present.

Adoption also challenges Robertson's portrayal of parent as commissioner, because it would promote a "widespread market in paid conception, pregnancies, and adoptions, the very antithesis of the current system."[13] Although Robertson sees no inherent problem in the emergence of such a market, he recommends that until such time as antiquated adoption laws are reformed, collaborative reproduction should be restricted to producing offspring genetically related to at least one parent. Otherwise,

11. Robertson, *Children of Choice*, p. 143.
12. Robertson, *Children of Choice*, pp. 142-43.
13. Roberson, *Children of Choice*, p. 143.

sufficient political opposition may be generated to restrict the use of reproductive technology, so in the meantime adoption should be "permitted to function independently with its own rules."[14] But the goal is eventually to collapse adoption into a comprehensive motif of procreative liberty in which commissioning becomes the sole criterion of parentage.

The problem that adoption poses to procreative liberty, however, is not merely one of a political tactic, but entails Robertson's move to redefine parentage solely in terms of the will, resulting in an inordinately thin account of the parent-child relationship. As Gilbert Meilaender has observed, "When we think of human beings chiefly as 'will,' as beings characterized by their interests, we see something true, but we miss much else."[15] What we miss are the social contexts and normative purposes that shape *what* we will and *how* we order our willing. Fixating on autonomous commissioners pursuing their reproductive interests not only distorts the relational character of parentage but also strips adoption of its inimitable quality. Although adoption is clearly associated with parentage, it nonetheless bears a moral significance and purpose that differs from procreative acts and purposes. Yet Robertson's thin rhetoric of rights and interests can neither acknowledge this distinction (other than as an expedient ploy) nor sustain the unique import of adoption, and thereby reduces it to a reproductive option. Describing this distinction and the distinctive quality of adoption requires a thicker moral vocabulary and grammar than that offered by procreative liberty, and to find a better-equipped alternative we must pay some attention to the social contexts and normative purposes which shape our understanding of parentage.

Procreative Stewardship

The theological framework of procreative stewardship provides a thicker moral vocabulary and grammar by emphasizing the continuity between procreation and child rearing in contrast to their casual separation in procreative liberty. The ordering of the biological and social aspects of parentage are in turn embedded within social spheres which presuppose this parental continuity, and it is in light of normative practices performed within these spheres that the distinctive moral significance of adoption is disclosed. I have developed a framework of procreative stewardship more

14. Robertson, *Children of Choice*, p. 144.
15. Meilaender, *Body, Soul, and Bioethics*, p. 88.

extensively elsewhere,[16] but its basic contours are outlined below by concentrating on the embodied character of procreation, and on marriage and family as the social spheres ordering the parental vocation and its practices.

It is odd that in Robertson's elaborate exposition of procreative liberty, little mention is made of the human body. Indeed, the body appears to be little more than a limitation to be overcome or a resource to be exploited. Commissioners encountering the limits of infertility or unsuitable partners may turn to collaborators to provide the required gametes or wombs. Yet even these bodily allusions are diluted, focusing as they do on discrete biological processes or materials. What Robertson fails to acknowledge is that even the most extensive forms of collaborative reproduction seek to assist, not displace, functions that can be performed only by embodied beings. Thus a biological bond between parents and children is rendered, ironically, an irrelevant consideration for those pursuing their *reproductive* interests.

In contrast, Meilaender contends that the biological bond reminds us that we are "embodied creatures who occupy a fixed place in the generations of humankind."[17] Lines of "kinship and descent" shape our identities by placing us within particular relationships and communities.[18] Parents and children are bound to persons not of their own choosing, reinforcing important lessons about the given character of human life. In addition, even though the "sexual union of a man and a woman is naturally ordered toward the birth of children," this "simple biological fact" is not "governed simply by the rational will."[19] A child is not merely bred into existence, but is the result of a relationship involving mutual self-giving and anticipation regarding the bonds with the child that unfold over time. Thus Meilaender maintains that it is "surely natural for husband and wife to desire a child of 'their own.'"[20]

This natural desire for offspring is expressed and ordered through the social institutions of marriage and family. If this were not the case, then parentage would refer to little more than instinctual drives associated with reproduction and nurturance, presumably providing too thin a foundation to carry the weight of Robertson's claim that discovering the

16. See Waters, *Reproductive Technology,* pp. 32-127.

17. Gilbert C. Meilaender, *Bioethics: A Primer for Christians* (Grand Rapids: Eerdmans, 1996), p. 13.

18. Meilaender, *Bioethics,* p. 13.

19. Meilaender, *Bioethics,* p. 14.

20. Meilaender, *Bioethics,* p. 13.

meaning of life depends on successfully pursuing one's reproductive interests. Rather, parentage signifies a complex ordering of biological *and* social affinities involving the roles of spouse, parent, and child, affinities which may be described as familial.

The need for ordering these affinities has been acknowledged consistently within the Christian tradition. Augustine, for example, asserted that the goods of offspring, fidelity, and sacrament are inherent to marriage.[21] Moreover, these goods not only benefit the children and spouses of particular families but also promote the common good. Thomas Aquinas would later refine this Augustinian framework by placing greater emphasis on the friendship between wife and husband.[22] In a more contemporary vein, recent Catholic teaching has stressed parity between the procreative and unitive dimensions of marriage,[23] while a number of Protestant theologians have reformulated Pauline and Augustinian themes regarding the one-flesh unity of marriage.[24]

The purpose of this brief excursion into a Christian understanding of marriage is to suggest that parentage is not a free-standing category but derives its intelligibility from both a prior marital relationship and anticipated familial association. Marriage provides a foundation for a family in which the parental vocation is properly practiced, and through which the virtues inherent to that vocation derive their content. James Gustafson, for example, identifies "mutual fidelity," "keeping promises," "attending to mutual needs," and "readiness to serve others" as the chief virtues and practices of marriage and family.[25] Or in theological terms, marital love unfolds into a parental love that in turn is enfolded into a

21. See Augustine, "On the Good of Marriage."

22. See Thomas Aquinas, *Summa Theologica*, "Supplement to the Third Part," qq. 41-68.

23. See, e.g., Pope Paul VI, *Humanae vitae*, Official Vatican website, http://www.vatican.va/holy_father/paul_vi/encyclicals/documents/hf_p-vi_enc_25071968_humanae-vitae_en.html, accessed 30 March 2004; and Pope John Paul II, *Familiaris consortio*, Official Vatican website, http://www.vatican.va/holy_father/john_paul_ii/apost_exhortations/documents/hf_jp-ii_exh_19811122_familiaris-consortio_en.html, accessed 30 March 2004. See also Cahill, *Sex, Gender, and Christian Ethics*, pp. 166-216, and Grisez, *Living a Christian Life*, pp. 553-752.

24. See, e.g., Karl Barth, *Church Dogmatics* (Edinburgh: T. &T. Clark, 1961), III/4:116-240; Oliver O'Donovan, *Marriage and Permanence* (Bramcote, U.K.: Grove, 1978); and Paul Ramsey, *One Flesh: A Christian View of Sex within, outside and before Marriage* (Bramcote, U.K.: Grove, 1975).

25. James M. Gustafson, *Ethics and Theology*, vol. 2 of *Ethics from a Theocentric Perspective* (Chicago: University of Chicago Press, 1984), p. 170; see also pp. 153-84. Cf. Waters, *Reproductive Technology*, pp. 40-49.

more expansive familial love. In the absence of marriage and family, parentage becomes a highly ambiguous category because it is torn from the social context which defines and delineates the parent-child relationship in terms other than those imposed by autonomous individuals who have successfully pursued their reproductive interests.

Marriage and family order a natural desire for offspring by acknowledging that they are themselves deeply embedded in affinities that are simultaneously and inseparably biological *and* social. In the absence of this presumptive ordering, the healthy desire for a child of one's own can be easily corrupted into a child one owns, a status not too far removed from the image of parent as commissioner. A child is *not* made or otherwise obtained by a parent,[26] but is entrusted to the care of parents who welcome the child into a sphere of familial love and care. Children do not belong *to* their parents, but rather children and parents *belong together* in a family. It is acknowledging that parentage is characterized by a complex nexus of given biological and social affinities constituting a family that makes adoption explicable as a uniquely moral act.

Adoption As a Moral Act

It might be assumed that adoption is unintelligible given the basic principles of procreative stewardship as outlined above. The foundational status and embodied character of the one-flesh unity of marriage seemingly require that parentage denotes a necessary biological bond between children and parents. Such an assumption, however, pays insufficient attention to the fact that this bond is expressed through the social spheres of both marriage *and* family. Thus adoption signifies what Oliver O'Donovan describes as a "pattern of representation by replacement" in which "the social parents of the child act as parents to one who has been begotten by others."[27] The act of adoption presupposes a moral response by representing the normative continuity between procreation and child rearing.

We may say, then, that adoption is motivated initially by *caritas* or charity. This does not imply that a child needing to be adopted is an object of disinterested beneficence on the part of adoptive parents. On the

---

26. See Oliver O'Donovan, *Begotten or Made?* (Oxford: Clarendon, 1984). See also Gilbert Meilaender, *Things That Count: Essays Moral and Theological* (Wilmington, Del.: ISI, 2000), pp. 101-10.

27. O'Donovan, *Begotten or Made?* p. 35.

contrary, the uniquely moral significance of adoption rests in the parents' commitment to build an enduring and genuinely parental relationship with a child not "their own," but with whom they will find their mutual belonging together as a family. The stress upon *caritas* emphasizes that adoption marks a moral response to an adopted child as a neighbor in need, rather than fulfilling the so-called reproductive interests of the adoptive parents. It is the need of a child to be placed and welcomed into a home that grants adoption its moral and legal status. Although the plights of childless couples and parents surrendering their children are often relieved, these are secondary effects rather than the primary purpose of adoption. If adoption is to embody a genuine pattern of representation through substitution, it must retain, again in O'Donovan's words, "an element which can only be described adequately as charity — a coming to the aid of natural parents, who have declared that they are unable to discharge their obligations to the child they have brought into life."[28]

If *caritas* or charity is to carry the weight I am placing upon it in portraying adoption as a uniquely moral act, then some further definition is required. Charity does not refer to an act which is entirely nonreciprocal, dispassionate, or self-sacrificial. If this were the case, then *caritas* would distort rather than clarify the complex motives underlying adoption. Adoption marks the creation of a genuine family, and not a disinterested provision of parental care. An adoptive family is *not* a small orphanage. Although charity seeks the good of the other, which may at times be expressed in self-sacrificial ways, adoptive parents are not dispassionate about their adopted children but hold the same parental expectations and fears, and share the full range of joys and anxieties, that might characterize any family.[29] Consequently, it should not be surprising that many, if not most, couples seeking to adopt an infant do so in response to infertility or have otherwise had natural parental longings frustrated. Yet it is precisely because of charity's emphasis on the *good of the other* that it is needed to preserve the moral integrity of adoption. The purpose of adoption is to provide for the welfare of the child, and not to satisfy the parental desires of the adopting couple. Although the motives of particular couples to adopt are admittedly complex, the moral and legal discourse employed to describe and regulate their acts needs to stress the priority of charity if adoption is to resist being reduced to a reproductive option. In

28. O'Donovan, *Begotten or Made?* p. 37.
29. See Gilbert Meilaender, *The Limits of Love* (University Park, Pa.: Pennsylvania State University Press, 1987), pp. 15-18.

terms of the two vignettes described above, for instance, it is the varying motives and procedures employed which disclose the contrasting accounts of what adoption means.

The questions of motive and procedures present the greatest challenge to the normative account of adoption developed in this essay. If there is not a necessary biological bond in the parent-child relationship, then have I not unwittingly slipped into the same trap of procreative liberty, namely, that parentage denotes an act of will? After all, even charitable acts are willful — adoptive parents must choose to admit needful children into their homes. Moreover, although adoption is a response to children in need, does not my privileging of marriage as the moral and social foundation of parentage undercut the efficacy of this so-called charitable response? Is there any reason to believe that only married couples are suitable candidates to adopt? In order to address these objections, I turn to the issues of single persons and same-sex couples as adoptive parents, and to the morality of adopting spare embryos. I have chosen these issues because in each instance they are unproblematic within the framework of procreative liberty, but appear to present distinct challenges to my normative account of adoption.

Single Parents and Same-Sex Couples

It would appear that given the basic principles of procreative stewardship, single persons and same-sex couples should be prohibited from adopting children. There are presumably both theological and prudential reasons why this is the case.

It could be argued that single persons and same-sex couples should not adopt because in both instances they fail to represent the most foundational aspect of parentage, namely, the one-flesh unity of marriage. In respect to single persons, one individual is forced to play the roles of two parents. Although this dual role-playing can be accomplished, it is nonetheless cumbersome and emphasizes the absence of the missing parent. There is an inherent relational symmetry among the child, mother, and father that should be preserved within adoptive families. In respect to a same-sex couple, they can represent only at best a simulacrum of marriage.[30] Marriage is a relationship between a man and a woman, thereby providing the foundation for the proper social ordering of procreation

---

30. They should presumably be regarded as single people cohabitating.

and child rearing. Although two parents are present in a same-sex couple, there is still parental role confusion resulting from the absence of a parent of a particular sex. Admittedly, a same-sex couple preserves a social symmetry among children and parents, but it fails to acknowledge that this symmetry is delineated along biologically differentiated lines.

It may also be objected that single persons and same-sex couples acting as adoptive parents confuse two distinctive vocations. Within the Christian tradition, a clear division has been drawn between singleness and marriage. Although the theological development of this distinction has a checkered history, it marks an attempt to define the two vocations as possessing respective sets of mutually exclusive practices and virtues. In short, the ways of singleness are not the ways of marriage, and their two paths cannot be traveled simultaneously. Singleness frees individuals to devote their time to the work of the church or other altruistic endeavors, whereas married couples are necessarily focused on child rearing and maintaining households. Moreover, the respective practices and virtues of singleness and marriage are derived from a more expansive and corresponding vocational witness. Marriage and family bear a providential witness given their task of ordering the transition of life from one generation to the next, whereas singleness bears an eschatological witness pointing to the end of creation's temporal unfolding in which the roles of spouse, parent, and child are supplanted by sisterhood and brotherhood in Christ.[31] The distinguishing witness of each vocation is one reason why illegitimacy and married couples refusing to be open to the possibility of offspring have proven problematic throughout much of the history of Christian moral theology. Consequently, single persons and same-sex couples acting as adoptive parents would only serve to confuse the distinctive and mutually exclusive qualities of their respective witness.

In addition, there is a prudential consideration that must be taken into account. Recent studies indicate that children reared in intact families (defined minimally as child, mother, and father living together) fare better along a wide range of criteria than their counterparts in circumstances deviating from this norm.[32] If adoption embodies a charitable response to neighbors in need, then it would be irresponsible to place children in environments where they may receive less effective parental care.

31. See Rodney Clapp, *Families At the Crossroads: Beyond Traditional and Modern Options* (Downers Grove, Ill.: InterVarsity, 1993).

32. For a summary of this literature, see Don S. Browning et al., *From Culture Wars to Common Ground: Religion and the American Family Debate* (Louisville, Ky.: Westminster/John Knox, 1997), pp. 55-58.

In response, I contend that the theological objection that adoption by single individuals and same-sex couples fails to represent the one-flesh unity of marriage is misplaced. Adoptive parents do *not* represent marriage, but represent *familial belonging* to the child. The objection is right in insisting that ideally the one-flesh unity of marriage provides the normative foundation of parentage, and that the resulting symmetry among children and parents denotes both social and biological affinities. But this structure is not an absolute prerequisite for providing a familial sphere of mutual belonging. If this were the case, then widowed or abandoned spouses and stepparents would be inherently unfit parents, a claim that one is hard-pressed to make on either theological or moral grounds.

The objection also fails to recognize that although adoption is a genuine form of parentage, it should not be construed as a substitute reproductive act. The adopted child does not signify a successful reproductive outcome. The familial symmetry invoked by the objection refers to what Meilaender describes as the natural desire of a couple for a child of "their own." Adoption, however, is not grounded formally in this desire but is an act of charity. In this respect, in ordering the natural desire for offspring, a couple undertakes the parental vocation prior to the birth of their baby, whereas adoptive parents undertake this vocation in response to a child who has already been born. In both instances, however, the parental vocation is embedded in and derives its intelligibility from the familial social sphere. As was argued in the preceding paragraph, since the ideal symmetry among children and parents is not an absolute prerequisite for the family, there is no compelling reason to presume that single persons or same-sex couples should be necessarily excluded as adoptive parents, so long as the *initial* motive is charitable rather than reproductive.

Consequently, the respective witness of either marriage or singleness is not compromised, because of the charitable nature of adoption. The objection is correct in insisting that marriage and singleness represent different vocations, otherwise the former cannot bear witness to the goodness of creation nor the latter to creation's destiny,[33] but it fails to acknowledge that adoption per se does not challenge the distinction, because it is an act representing parentage to a child in need rather than the

---

33. According to O'Donovan, the early church "conceived of marriage and singleness as alternative vocations, each a worthy form of life, the two together comprising the whole Christian witness to the nature of the affectionate community. The one declared that God had vindicated the order of creation, the other pointed beyond it to its eschatological transformation" (Oliver O'Donovan, *Resurrection and Moral Order: An Outline for Evangelical Ethics* [Grand Rapids: Eerdmans, 1986], p. 70).

44

culmination of a procreative act. The objection should be directed against assisted reproductive projects in which single persons serve as commissioners, gamete donors, or surrogates.

Portraying adoption as a charitable response to a child in need casts the prudential consideration in a different light. The substantial evidence indicating that children tend to fare better in intact families is readily granted and should not be dismissed casually, but these studies disclose general tendencies rather than particular cases. Placing adopted children exclusively in intact families does not guarantee that every child will receive optimal parental care. Indeed in some instances, especially in the case of older children who have been orphaned, prudence might dictate that single persons or same-sex couples who are related to or close friends of the natural parents are in the best position to adopt given their familiarity with the children. Moreover, the well-being of children is often "measured" in the absence of any strong normative claims regarding the nature of adoption. The principal motive driving natural or assisted reproduction is, for instance, different from that of adoption, thereby affecting the well-being of adopted children differently as well. In the absence of discerning this normative distinction, invoking the appearance (or irrelevance) of a preferred family structure becomes a crude political weapon used by partisans in the culture wars over so-called "family values," a move that serves to disregard the needs of adoptive children.

Spare Embryos

For the purpose of this exploration, "spare embryos" refers to embryos that have been produced outside a woman's body, and have not been selected for implantation.[34] These embryos are usually destroyed, although in some instances they are donated to individuals or couples pursuing assisted reproduction.

Within the framework of procreative stewardship, a case could perhaps be made that spare embryos should be made eligible for adoption. Given the prospect of imminent destruction, surely these embryos are neighbors in great need, and what more charitable response could be offered to them than the opportunity to develop and be born? Although

---

34. For the sake of simplicity, the following discussion will assume that the spare embryos in question are "healthy" candidates for implantation, and do not include embryos that have been excluded because they have tested positively for deleterious genetic traits.

adopting an embryo requires that it be implanted, gestated, and given birth, this should not be regarded as a reproductive process but as the necessary means to achieve the charitable end of adoption. Since adopting a child does not violate the biological symmetry of the family, then neither is it violated by adopting an embryo; it is merely applying the same principle, albeit at a much earlier stage in a child's development. Moreover, since marriage is not an absolute prerequisite for maintaining a family, many single persons and same-sex couples would be in a position to adopt (or assist others to adopt, by serving, for example, as a surrogate) spare embryos. In addition, adopting embryos would reinforce a key principle of procreative stewardship, namely, that children are not owned by their parents. Contrary to the tenets of procreative liberty, an embryo is not property that can be disposed of by its owner or commissioner. Requiring that spare embryos be made eligible for adoption could serve as a reminder that parents do not have the power of life and death over offspring.

I agree that spare embryos are neighbors in need, but, in spite of the foregoing, adoption is not a fitting response to their plight.[35] The argument asserts that implanting, gestating, and giving birth to spare embryos should not be construed as a reproductive project. Rather, they are the requisite means that must be employed to achieve the goal of adopting a child who would otherwise not be born. This stratagem, however, stretches the concept of adoption beyond the parameters of what it is intended to represent. Although adoption procedures may be initiated during a pregnancy, they are *not* instigated prior to a woman becoming pregnant. A woman agreeing to have an existing embryo implanted is not serving formally as a surrogate in respect to having the intention of surrendering the child upon birth,[36] but she is nonetheless providing a gestational service for an embryo with whom she shares no genetic relationship. What is being proposed is not so much adoption as an altruistically motivated form of collaborative reproduction. In order to adopt an embryo, the so-called adoptive parent must play a role similar to that of a commissioner overseeing a collaborative reproductive project. Consequently, the perception of embryos as property is reinforced rather than

---

35. For a discussion of the embryo as neighbor, see my essay on "Does the Human Embryo Have a Moral Status?" in *God and the Embryo: Religious Perspectives on the Debate over Stem Cells and Cloning*, ed. Brent Waters and Ronald Cole-Turner (Washington, D.C.: Georgetown University Press, 2003).

36. Unless the woman is serving as a surrogate for a woman or an infertile couple who are adopting the embryo.

challenged by the collaborative means required to make embryo adoption possible.

It is also not evident that charity can be extended to spare embryos. It is arguable that adoption denotes a charitable response to a *child* in need of parental care and familial belonging. It is not clear, however, that charity bids us to give every *embryo* an opportunity or chance to develop and be born. Such a charitable response would apply only if an ontological status is presumed that is equal to that of a child who has already been born.[37] No such presumption regarding the ontological status of the embryo underlies the framework of procreative stewardship outlined in this essay.[38] This should not suggest that embryos are excluded from the human community or rigorous moral regard, but simply acknowledges that they are not in need of immediate parental care. Nor does my reticence to stipulate an ontological status imply that the destruction of spare embryos is morally justified, but only that adoption should not be used as a tactic to circumvent the problem. Rather, attention should be directed toward regulating the use of reproductive technology in ways that lessen or eliminate the need to create spare embryos.

Revisiting the Tale of Two Adoptions

With the preceding discussions of procreative liberty and procreative stewardship in mind, we may now return to the tale of two adoptions in order to account for their contrasting motives and procedures. We will first examine the motives and then turn our attention to the procedures described in these vignettes. In addition, revisiting this tale will help clarify the principal argument that adoption is a uniquely moral act.

The first couple wants to have a second child by adopting an infant. Presumably the reason is not that the woman is unable or unwilling to become pregnant again. Rather, their decision is motivated by the need of a child to be placed in a family. The second couple pursues a private adoption in response to infertility. They admit they are desperate to have a child in order to fulfill an otherwise incomplete marriage. The first couple's decision marks a charitable response to a child in need, whereas the

---

37. See, e.g., John Berkman, "Adopting Embryos in America: A Case Study," *Scottish Journal of Theology* 55, no. 4 (2002): 438-60.

38. My reasons for stipulating agnosticism regarding the ontological status of the embryo are developed in Waters, *Reproductive Technology*, pp. 102-27.

second couple selects adoption as a means of satisfying their reproductive interests.

It would be a mistake simply to contrast the apparent altruism of one couple against the apparent selfishness of the other, because their respective motives are more complex than first meets the eye. The first couple does not stumble upon an orphaned infant, and out of sympathy or sense of religious duty bring her home where she can be clothed and fed. They had already decided that they wanted a second child, and adoption provided a means of implementing this decision in a way that also addressed other moral convictions they hold. Consequently, their decision to adopt was informed by other considerations that are self-regarding, a fact that does not detract from the charitable nature of their act, which can still be charitable even if it is not entirely dispassionate or sacrificial. Nor is the second couple simply indulging an egotistical self-fulfillment. As was argued above, it is natural that a couple should want a child of their own, and it is understandable that they would turn to adoption when this healthy desire is frustrated. Nonetheless, *how* a child is viewed differs remarkably in these two vignettes. For the first couple, the need of the child remains the paramount objective, while for the second couple their need to obtain a child is the principal consideration. Or to invoke an admittedly crude image, the first couple approaches the social service agency with the question, is there a child that needs to be adopted? Whereas the second couple issues their lawyer the command, find us a child.

The most striking contrast, however, is not the most conspicuous desires and commitments that form the respective motives to adopt but what is missing. The second couple pursues adoption to overcome their frustrated desire to have a child of their own. Although this is a good desire, the way they go about satisfying it is akin, or at least bears a resemblance, to a reproductive project. Adoption is employed as an alternative means to compensate for their frustrated attempts to reproduce. Consequently, what is never admitted into their range of consideration is that adoption is a moral act grounded formally in charity rather than a reproductive option to be exercised. In contrast, the first couple is committed from the outset to adopting a child in need. Although they want a second child, the goal they have established cannot be achieved through another means. Consequently, what is not entertained is the possibility that alternative reproductive options can be employed. If there were no children needing to be adopted, this couple would not simply fall back to a procreative option. The preceding discussion of embryo adoption helps to illuminate the differences in motive. The second couple would presumably be open to this option because it would satisfy *their* desire to obtain a child. Indeed, contracting a surrogate would not be entirely dissimilar to the relationship they formed with the pregnant woman who provided them with their child. The principal difference is that they did not initially commission her pregnancy. The first couple would not entertain this possibility because they are not embarked on a reproductive project; their overriding objective is to offer the hospitality of their home to a *child* in need.

We now turn our attention to the diverse procedures described in the vignettes. As will be recalled, the first couple undergoes an arduous process of inspection and introspection, whereas the second couple is subjected to little scrutiny. The most striking contrast is that in the former case adoption is predominantly a *public* act, while in the latter it is primarily *private*. The first couple must be declared publicly to be suitable parents before they are eligible to adopt. It is the social service agencies that are charged with this responsibility, and in doing so they are empowered to probe the motives of the couple and assess their capability to provide adequate parental care. In fulfilling these duties the agencies represent to the natural parents, adoptive parents, and the child the will and interests of the larger political community. Consequently, no private negotiation between the natural and adoptive parents is permitted, for such an act would negate the moral and legal rationale which adoption is intended to embody. In short, where the child needing to be adopted will be placed is the civil community's decision, and not the parents'. This is the case because the process is driven by the *best interests of the child,* which effectively renders the needs and wants of natural and adoptive parents mute if not irrelevant.

In contrast, the second couple is free to negotiate privately the terms of adoption with a pregnant woman who is unable to care for her child. The couple is not subjected to severe public scrutiny of their motives or ability to provide parental care, and the court plays the role of ensuring and validating that the terms of the agreement fall within specified legal constraints. Yet this means that the larger civil society and political community has no compelling interest or substantive role to play in determining where a child surrendered for adoption should be placed. Consequently, private adoption is spared the light of publicity, for it is predicated on meeting and matching the *needs of the adoptive and natural parents.*

The preceding discussion on single parents and same-sex couples again helps to illumine what is at stake in these different approaches to adoption. In the second story, it is irrelevant that the couple is married.[39] They are simply individuals, to invoke the jargon of procreative liberty, who are pursuing jointly their respective reproductive interests. In effect, they are commissioners of a reproductive project in which their chief collaborators are the lawyer and the pregnant woman. In the first story, the marital status of the couple is not irrelevant, but it is not the overriding consideration. At least in theory the child is placed in the best available home, a circumstance in which marriage may or may not prove to be the determining factor. The principal difference is that in the former case adoption is weighted toward signifying the successful conclusion of a reproductive project, whereas in the latter case adoption embodies to a greater extent a collective judgment that meets the best interests of the child.

The purpose for revisiting this tale of two adoptions is not to demonstrate the superiority of the British over the American option of private adoption. Both have their own particular sets of strengths and weaknesses. My intent is instead to illustrate the need for religious, moral, and legal forms of discourse that portray adoption as an act grounded primarily, though certainly not exclusively, in charity rather than reproduction. The fact that adoption is driven by a complex set of motives is readily granted; I am not arguing that only saints should be eligible to adopt. But there should be a public perception that the actual performance of adoption is a uniquely moral act that is sanctioned by both religious conviction and legal approbation. In the absence of such a public perception, the momentum of procreative liberty will prove irresistible, and adoption will be subsumed into a comprehensive market in which individuals select the most appropriate and expedient means for obtaining a child. And such an eventuality will, I fear, diminish rather than enhance the quality of both private life and the life of the public.

It may appear that this final section has led the reader far away from the issues of parentage and adoption that I am purporting to be investigating. Does the fate of civil society really hinge on preserving the charitable nature of adoption? No, but it is often the ordinary events associated with so-called daily living that disclose the fabric of our common life. As Augustine reminds us, a people is formed by and organized around the objects of their common love.[40] If above all else we love individual auton-

---

39. Assuming that the relevant legal jurisdiction permits single persons and same-sex couples to adopt.
40. See Augustine, *City of God,* 14.28.

omy and perceive the limits of natural necessity as a barrier to embracing what we love, then adoption will become but one among many options for how we pursue our respective reproductive interests. If, however, we love given bonds of affinity and perceive the natural necessity that makes them possible as a gift rather than a burden, then adoption will be preserved as a uniquely moral act that represents to children in need the unconditional offering of parental care, affection, and mutual belonging. Although preserving adoption as a charitable act will most certainly not determine the fate of civil society, it can serve as a reminder that the tasks of social and political ordering do not entail humans obtaining everything they will and want, but rather challenge humans to order their lives in accordance with the love that created, redeems, and sustains them.[41]

41. I am indebted to Gilbert Meilaender and Andy Watts for their comments on a previous draft of this essay.

3. Adoption and the Moral Significance of Kin Altruism

DON S. BROWNING

Adoption is a delicate issue. This is true for public policy and even more so for the fields of theological ethics and practical theology. I hold that these theological disciplines have a twofold task; they should first state a critically developed confessional view of the meaning of adoption and then articulate the implications and amendments that are appropriate and defensible for the wider public in a pluralistic society.

These are not easy tasks, especially in the present social context. The purpose, use, and justification for adoption in the face of roaring debates over the health of contemporary families and the appropriate use of reproductive technology make it analogous to the ball in a heated game of soccer. It can first be captured by one team and used to make a goal; it can next be stolen by the other side in its drive to score its own point. At one moment in the cultural debate, adoption can be invoked to justify all manner of family patterns alternative to the intact mother-father partnership. Arguments for adoption also can be employed to justify a much more expansive use of the reproductive technologies. On other occasions, adoption can be used to exemplify one of the few justifiable alternatives to the intact conjugal couple with children and employed to discourage almost all other alternatives.

The political and theological elasticity of the practice of adoption is due to certain failures in our moral and theological thinking. For example, many who enter the adoption debate have shortcomings in their wider analysis of the social and cultural context of the family; they have difficulties in understanding the meaning of adoption within broad cultural and social trends. Second, many contributors to the conversation are reluctant to make use of certain important distinctions, for example, the difference between moral and premoral goods and the difference between what Christians should rightly demand of themselves and what they can justifiably expect from the wider pluralistic culture. Even theological ethicists differ significantly in how they handle the question of adoption, although they all would claim to rely on the authority of the Christian tradition.

In this chapter, I hope to bring some order to the tensions in the moral-theological dialogues on adoption, or at least illustrate how order might be injected. I will do this by reviewing a small but influential number of contemporary Christian theological voices on the adoption issue.

Before launching into this discussion, I want to share a formative experience that has shaped my thinking about family and adoption. In the spring of 1991, the National Council of Churches sponsored a major conference on the family. It was held in Chicago and large numbers of people from all over the country attended. A consistent theme ran through many of the carefully selected plenary addresses. The message went like this: Sure, families are changing. There are more single-parent families, more divorces, more cohabiting couples, more children born out of wedlock, and more gay and lesbian families. Furthermore, there are many lonely single people who have no families at all. But do not worry. The church can and should become a big superfamily ready to receive and accept all disrupted families and all lonely individuals. One speaker drew analogies between a local neighborhood bar and the church. Just as a bar would accept, support, and in a way adopt all of its lonely customers, the church could do even better. It could become a great surrogate family offering symbolic and functional adoption to all isolated individuals and fractured families. The metaphor of adoption was used to promote a vague ideology of therapeutic acceptance as the cure for family disruption.

I was struck by the remarkable inadequacy of this solution. For years, I monitored the impact of the modern psychotherapies on culture, ecclesial practice, and modern theology itself. I believed in the power of psychotherapeutic acceptance and even the analogy that Tillich and others drew between it and Christian doctrines of grace and forgiveness.[1] I also believed that the church should invite, accept, and support all persons and all families willing to hear its message. But I also had become impatient with the over-extension in Christian theology of Carl Rogers's the-

---

1. Paul Tillich, "The Impact of Pastoral Psychology on Theological Thought," *Pastoral Psychology* 2, no. 101 (February 1960): 17-23. For my early favorable response to this line of thought, see Don Browning, *Atonement and Psychotherapy* (Philadelphia: Westminster, 1966).

ory of therapeutic acceptance or "unconditioned positive regard" and the way it worked to blunt ethical analysis and personal responsibility.[2] Therapeutic acceptance, as well as theological grace, was only effective, I believed, if it functioned against a clear ethical background that could articulate criteria for moral adequacy and therefore assign responsibility to individuals and communities. Under the cover of the idea of spiritual adoption, this conference was promoting a form of therapeutic acceptance as both the main and the only ecclesial and public policy for addressing the mounting problems facing families.

I noticed that the conference presented no real analysis of what was happening to families; we were told that society was changing, that societies always change, that change is generally good, and that change should not be resisted. No explanation of these changes was offered and no evaluation of these changes was presented. In the minds of the conference leaders, there seemed to be no qualitative differences between intact families and divorced families, children born within marriage and children born outside, children with fathers residentially present and those without their fathers, or single-parent families and two-parent families — that is, no differences that acceptance (i.e., adoption) by the church could not remedy. Isolation and stigmatization were the central problems of families, and loving inclusion was the cure for these problems. There were no more specific recommendations offered about how to lower the divorce rate, how to address teen pregnancies, how to bring fathers back into the lives of their children, how to prepare young people for better marriages, and how to create higher levels of equal regard and mutuality in marriages. There was no effort to address the growing tensions between work and family — what Habermas, to ratchet up the level of analysis, calls the colonization of the lifeworld by the technical rationality of market and state.[3] The interaction between acceptance and the metaphor of adoption had become, it seemed, a recipe for ecclesial and societal inaction. I was troubled.

---

2. Carl Rogers, *Client-Centered Therapy* (Boston: Houghton Mifflin, 1951), and "A Theory of Therapy, Personality, and Interpersonal Relationships," in *Psychology: A Study of a Science*, vol. 3, ed. Sigmund Koch (New York: McGraw-Hill, 1959).

3. Jürgen Habermas, *The Theory of Communicative Action* (Boston: Beacon, 1987), 2:196. Markets and bureaucracy can "colonize" our everyday lives by more and more dominating them with the cost-benefit logic of the market or the control mechanisms of state agencies and procedures.

Critical Familism and Adoption

The main concern of my early writing on families was the issue of family disruption itself. What is it? Is it a problem? What are the causes? What is an adequate practical-theological and moral-theological analysis of and response to current claims about growing family fragmentation? This was the concern of *From Culture Wars to Common Ground: Religion and the American Family Debate* (1997, 2000), the so-called summary volume of the first phase of the Religion, Culture, and Family Project.[4] The question of adoption was not at the center of our attention in that volume, although it was to some extent addressed. We certainly acknowledged that there is an important place for adoption in the Christian life.[5]

We hung a tag on the theological position on family issues that we developed; we called our position "critical familism." I have developed this concept in subsequent writings, principally in *Reweaving the Social Tapestry* (2001)[6] and *Marriage and Modernization* (2003).[7] Social-cultural analysis and theological-ethical retrieval has led me to believe that both church and society should promote the "committed, intact, equal-regard, public-private family."[8] I have envisioned this primarily as an *ecological* task requiring preparations by and resources from several interacting sectors of society.[9] The church should take leadership, but families also need the support of market, government, law, and the secular professions. By "intact," my colleagues and I meant that both church and society should attempt to encourage and support the husband-wife partnership and the offspring of such partnerships. "Intact" does not necessarily mean the modern nuclear family in its neolocality from extended family and its frequent isolation from other sources of social support. It means instead the integrity of the conjugal couple in either nuclear or joint-family arrangements. By using the phrase "critical familism," we wished to convey the task of vigilant critique of centers of power and distortion in culture, tra-

4. Don S. Browning, Bonnie Miller-McLemore, Pam Couture, Bernie Lyon, and Robert Franklin, *From Culture Wars to Common Ground: Religion and the American Family Debate* (Louisville, Ky.: Westminster/John Knox, [1997] 2000).

5. Browning et al., *From Culture Wars to Common Ground*, pp. 2, 178.

6. Don Browning and Gloria Rodriguez, *Reweaving the Social Tapestry: Toward a Public Philosophy and Policy of Families* (New York: Norton, 2001).

7. Don Browning, *Marriage and Modernization* (Grand Rapids: Eerdmans, 2003).

8. Browning et al., *From Culture Wars to Common Ground*, p. 2.

9. Browning et al., *From Culture Wars to Common Ground*, pp. 2, 306; Browning, *Marriage and Modernization*, pp. 24-29.

dition, market, government, and civil society that function to block or distort the free exercise of the love ethic of "equal regard," both within and between families. In asserting that this new family should be "public and private," we meant that husband and wife should in principle have full access to the privileges and responsibilities of both the public world of citizenship and the wage economy *and* the domestic world of intimacy, child care, and family maintenance.

The equal-regard family points to a theory of Christian love, one that can also be stated as philosophically relevant to society at large. We followed Louis Janssens, Paul Ricoeur, and several neo-Thomistic feminist theological ethicists in our understanding of Christian love as an ethic of equal regard.[10] Love as equal regard was for us what moral philosophers call a *mixed-deontological* concept. Meditations on the golden rule, the principle of neighbor love, and their extension into early Christian family ethics (Eph. 5:28) led us to see love as equal regard as the core of Christian ethics within the church, in the family, and in public affairs. It first means regarding the other as an end and never as a means alone; this principle is reversible and was interpreted by us to apply equally to other and self — "You shall love your neighbor *as* yourself" (Matt. 19:19). But we followed Janssens, Ricoeur, and some neo-Thomist feminists in going beyond a more strictly Kantian interpretation of equal regard after the fashion of Gene Outka[11] and attributed a strong teleological subdimension to the concept. *This was a move, as we will soon see, relevant to the adoption issue.*

We liked Ricoeur's way of stating the case for the mixed-deontological nature of love. With reference specifically to the golden rule, he follows Rabbi Hillel's formulation. Hillel argues that to do unto others as we would

10. Louis Janssens, "Norms and Priorities of a Love Ethics," *Louvain Studies* 6 (spring 1977): 209-37; Paul Ricoeur, "The Teleological and Deontological Structures of Action: Aristotle and/or Kant?" in *Contemporary French Philosophy*, ed. A. Phillips Griffiths (Cambridge: Cambridge University Press, 1987), pp. 99-112; Barbara Andolsen, "Agape in Feminist Ethics," *Journal of Religious Ethics* 9 (spring 1981): 69-81; Christine Gudorf, "Parenting, Mutual Love, and Sacrifice," in *Women's Consciousness, Women's Conscience: A Reader in Feminist Ethics,* ed. Barbara Hilkert Andolsen, Christine E. Gudorf, and Mary D. Pellauer (New York: Winston, 1985), p. 185.

11. Gene Outka, *Agape: An Ethical Analysis* (New Haven: Yale University Press, 1972). Outka is generally thought to have defined Christian love around Kant's teaching that morality involves a respect for self and other that can be universalized. This was what Outka meant by equal regard. A mixed-deontological view, on the other hand, retains their emphasis on equal respect but also tries to identify, as a subordinate interest, the other goods of life that should be equally distributed, a concern that most commentators feel is neglected by both Kant and Outka.

have others do unto us means doing *good* to others as we would have others do *good* to us.[12] Notice here the abstract reversibility of self and other; one finds this in both the biblical principles of the golden rule and neighbor love *and* Kant's categorical imperative that emphasizes respect for the humanity of both self and other.[13] But our view of love as equal regard went beyond abstract reversibility. Love as equal regard entails not only respect for other and self, it also requires theories of the *goods of life that actively should be promoted* within the context of this mutual respect.

This formulation opens the very important question of the *goods* of families and the *goods* of marriage, a question also relevant to the issue of adoption. The classic Christian tradition has listed three goods — fidelity between the conjugal couple, children and their education, and permanence (Aquinas meant by this sacramental permanence).[14] We tried to deepen this discussion of the goods of marriage and families. We were struck by the presence in the tradition of an implicit, and sometimes quite explicit, theory of kin altruism. This is the idea that in both creation as God intended it and in the rhythms of nature as revealed through naturalistic observation, it was commonly assumed that "natural" parents were more deeply invested in their children and, on average, more consistent sources of care and nurture than all substitutes. One can see this most distinctively where Aristotelian ethics influenced religious thought, whether in the ethics of the Christian Thomas Aquinas, the Jewish Maimonides, or the Islamic Al-Ghazzali.[15] There was no significant departure from this assumption in Protestant thought even though Aristotle's naturalism played a less significant role. This assumption emerges once again in the Catholic encyclicals from Leo XIII to Pius XI.[16] These Christian thinkers had no technical theory of kin altruism of the kind

---

12. Ricoeur, "Teleological and Deontological Structures," pp. 107-8.

13. Immanuel Kant, *Foundations of the Metaphysics of Morals* (Indianapolis: Bobbs-Merrill, 1959), p. 47.

14. Augustine, "On the Good of Marriage"; Thomas Aquinas, *Summa Theologica*, "Supplement to the Third Part," q. 42.

15. Thomas Aquinas, *Summa Contra Gentiles*, vol. 3, part 2, ch. 123; Maimonides, *The Code of Maimonides*, Book Four: *The Book of Women*, in *The Book of Marriage: The Wisest Answers to the Toughest Questions*, ed. Dana Mack and David Blankenhorn (Grand Rapids: Eerdmans, 2001), pp. 500-509; Al-Ghazali, *Book on the Etiquette of Marriage*, in *Marriage and Sexuality in Islam*, ed. Madelin Farah (Salt Lake City: University of Utah Press, 1984), pp. 48-126.

16. Leo XIII, *Rerum Novarum*, in *Proclaiming Justice and Peace: Papal Documents from Rerum Novarum through Centesimus Annus*, ed. Michael Welsh and Brian Davies (Mystic, Conn.: Thirty-Third Publications, 1981), pp. 3-39; Pius XI, *Casti Connubii*, in *The Papal Encyclicals*, ed. Claudia Carlen (Wilmington, N.C.: McGrath, 1981), pp. 391-414.

that today we find in evolutionary psychology. They had no theory of how shared genes between parents and offspring intensify the parental sense of investment in the children — parents' sense of identification with their offspring and the capacity to endure the hardship of parenting. But these thinkers did have everyday, naturalistic observations that children tend to look like their parents, and that this motivates parents to care for offspring out of a sense of preserving what is partially the parents themselves — what extends their "personality" and their "substance."

Kin Altruism As Finite Premoral Good

My colleagues and I handled kin altruism, whether derived from the theology and biopsychology of the tradition or from the insights of contemporary evolutionary psychology, as an important yet finite premoral good. We followed the definitions of "premoral good" that one can find in Janssens, Mary Midgely, and William Frankena.[17] Premoral goods are various finite objects, experiences, or tendencies that we experience as good in the sense of satisfying and enjoyable. They are the opposite of premoral evils or disvalues — objects, experiences, or tendencies that are unsatisfying or harmful. *Premoral goods are not fully moral goods.* A moral good, according to this line of thinking, is a disposition of the will to follow some principle that, if acted upon, would justly and productively organize a range of potentially conflicting premoral goods. That is the point; premoral goods can conflict and in this sense harm, if not destroy, one another. The moral good seen as a disposition and principle of free moral action is moral precisely in its capacity to organize, hierarchize, and harmonize competing premoral values, both within one's own life and in our lives with others.

The authors of *From Culture Wars to Common Ground*, although we were all liberal Protestants, followed the Catholic Thomas Aquinas and certain modern Thomists in viewing kin altruism as a highly important premoral good that should be protected and enhanced.[18] But it also was regarded as a finite good that can easily conflict with other finite goods.

17. Janssens, "Norms and Priorities," p. 210; Mary Midgley, *Beast and Man* (Ithaca, N.Y.: Cornell University Press, 1978), pp. 182-83; William Frankena, *Ethics* (Englewood Cliffs, N.J.: Prentice-Hall, 1973), pp. 9-10.

18. In addition to the position of Lisa Cahill, which I will review in this article, see Stephen Pope, *The Evolution of Altruism and the Ordering of Love* (Washington, D.C.: Georgetown University Press, 1994).

Hence, it is not an ultimate good that can always and everywhere trump all other goods.

It is not clear that the readers of *From Culture Wars to Common Ground* always understood our discussion of kin altruism as a finite, and even relative, good. For some readers, the fact that we even mentioned the importance of the kin altruism of natural parents was enough for them to conclude that we were deeming as grossly inferior if not morally defective all other family patterns where parents and children are not biologically related, including adoptive families. When properly interpreted, however, viewing kin altruism as a very important premoral good should allow one to give it a degree of centrality as a religio-cultural value without squeezing out all other organizations of affection and child rearing. Affirming it as a highly important premoral good should not lead to the automatic denigration of the relative goods found in other patterns.

On the other hand, acknowledging the relative goods in a variety of family patterns beyond the intact mother-father partnership should not make us disregard the importance of careful comparative analysis of the relative goods of different family patterns. This is why both church and society should take seriously recent research by Sarah McLanahan and Gary Sandefur,[19] Paul Amato and Alan Booth, [20] David Popenoe,[21] Mavis Hetherington,[22] and Mary Parks[23] showing that, on average, children growing up under the care of two biologically related parents do better in performing at school, relating to the job market, avoiding teen pregnancies, and forming marriages than those raised by single parents or stepparents. These too are goods that most people accept as important. Of course, it must be quickly added that many who grow up in disrupted families, even without regular contact with one of their "natural" parents (generally the father), often still do quite well in the external achievements

19. Sarah McLanahan and Gary Sandefur, *Growing Up with a Single Mother* (Cambridge, Mass.: Harvard University Press, 1994).

20. Paul Amato and Alan Booth, *A Generation at Risk* (Cambridge, Mass.: Harvard University Press, 1997).

21. David Popenoe, *Life without Father* (New York: Free Press, 1996).

22. E. Mavis Hetherington and John Kelly, *For Better or for Worse* (New York: Norton, 2002).

23. Mary Parks, "Are Married Parents Really Better for Children?" Center for Law and Social Policy: Policy Brief, May 2003, no. 3.

24. It should be noted that although children from intact families are two to three times more likely to do well in school, marriage, and work, the majority of children from disrupted families still do well (McLanahan and Sandefur, *Growing Up*, p. 43).

of their lives.[24] Furthermore, recent research demonstrates that adopted children do well on objective indices when compared to children raised by their biological parents.[25] This is explained partially by the high motivation, careful screening, and preparation of adoptive parents by adoption agencies. Also, from an evolutionary-psychological perspective, it is believed that humans have been selected for kin altruism over such long periods that the innate mechanisms for responding and bonding with children are in humans and can be activated, even if the child is not one's own.[26] But even then, as Judith Wallerstein has shown, many children of divorce separated from their biological parents have long-term subjective worries and doubts.[27] In addition, it seems to be a matter of continuing debate as to whether adopted children suffer inward anguish, self-doubts, and longings as a result of not knowing their biological parents.[28]

The distinction between moral and premoral goods can be used to clarify the claims about the moral relevance of the discoveries of sociobiology and evolutionary psychology. Ever since the early writings of sociobiologists such as E. O. Wilson, Richard Dawkins, and Richard Alexander;[29] philosophers such as Mary Midgley, Elliot Sober, and David Sloan Wilson;[30] and evolutionary psychologists such as David Buss, Robert Wright, and Steven Pinker,[31] these fields have made strong claims about the moral relevance of biological inclinations. More specifically, evolutionary psychologists have insisted that the twin realities of kin altruism and inclusive fitness (the tendency not only to preserve one's own

25. Peter Benson, Anu Sharma, and Eugene Roehlkepartain, *Growing Up Adopted: A Portrait of Adolescents and Their Families.* (Minneapolis: Search Institute, 1994).

26. Martin Daly and Margo Wilson, *Sex, Evolution, and Behavior* (Belmont, Calif.: Wadsworth, 1983), p. 291.

27. Judith Wallerstein, Julia Lewis, and Sandra Blakeslee, *The Unexpected Legacy of Divorce* (New York: Hyperion, 2000).

28. Betty Jean Lifton, *Twice Born: Memories of an Adopted Daughter* (New York: Penguin, 1977). For a more balanced statement of this point of view, see D. M. Brodzinsky, M. D. Schechter, and R. M. Henig, *Being Adopted: The Lifelong Search for Self* (New York: Anchor, 1992).

29. Edward O. Wilson, *On Human Nature* (Cambridge, Mass.: Harvard University Press, 1978); Richard Dawkins, *The Selfish Gene* (New York: Oxford University Press, 1989); Richard Alexander, *The Biology of Moral Systems* (Hawthorne, N.Y.: Aldine de Gruyter, 1987).

30. Midgley, *Beast and Man;* Elliott Sober and David Sloan Wilson, *Unto Others: The Evolution and Psychology of Unselfish Behavior* (Cambridge, Mass.: Harvard University Press, 1998).

31. David Buss, *The Evolution of Desire: Strategies of Human Mating* (New York: Basic, 1994); Robert Wright, *The Moral Animal* (New York: Pantheon, 1994); Steven Pinker, *How the Mind Works* (New York: Norton, 1997).

genes but also those of offspring, siblings, and cousins who carry our genes) are the foundations of morality.

Criminologist James Q. Wilson probably states this claim better than some of the evolutionary biologists. He believes that our preferential inclinations toward our own children and blood relatives sparked by kin altruism and inclusive fitness are the foundations of sympathy and thereby the main source of morality.[32] Kin altruism leads us to identify in special ways with the pain and elation of those who are partly us — our children, siblings, and so on. It leads us to regard them as we do ourselves. This is the core, he argues, of other important moral sentiments such as a sense of fairness, self-control, and duty.[33] These rudimentary sentiments can be analogically extended to others outside blood relations to wider social circles and therefore become the foundations of a more generalized social reciprocity. Frans de Waal in *Good Natured: The Origins of Right and Wrong in Humans and Other Animals* (1996) makes a similar argument.[34] Basically, Wilson and de Waal turn Richard Dawkins's "selfish gene" concept — the idea that our genes are only interested in their own individual well-being and immortality — on its head. The ideas of kin altruism and inclusive fitness show that creatures, even those who reproduce through sexual selection, have capacities for investment and sympathy in others, especially their own kin. This, Wilson and de Waal argue, is the foundation of other-regarding sentiments in general.

One does not have to determine either the scientific or moral adequacy of these arguments to examine their logic. *Claims about the importance of kin altruism to both parental investment and the development of moral sentiments are basically arguments at the premoral level.* The realities of kin altruism may prompt natural parents to be, on average, more invested in their offspring, but this investment does not automatically convert to full parental adequacy. In fact, in some cases, it may feed narcissistic strategies of manipulation and control that can be overtly destructive. In other cases, it can feed nepotism and tribalism. It may be true that kin altruism and inclusive fitness feed a primitive sense of sympathy, but a fully mature sense of equal regard, fairness, and duty require many social and cultural refinements beyond this elemental beginning.

Hence, in both cases — parenthood and more general morality — kin

32. James Q. Wilson, *The Moral Sense* (New York: Free Press, 1993), p. 30.

33. Wilson, *Moral Sense,* pp. 31-129.

34. Frans de Waal, *Good Natured: The Origins of Right and Wrong in Humans and Other Animals* (Cambridge, Mass.: Harvard University Press, 1996).

altruism may be a very important premoral good that is in some sense foundational. It is not exhaustive, however, of the full moral meaning of either parenthood or the mature ethical life. Nonetheless, kin altruism must be taken seriously as worthy of central cultural and religious appreciation and encouragement, as our religious traditions for the most part have tended to do.

Adoption and the Situation of Families

It is important to address the adoption issue with a careful analysis of the situation of families in rapidly modernizing countries such as the United States. In *From Culture Wars to Common Ground*, we dedicated a long chapter to this task. Personally, I am struck by how often scholars rush into family issues without careful analysis of what is happening. Many scholars see patriarchy as the major cause, and its dismantling as the major solution, of all family difficulties. This is an important part of the analysis, but this phenomenon needs to be set within a larger context. As Weber saw years ago, and Habermas and others more recently, the spread of technical rationality in market and government bureaucracy is clearly the most unsettling force today on families throughout the world.[35] A new means-end logic for the efficient enhancement of short-term satisfactions increasingly has colonized or dominated the lifeworld of day-to-day interactions — home, love, neighborhood, civil society — and led all of us to think more about mundane decisions in analogy to the cost-benefit logics of technical efficiency in market and bureaucracy. Rational-choice theorists explain family changes in terms of the declining economic dependence in the nineteenth century of the conjugal couple on extended family, and then, in the last half of the twentieth century, of the lessening financial dependence of wives on husbands because of women's entry into the wage economy.[36] These pressures, plus the customary problems of poverty (the recent relative decline of the salaries of working-class males), have undermined the role of economic interdependence in supporting marital and family stability.

Accompanying these economic and social-systemic transformations

35. Max Weber, *The Protestant Ethic and the Spirit of Capitalism* (New York: Charles Scribner's Sons, 1958), p. 182; Habermas, *Theory of Communicative Action*, 2:304, 307.

36. Gary Becker, *Treatise on the Family* (Cambridge, Mass.: Harvard University Press, 1991), pp. 347-61.

has been the increasing power, at least since the Enlightenment, of cultural individualism. This is a view of life that sees individual satisfactions and fulfillment as the primary goal.[37] Cultural individualism and the logic of market rationality should not be equated, but they clearly reinforce each other. Both function to destabilize the kin altruism and parental investments of the conjugal couple, and the consequences help explain the discouraging family trends summarized above. In addition, all of these changes unleashed new psychological turmoil. A profession of psychotherapy arose to help individuals and families cope with the ceaseless pressures of technical rationality and individualism. But psychotherapists generally rendered their assistance in terms of the very rationality and individualism that gave rise to these unsettling forces to begin with. Psychotherapy itself is in part a *techne,* and its guiding values, for the most part, have been distinctively individualistic.[38]

These changes mean that there are more broken families with children to adopt, more older childless couples who have waited too long and have missed the parental fulfillment of having children of their own, and more unmarried singles who think about adoption as a way to fulfill their parental inclinations. Some commentators, such as Stephen Presser in this volume, say that the adoption process itself is being sucked into the social and cultural dynamics of market and bureaucratic technical rationality.[39] Furthermore, some have cogently argued that the entire process of procreation, birth, and child rearing increasingly has come under the control of medical technology — that it has, in short, become "medicalized."[40]

The forces of technical rationality and individualism have inserted themselves into the realm of human procreation. Various birth control procedures have been available for decades. Now a whole slew of assisted reproductive technologies (ART) are obtainable, such as artificial insemination (AI), artificial insemination by husband (AIH), artificial insemination by donor (AID), in vitro fertilization (IVF), surrogacy, and still others.

---

37. Robert Bellah, Richard Madsen, William Sullivan, Ann Swidler, and Steven Tipton, *Habits of the Heart* (New York: Harper and Row, 1986), pp. 35-36.

38. See Don Browning, *Religious Thought and the Modern Psychologies* (Minneapolis: Fortress, 1987); Frank C. Richardson, Blaine J. Fowers, and Charles B. Guignon, *Re-envisioning Psychology: Moral Dimensions of Theory and Practice* (San Francisco: Jossey-Bass, 1999); Philip Cushman, *Constructing the Self, Constructing America: A Cultural History of Psychotherapy* (Cambridge, Mass.: Perseus, 1995).

39. Stephen Presser, "Law, Christianity, and Adoption," this volume.

40. Brent Waters, *Reproductive Technology: Toward a Theology of Procreative Stewardship* (Cleveland: Pilgrim, 2001), p. 14.

All of these technologies are available from many clinics for married or unmarried heterosexual couples, singles, and gay and lesbian couples in a new individualistic culture of "procreative liberty."[41] These technologies interacting with market rationality and cultural individualism have led, according to Brent Waters's excellent analysis, to a series of separations: the disconnection of sexual intercourse from marriage, procreation from sexual intercourse, parenthood from procreation, and child rearing from parenthood.[42]

All this means that the question of adoption must be located within the fuller context of significant new family disruptions as well as a new culture of procreative freedom. From one perspective, I would argue that this situation all the more requires new emphases on and methods for enhancing the integrity of the married conjugal couple and the on-average higher levels of the premoral good of kin altruism associated with this form of the family. On the other hand, in view of the actual reality of family disruption and larger numbers of homeless, abandoned, and suffering children needing care and support, this situation may require an *equally strong* cultural emphasis on the importance and dignity of adoption.

It is not a contradiction, as we will see below, to emphasize both directions simultaneously. Some analysts promote adoption but then fail to make the wider analysis of the reality and causes of more general family disruption. Hence, they regard a cultural emphasis on the equal-regard intact family as almost a threat to the cause of rendering adoption more culturally attractive. Others are so anxious to push for the revival and reconstruction of the intact family that they forget to address the importance of adoption. Both positions are finally wrongheaded. But if there is a need for adoption in face of the numerous reasons leading to family disruption, how does one build the case from a theological point of view — a case for the life of the church and a theological case for the role of adoption as a public practice in a pluralistic society?

In the remaining sections of this chapter, I wish to bring the concepts of critical familism into conversation with four recent theological-ethical views on the meaning of adoption. I do this, first, to make both appreciative and critical commentary on these important positions. I do it as well to enrich and extend critical familism on a topic about which it needs to say more.

41. Waters, *Reproductive Technology*, p. 19.
42. Waters, *Reproductive Technology*, pp. 15-17.

Ted Peters and an Eschatological Ethic of Adoption

Lutheran theologian Ted Peters in his *For the Love of Children: Genetic Technology and the Future of the Family* (1996) is a wonderful example of a position that draws advocacy of adoption into a collateral defense of progressive perspectives on the use of reproductive technologies.[43] There are few if any assisted reproductive technologies (ART) that Peters would not allow. This is because Peters sees no solid theological reasons for maintaining the unity between what the Christian tradition has called the *unitive* (the one-flesh melding of wife and husband) and the *procreative* (the birthing and education of children) aspects of covenanted marital love. For this reason, Peters is quite ready to allow into church and society Brent Waters's list of separations between sex and marriage, sex and procreation, procreation and parenthood, and parenthood and child rearing. Peters believes that traditional theological grounds for keeping these aspects of life in some kind of unity or interaction no longer have validity.

These reasons for keeping the unitive and procreative together have principally included natural law arguments widely used in Roman Catholic theology and "orders of creation" arguments used in Protestant theology. Roman Catholics actually use both kinds of arguments. For instance, Thomas Aquinas assumed that Genesis 1:28 ("Be fruitful and multiply") was addressed to male and female in the marital arrangement. Hence for him, marriage and procreation were willed by God at the foundations of creation — something of an order of creation.[44] But Aquinas spent much more time developing his natural law arguments for marriage. These said that the long period of human infant dependency requires the father to recognize that the child is part of his substance and should be cared for as he would care for himself. Furthermore, to address the dependency of both infant and mother, the father should join the mother-infant dyad, bond with consort and child, and assist with material and spiritual nurture.[45] Aquinas insisted that we love our children for two reasons — because they are part of us (both mother and father), and because they are part of the goodness of God (God's children) and should be cherished as such.[46] Clearly, the latter reason — the status of all children as reflective of

---

43. Ted Peters, *For the Love of Children: Genetic Technology and the Future of the Family* (Louisville, Ky.: Westminster/John Knox, 1996).

44. Aquinas, *Summa Theologica* (London: R. & T. Washbourne, 1917), "Supplement to the Third Part," q. 42, a. 2.

45. Aquinas, *Summa Contra Gentiles*, vol. 3, pt. 2, ch. 123.

46. Aquinas, *Summa Theologica*, vol. 2, part 2, q. 26, aa. 3, 8, 9.

the goodness of God — was the weightier reason for both Aquinas and the Christian tradition as a whole. From Aquinas's perspective, however, both reasons were theological. God was seen to work through the tendencies of nature just as God reveals God's purposes in the history of creation and salvation.

Both reasons, I might add, are central theological grounds for the love of our children from the standpoint of critical familism. Both reasons help us understand why marriage and procreation based on kin altruism should be central to church and public policy but why, as well, we need to cherish, preserve, and adopt all needy children, whether or not they are our own. Luther, it should be added, based his argument for the love of children principally on appeals to God's intentions in creation, but many commentators still detect remnants in his thought of classic natural law arguments as well.[47] I believe that Protestants and Catholics have available to them both of these theological arguments for the love of children. Of course, the naturalistic argument can be more readily used in public argument even if secularists reject the idea that God works through our kin-altruistic inclinations. This does not mean that the Christian framing of natural law argument is not valuable; indeed, it may be crucial for keeping the natural law argument from taking destructive directions.

But Peters is willing to jettison both types of theological argument — orders of creation and natural law. He is especially concerned to reject anything approaching a natural law argument. He derides what he calls the "inheritance myth" — any argument that the preferential attachments of parents for their children are due to a biological or genetic link.[48] Parenthood, especially fatherhood, is for him a completely social concept; it applies to those who actually love children and this incidental to their biological ties. Peters grounds the theology of adoption — his theological grounding for the love of all children — on eschatology. He writes,

> It is my proposal that the field of Christian ethics should be founded on our vision of the promised Kingdom of God. Ethics should be founded on eschatology. The world that constitutes our present reality is slated for transformation, a transformation promised to us by God and proleptically anticipated in the Easter resurrection of Jesus Christ.[49]

47. John McNeill, "Natural Law in the Teaching of the Reformers," *Journal of Religion* 26, no. 3 (1962): 168-82.
48. Peters, *For the Love of Children*, pp. 25-27.
49. Peters, *For the Love of Children*, p. 155.

But Peters does not view eschatology as fulfilling creation and nature, although much of the tradition actually does. For him, the transformations of God's kingdom that come from the future are totally disconnected from creation and nature. "We pass from being people of dust to people of heaven. We pass from being the children of Adam and Eve to becoming brothers and sisters of Christ."[50] Then we hear the culminating point: "Our definition or identity as human beings is determined not by the DNA we have inherited but rather by our vision of the network of relations that will constitute the Kingdom of God."[51]

What is this eschatological ethic that comes from the future and works without reference to nature or creation? It is first of all an ethic that assumes, and even celebrates, our increased freedom to make "choices" independent of the constraints of creation, nature, or tradition.[52] But choice, Peters acknowledges, requires criteria if it is to be responsible. He brings eschatology and Kant's categorical imperative together in a grand synthesis that emphasizes God's covenant with humans — but mainly a covenant that comes to us in God's eschatological action. Covenant is "a freely entered into promise to remain faithful . . . and should be applied to the relationship parents enter into with their children."[53] The content of this covenant goes like this: "God loves each of us regardless of our genetic makeup, and we should do likewise."[54] Or again, "[A] covenant to love children means that we will treat children as ends and not merely as means to fulfill someone else's desires."[55] It is striking that this position, in the final analysis, gives humans the freedom to choose, without constraints, whether to have children the "old-fashioned way" or use adoption, artificial insemination by donor (AID), surrogacy, gamete intrafallopian transfer (GIFT) (where neither the egg nor the sperm belong to the parents who will raise the child), or even cloning. Notice that adoption is lumped together as just one additional alternative reproductive strategy. Peters believes that his eschatologically stated imperative to love all children blocks the possibility of using these technologies to manipulate children for the sake of adult interests or to commodify them as we do our automobiles and clothes, always looking for the best model.

50. Peters, *For the Love of Children*, p. 155.
51. Peters, *For the Love of Children*, p. 155.
52. Peters, *For the Love of Children*, p. 3.
53. Peters, *For the Love of Children*, p. 3.
54. Peters, *For the Love of Children*, p. 4.
55. Peters, *For the Love of Children*, p. 3.

But this grand democracy of reproductive methods, as generous and attractive as it at first glance seems to be, has enormous problems. Peters is motivated to lift the cultural onus on adoption, and this is laudable. Certainly there are a range of reproductive technologies that can be used to enhance committed marital parenthood and the investments of kin altruism without resulting in Brent Waters's list of separations in the reproductive process. But the difficulties in Peters's position are of such magnitude that one cannot avoid the judgment that he has gone too far — too far for the *praxis* of the church and too far for the policies of the wider society.

First, Peters avoids developing his case within the context of a careful analysis of what is happening to families in modern societies. His position is, in brief, short on careful social analysis at either the theoretical or empirical level. He is concerned about the potential commodification of children but seems to have little interest in what the general forces of technical rationality, either in their market or in their state-bureaucratic form, are doing to promote family disruption, especially at the level of the integrity of the conjugal couple. He seems to have little understanding of how his lumping together adoption with all other presently possible assisted reproductive technologies could function as the crowning victory for technical rationality's colonization of the lifeworld. At the empirical level of analysis, he pays very little attention to the emerging social science literature that shows how, on average, children raised by biologically related parents in an intact relationship seem to do better in life on a variety of criteria.

Closely related to this is how Peters discerns our moral obligation to children. It is God's command from the future that we love children as ends and never treat them as means only. But should we be concerned about what is the *good* for children? Peters's eschatological Kantianism has the weakness of all forms of pure Kantiansim — it begs the question of the good for children other than the goal of respecting them as ends. In short, Peters has no theory of the premoral good for children. He claims that tradition, through such concepts as the orders of creation, does not show us what is good for children. Nature in the form of natural law arguments does not tell us what is good for children. Finally, the social sciences in their measurement of the conditions and consequences of various family arrangements do not for him tell us what is good for children. In the end, this leaves the ideas of love and respect as vacuous and without content, hardly enough to protect children from the commodification and manipulation that he fears.

Such a position, I fear, is not faithful to the Christian tradition. It is, however, even more fragile as a basis for public policy. It would seem to suggest that all of society would need to be converted to the expectations and moral predicates of Christian eschatology. Furthermore, his position is without definitions of the premoral goods for children — what makes them flourish, grow, and become mentally and physically healthy. If this is true, Peters's views would result in a public policy (especially in the present situation of growing technological dominance) that would sow even more seeds of reproductive disruption and confusion.

In the end, it would be better if Peters retained both the argument from created orders and the argument from nature. It is true that the idea of orders of creation can be misused. But it also can be employed by Christians as a powerful hypothesis of faith — one that can direct the imagination as it looks for other collaborating insights about the goods of life to be appreciated and preserved. The idea that covenant marriage is one of these orders — one of these plausibilities of faith — can be defended confessionally. It also is a fundamental human good that can be argued philosophically with the use of hermeneutic philosophy and the subordinate arguments of natural law and the human sciences. Philosophically, the idea of covenanted marriage has functioned, to use the terminology of Hans-Georg Gadamer, as a religio-cultural "classic" that has time and again been confirmed by intuition, reflection, and experience.[56] Natural law arguments of the kind used by Aquinas (the importance to dependent human infants of the supporting factors of parental certainty, kin altruism, and the bonding of parents) are a heuristic index or diagnostic, to use a phrase from Paul Ricoeur, about the natural energies taken up and organized by the covenanted marital relation.[57] These two resources help guide our "love of children" and give it content.

Clearly Peters is to some extent right: the element of respect for children as ends is the central component of love. Love as equal regard — so crucial to critical familism — holds this insight in common with Peters's

56. Hans-Georg Gadamer, *Truth and Method* (New York: Crossroad, 1982), p. 254.

57. The concept of diagnostic is Ricoeur's way of positioning the illuminating insights of natural explanation without obscuring the beginning of reflection in history and linguistic heritage. It is an anti-foundationalist way of handling natural sciences and would apply to the use by theological ethics of natural law. See Paul Ricoeur, *Freud and Philosophy* (New Haven: Yale University Press, 1970), p. 346. For an introductory discussion of the concepts of diagnostic and "distanciation" in Ricoeur, see Don Browning, "Ricoeur and Practical Theology," in *Paul Ricoeur and Contemporary Moral Thought*, ed. John Wall, William Schweiker, and David Hall (New York: Routledge, 2002), p. 260.

position. But the covenant of equal regard requires a teleological sub-moment — some view of the premoral goods of life and the premoral goods for children. I believe that the glorious title of Peters's book, "For the Love of Children," requires such teleological submoments before it can become an intelligible and trustworthy guide to family policy. Accepting my recommendations would lead him to cherish more the intact mother-father partnership, but at the same time to also honor adoption, appreciate ARTs that enhance covenanted marriage, and modify his enthusiasm for those ARTs that would undermine this relation.

Premoral and Moral Goods in Waters

There are, however, a variety of contemporary positions that are closer to the sensibilities of critical familism. But these positions are not identical to each other and not consistent with critical familism in all respects. Commenting on these admirable positions will teach us much and provide me with the opportunity to render critical familism's underdeveloped comments on adoption a bit more mature.

All of these perspectives share one thing in common; this is an emphasis on the religious and cultural centrality of what I have called the intact, equal-regard, mother-father partnership while, at the same time, commending the importance of adoption as a Christian obligation when needy children are at hand. Hence, the dual commitment that Peters finds contradictory is precisely what these thinkers believe the Christian faith makes possible. But this raises a variety of related questions. How do they each understand the appropriate theological grounds for adoption? How do they handle the crucial question of the relation of premoral and moral goods as these apply to the motivations for adoption? And, finally, how do they relate adoption to a variety of other strategies, methods, and technologies for reproduction?

In his recent *Reproductive Technology: Towards A Theology of Procreative Stewardship* (2001), Brent Waters has burst on the theological scene with a commanding perspective on these questions. His thesis is in the subtitle of his book. The fields of sexuality, love, procreation, adoption, and ART should be guided for Christians by the concept of procreative stewardship. What does it mean? First, it is the opposite of such positions as that of John Robertson, who would order procreation with the principles of procreative liberty — individual autonomy, individual fulfillment, and a sense of the ownership of one's body and one's offspring.[58] Procreative stewardship is based instead on the biblical idea that life (the life of the child and one's own life) are not our possessions to be disposed of as we please. They are, instead, gifts of God that are on loan from God and given to us to be cherished and nurtured.[59] The God-given context for the birth and nourishing of children is the covenanted marital relationship between husband and wife. Waters writes, "In being drawn toward each other as women and men, it is the one-flesh unity of marriage that expresses the fullest and deepest dimension of their fellowship. We may point to marriage as a sign, covenant and vocation bearing witness to a creation being drawn toward the expansive and enfolding love of its creator and redeemer."[60]

Furthermore, this one-flesh covenant between man and woman also includes the "unique one flesh of the child beyond them. In marriage a woman and man give birth to a child to whom both are related and drawn together in love and fidelity."[61] Humans — both parents and children — are not divisions of body and soul; rather they are "embodied souls and ensouled bodies."[62] We are more than our biology and more than our social relationships; we are creatures of God intended in creation to find our reproductive fulfillment in covenanted relations that include yet transcend both biology and finite loves in our relation with God. Waters admits that parenthood based on biological relatedness is important and should be promoted, but he does not directly employ the idea of kin altruism in either Aquinas or evolutionary psychology to amplify its relative importance. Biology, however, does not exhaust the meaning of parenthood, according to Waters. Waters makes a vague and unsystematic use of the concept of premoral goods when he describes the moral meaning of covenant. He writes, "A covenant entails the ordering of goods that are both internal and external to a relationship, binding its parties together by its imposed terms."[63] Waters seems to imply that the investment of kin altruism is one of those goods that are given organization by the marriage covenant, but he nowhere directly develops this idea. This will have consequence for a small reservation that I have about his position.

---

58. John A. Robertson, *Children of Choice: Freedom and the New Reproductive Technologies* (Princeton, N.J.: Princeton University Press, 1994).

59. Waters, *Reproductive Technology*, p. 3; many of these same points are made in Waters's "Adoption, Parentage, and Procreative Stewardship," this volume.

60. Waters, *Reproductive Technology*, p. 41.

61. Waters, *Reproductive Technology*, p. 42.

62. Waters, *Reproductive Technology*, p. 3.

63. Waters, *Reproductive Technology*, p. 41.

Waters believes in the moral obligation of Christians to adopt needy and abandoned children. But the Christian does this as a matter of "charity"; it is not a matter of personal fulfillment. "Adoption .. is not a reproductive option, but an act of charity (*caritas*)." Waters continues even more emphatically,

> The overriding consideration is the welfare of the child, not the plight of natural or adoptive parents. The intent is not to relieve natural parents of a burden they are unable to bear or to satisfy the parental desires of an infertile couple, but to find a suitable place of timely belonging for a child who would otherwise have none. This is why adoption is not restricted to infertile couples, for its purpose is not to obtain children but to place them in families.[64]

Waters is mildly critical of Roman Catholic moral theologians such as Germain Grisez and Lisa Cahill for recommending adoption as an alternative to third-party reproductive assistance for couples to fulfill their "generative" tendencies.[65] But let me be clear. Waters agrees with these thinkers: adoption is more Christian than the use of third parties. It is Grisez and Cahill's moral grounding that he questions. Charity should be the Christian motivation for adoption, not parental or generative self-fulfillment. All Christians should be willing to adopt when the need arises, not just the childless.

But this raises a series of important questions. Are we to conclude that when couples turn to adoption with the desire to fulfill their parental longings that they are always suspect from a Christian perspective? Does this mean that Christians should discourage this motivation in the general public? Should the charity that motivates adoption stand completely uninfluenced by our generative interests? Can charity build on, transform, and guide our generative interests? This raises the analogous questions: *What is Waters's understanding of love? Where does he stand in the great debate about the relation of eros* and *agape, of self-fulfillment and self-*sacrifice, in Christian love? It is with these questions in mind that I turn to a review of the commanding natural law perspective of Catholic moral theologian Lisa Cahill and the important covenantal position of Protestant Stephen Post.

---

64. Waters, *Reproductive Technology*, p. 73.
65. Waters, *Reproductive Technology*, p. 71.

Natural Law and Covenant in Cahill and Post

Cahill and Post share many things in common, including (like Waters) being contributors to this volume, but they develop their theological arguments in somewhat different ways. Both of them emphasize the religious and cultural priority of the covenanted conjugal couple.[66] Marriage is central for sexuality and child rearing for both of them. And each of them in some fashion takes seriously the good of kin altruism. Cahill does this by affirming the Aristotelian and Thomistic strand of thought that views the affections of natural parents as a seedbed of more generalized other-regard.[67] As does critical familism, Cahill also invokes the insights of evolutionary psychology about the nature of kin altruism; it is for her a naturalistic substratum of parental love, although it does not capture the full character of this love.[68] Post also makes considerable use of the idea of kin altruism, but often invokes the paradigms of history and the Bible more than either ancient or modern biology, although he gives modest attention to both. Post is struck by the innumerable uses of parental metaphors — God the father, God the mother, the solicitude of mother love, the forgiving father, and so on — that run throughout both ancient Hebrew and early Christian texts.[69] In fact, for Post, parental love and the male-female relation in covenant marriage reflect the very image of God as caring and loving parent — *in imagine Dei*.[70] Post makes much of the Greek concept of *storge*, a concept that points to the preferential and self-giving care and concern that parents have for their offspring.[71] We see this, he tells us, in the images of God delivered by tradition, and we experience it in our lives in families. This parental love is the foundation for the analogical spread of love to others outside the family. We first experience love in our own particular families and gradually learn to love others outside the family — especially if we believe that, in the end, like us they are all

66. Lisa Sowle Cahill, *Family: A Christian Social Perspective* (Minneapolis: Fortress, 2000), p. xi; Stephen G. Post, *More Lasting Unions: Christianity, the Family, and Society* (Grand Rapids: Eerdmans, 2000), p. 119.

67. Lisa Sowle Cahill, *Sex, Gender, and Christian Ethics* (Cambridge: Cambridge University Press, 1996), p. 71.

68. Cahill, *Sex, Gender, and Christian Ethics*, pp. 92-95.

69. Stephen G. Post, *Spheres of Love: Toward a New Ethics of the Family* (Dallas: Southern Methodist University Press, 1994), pp. 60-63. See also Stephen G. Post, "Adoption: A Protestant Agapic Perspective," this volume.

70. Post, *Spheres of Love*, p. 20.

71. Post, *Spheres of Love*, p. 63.

children of God and part of the grand family of God. And, as we will see, a similar view is held by Cahill.

Even though they both emphasize the priority of conjugal love and parenthood, they are both strong advocates of the Christian duty to adopt. In contrast to Peters, they do not see these two mandates as being in opposition. Both Cahill and Post, as with Waters, are opposed to the rush toward using the marvels of assisted reproductive technology. It should be observed, however, that Cahill pushes the limits of official Catholic teachings; she would permit the use of selected technologies that they have discouraged or forbidden. For instance, she approves the judicious use of contraception if it works to enhance the marital relationship and helps to space births for the good of the family as a whole. She also goes beyond church teachings in approving artificial insemination by husband (AIH), since it does not disturb marital commitment and can actually enhance the parental relationship. She agrees with Post, and indeed Waters, however, that any use of these technologies that introduces third parties or detracts from the integral relation between covenanted marital love, procreation, and child rearing should be resisted, both by the church and by the wider society.[72]

On the other hand, both Post and Cahill, in contrast to Waters, are proponents of the use of adoption for the realization of frustrated parental inclinations.[73] Post goes even further. He works hard to show why adoption is in no way inferior to parenting in intact families, and even argues for the moral acceptability of some parents voluntarily relinquishing their children for adoption when they do not have the means to sustain their offspring themselves.[74]

Cahill and Post use slightly different sources and theological methods in arriving at their respective positions. Cahill uses the resources of sacramental theology and natural law.[75] Post uses natural law thinking as well, but positions it as a subdimension of his covenant theology.[76] These

72. Cahill, *Sex, Gender, and Christian Ethics*, pp. 252-53.
73. Cahill, *Sex, Gender, and Christian Ethics*, p. 246; Post, *More Lasting Unions*, p. 123.
74. Post, *More Lasting Unions*, pp. 137-38. Post agrees with those spirited defenses of adoption such as Elizabeth Bartholet, *Family Bonds: Adoption and the Politics of Parenting* (New York: Houghton Mifflin, 1993). He is also for adoption for the good of the child rather than the legacy interests of the parents. For a history of these two motivations in culture and law, see Stephen Presser, "The Historical Background of the American Law of Adoption," *Journal of Family Law* 11, no. 2 (1972): 443-516.
75. Cahill, *Sex, Gender, and Christian Ethics*, pp. 46-50.
76. Post, *Spheres of Love*, pp. 85-88.

dual foci permit both Cahill and Post to give priority to "natural parents" but also to organize their kin investments into the more universalistic moral framework of the justice of the kingdom of God. This dual language also permits them to speak directly to the confessional life of the church as well as to the broader public. As a natural law theologian, Cahill takes the empirical needs and experiences of both children and adults with great seriousness. She believes that there are universal needs that cut across differing cultures, and, in contrast to Martha Nussbaum (with whom she otherwise has much in common), Cahill believes that kin-relatedness in parenting is one of those universals.[77] But Cahill is not a foundationalist. She does not move from the empirical analysis of experience directly to the assertion of norms.[78] Cahill assumes the historically mediated Genesis story of creation as a beginning point, that is, its affirmation of the male-female relation as reflective of *imago Dei* and its command to both men and women to multiply and have dominion. Natural law and empirical analysis are subordinate indices for her that provide further "good reasons" that help us see the plausibility of revelation and tradition.[79] These good reasons can and should be defended before wider, non-Christian publics and may often prove relevant to public policies in pluralistic societies.

Post, on the other hand, uses natural law and the empirical analysis of the social sciences in much the same way but within his covenant theology that puts the primary emphasis upon the command of God and our human response to this command. These moves by Cahill and Post make it easier for them to address their position on family and adoption to both ecclesia and public policy. They can do this with more ease than is the case with the more strictly confessional positions of Peters and Waters. The presence of a double language in Post and Cahill gives them extra flexibility in public debate.

This brings me to the last commonality of Cahill and Post: their understanding of the dialectical relation of kin altruism to more universal love and, as well, the dialectical relation of *eros* to the self-transcending character of Christian *agape*. Post has for several years investigated the relation between *agape* and *eros* — the relation of sacrificial love to self-love and the quest for self-fulfillment.[80] Post generally has opposed the view, often associated with Anders Nygren's magisterial interpretation of the history

---

77. Cahill, *Sex, Gender, and Christian Ethics,* p. 59.

78. Cahill, *Sex, Gender, and Christian Ethics,* p. 235.

79. Cahill, *Sex, Gender, and Christian Ethics,* p. 235.

80. Stephen G. Post, *A Theory of Agape: On the Meaning of Christian Love* (Lewisburg, Pa.: Bucknell University Press, 1990).

of Christian love,[81] that Christian love is mainly self-sacrificial love that completely transcends self-regard and self-love. To the contrary, Post identifies Christian love with the mutuality of the love commandment to "love your neighbor as yourself" (Matt. 19:19). This is close to the view in critical familism of love as equal regard. Post's view of love also retains, as does critical familism's theory of equal regard, a strong teleological sub-dimension. Post's view of love as mutuality builds on and analogically extends the motivations of kin altruism — the affections, investments, and solicitude of parental love extended outward from one's own offspring to all children everywhere. In contrast to Nygren, and in contrast to Peters and even Waters, the Protestant Post follows the core of the Catholic tradition that views universal love — even the love that leads to adoption — as the analogical generalization of kin altruism. *Eros* and *agape,* as well as kin altruism and self-transcending love, are dialectically related for Post. Post is also close to critical familism in holding a theory of mutuality and equal regard that requires the cross. For him, as it is for us, the cross is required in order to endure in the midst of sin and brokenness so that love as mutuality can be renewed and reinstated when threatened. The love that motivates adoption, for Post, should build on our innate, and sometimes frustrated, tendencies toward kin altruism, even though it must extend and stabilize these energies with the endurance of love inspired by the symbol of the cross. The two motivations can be brought together.

Cahill's view is similar. Cahill and Post allow the energies of kin altruism to come into play in adoption. Cahill writes about this in ways that, as we have seen, have elicited the critical response of Waters. In an effort to discourage forms of reproductive technology that undermine the one-flesh unity of the marital relation, Cahill believes that parents should see adoption as a creative way of "satisfying their generative impulses."[82] Waters believes that this dilutes the motivation of charity. It should be noticed, however, that Cahill holds that adoption should not be motivated for Christians by parental needs alone; it must be motivated by our sense of solidarity with others as children of God and persons for whom Christ died — truths symbolized in the Christian common meal.[83]

---

81. Anders Nygren, *Agape and Eros* (Philadelphia: Westminster, 1953).

82. Cahill, *Sex, Gender, and Christian Ethics,* p. 247.

83. Cahill, *Family,* pp. 42-44. It is my reading of Timothy Jackson's position that he too would place the primary emphasis on the needs of the child and the agapic love of the adopting parent but would not necessarily eliminate, as a secondary grounds for adoption, the needs for generative fulfillment of the adopting parent. See his "Suffering the Suffering Children: Christianity and the Rights and Wrongs of Adoption," this volume.

In short, Cahill and Post implicitly maintain the distinction between premoral and moral goods that I developed earlier in the paper. This helps them both appreciate kin altruism as a very important premoral good — a good that more fully Christian moral acts build on, analogically extend, and in partial ways transcend. For these two theologians, the satisfaction of generative inclinations can be a partial ground for adoption for Christians *and* for wider public policy. But kin altruism always needs to be extended, both for the task of parenting our own biological children and as a ground for adoption. As Waters says, the adoption element must enter for Christians into the parenting of their own offspring. Our children are both products of our own genes and gifts of God. Fully to recognize them as gifts is also to acknowledge the element of adoption in every act of parenting.

The Christian should support public policies that promote adoption. In the present context of world family disruption, the need is great. But this raises the question, what can be the grounds for adoption, other than fulfilling generative needs alone, in public policy? Cahill believes rational deliberation is a resource. She believes that the expansion of altruism beyond our own children is possible on other than Christian grounds. She writes, "A judgment in favor of inclusive altruism can, of course, be supplied by a religious tradition like Christianity. I maintain that it can also be arrived at inductively, consensually, and experientially by public and dialectical reflections on nature and conditions of a humane society."[84]

This may be true. Christians can, and should, acknowledge that there may be other than Christian ways to justify and inspire the adoption of the needy. Admitting this should not undercut the Christian belief that acknowledging children as gifts of God, God's children, and objects of Christ's love — hence as persons we too should love and cherish — provides even profounder reasons for adoption.

84. Cahill, *Family,* pp. 10-11.

4. Navigating Racial Routes

SANDRA PATTON-IMANI

ELISA: So like when I got to college that's when it was like such a huge culture shock. It's like suddenly realizing you're Black, but not knowing what that meant. Or having to interact with other Black people. It was really really hard. And that's where a lot of the anger came from, 'cause I suddenly was faced with everything I missed out by being with White people and not knowing who I was or having cultural identity. It's like even now, as much as I've grown it's something I'll never be able to get back. And I think, you know, I go back and forth about this. Obviously I'm grateful for them giving me a home. And I'm successful and I wouldn't be here, most likely if I was bounced around in foster homes. That's what my mom always says. [inaudible] I definitely believe Black kids should be adopted by Black parents. I mean, there's just such a huge hole. And there's just so much — no matter how much I read or learn or study I'll never get it back. And I just hate that.

SANDI: What things were a culture shock to you?

ELISA: You know, the way people talk, the way people acted. It's hard to explain. It's just like this confidence — I don't even know if confidence is the right word. . . . Like I'm real shy and reserved, whereas my friends and my boyfriend they just don't — there's like an inner strength. I'm missing that I think for a lot of reasons.

This chapter originally appeared in *BirthMarks: Transracial Adoption in Contemporary America,* by Sandra Patton (New York: New York University Press, 2000), pp. 62-98, 195. Reprinted by permission.

Culture shock is a term used to describe the bewilderment and distress individuals often experience upon traveling to a foreign land. It occurs when a person's assumptions and expectations about self, others, and reality fail to provide the information necessary for cultural interaction and survival. Elisa experienced this sort of disorientation on several levels. The assumptions she had learned to make about herself while living in a White family and community were inconsistent with others' social expectations of her as a Black woman in her new college setting. There was a dissonance between her social expectations — "the way people talk, the way people acted" — and the skills she needed to comfortably interact with the Black community at her college. She felt like a foreigner, an outsider in the cultural group to which she was supposed to belong. This sense of dislocation stemmed from her rather unique social location as the Black child of White parents. Transracial adoption violates what we typically think of as the normal familial channels of socialization and enculturation.

What does it mean to have a racial identity? What cultural skills and cognitive maps does a person need to successfully navigate through contemporary U.S. society as an African American? How is identity — one's conception of self — connected to cultural knowledge and social policy? What does Elisa's sense of culture shock say about the way race is constructed in the United States? Culture shock points to the sense of displacement at the heart of transracial adoptees' identities. Their existence as African Americans in White families disrupts mainstream assumptions about race, family, and identity. Their self-definitions often challenge the way other people classify them with regard to racial identity. Indeed, their sense of self testifies to the hybridity of identity.

In this chapter I consider the identities of transracial adoptees in light of the social controversy over this issue: the development of a positive sense of racial identity and the acquisition of survival skills for dealing with racism. Important as these questions are in considering the effects of adoption and welfare policies in the lives of children, however, the lives of Black children raised in White families are profoundly significant in broader ways as well. I argue that, though the social locations of transracial adoptees are somewhat unique, their life stories raise challenging and intriguing questions about how race is structured, how social policy shapes individual identities, the way kinship is socially structured and made meaningful, as well as how individuals — whether adopted or not — construct a meaningful sense of self in a swiftly changing society rife with contradictory prescriptions for self-definition and presentation. I argue that everyone navigating life in the contemporary United States needs to learn survival skills to cope with cultural diversity, oppression, and power inequalities; all contemporary "American" identities are multicultural; all our identities — whether adopted or nonadopted — are constructed and maintained in interaction with social institutions and public policies; and finally, who we are is the result of a complex process involving continual social construction and cultural negotiation that cannot be neatly labeled to fit the categories on census forms or social science surveys. To be sure, the struggle for identity is often more difficult and painful for members of racial-ethnic minorities in the racially stratified United States. The process of navigating through life is highly variable, depending on one's social location in the power structure. In arguing that everyone needs survival skills to navigate the contemporary racial terrain, I am proposing that such skills vary widely according to the specificities of identity — race, gender, class, age, disability, and sexual orientation. In fact, the nature of the struggle, the need for survival skills, and the ways one uses these skills vary with one's location in the power structure.

The life stories chosen here are drawn from interviews with twenty-two transracial adoptees — Black and mixed-race children adopted by White parents — conducted between 1994 and 1996. I conducted follow-up interviews in 1998 and 1999. Twelve of the interviewees lived on the West Coast, and ten resided in the Mid-Atlantic region of the United States.[1] All of them were eighteen years or older at the time of the interview, with the majority between twenty-two and thirty. Five of the twenty-two interviewees were men, while seventeen were women. With the exception of one man, who was a senior in high school at the time, all my informants were employed, and all but two had attended college for some period of time. I interviewed each adoptee at least once for at least one hour; most of the interviews ranged from one and a half to two hours, though a few ran as long as three hours. I conducted follow-up interviews with several key informants, and interviewed the parents of seven adoptees. I draw on interviews with key informants to illuminate the central issues that emerged from their lives, and on the broader sample to illustrate the range of experiences represented by the people I spoke with. The names of the adoptees have been changed, as have other identifying facts.

1. I found my informants through various sources. Many were referred to me by friends and acquaintances who were aware of my research. Often one informant led me to others. Several people were referred to me by social workers that I interviewed. This word of mouth process provided me with a number of informal social groupings of adoptees and adoptive families, as well as several individuals who were not socially connected to other transracial adoptees.

As we will see in this chapter, the experiences of the twenty-two people I interviewed varied widely in some ways, and were profoundly consistent in others. Clearly, one cannot hope to assemble twenty-two people who "represent" the experiences of all transracial adoptees in the United States. This was not my goal. I did, however, seek to interview people whose lives represented a broad range of experiences as African Americans raised by White parents. My goal has been to explore in depth the lives and identities of those I interviewed, focusing on the processes by which they constructed and maintained a meaningful sense of self. In approaching their lives in cultural, social, and political contexts I have sought to understand the dynamic interplay of identity, family, culture, and social structure. I begin with a discussion of survival skills and cultural knowledge, and continue with a consideration of adoptees' identities as multiply defined and multiracial. Finally, I consider the processes by which the adoptees I interviewed constructed a meaningful sense of self.

Survival Skills and Cultural Knowledge

The question of whether or not White parents can and/or do impart survival skills to deal with racism to their Black children has been central in public debates regarding the appropriateness of transracial adoption. This issue also speaks to broader questions about the maintenance of ideology at the level of individual experience, and the ways in which individuals are able to resist power-infused social narratives of subordination. The work of W. E. B. Du Bois is a useful place to start in considering questions about race, oppression, and consciousness. In 1903 Du Bois wrote that the American of African descent was

> born with a veil, and gifted with second-sight in this American world, — a world which yields him no true self-consciousness, but only lets him see himself through the revelation of the other world. It is a peculiar sensation, this double-consciousness, this sense of always looking at one's self through the eyes of others, of measuring one's soul by the tape of a world that looks on in amused contempt and pity. One ever feels his twoness, — an American, a Negro; two souls, two thoughts, two unreconciled strivings; two warring ideals in one dark body, whose dogged strength alone keeps it from being torn asunder.[2]

2. W. E. B. Du Bois, *The Souls of Black Folk* (New York: Penguin, 1903), p. 5.

Du Bois's concept of "double-consciousness" addresses a central aspect of contemporary scholars' questions about the way oppressive systems of cultural meaning are both maintained and resisted at the individual level. Du Bois articulated both the negative and positive effects of this state of being. Seeing oneself and the world through the eyes of one's oppressor, he wrote, led to an internalization of the negative cultural messages that justified inequality and an alienation from self. Du Bois characterized the positive effects as the gift of "second sight," an ability to recognize the inconsistencies of racial ideology. Contemporary scholars have interpreted this second sight as a necessary "survival skill" for members of racially oppressed groups living in a racially stratified society. Examples of such survival skills include the methods of deconstructing and delegitimating racial stereotypes and racist treatment, resistance and subversion, the ability to deal with a variety of cultural settings, and the ability to anticipate and read cultural signals, as in the behavior of police.

In a discussion of parenting in Black families, Marie Ferguson Peters explains that:

> Black families encourage the development of the skills, abilities, and behaviors necessary to survive as competent adults in a racially oppressive society, and a number of studies have investigated the characteristic, often culture-specific, child-rearing behaviors and survival mechanisms which enable Black parents to cope with everyday exigencies or with crisis situations.[3]

The central questions in the public debate have been whether or not White parents can raise Black children with a positive sense of African American identity, and teach their children the survival skills they will need although they themselves had never experienced racism personally. The majority of people I interviewed felt that the socialization they had received from their parents was often inadequate when they experienced a racist incident. While they acknowledged that their parents had done their best and given them whatever cultural knowledge they were *able* to give, most of my interviewees had found it necessary to learn and incorporate their own survival skills to navigate the contemporary multicultural landscape. While everyone I talked to had struggled with this issue in varying degrees, most had acquired satisfactory methods of coping.

3. Marie Ferguson Peters, "Parenting in Black Families with Young Children: A Historical Perspective," in *Black Families,* ed. Harriette Pipes McAdoo, second ed. (Newbury Park, Calif.: Sage, 1988), p. 233.

Brian Scott, a twenty-five-year-old transracial adoptee at the time of our interview who was raised in the diverse community of Berkeley, California, directly addressed the question of whether or not White parents could impart such coping mechanisms to their Black children:

SANDI: Do you feel like they gave you any of those skills?

BRIAN: Nope. I don't think they could, 'cause they've never been there. And a White person will never be there. I mean, White people go to Africa and they're in charge! I don't know how that happened. [wryly]

SANDI: That is really well-put.

BRIAN: You know? You can see it and you can talk about it, and you can — like my dad went to the "I Had a Dream" March in the Civil Rights .. and he got whupped by the police in Alabama. Stupid ass strayed from the Civil Rights bus, and said, "I'm gonna go look at Alabama" by himself. They beat him up and said, "We're gonna throw you in the river with some cement if we ever catch you again." But he'll never have walked into a store and be treated like they treat a Black person — watched, you know, handed a bill before you eat — "pay now." You know? He just never will go through that. He can see it all he wants. He can't tell me how to deal with it; he couldn't and he didn't tell me how to deal with it. You know? Here in Berkeley I went to a store — New West — a couple years back when those were just coming in, and I had to go get something. My grandpa took me to New West to get some jeans. You know. Paying for 'em with a credit card, and the lady's taking a helluva long [time] to process the credit card. What the hell is she doing? It's fifteen minutes, and you gotta punch a number. And I'm sittin' here — Gramps is loaded [rich] — I know it's not [a problem with] his credit card. The police show up. She was like I held my grandpa hostage. And you know, my dad will never go through something like that because he's White. You know what I'm saying? It just doesn't happen. When police pull him over they don't pull their guns on him. They talk to him like a respectable person. So he couldn't teach me that. And I don't think he wanted to even *see* what he couldn't teach me, and *needed* to teach me. I mean, I think that's the hardest thing for White people, is they — the good people — they don't want to have to think it's really like that. You know? I mean, they really don't. And they want to believe that the police aren't like that.

Brian's story demonstrates the powerful role of media images and public narratives in the social construction of race and identity, and conveys the embodied aspects of racial identity. A Black male body carries a different social message than does a White male body. These racial codes of social identity are conveyed and understood through public narratives of race that shape the way people are seen and treated in everyday social interactions. A Black man has to deal with such encounters, which often involve police, throughout his lifetime. Thus, of necessity his sense of self is constructed and maintained in interaction with public narratives which define Black males through crime, unemployment, drug addiction, and gang violence.

Brian was not alone in having to define himself against and through such social narratives. All Black men living in the contemporary United States are, in varying degrees, affected by such stereotypical images. Yet his situation was complicated by the fact that he was raised in a White family, and thus grew up with a White man as his familial role model. As he so vividly illustrated, his father couldn't teach him what he had never experienced or even learned to see himself: "When police pull him over they don't pull their guns on him. They talk to him like a respectable person." Brian was tacitly and unconsciously taught to walk through the world as if he had the privilege of White skin and its attendant social meanings. Although Brian was also a respectable person, he had learned through encounters like the one he described that he must constantly navigate the distance between his sense of self as a respectable person and the dangerous images others often had of him. In popular narratives Black skin is not a signifier of respectability.

Popular ideological narratives often locate the meaning of "authentic Blackness" in images of inner-city gangsters and teenage mothers. In her analysis of the Anita Hill–Clarence Thomas controversy, cultural studies scholar Wahneema Lubiano discusses racial narratives in relation to perceptions of social reality. Though she specifically addresses Black women, her observations apply equally to Black men:

> Categories like "black woman," "black women," or particular subsets of those categories, like "welfare mother/queen," are not simply social taxonomies, they are also recognized by the national public as stories that describe the world in particular and politically loaded ways — and that is exactly why they are constructed, reconstructed, manipulated, and contested. They are, like so many other social narratives and taxonomic social categories, part of the building blocks of "reality" for many people; they suggest something about the world; they provide simple, uncomplicated, and often wildly (and politically damaging)

inaccurate information about what is "wrong" with some people, with the political economy of the United States.[4]

Transracial adoptees must interact with this racial narrative in constructing a meaningful sense of self. Most of the adoptees I interviewed had, at various moments in their lives, found it necessary to question their own sense of themselves as African Americans in relation to such dominant media images. A number of them cited television images of Blacks as their primary exposure to African American people and culture as they were growing up. One woman explained that because most of her childhood ideas about African Americans came from television, she thought all Blacks were poor and uneducated. As a child she thought she had better marry a White man to make sure she didn't live in poverty. Feminist cultural critic bell hooks discusses White viewers of Black images on television as follows:

> Many white folks who never have intimate contact with black folks now feel that they know what we are like because television has brought us into their homes. Whites may well believe that our presence on the screen and in their intimate living spaces means that the racial apartheid that keeps neighborhoods and schools segregated is the false reflection and that what we see on television represents the real.[5]

Hooks points out that televised views of Black life likely shape the racial perspectives of many Whites who have little or no social interaction with Black folks. If this is true for Whites, perhaps it is true for many transracial adoptees as well. How do you construct a positive sense of African American identity if your family is White, the community you live in is predominantly White, and many of the media images you are exposed to equate Blackness with poverty, crime, drug addiction, gang violence, and single-parent families? In such a situation one of the survival skills a Black adoptee needs is a critical consciousness that will help him or her deconstruct such racial representations and the power relations embedded within them. Transracial adoptees must learn to say not only, "That is not me," but also, "That is not 'authentic' Blackness."

---

4. Wahneema Lubiano, "Black Ladies, Welfare Queens, and State Minstrels: Ideological War by Narrative Means," in *Racing Justice, Engendering Power: Essays on Anita Hill, Clarence Thomas, and the Construction of Social Reality,* ed. Toni Morrison (New York: Pantheon, 1992), pp. 330-31.

5. bell hooks, *Killing Rage: Ending Racism* (New York: Henry Holt, 1995), p. 112.

SANDRA PATTON-IMANI

In their discussion of Black families, socialization, and identity development, James Jackson, Wayne McCullough, and Gerald Gurin explain:

> The minority family is the important agent of socialization, for it is within the family context that the individual first becomes aware of and begins to grapple with the significance of racism and discrimination. The intrafamilial socialization of group and personal identity has considerable bearing upon personal functioning in a society that cultivates negative conceptions of minority group members through direct interaction, the media, and institutional barriers.[6]

This is not to suggest that White parents are *incapable* of teaching such survival skills. We must acknowledge, however, that a critical consciousness about race and racism has to be learned. It is possible, and is indeed quite common, for White people to grow up in the United States with little or no contact with people of color, no suggestion that social reality is perceived differently from social locations other than their own, and/or no awareness that racism still operates at multiple levels in contemporary society. In fact, many of the messages aimed at Whites in mainstream public discourse support and foster the view that racial inequality was eradicated by the civil rights movement, and that the United States is a "color-blind" society. There are countless channels through which Whites can and do bring a critical perspective to bear on race relations and media representations of racial-ethnic minorities. When transracially adoptive parents take the opportunity to educate themselves and their children, to (re)locate their families to racially diverse communities, and to grapple with the sticky, often painful, issues that arise in multiracial families, their children benefit tremendously. Indeed, this is a critical factor for transracial adoptees.

Thirteen of the twenty-two people I interviewed were raised in predominantly White communities in families that made little or no effort to diversify their social world. The levels of struggle and pain my informants experienced around issues of racial identity and racist treatment were related to their parents' attitudes and awareness about racial issues and the racial makeup of the communities in which they lived. All the adoptees I spoke with experienced their sense of identity as an "issue" that had to be

6. James S. Jackson, Wayne R. McCullough, and Gerald Gurin, "Family, Socialization Environment, and Identity Development in Black Americans," in *Black Families,* ed. Harriette Pipes McAdoo, second ed. (Newbury Park, Calif.: Sage, 1988), pp. 244-45.

dealt with, yet their responses to this varied. These findings are consistent with those of Ruth McRoy, Louis Zurcher, Michael Lauderdale, and Rosalie Anderson in their studies of transracially adopted children. They found that

> The children whose families were residing in integrated areas, who attended racially integrated schools, and who had parents who acknowledged their children's racial identity, tended to perceive themselves as black persons and to feel positively about it. Those children who had little, if any, contacts with blacks tended to develop stereotyped impressions of blacks and were likely to feel they were "better off" in a white adoptive family than in a black adoptive family. . . . Such children were likely to act as similarly as possible to their white peers and white family members and to renounce any similarities or allegiances to blacks.[7]

It is difficult to separate the intertwined issues of racial identity and survival skills. Adoptees who had been surrounded by Whites all their lives and had never learned to critically appraise representations of African Americans in the mass media, books, toys, and social attitudes tended to be the most White-identified and most accepting of negative, stereotypical views of Blacks. Their coping mechanisms to survive the onslaught of racist attitudes, treatment, and representations they encountered involved distancing themselves from Blackness and embracing Whiteness — they largely accepted representations of African Americans as truth and posited themselves as "exceptions" who were "different" from other Blacks. On the other hand, those who acquired a critical perspective to deal with racial representations and racism as a systemic issue developed survival skills that both allowed them to question and criticize racist images and narratives *and* to define positive, healthy views of themselves as African American and/or biracial people.

Kristin Rhineholt and her three transracially adopted brothers (none related biologically) were raised in a nearly all-White community in Pennsylvania. Kristin and her older brother Nicholas were strongly White-identified. Nicholas, the only Black member of the police force in a small East Coast town, saw racism as a learned condition taught in Black fami-

7. Ruth G. McRoy, Louis A. Zurcher, Michael L. Lauderdale, and Rosalie N. Anderson, "The Identity of Transracial Adoptees," *Social Casework: The Journal of Contemporary Social Work* 65, no. 1 (January 1984): 34-39. See also, by the same authors, "Self-Esteem and Racial Identity in Transracial and Intraracial Adoptees," *Social Work* 27 (November 1982): 522-26.

lies that was used as an excuse for thinking *"they"* were inferior or explaining why *"they"* hadn't succeeded. Kristin unquestioningly accepted stereotypes associating African Americans with poverty, lack of education, and the enjoyment of particular kinds of foods — watermelon, fried chicken, collard greens, and orange soda. There was a seven-year gap between Kristin and her two eighteen-year-old brothers, and my interview with one of them, Steve, indicated that the family had dealt with racial issues differently with the two younger siblings. Steve was significantly more comfortable with himself as an African American. The following excerpt from an interview with Kristin, however, illustrated the connections between race, representation, and the formation of her White-identified consciousness:

SANDI: What about like books and toys, things like that?
KRISTIN: We had both.
SANDI: Black dolls?
KRISTIN: Um hmm. But then again, people are appalled at *Little Black Sambo*. She read that to us.
SANDI: Really?
KRISTIN: Oh yeah. I like it. And I don't see what other people see.
SANDI: I don't think I've ever actually read the story. I've just heard a lot about it.
KRISTIN: Really? It's a good book. And she used to do voices to Brer Rabbit. Ya know. It was never an issue of, "Oh, this shouldn't be read." You know, stuff like that.

Little Black Sambo has been held up as an intolerably racist children's book. "Sambo" is a caricature of Blacks as buffoons whose roots lie in the nineteenth-century racist theater tradition of minstrelsy. The thrust of the plot is that Sambo is stupid enough to allow tigers to repeatedly trick him out of the new clothes his mother has just given him. The Sambo character in the children's story also represents the racist stereotype of the "pickaninny," typically a scantily clad, unkempt, wild-looking, animal-like Black child. Kristin was clearly aware that the book had been criticized, but emphasized that she liked it. The key phrase here was, *"I don't see what other people see."* Her parents did not teach her to recognize racist stereotypes.

Kristin's and Nicholas's experience represented one end of the spectrum. While a number of other families did little to teach their children critical race skills, most of the adoptees went searching for their own racial enculturation at different points in their lives. Only four of the twenty-two people I interviewed were primarily White-identified and had not felt the need to learn more about Black culture and become more comfortable with themselves as African Americans. Eight of the adoptees I interviewed were raised in diverse communities; of these, the parents of five were aware of the need to teach their children survival skills and to engage the family in multiracial groups and activities. These five represented only three sets of parents, however — there were two sets of siblings among them. Andrea and Erika Bailey were both adopted from Africa and were raised in Los Angeles. Both their parents were academics whose specializations focused on Africa, and both had been deeply committed to movements for social justice in the United States. While Andrea and Erika had not been immune to struggles over identity issues, they had been given a solid foundation that included an understanding of racism and oppression, as well as an appreciation of African and African American cultures. Andrea explained:

ANDREA: Do I have the survival skills to respond to racism? Oh yeah.

SANDI: So how did your parents deal with racism? Can you think of the ways that they taught you about it?

ANDREA: These are hard questions.

SANDI: I know. Sorry.

ANDREA: It's just they're large in scope. Well, to answer the first question — Have I been able to deal with the survival skills? — I'd say most definitely, because I consider myself well-educated from a very progressive family, so I know issues that are out there. I know how to defend myself. I know that I have resources. Which I might not feel like I had if I was in a different environment, and if I didn't watch and learn from the ways my parents handled different situations. You know? So yes, I can survive. In terms of how they've dealt with racism, racism in the small, as how it affects our family or racism in the broader spectrum?

SANDI: However you have felt it.

ANDREA: Well, my parents have actively fought against that, just being the progressives that they are. They actively wanted to — I don't know. In their literature, in their readings, I may not have necessarily always understood what they were talking about at dinner time and stuff like that but you know, it was always about social causes, trying to get me and my sister to immerse ourselves in those causes as well. So it wasn't just E.R.A. and Women's Rights and stuff that we were a part of. I remember once I was in junior high I think. I was in this young people's theater company, and we were putting on this play. I forget the name of the play, but I got this really big part, but it was the part of a servant. But it wasn't stereotypically designated for an African American's role. It was actually an Irish part, but you know, I got this part and my parents told me I couldn't do it. They told me I couldn't be in the play if I did it. And I didn't understand it. And I was like —

SANDI: Oh wow.

ANDREA: You know, it's just any part. It's not anything racial. And I remember we got into big fights about it, so I never — I didn't take the part. But I remember that was — I remember that was one of the first times I remember really race and racial issues really affecting myself.

SANDI: Did you understand why?

ANDREA: At the time I didn't. At the time I just thought they were being extreme, and they didn't understand that the part was just a part. But you know, I can understand why.

SANDI: Looking back on it now, do you think they made the right decision?

ANDREA: Uh, yeah, sure. Um, I think yeah.

Andrea's parents were clearly aware of the history of Black representation in the American media. For many years the only roles available to African Americans in film and television were as servants. Even now one of the most prevalent roles available to Black actors is a variation on the mammy/servant stereotype whose primary concern is the well-being of White folks.[8] Andrea was also confident about dealing with racist attitudes and treatment. Importantly, she was raised with an understanding of race and inequality as *systemic* issues. In contrast to many of my informants, this provided her with an explanatory system that did not blame and stigmatize African Americans for being poor and having access to fewer social resources. Unlike explanatory systems that locate racism in the ignorance of individuals, her racial analysis was grounded in a critique of social structure. This gave her a way of understanding racial dif-

8. See Robert Gooding-Williams, "Look a Negro!" in *Reading Rodney King/Reading Urban Uprising*, ed. Robert Gooding-Williams (New York: Routledge, 1993); Sau-ling C. Wong, "Diverted Mothering: Representations of Caregivers of Color in the Age of 'Multiculturalism'," in *Mothering: Ideology, Experience, and Agency*, ed. Evelyn Nakano Glenn, Grace Change, and Linda Rennie Forcey (New York: Routledge, 1994).

ference and inequality without requiring her to define herself as "not Black" in order to maintain a positive sense of self.

Transracial adoptees are not alone in needing to learn survival skills. We all construct our sense of self and others through interaction with public discourse about identity and "difference." As I noted at the start of this chapter, such critical skills for "reading" and deconstructing racial representations are invaluable for members of all racial and ethnic groups in the racially stratified United States. As the work of multiracial feminists and race relations theorists has demonstrated, questions of power are relational; we all exist in complex webs of power relations that vary according to our multiple identities and social locations. Racial-ethnic identities are not monolithic, but are experienced differently on account of differences in gender, class, sexual orientation, age, and disability. Sociologist Howard Winant explains that

> Nearly a century ago Du Bois analyzed "double consciousness" as a basic tension in black identity produced by the painful but ineluctable presence within black subjectivity of white attitudes and prejudices. Today we may reasonably extend this insight to propose the existence of a "multiple consciousness" through which most North Americans necessarily experience their racial identities.[9]

In my view, learning to untangle ideological narratives of "difference" from the actual diverse range of identities we embody and encounter in others is a necessary survival skill for all of us living in the United States. Whites need to learn how to decenter Whiteness as normal, as generically human, and above all, as innocent. Indeed, the acquisition of such deconstructive skills would likely contribute to the survival of our society and to all of us living in it.

Black/White/Biracial: Multiply Defined Identities

SAM: but because I was so clearly unidentified — I mean, even now nobody ever thinks I'm Black. I'm at my darkest now because I hung out at the beach all summer — well, not all summer, two weeks. [We both laugh.] .. So in the winter when I'm much lighter, you know, I'm taken either for Jewish or French or Hispanic. I'm taken for East

9. Howard Winant, *Racial Conditions: Politics, Theory, Comparisons* (Minneapolis: University of Minnesota Press, 1994), pp. 53-54.

Indian a lot. I have a lot of East Indian friends, so when I'm with them. Whenever we travel, no matter where we go, if we're in Mexico I'm Mexican. If we're in Guatemala I'm Guatemalan. If we're in Equador I'm Ecuadorian. So, um, in some ways it's been — once I passed out of adolescence and I felt more of a whole person, just in general, then it became something I could play with. I don't ever say I'm anything but what I am, but it's something that has become more — it's just more comfortable than having to defend — not defend myself, but just being questioned all the time. Whenever I went to a new town — I jumped around from college to college for a couple years — I would get questioned. You know, people would come up to me in like a bank line and ask me what my identity was. I'm serious. You know, it was just like it was constant for a while.

The changeling quality of Sam Bennett's racial identity was shared by a number of the adoptees I interviewed. Yet, even among those who were more easily categorized as Black, many had developed multiply defined selves. Many people who do not live on the "color line" view race and racial identity as biological or even cultural givens. As I have discussed, however, the lives of transracial adoptees problematize such assumptions.

There are different approaches to studying racial identity. Perhaps the most widely known is the psychological research of William Cross, Janet Helms, and T. A. Parham, who track the development of racial identity through a stage model.[10] Though some of my informants narrated their identity progression through a similar set of stages, I was struck by the depth and diversity of their experiences. I take a life-history approach that focuses on the insider's view — the ways in which people experience themselves in relation to family, community, culture, and society. This perspective allows me to consider the multiplicity of identities each person assumes by exploring the various systems of cultural meaning they draw on in the course of their lives. A number of cultural anthropologists have used this "person-centered" approach to ethnography, in which, as John Caughey explains,

10. Psychological stage theories track the development of individual identity through a series of four or five stages from a point at which people accept a negative stereotypical understanding of Blackness to one at which they define a positive sense of racial identity. See William E. Cross, *Shades of Black: Diversity in African-American Identity* (Philadelphia: Temple University Press, 1991); Janet E. Helms, *Black and White Racial Identity: Theory, Research, and Practice* (New York: Greenwood, 1990); T. A. Parham, "Cycles of Psychological Nigrescence," *The Counseling Psychologist* 17, no. 2 (1989): 187-226.

We see that we need to attend to the fact that it is not only modern communities but modern individuals that are multicultural. That is, contemporary Americans are likely to think about themselves and their worlds in terms of several different cultural models and also to play multiple social roles which are associated with and require operating with diverse and often contradictory systems of meanings.[11]

This approach is particularly relevant to a consideration of transracial adoptees, whose lives have been structured by multiple systems of cultural meaning. With a few exceptions, most of my informants actively sought out African American cultures and communities in their struggle for self-understanding and social survival. As anthropologist Ward Goodenough explains, "A person may not only attribute different systems of standards to different sets of others, he may also be competent in more than one of them — be competent, that is, in more than one culture."[12]

My informants' social location as Black children of White parents placed them in the rather unique position of having, as many of them expressed it, "insider" access to both African American and White cultures in the cultural and historical era following the civil rights movement. Even Kristin Rhineholt, the most White-identified among them, said that though most comfortable in the company of White people and most conversant in that cultural meaning system, as a person with brown skin she was typically treated like other African Americans, and thus felt she was "sitting on the fence."

Transracial adoption in the late 1960s occurred alongside another social change with regard to race and family. The landmark Supreme Court ruling in *Loving v. State of Virginia* in 1967 removed the last legal barriers to interracial marriages, and the first generation of children from these marriages had come of age at the same time as the largest cohort of transracial adoptees. Though the number of multiracial births in the United States was only 3.4 percent of all births in 1989, for the first time in history the rate of bi- and multiracial births was increasing at a greater rate (260 percent) than that of single-race births (15 percent).[13]

11. John L. Caughey, *Imaginary Social Worlds* (Lincoln: University of Nebraska Press, 1984), p. 129.

12. Ward H. Goodenough, *Culture, Language, and Society,* second ed. (Menlo Park, Calif.: Benjamin/Cummings, 1981), p. 99.

13. Maria P. P. Root, "The Multiracial Experience: Racial Borders As a Significant Frontier in Race Relations," in *The Multiracial Experience: Racial Borders As the New Frontier,* ed. Maria P. P. Root (Thousand Oaks, Calif.: Sage, 1996), p. xiv.

Along with these demographic shifts has come a new wave of scholarship, autobiography, and movements for the recognition of multiply defined people and families.[14] G. Reginald Daniel discusses multiracial individuals as follows:

> The psychosocial configuration of their identity is premised instead on a style of self-consciousness that involves a continuous process of "incorporating here, discarding there, responding situationally." Because the contemporary blended individuals maintain no rigid boundaries between themselves and the various contexts within which they operate, their identity has no fixed or predictable parameters. They are liminal individuals whose identity has multiple points of reference and, yet, has no circumference, due to the fact that it manifests itself on the boundary.[15]

Daniel's description suggests that, like transracial adoptees, multiracial individuals juggle a diverse repertoire of cultural meaning systems during the course of their lives. This sense of liminality, or as Gloria Anzaldua puts it, "mestizo" identity,[16] was evident in most of my informants' life stories. Of the twenty-two adoptees I interviewed, sixteen had birth parents of different races; only six had two Black birth parents. While there are parallels between multiracial individuals raised in their birth families

14. Maria P. P. Root, ed., *Racially Mixed People in America* (Newbury Park, Calif.: Sage, 1992); Root, "The Multiracial Experience"; Naomi Zack, *Race and Mixed Race* (Philadelphia: Temple University Press, 1993); Naomi Zack, ed., *American Mixed Race: The Culture of Microdiveristy* (Lanham, Md.: Rowman and Littlefield, 1995); Maureen T. Reddy, *Crossing the Color Line: Race, Parenting, and Culture* (New Brunswick, N.J.: Rutgers University Press, 1994); Shirlee Taylor Haizlip, *The Sweeter the Juice: A Family Memoir in Black and White* (New York: Simon and Schuster, 1994); Lise Funderburg, *Black, White, Other: Biracial Americans Talk about Race and Identity* (New York: William Morrow, 1994); Gregory Howard Williams, *Life on the Color Line: The True Story of a White Boy Who Discovered He Was Black* (New York: Dutton, 1995); Barack Obama, *Dreams from My Father: A Story of Race and Inheritance* (New York: Times Books, 1995); Judy Scales-Trent, *Notes of a White Black Woman: Race, Color, Community* (University Park, Pa.: University of Pennsylvania Press, 1995); James McBride, *The Color of Water: A Black Man's Tribute to His White Mother* (New York: Riverhead, 1996); Scott Minerbrook, *Divided to the Vein: A Journey into Race and Family* (New York: Harcourt Brace, 1996); and Becky Thompson and Santeega Tyagi, eds., *Names We Call Home: Autobiography on Racial Identity* (New York: Routledge: 1996).

15. G. Reginald Daniel, "Black and White Identity in the New Millennium: Unsevering the Ties That Bind," in *The Multiracial Experience: Racial Borders As the New Frontier,* ed. Maria P. P. Root (Thousand Oaks, Calif.: Sage, 1996), p. 134.

16. Gloria Anzaldua, *Borderlands/La Frontera: The New Mestiza* (San Francisco: Spinsters/Aunt Lute, 1987).

and transracial adoptees, there are significant differences as well. While both multiracial individuals and adoptees such as my informants occupy a space on the social "boundary," their experiences differ, often in profound ways, because nonadopted people are usually raised with their birth families. The identity issues are complicated for adoptees not only by the absence of their birth families, but also by the absence of any significant biological or medical history (except in the case of one informant, whose adoption was open). Also, transracial adoptees lack a familial socialization in African American culture.

The people I interviewed responded to these circumstances in a variety of ways, constructing and defining complex, multifaceted senses of self. While their racial identity was fluid and contextual, their primary self-definitions frequently diverged from the official definition of race by adoption agencies, based on the races of their birth parents. Of the six adoptees with two Black birth parents, two were primarily White-identified. Among the group of sixteen whose birth parents were of different races, two were principally White-identified. The remaining four with two Black birth parents were Black-identified. Five adoptees whose birth parents were not of the same race were Black-identified. These adoptees explicitly defined themselves as Black, often reasoning that they were seen and treated as Black, regardless of the race of their birth or adoptive parents. This sense of identification was usually articulated as a conscious choice to learn about and participate in African American cultural traditions, to celebrate African and Black American history, and to resist White cultural ideology. The remaining eight, all of whom had birth parents of different races, defined themselves as mixed or biracial. Thus, of the twenty-two people I interviewed four were primarily White-identified, nine were Black-identified, and nine saw themselves as multiracial. Significantly, all of them recognized the "constructedness" of such racial categories and were clear that their self-definitions were based on cultural *choice* rather than unproblematically given. These configurations clearly revealed the separation of biological and cultural factors in assigning racial identity; indeed, the force most evident in the construction of the identities of adoptees was *social structure* — adoption agencies and the public policies which governed their practice.

In recent years ethnographers, feminists, and other cultural studies scholars have emphasized the contextual and relational character of identity. With regard to ethnographic method, increasing attention has been paid to the ethnographer's presence in shaping the self-narratives of the people being interviewed. Renato Rosaldo explains:

> The study of differences, formerly defined in opposition to an invisible (ethnographic, authorial) "self," now becomes the play of similarities and differences relative to socially explicit identities. How do "they" see "us"? Who are "we" looking at "them"? Social analysis thus becomes a relational form of understanding in which both parties actively engage in "the interpretation of cultures."[17]

Indeed, my interviews were contextual, relational, interactive moments of identity construction and definition for both my interviewees and myself. Not only did I provide my interviewees an occasion for self-reflection and the articulation of self, but my identity as an adoptee gave them a listener and questioner who was an "insider." The sense of validation was powerful for me as well, as each of us participated in a unique dialogue in which another person "got it" — an "insider's view" of adoption. Certainly, there were profound differences among the group of people with whom I spoke, but some foundational assumptions seemed present in almost every encounter. All of us carried the stigma of having been "given up" or "relinquished" or "abandoned." For all of us, biology was absent from the experience of kinship and thus fully separated from our cultural, emotional, and experiential understandings of family. We each had a sense that our identities were not "natural," but rather, contingent and constructed. We knew that we could easily have grown up in other families, and thus have been entirely different from the selves we now knew.

The relational definition of self was particularly interesting with regard to my interviewees' understandings and articulations of the "constructedness" of racial categories. One subject that came up repeatedly with the women I interviewed was the "hair issue." Many of them described the problems their mothers had in caring for their hair — "Black hair" often demands a different kind of care than "White hair." Some of their mothers learned, while others took them to hairdressers or family friends. The majority of the women I spoke with had one White birth parent, and thus many of them had what has often problematically been referred to as "good hair," curly and/or frizzy as opposed to "kinky."[18] We often bonded over hair issues. Many of the women and I had similar curl-frizz ratios, and this was frequently commented on. Such comments were not casual, however, but deliberately made, to illustrate the arbitrary so-

17. Renato Rosaldo, *Culture and Truth: The Remaking of Social Analysis,* second ed. (Boston: Beacon, 1993), pp. 206-7.

18. The term "good hair" derives from a perspective that values light skin and hair that is closer to that of European Americans.

cial distinctions drawn between racial groups. Skin color became another point of comparison used to highlight the gaps between actual skin tone and the constructed categories of Black and White. Many of those I interviewed had such light skin that the differences between us were very slight. (I have very pale skin.) They often pointed this out, or sometimes would refer to my skin color in describing a sibling. One woman showed me both color and black and white photos taken throughout her life to demonstrate that unless she was tanned, it was very difficult to tell she was African American.

I will now turn to excerpts from interviews with four women who defined and discussed their identities in distinct ways. Andrea Bailey addressed the difficulties she had had in dealing with identity issues. Cat Benton discussed her identity as a biracial woman. Karinne Randolph emphasized the importance to her of defining herself as Black. Finally, Kristin Rhineholt articulated a White-identified sense of self.

Andrea was a twenty-five-year-old woman who had been adopted into her family at the age of two. She and her older sister Erika (not biologically related) were adopted from an orphanage in Africa, and were raised in the Los Angeles area. As I discussed earlier, their parents, academics whose work focused on Africa, made great efforts to raise them in a racially diverse community with an awareness and understanding of their African heritage and racial issues in the United States. What was striking about Andrea's experiences was that though her parents did "all the right things" with regard to race, she still struggled over her racial identity and the sense that she did not belong anywhere socially. She emphasized: "I don't fit in right now. I don't fit in anywhere really." In the following excerpt, she discussed the enormity of racial issues in her life:

SANDI: Do you ever think about how it would have been if you had been adopted by a Black family?

ANDREA: Umhm.

SANDI: What do you imagine?

ANDREA: Life would be easier.

SANDI: Really?

ANDREA: Sometimes. The identity problems I'm having would not exist, I don't think. They might. But I'd feel, I guess, like I belonged a lot more than I do now.

SANDI: Do you have any sense of what is about race and what is about adoption?

ANDREA: I think for me, I'd say that about 95 percent of it is about race.

I feel like . . . It's contradicting because I feel like I have this perfect life in terms of a stable family that loves me and would do anything for me and I would do anything for them. And that if I compare my life with that of my friends who have not had the same situations, or life events that I've had, I'd say that I have one of the more stable families, more open and communicative. And parents with good politics and all that kind of stuff. And I think that — I don't think it's an adoption thing. I think it's a transracial adoption thing, because the feelings that I've had toward my family have been mostly — well, up until I was able to notice or truly understand the profound differences, the issues surrounding transracial adoptions — it really was normalcy for me. So normal that it would anger my sister, because I would treat them — I would take them for granted. I think if I was older when I was adopted issues of adoption might be more profound.

Andrea's sense of the stability of her family in contrast with her angst over her racial identity spoke to the pervasiveness and, perhaps, the inevitability of such struggles among transracial adoptees. All twenty-two adoptees discussed race and racial identity as issues that demanded their attention. While some, like Andrea, were contending with their sense of self as racial beings at the time of the interview, others felt they had passed through their most tumultuous years and had come to some kind of self-understanding and definition.

Cat Benton was a twenty-three-year-old biracial woman who was adopted into her White family — her father, mother, and their birth son — as an infant. She was raised in the multiracial city of Oakland, California, where she was residing when I interviewed her. More than any other informant, she grew up immersed in both Black and White cultures. She discussed her sense of self as biracial in the following passage:

SANDI: So when you think about your identity, how do you define your identity? Not necessarily in terms of race, but let me ask you about who you are.

CAT: A few years ago I would have been — well, you would've had to figure out — if you asked me on this day I would say something different, but because of the exposure and the experiences and the people I've been around I have to say that being Black and White — of some Black and some White — whatever that is, biracial, having one parent one, one parent the other is a unique background, is its own background, its own culture. I don't mean biracial period — Black and Hispanic, White and something — I mean Black and White is a separate background. And I consider myself biracial, Black and White.

SANDI: So what does that give you and not give you? What does it lack and what does it have?

CAT: Um, it has an understanding that no other culture can understand. There's no other culture that can truly understand and feel at home being around two different — being around these two groups of people. It lacks a lot because you never feel like — you never totally fit in anywhere unless you're with other mixed people. And it does work in other mixes. When you come across that Black and White person it's like "What's up? You know me and I know you. Don't try to front, ya know." And most mixed people try to identify one way or the other. There are not very many people who I know who identify as a mixed person, biracial Black and White person. More and more I come across that, especially in Berkeley. Yeah, no matter where you were raised, I mean, depending on the color of your skin and maybe if you're thinking of yourself as all this or all this, if you are in tune with the fact that you are biracial and are strong on both sides, you're never gonna feel all the way comfortable here and you're never gonna feel all the way comfortable there. And that's what it lacks. And society craves that, society — "Label yourself? What are you?"

SANDI: Check that box!

CAT: Other!

Cat enjoyed playing with traditional racial categories and mixing them up. This discussion was notable for her engagement with questions of culture, though there was an interesting slippage between her biological definition as biracial — having one Black and one White birth parent — and the cultural familiarity with both groups that she acquired as a member of a White family living in a racially diverse neighborhood. She defined being biracial as having "its own background, its own culture." Thus, she identified three cultural meaning systems in her life: biracial, Black, and White. She was exposed to these systems of meaning in the family and community she was raised in; as she intimated, biracial culture was alive and well in Berkeley, California. These meaning systems, along with others she drew on, constituted her own repertoire of cultural tools for navigating the borderlands she inhabited. Rosaldo discusses the crossing of cultural demarcations as follows: "The result is not identity confusion but play that operates within, even as it remakes, a diverse cultural repertoire. Creative processes of transculturation center themselves along literal and figurative borders where the 'person' is crisscrossed by multiple identities."[19]

Adoptees who defined themselves as mixed or biracial did so on the basis of the racial identifications of their birth parents. They were, however, also biracial or multicultural in terms of their engagement with various systems of cultural meaning. All of them were raised to be culturally proficient in "mainstream" White cultures, yet they had all sought out some exposure to Black communities and cultures. Such exploration was minimal for a few, but more substantial for others. For some, the experience of going away to college provided new social opportunities in more diverse settings than those in which they had been raised. Some searched for their birth parents as a means of establishing a connection with their Black families.

Eight of the people I interviewed defined themselves as Black, a number of them reasoning that as they were seen as Black by others, it was important that they take an affirmative stand regarding Black identity. Karinne Randolph, the child of an interracial relationship, was adopted into a large family with other transracial adoptees at eighteen months of age. She was raised in a racially diverse city in Pennsylvania, where she lived and worked as a social worker when I interviewed her. Her parents had raised her and her siblings in a mixed neighborhood, where they attended diverse schools. The parents' social group included both Whites and African Americans, and they encouraged their children to explore Black culture as much as they wished. In the excerpt below, Karinne discussed the importance of defining herself as African American:

SANDI: So when did you come to this decision or this understanding of yourself as African American rather than mixed?
KARINNE: In high school. I know I did that in high school, but I became more serious about it in college. I think lots of people do that in college. They really go there to try and find themselves, so to say. I think we're just a bunch of big babies trying to define ourselves. And part of it's that and part of it's that I'm an adult now. I can't be wishy-washy about this for the rest of my life. I have to make a firm decision. I believe in you know, identifying what the problem is and dealing with it head-on, and taking care of it. It's kind of hard to say that about something so deep like this, but I made a conscious decision

19. Rosaldo, *Culture and Truth*, p. 216.

probably in eighth grade to really try to focus on that. I think it went back and forth for a lot of years depending on what the circumstances were at the time. Whether I was liking someone specific at the time or whatever. Because of the way I [inaudible] I felt I really needed to make a decision. And I think that with adult African American adoptees, if you live with White parents you either make the decision that it doesn't matter, and you end up with someone who's White. Or you make a decision that it does matter, and that your generations are going to be affected because of the decisions that you make, that you really go the way that you feel in your heart. Like if you really feel that you're African American and you're proud of that, that's just what you do. That's the decision I made for me. I can't talk for anybody else. That's just what I perceive in them.

This definition of self shaped different aspects of her life. For example, it was important to her that she raise her daughter with a strong sense of African American culture. She was engaged in a continual process of education, from history and culture to cooking practices. She was very involved in the Black church she belonged to, and worked in a predominantly Black social service agency. She emphasized that she was comfortable and familiar with White culture as well, but drew her strength from the cultural traditions of African Americans.

The lives of transracial adoptees raise interesting questions about how racialized meanings of self are constructed, disseminated, and maintained through social institutions and public policies. The adoption system in the United States is geared toward the reproduction of normalized, naturalized nuclear families. In fact, historically it has developed as a means of reproducing White middle-class families headed by heterosexual married couples. It is useful therefore to ask what kinds of identities are being socially constructed through the placement of Black children in these families. Thus far, in this section I have discussed the lives of adoptees whose parents were conscientious about raising them in a racially diverse community and gave them the opportunity to become familiar with African American cultures. Now I turn to the experiences of a woman who did not have such social options.

Kristin Rhineholt, a twenty-five-year-old transracial adoptee, was the birth child of two African Americans. She was raised, along with her three transracially adopted brothers, by White parents in a nearly all-White Pennsylvania community. In the following excerpt, she discussed her racial identity in these terms:

KRISTIN: And people have said to me, they're like "You talk funny." I'm like "What do you mean I talk funny? I talk properly." And, I mean, that was one thing I hated my parents for — you couldn't have a sentence at the table without them saying, "It's Nicholas and I." You know, things like that. I'm like, "God Mom, Nicholas and *me!*" You know? I want to say whatever I want to say, but my command of the English language is pretty good. And I don't have the typical Black slang and accent and whatever. And I guess maybe I'd have that [if raised in a Black family]. And my friends laugh at me when I try and do it, just to mess around. They're like, "Kristin, please stop." Or like when Blacks talk to me sometimes I'll be like, "What? In English? I don't know what you're saying." And so I think about — would I have talked like that?

SANDI: So do people tell you you "sound White"?

KRISTIN: Oh yeah. Like I don't think anybody ever would ever mistake me for being Black if they never saw me. Never. Never in a million years.

SANDI: Huh. That's interesting though, the way you put that — "mistake" you for being Black. Like you're not really —

KRISTIN: That's true.

SANDI: That's interesting. A little slippage there.

KRISTIN: Yeah. Okay, rewind.

SANDI: Well, so, play with that a little bit. I mean *what are you?* Like if — I don't know I just came from interview —

KRISTIN: Shelley?

SANDI: Yeah. And she said people all the time — because she's very light-skinned — ask, "What are you?" If somebody asked you that —

KRISTIN: No, no. [meaning no one would ask that, because of her dark skin]

SANDI: Well, I'm asking you. "How do you self-identify?"

KRISTIN: Well. [pause]

SANDI: Or who are you?

KRISTIN: [pause] I would probably say I'm White with very, very dark skin.

SANDI: Really?

KRISTIN: Yeah. I think that for the most part that's the only part of me that I feel — I mean, obviously everyone knows, 'cause they look at me. But I think yeah, that would be the only way you'd know.

SANDI: That's a really powerful statement. So in a sense, you're saying you're making a real distinction between skin color and the way you see the world.

KRISTIN: Uh. [pause] Um. I don't know.

SANDI: Well, so like what does it mean to be *really Black* in that perspective?

KRISTIN: Well, I mean, I think — I guess there's a lot — but I think of stereotypes. And that's a very — I mean, to me stereotypes come to be because they're very prevalent in an area. And that's, I mean I think of the stereotypical [pause] — I mean I think it's [pause] — I don't think — I don't know what my life would've been like. I don't. But I don't — A lot of time I don't think I would have been as — not as smart — [pause] but as intelligent, I guess. I mean, that's weird, but . . .

This story can be read through a number of frames. In terms of Du Bois's schema, Kristin had internalized oppression. She accepted stereotypical representations of Blacks as true, and was thus alienated from, or had not developed, that part of herself. In the late twentieth century this alienation from self — the negative aspect of Du Bois's concept of double-consciousness — emerged through the inscription of the language and knowledge of Whiteness through the media, public policy, social institutions, social interactions, and familial socialization. Racial hegemony is maintained through the interaction of individual consciousness with cultural meaning systems, public knowledge, and media representations.

From an anthropological perspective, Kristin's social location in a White family and community had provided her with a set of cultural meaning systems that are usually only available to Whites. To her, these mainstream systems of cultural meaning seemed *natural;* indeed, she explained that she often *forgot* she was Black until someone else reminded her. She experienced a gap between the identity she had constructed through the cultural meaning systems available to her and the way she was seen and treated by the world.

This sense of disjuncture between identity and culture is felt and articulated *linguistically*. Kristin was referring to the racialization of language in her discussion of sounding White because she spoke "properly." In social interaction language indicates one's race and class — people "sound White" or "sound Black," depending on the cadence and accent of the speech and the relative use of "proper" English versus "slang." Kristin made an explicit connection between language, race, and identity when she said, "Oh yeah. Like I don't think anybody ever would ever mistake me for being Black if they never saw me. Never. Never in a million years." The use and understanding of language define insider versus outsider status in different class and racial-ethnic groups. Kristin's command of standard English and her inability to "sound Black" located her linguistically as White and middle class, while her inability to understand the English of some Blacks defined them as other in relation to herself.

This connection between self, language, and culture was explicit in Kristin's discussion of both sounding White and defining herself as "White with very, very dark skin." Mark Poster discusses language and identity as follows: "The individual wrestles with self-constitution through the manipulation of symbols, through carefully elaborated and systematized rules of formation, enunciative statements, and so forth."[20] Kristin's construction of self had been inscribed with the language of Whiteness. The symbols and statements that defined and made meaningful her perceptions of herself and her world taught her to see the world from the perspective of White power, privilege, and innocence. Her *subjectivity* saw Whiteness as self, and Blackness as other. Her views of African Americans had been primarily shaped through media stereotypes, and in fact she said there were times when she found herself thinking racist thoughts about other African Americans. She had learned to view herself as unconsciously White; this *natural and normal* self-concept as White was facilitated by the widespread representation of Whiteness as generic humanness. In her own consciousness she belonged to the unmarked category of humanity. She articulated her sense of racial identity in the following excerpt:

KRISTIN: Uh. Well, I think it comes back to, you see talk shows where you've got transvestites or where men have said, "I am a woman in a man's body." And I feel like I've been conditioned White, and I am White in a Black body.

Kristin's experience points to the profoundly *racial* character of contemporary prescriptions for identity, through the marking of her difference and the gap between her self-knowledge and the ways she was perceived and treated.

---

20. Mark Poster, "Foucault and the Problem of Self-Constitution," in *Foucault and the Critique of Institutions,* ed. John Caputo and Mark Yount (University Park, Pa.: Pennsylvania State University Press, 1993), p. 79.

SANDI: You said, when you started on this little stream, that you have your troubles. Do you mean in terms of racial identity or — ?

KRISTIN: Oh yeah, definitely.

SANDI: So how would you express that?

KRISTIN: You mean like, what do I mean?

SANDI: Yeah.

KRISTIN: Well, I think I might have said it earlier, but I mean, definitely, I forget. And I mean it's like, it's almost like a *double life*. Because sometimes I can't get away from it. Everyday I look in the mirror there's this brown skin. But at the same time, I forget until someone reminds me, like, "Hey, you're Black. You can't do that."

SANDI: So what are some of the ways you get reminded?

KRISTIN: When . . . When like people will call me nigger, and I'm like, "Me?" Or like, "Oh yeah. sh-keh [sound meant to signify being hit with something]. But things like that where — or, that's probably the biggest, but, I mean, or the looks you get. I mean, I don't get them as much anymore because I think I'm old enough that my mom and I probably look like just friends walking through the mall or something like that. But when I was younger it's like the looks, like, "Who's that Black girl with that blond, blue-eyed woman?" You know, and it's right there. It's a reminder.

Her experiences illustrate how deeply racialized social interactions are in this country. Kristin's physical presence, her Blackness, spoke through the metalanguage of race, disrupting her unconscious sense of White privilege in the nearly all-White settings she found herself in.

This passage calls to mind the works of both W. E. B. Du Bois and Frantz Fanon. The *doubleness* Kristin spoke of was the disjuncture between her internal view of herself as generically and fully human — which in her racial meaning system signified White — and the *otherness* she felt when someone reminded her, "Hey, you're Black. You can't do that." Fanon captured this social *othering* in his phrase, "Look, a Negro!" In *Black Skin, White Masks* he considers the contrasts between his personal sense of himself and his physical presence, and the objectifying "look" of Whites that he calls the "racial epidermal schema."[21] By this he means the *racial gaze* — a set of ideological assumptions and narratives that are culturally available to Whites and others for use in affixing meaning to Black bodies.

21. Frantz Fanon, *Black Skin, White Masks,* trans. Charles Lam Markmann (New York: Grove, 1967), p. 112.

Fanon explains that such visual assaults on his personhood are driven by "legends, stories, history, and above all, *historicity*" that narrate the meanings of Black skin others impose on him.[22] Robert Gooding-Williams explains:

> Fanon describes the experience of being subjected to the racial epidermal schema as that of being physically fastened or affixed to an image of oneself; one feels as if one had acquired a second epidermis (hence the concept of a racial *epidermal* schema) that had been superimposed on one's body and then come to haunt it like a shadow.[23]

For Kristin there was another complexity. She had been socialized with a subjectivity that valued Whiteness and devalued Blackness, and thus had largely internalized the social narratives attributing social dysfunction to African Americans. Thus, the racializing gaze was self-inflicted as well: "Because sometimes I can't get away from it. Everyday I look in the mirror there's this brown skin." As Fanon stressed, what that brown skin means is culturally and historically specific, and is powerfully and painfully conveyed through social narratives. This is evident from the list of characteristics he "discovered" when he turned the racial epidermal schema on himself:

> I subjected myself to an objective examination, I discovered my blackness, my ethnic characteristics; and I was battered down by tom-toms, cannibalism, intellectual deficiency, fetishism, racial defects, slaveships, and above all else, above all: "Sho' good eatin."[24]

In describing how she imagined her life might have been either if she had been raised by her birth parents or been adopted by a Black family, Kristin explained that she would probably have liked fried chicken, watermelon, collard greens, and orange soda. She thought she would have been less intelligent than she was. She assumed she would have been poor, and thus would not have learned how to play the piano or to swim, or had good educational opportunities. Having grown up surrounded only by Whites, Kristin's views of African Americans were rooted in ideological narratives about racial difference available in literature, popular culture,

---

22. Fanon, *Black Skin, White Masks*, p. 112 (emphasis in original).

23. Gooding-Williams, "Look a Negro!" p. 164 (emphasis in original). I am indebted to Gooding-Williams's brilliant use of Fanon in his analysis of the Rodney King verdict.

24. Fanon, *Black Skin, White Masks*, p. 112.

news media, and cultural lore. There was no one in her life to counter such racial fables.

I imagine that some people in favor of "color-blind" adoptions might dismiss these issues. Kristin was a college graduate, was steadily employed, had a close relationship with her family, and led a stable life. Yet race was a major issue for her. Although being White-identified did not present her with insurmountable problems, there were aspects of it that steadily eroded the edges of her self-esteem. Her primary adaptational strategies had involved defining herself as different from most African Americans. This tactic was ineffectual, however, in situations in which others "reminded" her she was Black.

Adoption across racial, ethnic, and cultural lines constructs lives that question some of American society's basic assumptions about what constitutes identity. Was Kristin "really Black," if she saw herself as "White with very, very dark skin," was uncomfortable with African Americans, and had no insider knowledge of Black culture? What does race mean in this context? Recently, I found myself in a casual conversation with someone about these issues. I had relayed the stories of a few transracial adoptees as well as my own experience of discovering in adulthood that I was "half Jewish." I asked rhetorically, "What does it mean then that I'm supposedly half-Jewish, but didn't grow up with that cultural knowledge?" To my surprise, the man I was speaking with answered bluntly, "It means you would have been killed in Nazi Germany." The Third Reich defined a Jew as someone with at least one Jewish grandparent. A contemporary anti-Semitic White supremacist would not care whether or not I *defined* myself as Jewish; racial hatred operates on absolutes. Being adopted provides no exemption; such lines are drawn in "blood."

Clearly, transracial adoptees do not have the choice of defining themselves out of the category Black. We live in a social world organized around racial-ethnic categories, and we are seen and treated by others according to the categories we *appear* to fit and the cultural meanings attached to such classifications. While Kristin's story was rather unique with regard to her full identification with Whites and self-distancing from African Americans, her experience was illustrative of my other informants' experiences as well. At some point in their lives they had all felt a jarring sense of disjuncture between their view of themselves and the ways they were seen and treated by people outside their families. Throughout their lives they had had to learn to adapt to a world that recognized the social meanings of racial difference and racism, and often translated those ideologies into actions and utterances.

Routes of Identity

LYNN: I had decided to do a Black Studies minor, but continued to take like all these classes in Black Studies. Because I thought, "At least I better get educated, so I know what this is about." I took an Intro to the Black Woman, or whatever — uh, Black Women in America with this professor that was wonderful. And so I started reading all that literature. And it just didn't add up in my head, that somehow someone had missed my education. Why didn't I know this stuff before? Why was I denied access to the Black community before? So, of course, I blamed my parents.

Lynn described this time in her life as her "radical Black phase," a time when she questioned the racial assumptions she had been raised with, immersed herself in African American culture and history, and became part of the Black community at her school. Her immersion in Black cultures was a search for an understanding of identity.

Like most of the people I interviewed, Lynn found her parents' socialization around issues of race to be inadequate. It is important to contextualize my informants' familial experiences within a broader societal framework. In public discussions of transracial adoption the question of *culture* is too often addressed solely at the individual and familial level. Access to and awareness of Black culture is also a structural issue. Lynn's parents, like most White folks who grew up and were educated in the 1950s and 1960s, lived in predominantly segregated communities and went to schools in which little attention, if any, was paid to African American history or culture.

Indeed, in the 1970s when Lynn and her siblings were growing up, the area in which they lived on the West Coast was still profoundly segregated. When schools were desegregated by busing, the class differences between Lynn and the Black children new to the school seemed so stark that she found herself more comfortable in her already established friendships with Whites. By the time she got to college she knew who Sojourner Truth, Harriett Tubman, and Frederick Douglass were; as she put it, she knew the "biggies," but had little knowledge beyond this of Black culture or history. Having been raised in a middle-class White family and community, however, she was well-versed in White culture and history. It was in college that she began to explore African American history and culture, and to question the way she had been raised.

It was often upon leaving home that the transracial adoptees I interviewed first began to grapple with the social and personal meanings of being Black in the contemporary United States. Several of my informants went through a similar process of exploration by dating men their parents tacitly regarded as "too Black" — more in terms of culture and politics than of skin color. One woman became a member of the ballet troupe, the Dance Theater of Harlem. Lynn's story illustrates the power of self-discovery and transformation that is often involved in such a quest. In the following excerpt, she discussed her second semester in college, which she spent in Paris. Just before leaving school for the semester she began dating a South African man.

LYNN: And I had a Black friend, like my [with emphasis] *first Black friend,* who I'm still friends with.

SANDI: God, you gave me chills. I mean, to be a sophomore in college, or whatever, and to have your first Black friend is really — that's really powerful.

LYNN: As a freshman in college. Yes. So Amanda Williams, who I'm still friends with, and who still drives me insane — but we were actually roommates when we were in Paris together. And she gave me some James Baldwin to read. So I read that and I thought about it. And she let me read like part of her journal. She kept a journal and she wrote poetry, and really a lot of it was about what it was like being Black on an all-White campus, or being Black on this tour. I mean it was really interesting. She's a really bright woman. I mean, she's working on her doctorate in chemical engineering. I mean, she's very smart. So I was reading this stuff, and started thinking, "huh." And then I thought I should read some stuff about South Africa if I'm going to date this guy, so I started to buy books. I started to read books about Nelson Mandela being on Robbens Island. And that started me thinking, "Why are White people doing this to Black people?" Um, and then I came back and went back to school. And Louis and I lived together. And Louis — it was interesting too — because he was of mixed race heritage. They call it "colored" in South Africa. But he was half Indian. His family had — they were Malay, and from New Delhi. And then his father was Sutu, so African. So within their own family they had this dichotomy between races, which in South Africa, as you can imagine, was really really strong. So Louis was the most self-righteous Black person I had ever met in my life. He just really really believed he was Black, and he looked Indian. So people always said, "Oh you're Indian." And he always said [with emphasis],

"No, I'm *African*." And that completely, like changed my frame of mind. And he was — considered himself a Marxist, to top it off. So he's like espousing Marxist ideology all the time. This is the guy I got engaged to. And you know we had an awful marriage, but it completely transformed my identity. I mean, most of my friends at the university were Africans, so on some level they did not make that color differentiation. You know that color stratification within the Black community. Because Africa, the continent is made up of all sorts of people. And so we moved — I mean we had friends who were South Africans and from Nigeria and Ethiopia. So we had this group of African people — and Liberia — who we're buddies with. And they were pretty radical. And then we started to — we used to go down to African Heritage House. I used to go down with him, and then I started going to the meetings. And then they would have sisters meetings, and so I would go to those. And I started taking — I remember, I'm so embarrassed I ever said this. I took this Intro to the Black Novel class in the Black Studies Department. It was the first semester I got back to school after being in Europe. And the teacher said, "Why are you here?" And everybody else had to go around and say — And I said, "Well, I'm here because I want to learn something about my cultural identity." Which you know, in that context was probably a little — they were probably like, "What the hell is she talking about?" Because they didn't know where I was coming from. You know, I started to read, you know, Black writers for the first time. I mean, I knew who Harriett Tubman was and my mother gave me a book on Sojourner — I knew who Sojourner Truth was 'cause my mom gave me a book on her. They were like these isolated — I knew who Frederick Douglass was. I mean, I knew the biggies. . . . So I started you know, Ralph Ellison. And reading this stuff that I didn't even know existed, and reading Black poetry. And it was really powerful.

SANDI: I bet.

LYNN: And so then I became — not to like my White family so much. And it became really hard for me to reconcile being — getting radicalized with this White, upper-class, elite — which my family had become by that point — family.

This was how Lynn constructed her roots. She explored the routes of Black culture as they intersected the various pathways she walked. During her "radical Black phase" she explored and claimed an insider view of

Black cultures, and since then has also come to embrace the mainstream White cultural meaning systems with which she was raised.

While transracial adoptees deal with specific questions of racial identity, such explorations of and shifts in sense of self are not unusual for nonadoptees in their early adult years. Many people feel compelled to define themselves differently from the way they were raised, and often go through a period of anger at their parents for not fulfilling their needs. In no way do I wish to diminish the importance of the needs of transracial adoptees to live in racially diverse communities, attend diverse schools, and be part of families — of whatever race — that give them some knowledge and a sense of belonging in whatever racial-ethnic groups they are a part of. I simply wish to place the identity quests of my informants in sociocultural context.

Conclusion

It is useful to step back for a moment to consider these allegories of identity in a broader milieu. Adoptees are certainly not alone in feeling that they don't know who they are. Identity politics, coming of age stories, identity crises, coming out stories, midlife crises, and spiritual transformations saturate both the public discourse and private lives.

The stories I have discussed in this chapter indicate the power of social institutions in constructing and shaping individual lives and identities. Transracial adoptees' identities are constructed through the discourse of the child welfare system; such people are written into being as culturally and discursively White, yet are physically viewed as Black. They began as Black infants or young children placed into subject positions mapped out as White and middle class. A few of the adoptees I interviewed had lived in a homogeneous White social world, only moving outside the lines when other people challenged their social status as symbolically White. Some of my informants took it upon themselves to explore and discover their identities as African Americans. Others had parents who had raised them in diverse, multiracial communities.

The disjuncture between the identities prescribed by their social locations and their apparent Blackness demonstrates the constructedness of racial meaning, and suggests the power of social institutions and ideological cultural meaning in guiding and shaping the identities of all individuals in the contemporary United States. For while people who were not adopted cannot point so easily toward the role of the state in determining who they are, I would argue that lives and identities are continually and subtly shaped and constructed in interaction with myriad social institutions that our cultural assumptions about individuality typically prevent us from seeing.

I have addressed the two primary issues in the public dialogue over transracial adoption, namely, survival skills and racial identity. The adoptees I interviewed struggled profoundly with these issues. Their narratives also show that there are effective ways of dealing with such concerns, however. I conclude with Cat Benton's perspective on the practice of transracial adoption.

> CAT: If I could say one thing — and this is just a message to parents that want to adopt. What is it I want to say? There's no way that you can give that child everything that child needs. Be aware that that child needs a lot more than love. Be aware that that child needs to know where he or she came from. If you can have an open adoption do it. Or at least keep contact with the birth parents so they can find them one day. And [pause] understand that your child is being brought into your home with a dysfunction; they are not a normal child — quote unquote "normal." They are entering your home with a dysfunction.
>
> SANDI: Because it's an adoption?
>
> CAT: Because it's an adoption. I went to a palm — I didn't go to a palm reader, but there was a palm reader at this party, and there was four adoptees at this party. And she was hired for like three hours to read everybody's palms briefly. And when she got to mine — I was one of the last people — and she said, "God, I keep coming up against this abandonment issue." And she said, "You know you went home with the wrong family from the hospital." And so I really — I believe it's in our bones; it's in our makeup; it's in our lives. There's nothing we can do about it. So, understand that your child needs more than you can give it, and you can never fulfill what your child needs, but do your best to educate your child on where they come from. And think about therapy and groups and people that are like them.
>
> SANDI: What about at the policy level? Do you think that they should be made easier for people? Should it stay the same? Should it be made harder?
>
> CAT: Adoption?
>
> SANDI: Whites adopting Black kids, or children of color.
>
> CAT: Oh. Um, I think that it should be made easier, but there should be

some sort of class, or some sort of educational — And there should be some sort of interaction with adoptive — new adoptive parents — to parents that have raised adoptees. You know, some sort of an educational thing going on. When you — you know you have to have a license to drive, you don't have to have a license to be a parent. And I'm not sure what they go through to screen you to be an adoptive parent, but um, it shouldn't be hard in the sense that they're a Black child coming into a Black family. It should be harder in the sense of — Do *you know* what you're getting into? "Oh I want to give love to some child!" Well, that's not enough.

SANDI: So at the same time that you're saying that and that it's deadly to do this, you're saying it should be made easier?

CAT: Umhmm.

SANDI: How do you resolve that?

CAT: Easier in the sense that I don't think that because the family is White — The reasons that I think it's hard now are racist issues, not realistic issues. I think that it should be made easier in the sense of just because this child is Black and just because this family is White it's not okay. That's not what I'm saying. I'm saying it should be okay, but society is screwed. And because of that and because of the adoption issue itself, it should be harder in the sense of [pause] educating those parents and saying, "This is really what you're getting into." And, "Are you capable of that? Are you capable of giving this child what he needs?" Not harder in the sense that you're White and he's Black and shouldn't be with that family. Harder in the sense of really taking a look at it and saying, "This is what this child needs. Are you financially and emotionally prepared to give that to that child?" And if you're not you can't do it.

What seems clear from the lives of those I interviewed is that when transracial adoptions are *necessary* families should be chosen carefully, and should be educated as to the particular needs that child may bring to the family, as well as the way the presence of a person of color will change the family.

II. Theological Perspectives

5. A Conversation We Ought to Be Having over Adoption

JEFFREY STOUT

Hardly anybody opposes adoption per se. The main question being debated — sporadically and unproductively — is, who may adopt whom under what circumstances? The debate is troubling for two reasons that I shall touch on here: first, because of its tendency to degenerate into culture-war nastiness concerning family values and same-sex coupling; and second, because of its failure to confront our religious differences honestly and helpfully. There are also other reasons, which bear more on race and class than on gender and religion, but I must leave these for another occasion.

It seems clear that the major obstacle to full-fledged legal recognition of same-sex marriage as a legitimate context for adoption in this country is Christian opposition to it. Any citizen who favors such recognition, as I do, has an interest in looking into the reasons that lead some Christians to oppose it. But liberal political philosophers have largely evaded serious conversation with such Christians, and have encouraged their readers and students to view such conversation as essentially pointless or impossible. In this chapter I want to call this evasion into question.

Christianity, being a "religion of the Book," attributes moral authority to the Bible. It has traditionally encouraged its members to live their entire lives, not least of all their political lives, in light of what the Bible says. We should not find it surprising, then, that the reasons Christians give for opposing same-sex marriage — and thus for opposing adoption in the context of same-sex marriage — are often biblical reasons.

Many American Christians hold that the Bible rules out same-sex coupling as such. They then argue as follows: Marriage, in biblical terms, is the only legitimate context for one-flesh union and for the raising of children. The secular liberals who favor adoption by anyone other than a married heterosexual couple are therefore in the process of depriving our society of its true basis in biblical faith. Americans have traditionally been a "people of the Book." If secular liberalism has its way, they will cease to be. Thanks to the grip that liberals have on our legal institutions, the entertainment industry, and higher education, the very institution of marriage is in the process of becoming incoherent. The children who find themselves in the resulting ersatz families are only the most salient victims of the new secularism. Any child who grows up in a society that recognizes same-sex marriages as authentic and allows same-sex couples to adopt children is likely to be badly confused about what marriage is.

We are all familiar with some version of this conservative argument. It is a staple of the culture wars. How do secular liberals respond to it? Not, for the most part, by criticizing the argument on its own terms, but rather by insisting that Christians should keep their religious opinions to themselves. The focal point of the debate immediately shifts from marriage and adoption to the question of religion in the public square. If religious reasons can be excluded as inappropriate in the context of public controversy, the issue of adoption boils down to the question of how to foster some measure of family stability for the raising of adopted children while allowing individuals maximal freedom to couple as they choose. But why should religious reasons be excluded?

Richard Rorty answers this question in a widely discussed essay, "Religion As a Conversation-Stopper," in which he appeals to "the Jeffersonian compromise" between the Enlightenment and the religious.[1] This compromise, which Rorty sees as essential to maintaining a stable political order under modern conditions, allows citizens to hold religious views as long as they keep them private. Citizens violate the Jeffersonian compromise when they express their religious views in public as reasons for their political conclusions. When Rorty says that religion is a conversation-stopper, he means that offering a religious reason for a political conclusion — such as a restriction on who may adopt whom — is likely to bring the public discussion of policy to a halt. The problem, he thinks, is that nobody knows how to argue productively over the acceptability of religious premises. Rorty's

1. Richard Rorty, "Religion As a Conversation-Stopper," in *Philosophy and Social Hope* (London: Penguin, 1999), pp. 168-74. Since I wrote this essay, Rorty has responded to it by modifying his position somewhat. See Richard Rorty, "Religion in the Public Square: A Reconsideration," *Journal of Religious Ethics* 31, no. 1 (spring 2003): 141-49. I shall have to defer taking up his modified position until some other occasion.

practical advice can be summed up in a line from Whitman's *Leaves of Grass:* "Argue not concerning God."[2]

Rorty's reason for this view is essentially pragmatic. The political discussion goes better when citizens abide by the Jeffersonian compromise and keep their religious opinions out of the public square. We all have an interest in keeping the public discussion of public policy going. If religion is essentially a conversation-stopper, we all therefore have a reason to keep our religious opinions to ourselves. Otherwise, we risk having the discussion break down, as it did during the religious wars of early modern Europe.

It seems odd for a pragmatist like Rorty to be claiming that religion is essentially anything, let alone a conversation-stopper. From a pragmatic point of view, the conversational utility of appealing to religious premises can be expected to depend on the situation. Moreover, Rorty seems to have forgotten how he defined "conversation" in the book that brought him to public prominence, *Philosophy and the Mirror of Nature.*[3] In that book, he contrasted conversation with "normal discourse." In normal discourse, one always knows how to settle disputed points. Conversation is what we need when we don't know how to resolve a controversy by appeal to agreed-upon rules or principles.

Philosophy, at its best, helps us transcend the failures of normal discourse by keeping a conversation going, despite the clash of apparently incommensurable premises. Conversation is what Rorty used to call the mode of discourse we need when people employing different vocabularies reach a momentary impasse.[4] But if this is what "conversation" means, then conversation need not come to a halt when religious premises are introduced into a political argument.

Normal discourse might well break down under such circumstances — for the simple reason that members of our society do not share the same religious commitments. Conversation, however, is the art of responding to such impasses creatively. The "edifying" philosopher's vocation is to practice this art in such a way that others can be drawn into it, thereby transforming an impasse into an opportunity for a different, more exploratory, improvisational discussion that aspires to attain wisdom. I think here of the point in one of Plato's early dialogues where

2. Walt Whitman, *Whitman: Poetry and Prose,* ed. Justin Kaplan (New York: Library of America, 1982), p. 11.

3. Richard Rorty, *Philosophy and the Mirror of Nature* (Princeton, N.J.: Princeton University Press, 1979).

4. Rorty, *Philosophy and the Mirror of Nature,* pp. 389-94.

Euthyphro realizes, thanks to Socrates' rigorous questioning, that piety cannot be defined simply as what the gods love. Euthyphro falls silent, unable to go further on his own. But Socrates, an edifying philosopher if ever there was one, finds a way to get the dialogue going again.[5]

Normal discourse does tend to break down when latter-day Euthyphros introduce religious premises into the debate over who may adopt whom. But what would happen if, instead of chastising such people for appealing to the Bible in a public debate, we tried to initiate a Socratic conversation with them about what the Bible means? What if we challenged them to live up to the deepest of the convictions they express — to be more, rather than less, theological?

I will return to these questions in a few paragraphs. But first I want to take note of the somewhat more plausible versions of secular liberalism associated with the work of John Rawls. I say "versions" in the plural because Rawls changed his mind over time on both the sort of liberalism he was trying to formulate and the role of religious reasons in public debate.

In his first book, *A Theory of Justice,* Rawls argued for a form of secular liberalism that derived largely from his reading of the greatest theorist of the social contract, Immanuel Kant.[6] But he later came to believe that it would be unrealistic to expect everyone to accept his own Kantianism as *the* public framework for political deliberation. Given that reasonable people can disagree over Kantianism as much as they disagree over Augustinianism, Rawls realized that it would be *unfair* to build any such comprehensive doctrine into the basis of political deliberation. That is why Rawls endeavored, in his later work, to articulate a more modestly *political* liberalism — a framework for public reason that did not presuppose his own secularism.[7]

It is not clear, however, that he succeeded in securing the sort of independent basis for political deliberation that he sought. At any rate, he did not succeed in persuading his religious critics that he had done so.[8]

---

5. Plato, *Euthyphro, Apology, Crito,* trans. F. J. Church, rev. by Robert D. Cumming (Indianapolis: Bobbs-Merrill, 1956), pp. 13-14.

6. John Rawls, *A Theory of Justice* (Cambridge, Mass.: Harvard University Press, 1971).

7. John Rawls, *Political Liberalism,* paperback ed. (New York: Columbia University Press, 1996), and *Collected Papers,* ed. Samuel Freedman (Cambridge, Mass.: Harvard University Press, 1999), chs. 15-27.

8. For two examples, see Nicholas Wolterstorff, "The Role of Religion in Decision and Discussion of Political Issues," in *Religion in the Public Square: The Place of Religious Convictions in Political Debate,* by Robert Audi and Nicholas Wolterstorff (Lanham, Md.: Row-

Some of those critics persist in viewing him as the quintessential secularist. Perhaps he wanted to achieve a form of liberalism that did not presuppose a comprehensive secularist outlook, but in their view his "political liberalism" still left the essentials of his old secular liberalism intact.

What role, exactly, did his political liberalism envisage for religion in public debate? Rawls initially defended a relatively restrictive view — namely, that when discussing or deciding constitutional essentials or matters of basic justice, one ought to reason solely from principles that no reasonable person could reasonably reject. Such principles promise to put political deliberation on a fair basis. They define the social contract of political liberalism.

According to Rawls, agreeing to restrict oneself to reasoning on the basis of principles that no reasonable person could reasonably reject shows respect for other people. It does so because they, too, will buy into the social contract that restricts their reasoning in this way — at least if they are being reasonable. A political order founded on this sort of social contract is one in which all reasonable citizens accept the freestanding rational basis of the laws that coercively constrain them.

What does this view imply for the use of religious premises in political discussion? It seems clear that religious premises are not able to pass muster as principles that no reasonable person could reasonably reject. Religious premises are such that reasonable people disagree over them. By "reasonable" people, Rawls means people interested in finding a way to live cooperatively by following agreed-upon rules. People who are reasonable in this sense adhere to various comprehensive outlooks, some of them religious outlooks, like Christianity or Islam, others of them secular outlooks, like Peter Singer's utilitarianism. Rawls concluded that fairness requires us to bracket all comprehensive outlooks, religious or secular, when deliberating on constitutional essentials or matters of basic justice.

Rawls's critics argued that this formulation of his view was too restrictive. Doesn't it imply that Lincoln's Second Inaugural Address and King's most influential speeches violated the norm of fairness by introducing religious reasons improperly into a public discussion? Rawls replied that these justly famous examples of political oratory were not obviously concerned with constitutional essentials and matters of basic justice. But he still found them sufficiently troubling, as potential

---

man and Littlefield, 1997), pp. 67-120, and Timothy P. Jackson, "To Bedlam and Part Way Back: John Rawls and Christian Justice," *Faith and Philosophy* 8, no. 4 (October 1991): 423-47.

counterexamples, to alter his position a bit. In the paperback edition of *Political Liberalism* and in his important paper "The Idea of Public Reason Revisited,"[9] he conceded that one may introduce religious premises into one's reasoning on constitutional essentials and matters of basic justice *provided* that one is committed to offering eventually reasons that appeal strictly to principles that no reasonable person could reasonably reject. This is known as the "proviso." Religious reasons, according to this revised version of Rawls's position, function at best as I.O.U.'s. You may offer them initially, if you want, but only if you commit yourself to offering eventually reasons of a different kind — a *liberal* kind, a kind of reason bleached of all reliance on comprehensive doctrines, religious or secular.

What Rorty calls the Jeffersonian compromise and what Rawls calls the social contract are two names for roughly the same thing. Both of these philosophers have assumed that it's going to be possible, ultimately, to resolve our disputes over fundamental issues by relying on a basis of premises that are independent of our religious commitments and other comprehensive doctrines. But it is not clear that there is such a basis, and on the pragmatic and holistic view of reasoning that Rorty and Rawls share, it isn't clear that there could be. Why should we believe that the basis being proposed by these philosophers is independent of religious disputes in the way they suppose? Why should we believe that there are any principles that no reasonable person can reasonably reject?

It should not be surprising, it seems to me, that many biblically oriented citizens see the framework favored by Rorty and Rawls as an expression of secularism, as an unfair attempt on the part of the nonreligious liberal elite to deprive religious citizens of the religious grounds of their political reasoning — in effect, to shut them up. What happened to freedom of religion? What happened to freedom of expression? Rorty and Rawls seem to be implying that we have these freedoms but should refrain from exercising them in public discussion of political fundamentals. It seems to me that this view would seem as odd to Emerson, Thoreau, and Whitman as it would to Jonathan Edwards.

In my book *Democracy and Tradition,* I argue in some detail that Rorty's Jeffersonian compromise and Rawls's social contract fail to provide adequate models of public discussion.[10] The liberal professors should stop trying to impose their own sense of decorum on a populace ani-

9. Rawls, *Collected Papers,* ch. 26.
10. Jeffrey Stout, *Democracy and Tradition* (Princeton, N.J.: Princeton University Press, 2004), ch. 3.

mated with the idea of free expression. It is true that introducing religious premises into a political argument sometimes gets the discussion off track or signals a disposition to treat other people disrespectfully. But in my view, the liberal professors have succeeded only in fueling religious resentment of liberalism.[11] The remedy for this, it seems to me, is to restore the link in political theory between liberal democracy and Socratic conversation.

Think back to the exchange between Socrates and Euthyphro. When Euthyphro appeals to Hesiod's stories about the gods, which are authoritative for him in the way that the Bible is authoritative for today's Bible-thumpers, Socrates does not chastise him for appealing to religious premises in justifying a legal conclusion in the case against his father. Socrates does not try to shut Euthyphro up, but instead tries to get him to talk in greater depth. He questions Euthyphro in a way that compels him to make explicit what his professed commitments actually presuppose. In the process, the difficulties in Euthyphro's outlook are made manifest. Euthyphro discovers that it can be more painful to be taken seriously by Socrates than to be laughed at when speaking religiously in the assembly. It is not Socrates but Euthyphro who eventually brings the conversation to an end by claiming to be too busy to pursue the questioning further.[12]

A Socratic response to the biblically oriented citizens among us would be to encourage them to speak their minds on topics like adoption and then subject their arguments to respectful but stringent questioning. If it is true that Christian arguments from biblical authority constitute the main obstacle to legal recognition of same-sex marriage in the United States, then why not encourage Christians to state those arguments openly? How else are they to be subjected to critical scrutiny? Rorty grants that there is no way to prevent people from allowing their religious commitments to influence their political conclusions. But his "don't ask, don't tell" strategy concerning religious premises has the effect of leaving highly consequential theological commitments in the shadows.

It would be better, it seems to me, to begin a serious conversation about sexuality, marriage, and adoption in which we all felt free to express our comprehensive views as fully as we wished while also feeling free to offer respectful criticism of each other's premises. In this way, we could show each other respect: first, by expressing the reasons that actually

11. I discuss John Milbank, Alasdair MacIntyre, and Stanley Hauerwas as embodiments of this resentment in *Democracy and Tradition*, chs. 4-7.

12. Plato, *Euthyphro*, p. 20.

move us to reach our conclusions, and second, by challenging the reasons our neighbors offer *on their own terms*. It is hard to know what those terms are unless they are expressed in public.

The sort of exchange that I am calling for does not proceed from principles that no reasonable person can reasonably reject. If, on a given issue, we find that we are able to resolve our disagreements on the basis of considerations we all accept, so much the better. But if we are unable to find an essentially common basis for our arguments, this should not prevent us from conversing, as long as we proceed respectfully and dialectically. Conversing in this sense involves expressing ourselves as fully as we wish and challenging other commitments on their own terms. Full disclosure of premises and immanent criticism go hand in hand. Let us call the model I am proposing "Socratic," to distinguish it from the Jeffersonian compromise and social contract models.

The greatest moral breakthrough in American history was the collapse of widespread acceptance of slavery. One of the things that made this breakthrough possible was the criticism of biblically grounded arguments for the propriety of slavery. Christian abolitionists brought careful and rigorous criticism to bear on the pro-slavery arguments of their fellow Christians. For this to happen, the latter arguments had to be expressed publicly. Despite the significance of liberation from slavery in the Exodus story, the Bible largely takes slavery for granted as one of the given structures of the social order. If abolitionism was to win ground, there had to be a conversation about the widespread assumption that God had punished blacks as "Hamites" and about St. Paul's advice that slaves should obey their masters.

We are in roughly the same situation today with respect to the debate over adoption. If same-sex marriage is going to win ground as an appropriate context for the raising of adopted children, there needs to be a conversation about the sin of Sodom, the abominations of Leviticus, and St. Paul's condemnation of men who commit unnatural acts with men. Theologians have already done much to challenge received opinion on these points of biblical interpretation, but the public conversation has barely begun.

The theological scholarship that I am referring to does not take a liberal conception of freedom as its point of departure and simply discard all biblical passages that restrain sexual permissiveness. To the contrary, the theological scholarship that matters most in this context is the most seriously and rigorously biblical in orientation — the sort that cannot honestly be dismissed by theologically conservative Christians as secular liberalism in drag. Orthodox Christians could dismiss the first wave of Christian defenses of same-sex coupling in this way. But in the last several years, something of great public importance has been happening in theology. Deeply biblical, *theologically* conservative critiques of the church's traditional stances on same-sex coupling and same-sex marriage have emerged. These critiques begin with Socratic questioning of *culturally* conservative assumptions about the Bible. They have much to teach the philosophers about how to conduct a conversation.

Mark D. Jordan has contributed to this development in two important ways: first, by using his consummate skills as a historian to show that Christian attitudes toward the "sin of Sodom" actually took shape in the medieval period for reasons that were neither especially coherent nor essentially biblical; and second, by arguing on theologically conservative grounds for a view of the Holy Spirit that challenges the Vatican's practice of silencing gay priests.[13]

Given our interest in fostering a fruitful public conversation about adoption in particular, an American theologian who merits especially close attention is Eugene Rogers. The most effective response to Christians who infer culturally conservative conclusions on adoption from theologically conservative premises is to ask them how they propose to respond to Rogers's book *Sexuality and the Christian Body: Their Way into the Triune God.*[14] Rogers's book, to my eye, is the most profoundly Trinitarian treatment of sexuality and marriage in recent times. It makes the prooftexting of most culturally conservative Christians seem downright untheological by comparison.

Rogers aims to make explicit the parallels between what the Bible says about slavery and what it says about same-sex coupling. Theologically liberal scholars have taken this tack before, in the hope of downgrading the authority of the latter passages to the level that the former enjoy in the contemporary church. But Rogers goes on to probe what the alleged unnaturalness of same-sex coupling ought to signify in a biblical context. The Bible does not present Jesus as the natural offspring of Mary

---

13. On the first point, see Mark D. Jordan, *The Invention of Sodomy in Christian Theology* (Chicago: University of Chicago Press, 1997). On the second, see Jordan, *The Silence of Sodom: Homosexuality in Modern Catholicism* (Chicago: University of Chicago Press, 2000). See also Jordan, *The Ethics of Sex* (Oxford: Blackwell, 2002).

14. Eugene F. Rogers Jr., *Sexuality and the Christian Body: Their Way into the Triune God* (Oxford: Blackwell, 1999). I discuss Rogers at greater length in my essay "How Charity Transcends the Culture Wars: Eugene Rogers and Others on Same-Sex Marriage," *Journal of Religious Ethics* 31, no. 2 (summer 2003): 169-80.

and Joseph. Matthew gives Jesus a genealogy that includes no fewer than four irregular sexual unions. When St. Paul says in Romans 11 that God "grafts" the Gentiles onto the people of Israel, thus bringing the Gentiles into the covenant, he alludes to the grafting of wild branches onto a domestic olive tree, which is hardly a natural act. Who achieves this grafting, this unnatural union? Jesus Christ, who is himself conceived outside "natural" human wedlock.[15]

If you had read only the standard treatises on natural law and the standard biblical passages on unnatural coupling, you would be likely to miss the broader biblical significance of the natural and the unnatural. The context is further complicated by Galatians 3, where Paul says that "[t]here is no longer Jew or Greek, there is no longer slave or free, there is no longer male and female; for all of you are one in Christ Jesus" (v. 28 NRSV). All of these distinctions dissolve when human beings are taken up into God's Trinitarian life. Galatians 3 is the very passage that eventually persuaded American Christians to abandon traditional tolerance of slavery. In Rogers's work, it also becomes a key consideration in the debate over same-sex marriage.[16] If there is no longer male and female in Christ, if *God* practices the art of unnatural union, how is a culturally conservative position on same-sex marriage to be justified theologically?

How does God incorporate the Gentiles into the covenant? *Not by begetting them as God's natural children, but rather by adopting them.* The hospitality of adoption is, for Rogers, the biblical model for salvation of the Gentiles. What does this have to do with the sin of Sodom? Rogers points out, tellingly, that the story of Sodom and Gomorrah "provides a contrast to" an earlier story about Abraham and the promise of Isaac. "In the first case, Abraham shares hospitality with the Trinity and receives the promise of a covenant. In the contrasting case, the Sodomites greet the visitors with violence."[17] The sin of Sodom is violent inhospitality, the opposite of what Abraham shows to "the three angels who appeared to him at the oaks of Mamre,"[18] the opposite of what God does by adopting the unnatural Gentiles unnaturally into the covenant.

These arguments and ideas are too important to leave behind the closed doors of divinity schools and departments of religion. Scholars

15. For the point about the genealogy given in Matthew, see Rogers, *Sexuality and the Christian Body*, pp. 3, 188, 243-44; for the point about grafting, see pp. 3, 27-28, 51, 64-66, 177-79, 208, 273.

16. Rogers, *Sexuality and the Christian Body*, pp. 34-38, 142-43.

17. Rogers, *Sexuality and the Christian Body*, p. 260.

18. Rogers, *Sexuality and the Christian Body*, p. 258.

like Jordan and Rogers are showing the rest of us what it would look like to *converse* with the religious assumptions of our fellow citizens. To do so is to take those citizens seriously on their own terms, to show them respect and a kind of conversational hospitality, to adopt them into the public as conversation partners who ought to be heard from. One need not share their assumptions to examine them. Socrates did not agree with Euthyphro, after all.

6. Adoption, Personal Status, and Jewish Law

MICHAEL J. BROYDE

Judaism did not recognize the Roman institution of adoption since the Roman concept is directed toward substituting a legal fiction for a biological fact and thus creating the illusion of a natural relationship between the foster parents and the adopted son. Judaism stated its case in no uncertain terms: . . . the natural relationship must not be altered. Any intervention on the part of some legal authority would amount to interference with the omniscience and original plan of the Maker. The childless mother and father must reconcile themselves with the fact of natural barrenness and sterility. Yet they may attain the full covenantal experience of parenthood, exercise the fundamental right to have a child and be united within a community of I-thou-he. There is no need to withhold from the adopted child information concerning his or her natural parents. The new form of parenthood does not conflict with the biological relation. It manifests itself in a new dimension which may be separated from the natural one.

RABBI JOSEPH B. SOLOVEITCHIK[1]

1. Rabbi Joseph B. Soloveitchik, *Family Redeemed: Essays on Family Relationships,* ed. David Shatz and Joel Wolowelsky (New York: Meorot Harav Foundation, 2002), pp. 60-61.

This chapter is prepared as part of the Center for the Interdisciplinary Study of Religion project on "Sex, Marriage, and Family." Special thanks is extended to Nicole Brandi for her research assistance.

There are two basic models of adoption found in legal systems. One framework has a full legal category of adoption, by which children become — as a matter of law — as if they were born to the adoptive parents. The other construct has no legal category of adoption at all and denies that children become as a matter of law as if they were born to the adoptive parents, but instead views such situations as a form of raising the children of another, or long-term foster care. Jewish law (like Islamic law[2] and the common law[3]) does not have a category of adoption,[4] but merely of foster care. Modern American law[5] (like the Code of Hammurabi,[6] Roman law,[7] and the Napoleonic code[8]) has full legal adoption. The differences between these two approaches are quite dramatic. This chapter will focus on Jewish law, and will allow the reader to see how Jewish law — with no legal category of adoption — addresses situations where children need a new home.

Why Is There No Adoption in Jewish Law?

Jewish law *(halakha)*[9] did not and does not have a court system with its juridical authority grounded in the right to change people's family law sta-

2. D. Marianne Brower Blair, "The Impact of Family Paradigms, Domestic Constitutions, and International Conventions on Disclosure of an Adopted Person's Identities and Heritage: A Comparative Examination," *Michigan Journal of International Law* 22 (2001): 646.

3. C. M. A. McLauliff, "The First English Adoption Law and Its American Precursors," *Seton Hall Law Review* 16 (1986): 659-60. It was not until the late 1920s that adoption became possible in England without a special act of Parliament.

4. Indeed, as noted by Rabbi Ben Tzion Uziel, 2 *Sha'arei Uziel* 185(7), the Hebrew term for adoption *("imutz")* (derived from Ps. 80:16) connotes the grafting of a branch onto a tree and is a misnomer in Jewish law. The classical term used in Jewish law ought to be *benai amunim*, which means "the children of people who raise them."

5. See for example, Ruth Arlene W. Howe, "Adoption Practice, Issues and Law, 1958-1983," *Family Law Quarterly* 17 (1983): 123-97.

6. *The Code of Hammurabi, King of Babylon: About 2250 B.C.*, ed. Robert Francis Harper (Chicago: University of Chicago Press, 1904), §§185-86.

7. See John Francis Brosnan, "The Law of Adoption," *Columbia Law Review* 22 (1922): 332-42; Leo Albert Huard, "The Law of Adoption: Ancient and Modern," *Vanderbilt Law Review* 9 (1956): 743 (summarizing various ancient adoption laws).

8. Huard, "Law of Adoption," p. 743.

9. "Jewish law," or *halakha*, is used herein to denote the entire subject matter of the Jewish legal system, including public, private, and ritual law. A brief historical review will familiarize the new reader of Jewish law with its history and development. The Pentateuch (the five books of Moses, the Torah) is the touchstone document of Jewish law and, according to Jewish legal theory, was revealed to Moses at Mount Sinai. The Prophets and Writ-

tus. When disputes arise in family matters, they are treated as factual disputes under the law — but basic status issues cannot be changed by the legal system or judicial decree. Mother and father (and, by extension, brothers and sisters), once determined at birth, remain parents (and blood relatives), and cannot have that status removed. Indeed, the inability of the court system to change personal status is a general theme of all of Jewish family law.

Four examples — from dramatically different areas and eras of Jewish family law, but all sharing the basic model of family law as status issues — make this clear within Jewish law. The first example is from the most basic area of family law, namely, marriage and divorce. As the Tal-

---

ings, the other two parts of the Hebrew Bible, were written over the next seven hundred years, and the Jewish canon was closed around the year 200 B.C.E. The time from the close of the canon until 250 C.E. is referred to as the era of the *Tannaim*, the redactors of Jewish law, whose period closed with the editing of the *Mishnah* by Rabbi Judah the Patriarch. The next five centuries were the epoch in which the two Talmuds (Babylonian and Jerusalem) were written and edited by scholars called *Amoraim* ("those who recount" Jewish law) and *Savoraim* ("those who ponder" Jewish law). The Babylonian Talmud is of greater legal significance than the Jerusalem Talmud and is a more complete work.

The post-Talmudic era is conventionally divided into three periods: (1) the era of the *Geonim*, scholars who lived in Babylonia until the mid eleventh century; (2) the era of the *Rishonim* (the early authorities), who lived in North Africa, Spain, Franco-Germany, and Egypt until the end of the fourteenth century; and (3) the period of the *Aharonim* (the latter authorities), which encompasses all scholars of Jewish law from the fifteenth century up to this era. From the period of the mid fourteenth century until the early seventeenth century, Jewish law underwent a period of codification, which led to the acceptance of the law code format of Rabbi Joseph Karo, called the *Shulhan Arukh*, as the basis for modern Jewish law. The *Shulhan Arukh* (and the *Arba'ah Turim* of Rabbi Jacob ben Asher, which preceded it) divided Jewish law into four separate areas: *Orah Hayyim* is devoted to daily, Sabbath, and holiday laws; *Even Ha-Ezer* addresses family law, including financial aspects; *Hoshen Mishpat* codifies financial law; and *Yoreh Deah* contains dietary laws as well as other miscellaneous legal matter. Many significant scholars — themselves as important as Rabbi Karo in status and authority — wrote annotations to his code, which made the work and its surrounding comments the modern touchstone of Jewish law. The most recent complete edition of the *Shulhan Arukh* (Vilna: Ha-Almanah veha-Ahim Rom, 1896) contains no less than 113 separate commentaries on the text of Rabbi Karo. In addition, hundreds of other volumes of commentary have been published as self-standing works, a process that continues to this very day. Besides the law codes and commentaries, for the last twelve hundred years Jewish law authorities have addressed specific questions of Jewish law in written *responsa* (in question and answer form). Collections of such *responsa* have been published, providing guidance not only to later authorities but to the community at large. Finally, since the establishment of the State of Israel in 1948, the rabbinical courts of Israel have published their written opinions deciding cases on a variety of matters.

mud explains, marriage and divorce are essentially private acts (or contracts) which do not require a court system, permission from a judge, or a license from government.[10] Courts cannot create marriages or end them. Court-ordered annulments or divorce are essentially beyond the reach of Jewish law or a Jewish law court.[11] A Jewish court can, in exceptional situations, order a husband to give a Jewish divorce, and a wife to accept one, but it cannot grant the writ of divorce itself. Marriage and divorce are private status issues and fundamentally beyond the reach of the Jewish court systems to change.[12]

Another example is in the modern Jewish law discussion of artificial insemination. Although there is a wide-ranging debate within Jewish law about the propriety of such conduct, no one proposes that a husband who consents to the artificial insemination of his wife with sperm other than his own is the father of the resulting baby, as he is not such as a matter of fact.[13] A similar discussion takes place in the area of surrogate

10. For a discussion of this, see Michael Broyde, *Marriage, Divorce and the Abandoned Wife in Jewish Law: A Conceptual Approach to the Agunah Problems in America* (Hoboken, N.J.: KTAV, 2001).

11. The Talmud recounts six cases of annulment, three of which were pre-consummation, and thus suspect, and three of which involved duress in the creation of the marriage, thus causing the marriage to be naturally void. (The absence of court jurisdiction in marriage and divorce created the problem of abandoned wives and husbands who were stuck in a marriage where their spouse was not present; this is beyond the scope of this chapter.)

12. This stands in sharp contrast to American law. As is noted in American Jurisprudence (American Jurisprudence 2d Criminal Law, 21A §1034), civil death (the depriving of one's rights as a citizen) as a punishment for a crime whose sentence is life imprisonment historically included the dissolution of one's marriage, *whether or not either spouse wished the marriage to be dissolved.* Even if neither spouse wished the marriage to be dissolved, it could still be dissolved. As is stated in American Jurisprudence:

> Some statutes provide that when either spouse is sentenced to life imprisonment the marriage is automatically dissolved, without any judgment or legal process, and that a subsequent pardon will not restore conjugal rights. The same result has been reached under a statute merely declaring such persons civilly dead, where the statutes declaring a marriage of one who has a living spouse to be void, and to constitute the crime of bigamy, expressly except cases in which the living spouse has been sentenced to life imprisonment. *It has been held that dissolution of the marriage takes place without the necessity of any election on the part of the other spouse.* (Emphasis added)

It is part of the punishment for the crime that causes the marriage to be dissolved.

13. Four basic positions exist:

The first position, referred to as the position of Rabbi Moses Feinstein as a result of his vigorous advocacy of this position, is that artificial insemination is permitted and that

motherhood (and cloning).[14] Biological fatherhood and motherhood are status issues in Jewish law and beyond judicial re-ordering.

Yet another example is the discussion of child custody (which will be elaborated in the section on "Jewish Law and Adoption" in this chapter). Although there is a wide-ranging and intense dispute among various Jew-

---

the paternity of the child is established by the genetic relationship between the child and the father (sperm donor). Thus he who donates the sperm is the father. Furthermore, Rabbi Feinstein is of the opinion that the act of artificial insemination does not violate Jewish law, and does not constitute an act of adultery by the woman, if she is married. See Moses Feinstein, *Iggrot Moshe*, 1 *Even Ha-Ezer* 10, 71; 2 *Even Ha-Ezer* 11; 3 *Even Ha-Ezer* 11. For another vigorous defense of his position, see M. Feinstein, *Dibrot Moshe, Ketubot* 233-48.

The second position, of Rabbi Joel Teitelbaum, is identical to that of Rabbi Feinstein's in acknowledging that the genetic relationship is of legal significance and the paternity is established solely through the genetic relationship. He also maintains, however, that the genetic relationship predominates to establish illegitimacy and the legal impropriety of these actions. Thus, heterologous artificial insemination is an act of adultery. See J. Teitelbaum, 2 *Divrei Yoel* 110, 140. (Both Rabbi Feinstein and Rabbi Teitelbaum agree on how paternity is established; however, they differ as to how illegitimacy is established.)

A third view is that of Rabbi Eliezer Waldenberg. He is of the opinion that an act of adultery occurs, not through the genetic mixing of sperm that is not the husband's with the wife's egg, but rather by the act of heterologous insemination itself; this act is physically analogous to adultery and is not permitted. This view is not based on the presence or absence of genetic relationships between child and husband but rather upon Rabbi Waldenberg's belief that the injection of sperm into another man's wife is, itself, a prohibited form of adultery. Furthermore, Rabbi Waldenberg maintains that this conduct is also a violation of the rules of modesty, which are of rabbinic origin. See E. Waldenberg, "Test Tube Infertilization," *Sefer Asya* 5 (1986): 84-92, and 9 *Tzitz Eliezer* 51:4.

A fourth position is advocated by Rabbi Jacob Breish, who maintains that heterologous insemination is not an act of adultery, and no biblical violation occurs; the sperm donor is the father. Nonetheless, he maintains that "from the point of view of our religion these ugly and disgusting things should not be done, for they are similar to the deeds of the land of Canaan and its abominations." See Jacob Breish, 3 *Helkat Yakov* 45-48 (quote on 46); similarly, see Rabbi Yehiel Yaakov Weinberg, 3 *Sredai Aish* 5.

Indeed, the outlier position in Jewish law is that the person who injects the sperm is the legal father, since he or she is committing the adultery (see Yoram Shapiro, "Artificial Insemination," *Noam* 1 [1957]: 138-42). This position has been widely attacked as it seems to be based on what on its face is an illogical position — that neither the genetic father nor the husband of the wife would be considered the father of the child; see Menachem Mendel Kasher, "Artificial Insemination," *Noam* 1 (1957): 125-28, and Jacob Breish, 3 *Helkat Yakov* 47. Even this view, however, is consistent with the basic model of Jewish law: fatherhood, once established, is unchangeable.

14. See Michael Broyde, "Cloning People: A Jewish View," *Connecticut Law Review* 30 (1998): 503-35, and "The Establishment of Maternity and Paternity in Jewish and American Law," *National Jewish Law Review* 3 (1988): 117-52.

ish law decisors of the medieval era as to whether Jewish law can ever take custody of children away from fit parents and give the children to more fit "strangers" (such as grandparents), it is always made clear in the discussion that the basic issue is of "mere" custody, and not who is the parent. Fundamental notions of parenthood are immutable.[15]

A further example is sex-change surgery. According to Jewish law, the removal of sexual organs is prohibited; hence, sex-reassignment surgery is prohibited for men according to biblical law,[16] and it is disputable whether the removal of sexual organs is a biblical or rabbinic prohibition for women.[17] What is the status of a person who actually has such an operation? Jewish law is clear that a person who has a sex-change operation does not, in fact, change his or her gender according to Jewish law. Gender, too, is immutable. The earliest discussion concerning the sexual status of a transsexual is found in the twelfth-century commentary of Rabbi Abraham Ibn Ezra,[18] where he, quoting eleventh-century authority Rabbenu Hananel, states that intercourse between a man and another man in whom the sexual organs of a woman have been fashioned constitutes a violation of the biblical prohibition of homosexuality, despite the presence of apparently female sexual organs. Thus, Ibn Ezra rules that sexual status cannot be changed surgically, for if this person were now legally a woman, no violations of the sodomy laws could occur. This view is, indeed, the view accepted by Jewish law authorities.[19] Sexual status

15. For more on this, see Eliav Shochatman, "The Essence of the Principles Used in Child Custody in Jewish Law," *Shenaton LeMishpat HaIvri* 5 (5738): 285-301 (Hebrew), and Ronald Warburg, "Child Custody: A Comparative Analysis," *Israel Law Review* 14 (1978): 480-503.

16. See Lev. 22:24 and Babylonian Talmud, *Shabbat* 110b.

17. Compare Tosaphot, commenting on Babylonian Talmud, *Shabbat* 110b, s.v. *v'Hatanya* (rabbinic violation), with Maimonides, *Mishneh Torah, Sefer Kedushah, Hilkhot Isurei Biah* 16:11 (biblical prohibition).

18. Ibn Ezra (1089-1164) of Toledo, Spain, was a well-known biblical commentator; see his commentary on Lev. 18:22.

19. A contrary view is taken by Rabbi Eliezer Waldenberg, 10 *Tzitz Eliezer* 25:26, 6, but his analysis is difficult to accept and might be limited to this person's ability to stay married, rather than a general gender classification. Rabbi Waldenberg's view is widely disagreed with. See, e.g., F. Rosner and M. Tendler, *Practical Medical Halacha* (New York: Rephael Society, Medical-Dental Section of the Association of Orthodox Jewish Scientists, 1980), p. 44.

When discussing transsexual surgery, it is important to note that the law concerning children born with ambiguous sex status is different from that of sex-reassignment surgery in an adult. When a child is born genetically of one sex but with the outward physiological

cannot be changed.[20]

Thus, understanding how Jewish law has consistently viewed its own judicial and legal power in the area of family law allows adoption to be placed in context. Jewish law views status issues as matters of natural law, which can be adjudicated by a Jewish law court when in dispute,[21] but cannot be changed once established.[22]

---

signs of another sex, it is permitted to remove the outward sex organs and to harmonize the physiological appearance of the sex organs with the genetic sex status. That is not considered a violation of Jewish law, as the sex organs are not in fact genuine sex organs capable of reproduction. This would also be the case for a person whose general physiological appearance is not in harmony with his genetic status. It is not true, however, of a person whose genetic and physical appearance is not in harmony with his perceived psychological status. See Rosner and Tendler, *Practical Medical Halacha,* pp. 43-45; Moshe Steinberg, "Change of Sex in Pseudo-Hermaphroditism," *Asya* 1 (1976): 142-53.

20. American law does allow for sex change. One of the first American cases to discuss the status of such persons is a New Jersey case, *M.T. v. J.T.,* 355 A.2d 204, 140 N.J. Super. 77 (1976), where a wife filed a complaint for support and maintenance against the husband she was now separated from. In defense to the action for nonsupport, the husband asserted that his wife was a male and hence their marriage was void. He maintained that his wife was a former male who had "successfully" undergone sex reassignment surgery before the marriage. He maintained, however, that the law still categorized "her" as a male. Thus, since New Jersey does not recognize marriages between two members of the same sex, the marriage was void. The New Jersey Superior Court ruled that "where a transsexual was born with physical characteristics of a male, but successful sex reassignment surgery harmonized her gender and genitalia so that she became . . . a woman, such transsexual thereby became a member of the female sex for marital purposes and subsequent marriage to a male was not void" (American Jurisprudence 2d Marriage, 52 §50 [citing *M.T. v. J.T.,* 355 A.2d 204, 140 N.J. Super. 77 (1976)]). The New York Supreme Court agreed with this view in ruling in the famous case of *Richards v. United States Tennis Association,* 93 Misc. 2d 713, 400 N.Y.S.2d 267 (Sup. Ct. 1977), in which Richards sued the U.S.T.A. over its denial of permission for "her" to play professional tennis as a woman, after she underwent sex-reassignment surgery. The court ruled that the law must reflect the successful sex-reassignment surgery when it is done properly and for an appropriate medical reason. This is now the accepted law; see *In re Heilig,* 816 A.2d 68 (Md. 2003) and *In re Estate of Gardiner,* 22 P.3d 1086 (Kan.App., 2001).

21. Such as uncertain paternity; see *Shulhan Arukh, Even Ha-Ezer* 3:8.

22. This is not the model with which Jewish law views monetary matters, where a Jewish law court has the right of eminent domain to transfer property (thus providing a basis for regulating all financial matters), or ritual law, where decisors of Jewish law are allowed to add observances or suspend them. Although this matter is far beyond the reach of this chapter, grasping when and in what areas of law any given legal system perceives activism as a value is quite crucial to understanding the values of the system.

The Theoretical Basis for Parental Custody:
The Predicate to Adoption

The initial question in all adoption determinations is frequently unstated: by what "right" do natural parents have custody of their children? As explained below, two very different theories, one called "parental rights" and one called "best interest of the child," exist in Jewish law. These two theories are somewhat in tension, but they lead to similar results in many cases, as the best interests of the child will often coincide with granting parents rights. Asking by what right parents have custody of their children is simply another way of considering when they should not.

There is a basic dispute within Jewish law as to why and through what legal claim parents have custody of their children. Indeed, this dispute is crucial to understanding why Jewish law accepts that a "fit" parent is entitled to child custody — even if it can be shown that others can raise the child in a better manner.[23] It also sets parameters for when adoption is proper.

Rabbi Asher ben Yehiel (R. Asher),[24] in the course of discussing the obligation to support one's natural children, advances what appears to be a naturalist theory of parental rights. R. Asher asserts two basic rules. First, there is an obligation (for a man)[25] to support one's children, and this obligation is, at least as a matter of theory, unrelated to one's relationship — or lack thereof — with the child (custodial), with one's wife (marital), or with any other party.[26] A man who has children is biblically

---

23. This chapter will not address the extremely important question of *how* Jewish law determines parental fitness; for an excellent discussion of that topic, see Rabbi Gedalya Felder, 2 *Nahalat Tzvi* 282-87 (second ed.), where he discusses the process that should be used by a beth din to make child custody determinations. Rabbi Felder discusses the practical matters involved in such determinations, and he adopts a format and procedure surprisingly similar to that used by secular tribunals in making these determinations. He indicates that the beth din should interview the parents, consult with a child psychologist, and conduct a complete investigation.

24. Known by the Hebrew acronym "Rosh," R. Asher (1250-1327) was a late Tosaphist who emigrated from Franco-Germany to Barcelona, then Toledo, Spain.

25. R. Asher might claim that the Talmudic rule which transferred custody of children (of certain ages) from the husband to the wife did so based on a rabbinic decree, and that this rabbinic decree gave the custodial mother the same rights (but not duties) as a custodial father; for a clear explication of this, see Rabbi Shemuel Alkalai, *Mishpatai Shemuel* 90.

26. Rabbi Asher ben Yehiel, *Responsa of R. Asher (Rosh)* 17:7; see also Rabbi Judah ben Samuel Rosannes, *Mishneh Lemelekh, Hilkhot Ishut* 21:17.

obligated to support them. Following logically from this rule, R. Asher further states[27] that, *as a matter of law,* the parents are always entitled to custody against all others.[28] Of course, R. Asher would agree that in circumstances in which the father or mother are factually incapable of raising the children — are legally unfit as parents — they would not remain the custodial parents.[29] He appears to adopt the theory, however, that the father and mother are the presumptive custodial parents of their children based on their obligations and rights as natural parents, subject to the limitation that even natural parents cannot have custody of their children if they are factually unfit to raise them.[30] While this understanding of the parents' rights is not quite the same as a property right, it is far more a right (and duty) related to possession than a rule about the "best interest" of the child. The position of R. Asher seems to have a substantial foundation in the works of a number of authorities.[31]

27. *Responsa of R. Asher,* 82:2.

28. In any circumstance in which a marriage has ended and the mother is incapable of raising the children, the father is entitled to custody of his children, even if one were to agree that the children would be "better off" being raised by grandparents. Much of this basic dispute can be found in American law as well. *Painter v. Bannister,* 140 N.W. 2d 152 (Iowa 1966) typifies the best interest of the child cases, in that the court removed a child from the custody of a fit father and gave custody to more fit grandparents. The tradition of this form of custody determination is quite old and can be found in the English common law; see *Shelly v. Westbrooke,* 37 Eng Rep 850 (1817). A contrary view is found in *Pusey v. Pusey,* 728 P2d 117 (Utah 1986), and can be implied from the recent Supreme Court decision in *Troxel v. Granville,* 120 Sct 2054 (2000).

29. This could reasonably be derived from the Babylonian Talmud, *Ketubot* 102b, which mandates terminating custodial rights in the face of life-threatening misconduct by a guardian.

30. In cases of divorce, in situations where the Talmudic rabbis assigned custody to the mother rather than the father, that custody is based on a rabbinically ordered transfer of rights, and the mother gets custody, even if the children are best served by another. For a longer discussion of this issue, see *responsa* of Rabbi Ezekiel Landau, *Nodah BeYehudah, Even Ha-Ezer* 2:89, and Rabbi Yitzhak Weiss, *Minhat Yitzhak* 7:113, where these decisors explicitly state that even in cases where the mother was assigned custodial rights, the father has a basic right to see and educate his male children, and if this right is incompatible with the mother's presumptive custody claim, his rights and obligations supersede hers and custody by the mother will be terminated.

31. See, e.g., Rabbenu Yeruham ben Meshullam, *Toldot Adam veHava* 197a in the name of the *Geonim,* Rabbi Isaac deMolena, *Kiryat Sefer* 44:557 in the name of the *Geonim,* and Rabbi Joseph Gaon, *Ginzei Kedem* 3:62, where the theory of custodial parenthood seems to be based on an agency theory derived from the father's rights. R. Asher, in his theory of parenthood, seems to state that typically the mother of the children is precisely that agent. When the marriage ends, the mother may — by rabbinic decree — continue, if she wishes, to

There is a second theory of parental custody in Jewish law, the approach of Rabbi Solomon ben Aderet (Aderet).[32] Aderet indicates[33] that Jewish law always accepts — as a matter of law — that child custody matters be determined according to the "best interest of the child." Thus, Aderet rules that in a case where the father is deceased, the mother does not have an indisputable legal claim to custody of the children. Equitable factors, such as the best interest of the child, are the *sole* determinant of custody. This *responsum* is generally read as a theory for all child custody determinations.[34] Aderet maintains that all child custody determinations involve a single legal standard — the best interest of the child — regardless of the specific facts involved, and this is the standard to be used to place children in the custody of nonparents as well. According to this approach, the "rules" that one encounters in the field of child custody are not really "rules of law" at all, but rather the presumptive assessment by the Talmudic Sages as to what generally is in the best interest of children.[35]

An enormous theoretical difference exists between R. Asher and Aderet. According to R. Asher, parents[36] have an intrinsic right to raise their progeny, unless unfit. In order to remove children from parental custody, it must be shown that these parents are unfit to be parents and that

---

be the agent of the father, because Jewish law perceives being raised by the mother (for all children except boys over six) as typically more appropriate than being raised by the father.

Interestingly, a claim could be made that this position was not accepted by Rabbi Yehuda ben R. Asher, one of Rabbi Asher's children; see *Zikhron Yehuda* 35 quoted in *Beit Yosef, Tur, Hoshen Mishpat* 290.

32. Known by the Hebrew acronym "Rashba," Rabbi Aderet (1235-1310) of Barcelona, Spain, was an eminent and prolific decisor.

33. *Responsa of Rashba Traditionally Assigned to Nahmanides*, 38. Throughout this chapter, the theory developed in the *responsa* is referred to as Rashba's, as most latter Jewish law authorities indicate that Rashba wrote these *responsa* and not Nahmanides; see Rabbi David Halevy, *Turei Zahav, Yoreh Deah* 228:50, and Rabbi Hayyim Hezekiah Medina, *Sedai Hemed, Klalai Haposkim* 10:9 (typically found in volume nine of that work).

34. For example, see *Otzar HaGeonim, Ketubot* 434, where this rule is applied even when the father is alive.

35. See Warburg, "Child Custody," pp. 496-98, and Shochatman, "Essence of the Principles Used in Child Custody," pp. 308-9.

36. It is my opinion that later authorities disagree as to the legal basis of the mother's claim. Most authorities indicate that the mother's claim to custody of the daughter is founded on a transfer of rights from the father to the mother based on a specific rabbinic decree found in the Talmud. On the other hand, many other authorities understand the mother's claim to custody of boys under six to be much less clear as a matter of law and are inclined to view that claim based on an agency theory of some type, with the father's rights supreme should they conflict with the mother's.

some alternative arrangement to raise these children consistent with the parents' wishes and lifestyle (either through the use of relatives as agents or in some other manner[37]) cannot be arranged.[38] According to Aderet, the law allows the permanent transfer of custodial rights (quasi-adoption) in any situation where it can be shown that the children are not being raised in their best interests and that another would raise them in a manner more in line with those interests.[39]

This legal dispute is not merely theoretical: the particular *responsa* of Rabbis Asher and Aderet, elaborating on these principles, present vastly differing rulings as a result. R. Asher rules that as a matter of Jewish law, custody is always to be granted to a parent (unless he or she is unfit); quasi-adoption is a last resort; Aderet rules that when the father is deceased, typically it is in the best interest of the child to be placed in quasi-adoption with male relatives of the father rather than with the mother. To one authority, the legal rule provides the answer; to another, equitable principles relating to best interest do.

These two competing approaches provide the relevant framework to analyze many of the theoretical disputes present in prototypical cases of child custody disputes that often form the predicate to quasi-adoption in the Jewish tradition. According to one theory, children are taken from their parents only in cases of categorical unfitness; according to the other approach, quasi-adoption is *always* proper if it is in the "best interests of the child."

37. For example, sending a child to a boarding school of the parent's choosing; see, e.g., 4 P.D.R. *(Piskai Din Rabbani)* 66 (1959), where the rabbinical court appears to sanction granting custody to the father, who wishes to send his child to a particular educational institution (a boarding school) which will directly supervise the child's day-to-day life.

38. It is possible that there is a third theory also. Rabbenu Nissim (Hebrew acronym "RaN," commenting on Babylonian Talmud *Ketubot* 65b), seems to accept a contractual framework for custodial arrangements. R. Nissim appears to understand that it is intrinsic in the marital contract *(ketubah)* that just as one is obligated to support one's wife, so too one is obligated to support one's children. This position does not explain why one supports children born out of wedlock (as Jewish law certainly requires; see *Shulhan Arukh, Even Ha-Ezer* 82:1-7) or what principles control child custody determinations once the marriage terminates. *Mishneh LeMelekh, Hilkhot Ishut* 12:14 notes that R. Nissim's theory was not designed to be followed in practice.

39. As a matter of practice, this would not happen frequently. Indeed, I have found no *responsa* which actually permit the removal of children from the custody of parents who are married to each other.

Jewish Law and Adoption

Although the institution of adoption, through its widespread use in Roman law,[40] was well known in Talmudic times, the redactors of Jewish law willfully refused to recognize such an institution within Jewish law. Rather, they created an institution which they called "A Person Who Raises Another's Child,"[41] which is quasi-adoption. Unlike either Roman law or current adoption law, this institution does not change the legal parents of the person whose custody has changed.[42] One who raises another's child is an agent of the natural parent; and like any agency rule in Jewish law,[43] if the agent fails to accomplish the task delegated, the obligation reverts to the principal. Thus, the biblical obligations, duties, and prohibitions of parenthood still apply between the natural parents and the child whose custody they no longer have.[44]

This is not to diminish the value of this form of quasi-adoption. Indeed, the same Talmudic statement that denies adoption posits that such conduct is meritorious (and thus encouraged). Rabbi Samuel Eliezer Edels,[45] in his commentary on this passage in the Talmud, notes that the value and importance of raising others' children is not limited to orphans, but applies also in situations where the children's parents are alive but cannot take care of the children.[46] Those who raise the child of another are still obligated in the duty of procreation, however, and do not fulfill their obligation through this quasi-adoption. The rationale for this is clear: while raising the child of another is meritorious conduct, this proper deed is not an act of procreation, and these are not the natural

40. Frederick Parker Walton, *Historical Introduction to the Roman Law,* fourth ed., rev. (Edinburgh: W. Green and Son, 1920), p. 72.

41. See Babylonian Talmud, *Sanhedrin* 19b. This is viewed as a righteous deed; see *Exodus Rabbah,* ch. 4.

42. Although it is true that there are four instances in the Bible in which adoptive parents are called actual parents; see 1 Chron. 4:18, Ruth 4:14, Ps. 77:16, 2 Sam. 21:8. These are assumed to be in a nonlegal context. See Babylonian Talmud, *Sanhedrin* 19b.

43. Israel Herbert Levinthal, *The Jewish Law of Agency, with Special Reference to the Roman and Common Law* (New York: [printed at the Conat Press, Philadelphia], 1923), pp. 58-73.

44. J. Karo, *Shulhan Arukh, Even Ha-Ezer* 15:11.

45. Known by the Hebrew acronym "Maharsha," R. Edels (1555-1631) wrote his famous analytical commentary on the Talmud while an active communal leader of Eastern Europe (in what is now Poland). Interestingly, he adopted the surname Edels in tribute to his mother-in-law Edel, who covered all the expenses of his yeshiva in Posen for some twenty years.

46. *Commentary of Maharsha,* Babylonian Talmud, *Sanhedrin* 19b.

children of the person caring for them and cannot take the place of one's obligation to procreate.[47]

In modern times, the erudite reflections of noted Talmudist and philosopher Rabbi Joseph B. Soloveitchik sum up the Jewish law view, and it is worth quoting at greater length from the passage cited at the beginning of this chapter:

> Judaism saw the teacher as the creator through love and commitment of the personality of the pupil. Both become *personae* because an I-Thou community is formed. That is why Judaism called disciples sons and masters fathers. . . . Our Talmudic sages stated, "Whoever teaches his friend's son Torah acquires him as a natural child" (Sanhedrin 19b). . . . Judaism did not recognize the Roman institution of adoption since the Roman concept is directed toward substituting a legal fiction for a biological fact and thus creating the illusion of a natural relationship between the foster parents and the adopted son. Judaism stated its case in no uncertain terms: what the Creator granted one and the other should not be interfered with; the natural relationship must not be altered. Any intervention on the part of some legal authority would amount to interference with the omniscience and original plan of the Maker. The childless mother and father must reconcile themselves with the fact of natural barrenness and sterility. Yet they may attain the full covenantal experience of parenthood, exercise the fundamental right to have a child and be united within a community of I-thou-he. There is no need to withhold from the adopted child information concerning his or her natural parents. The new form of parenthood does not conflict with the biological relation. It manifests itself in a new dimension which may be separated from the natural one. In order to become Abraham [a spiritual parent], one does not necessarily have to live through the stage of Abram [a biological parent]. The irrevocable in human existence is not the natural but the spiritual child; the threefold community is based upon existential, not biological, unity. The existence of I and thou can be inseparably bound with a third existence even though the latter is, biologically speaking, a stranger to them.[48]

---

47. *Shulhan Arukh, Even Ha-Ezer* 1:3-6. A contrary view is taken by Rabbi Shlomo Kluger in his commentary on *Shulhan Arukh, Even Ha-Ezer* 1:1. He posits that adoption is a form of procreation, since without the adult's actions these children would die. His opinion has been widely discredited.

48. Soloveitchik, *Family Redeemed*, pp. 60-61.
Contrasting the view of Jewish law with American law is deeply illuminating of both

Rabbi Soloveitchik's view — fully reflective of the Jewish legal tradition — is that the process of quasi-adoption is special, sacred, a manifestation of holiness, and covenantal. It is such precisely because it is one of choice, like a student-teacher relationship,[49] and thus different from (and not to be confused with) natural parenthood, which lacks these basic covenantal components. Biological relationships (such as the parent-child relationship) are less covenantal in nature — because of the absence of choice —

---

systems. Between 1860 and the end of World War II, all states passed adoption and child welfare acts which closely scrutinized requests for adoption. Their basic theme and thrust was that "[a]doption laws were designed to imitate nature" (Sanford N. Katz, "Re-Writing the Adoption Story," *Family Advocate* 5 [1982]: 9-10). They were intended to put children in an environment where one could not determine that they had been adopted; even the children themselves many times did not know. The law reflected this, and severed all parental rights and duties with an adopted child's natural parents and reestablished them in total with the adoptive parents, as per the Roman model of adoption law. Significant change in adoption practice has occurred in the last thirty years, the most important regarding the ability or propriety of a state to seal its adoption records — an issue which goes to the very heart of the current American approach to adoption. If adoption records cannot or should not be sealed, then it is beyond the state's power to create an adoption system which effectively mimics the creation of a new parental unit, since the children will become aware of the fact that they have biological parents separate from their adoptive parents. Historically, almost all states sealed adoption records and provided virtually no access. The original birth records were sealed, and if, by coincidence, the adopted child was to meet and marry a natural sibling, the state would permit such a marriage since the adopted child would have no legal relationship with his or her natural family. The "right to know" controversy has resulted in a number of states granting adoptees (upon attaining their majority) access to all the information collected. Once children have a right to know who their natural parents are, the adoption law must reflect the dichotomous relationship between one's natural parents and one's adoptive parents; see, e.g., Carol Amadio and Stewart Deutsch, "Open Adoption: Allowing Adopted Children to 'Stay in Touch' with Blood Relatives," *Journal of Family Law* 22 (1983): 59-93. These tensions have not yet been resolved in American law. Most states still ascribe to adoption law the ability to totally recreate maternal and paternal relationships notwithstanding the knowledge of one's biological parents. Along with their ability to completely recreate parental relationships, states also maintain the ability to legally destroy any such relationships. It is well within the power of the state to not only create new parental rights and duties, but also to remove the rights of a parent toward a child and the duties of a parent to a child as well.

49. Rabbi Soloveitchik quotes as a proof-text Maimonides, who states, "This obligation [of teaching Torah] is to be fulfilled not only towards one's son and grandson. A duty rests on every scholar in Israel to teach all disciples, even if they are not his children, as it is said, 'and you shall teach them to your children' (Deut. 6:7). The oral tradition teaches: 'Your children' includes your disciples, for disciples are called children as it is said: 'And the sons of the prophets came forth' (II Kings 2:3)" (*Hilkhot Talmud Torah* [The Laws of Torah Study] 1:2, quoted in Soloveitchik, *Family Redeemed,* p. 60).

than relationships of selection (such as husband and wife, student and teacher, or, as Rabbi Solovietchik highlights, adoptee and adopter) precisely because the central characteristic of covenant is selection and choice.[50]

Quasi-Adoption As Granting Some Parental Rights

Even as the Jewish tradition does not have an institution of real adoption, certain nonbiblical aspects of parenthood established by the rabbis of the Talmudic era have been connected to custody rather than parenthood, and thus have been granted to adoptive parents. For example, in Talmudic times it was decreed that the possessions, earnings, and findings of a minor child belong to his or her father.[51] Although the wording of the Talmud refers only to father, it is clear from later discussions that this law applies to anyone who supports the child, such as adoptive parents.[52] The reason for the rabbinic decree is that it was equitable that one who supports a child should receive the income of that child.[53] Thus, a financially independent minor does not transfer his or her earnings to his or her parents.[54] Similarly, the earnings of an adopted child go to his or her adoptive parents since the rationale for the decree applies equally well to biological and adopted children.[55] A similar line of reasoning allows adoptive parents to redeem their adopted son if he is a first-born (to his natural parents).[56]

One who raises another's child does not assume the biblical prohibitions or obligations associated with having a child of one's own, however. For example, regardless of who is currently raising the child, it is never permitted for a natural parent to marry his or her child; on the other hand, the assumption of custody cannot raise to a biblical level the prohibition of incest between a parent and the adopted child.[57] Indeed, the Tal-

---

50. It is for this reason that the Jewish prophets always analogized God's relationship with the Jewish people to that of a husband and a wife and not a parent and a child.

51. Babylonian Talmud, *Baba Metzia* 12b.

52. J. Karo, *Shulhan Arukh, Hoshen Mishpat* 370:2.

53. J. Falk, *Meirat Einaim*, commenting on J. Caro, *Shulhan Arukh, Hoshen Mishpat* 370:2.

54. J. Karo, *Shulhan Arukh, Yoreh Deah* 370:2.

55. J. Karo, *Shulhan Arukh, Yoreh Deah* 370:2; Z. Mendal, *Ba'er Haytaiv,* §4, on J. Karo, *Shulhan Arukh, Yoreh Deah* 370:2.

56. David Tzvi Hoffman, *Melamed Lehoil, Yoreh Deah* 97-98.

57. By inference the same can be said of adoptive siblings; see Hoffman, *Melamed Lehoil, Yoreh Deah* 15:11 ("It is permitted to marry one's adopted sister.")

mud explicitly discusses whether or not adopted children raised in the same home may marry each other, and concludes that such marriages are permitted.[58] One medieval authority, Rabbi Judah of Regensberg,[59] decreed that such marriages not be performed,[60] but this decree has not been generally accepted,[61] and in situations where there is a known, open adoption, such marriages are permitted.[62]

Other examples of adoptive parents being treated as natural parents can be found in the areas of ritual law. For example, while the rabbis prohibited two unrelated unmarried people of the opposite sex from rooming together alone (in Hebrew, the laws of *yihud*),[63] it is widely held that these rules do not apply in the adoption scenario. Although some commentators disagree,[64] many maintain that it is permissible for an adopted child to room and live with his adopted family,[65] notwithstanding the *prima facie* violations of the prohibition of isolation.[66] As one authority has noted, without this lenient rule, the institution of raising another's child would disappear.[67] The same is said for the general prohibition of people unrelated to each other engaging in kissing or hugging, which these same authorities permit in situations where the relationship between the adoptive parents and the child is functionally similar to a natu-

---

58. Babylonian Talmud, *Sotah* 43b.

59. Also known as Rabbi Judah HaHasid (the Pious). He was a renowned ethicist and scholar of the Rhineland Jewish community (1150-1217).

60. Judah of Regensberg, *Sefer Hasidim*, Comm. 29. See also Babylonian Talmud, *Sotah* 43b.

61. See Moses Sofer, *Responsa* 2 *Yoreh Deah* 125.

62. See *Minhat Yitzhak* 4:49. Although legally permitted, few such marriages are actually performed; however, there was a time when such was exactly the motive of people who raised children other than their own in their household.

63. J. Karo, *Shulhan Arukh, Even Ha-Ezer* 22:2. According to one commentator, this rabbinic prohibition even included the rooming together of a married woman with a man not her husband. See Maimonides, *Mishneh Torah, Sefer Kedushah, Hilkhot Isurei Biah* 22:2.

64. M. M. Schneersohn, *Zikhron Akedat Yitzhak* 4:33-37. For a complete list of those authorities taking this position, see Israel Berzon, "Contemporary Issues in the Laws of Yichud," *Journal of Halacha and Contemporary Society* 13 (1986): 108.

65. This, for example, occurs when a couple adopts a boy, and the boy's adoptive father later dies, leaving the adopted child living alone with a woman not his natural mother.

66. See E. Waldenberg, 6 *Tzitz Eliezer* 40:21; C. D. Halevi, *Aseh Lekha Rav* 194-201. Rabbi Joseph B. Soloveitchik has also been quoted as permitting this. See Melech Schacter, "Various Aspects of Adoption," *Journal of Halacha and Contemporary Society* 4 (1982): 96. Rabbi Feinstein has also commented on this issue; see M. Feinstein, *Iggrot Moshe* 4 *Even Ha-Ezer* 64:2.

67. E. Waldenberg, 6 *Tzitz Eliezer* 226-28.

ral relationship.[68] The basic argument is simple: One's children are exempt from the general prohibitions of physical interactions with the opposite sex, as no erotic intent is generally present. The same is true for quasi-adopted children.

Another example of a change in Jewish ritual law as a result of the quasi-adoption of a child appears in the obligation of mourning. Adopted children are no longer obligated to, for instance, recite the mourner's prayer *(kaddish)* upon the death of their natural parents — instead, there is an incumbent obligation to mourn upon the death of their adoptive parents.[69] This is so because the institution of mourning as we know it is totally rabbinic in nature, and seems to be a proper reflection of the sadness one feels when the person who raised one passes on.[70] Numerous other examples exist of rabbinic institutions that are not strictly applied in the context of raising another's child, since Jewish law would like to encourage this activity.[71]

Notwithstanding the high praise Jewish law showers on a person who raises another's child,[72] it is critical to recognize that the institution of "adoption" in Jewish law is radically different from the adoption law of American jurisdictions. In Jewish law, adoption operates on an agency theory. The natural parents are always the parents; the adoptive parents never are — they are merely agents of the birth parents (or the rabbinical courts). While a number of incidental areas of parental rights are associated with custody and not natural parenthood, they are the exception and not the law. In the main, Jewish law focuses entirely on natural relationships to establish parental rights and duties. Jewish adop-

---

68. This matter is conceptually easier in my opinion, as nonsexual touching is arguably permitted anyway in Jewish law, and the essential characteristic of this touching is that it is nonsexual. For more on this topic, see Babylonian Talmud *Kiddushin* 81b, and Rashi, Tosaphot, Ritva, and Yam Shel Shlomo *ad locum; Shulhan Arukh, Even Ha-Ezer* 21, 4-7; Gr"a, *Even Ha-Ezer* 21:19; *Pit'hai Teshuva, Even Ha-Ezer* 21:3 and *Iggrot Moshe,* 2 *Even Ha-Ezer* 14. For an article on this topic in English, see Rabbi Yehuda Herzl Henkin, "The Significant Role of Habituation in Halakha," *Tradition* 34 (2000): 3-40.

69. M. Sofer, *Responsa,* 1 *Orah Hayyim* 174. Rabbi Sofer also notes the praise Jewish law lavishes upon one who raises another's child.

70. This issue is in dispute. Compare J. Karo, *Shulhan Arukh, Yoreh Deah* 398:1 with M. Isserles, commenting on J. Karo, *Shulhan Arukh, Yoreh Deah* 399:13.

71. See generally J. Karo, *Shulhan Arukh, Orah Hayyim* 139:3. See also A. Auli, *Magen Avraham,* commenting on Karo's *Shulhan Arukh, Orah Hayyim* 139:3, and M. Feinstein, *Iggrot Moshe,* 1 *Yoreh Deah* 161. For a summary of various laws of adoption, see Schacter, "Various Aspects of Adoption."

72. See Babylonian Talmud, *Sanhedrin* 19b.

tion looks much more like long-term foster care than like classic American adoption.

Open versus Closed Adoption

Secretive adoptions have always taken place in every society and every culture,[73] and there is a case history of such in the Jewish legal tradition as well.[74] Given the Jewish law view that adoption is really a misnomer, and that quasi-adoption and long-term foster care are better terms, the Jewish tradition favors "open" rather than "closed" adoptions: children always need to know that their current caretakers are not their parents. This point is first addressed directly by Rabbi Moses Sofer,[75] who notes that many different aspects of Jewish law are predicated on an awareness of who one's progeny are, and when people are raising other children in their home, they bear a duty to not hide that fact.[76] Similar views are expressed by many different authorities of the last century.

Rabbi Moses Feinstein, one of the leading decisors in America in the last century, notes in his *responsa*[77] that it is obvious that Jewish law mandates that the identity of the natural parents be shared with an adopted child, when the identity is known. Rabbi Feinstein posits that without this knowledge, such a child will never be certain of whom his or her natural siblings are and might[78] enter into an illicit marriage with a natural

73. See, for example, Lucy S. McGough and Annette Peltier Falahahwazi, "Secrets and Lies: A Model Statute for Cooperative Adoption," *Louisiana Law Review* 60 (1999): 13-90.

74. See Rabbi Hayyim Bachrach, *Havot Yair* 92-93. These *responsa*, from just before the dawn of the eighteenth century, recount the story of a couple who (it was claimed) switched children with their maid after one of their own children died. Needless to say, many difficulties and questions arose from these actions. The solution advocated by one of the rabbis in this *responsa* is second-guessed by Rabbi Moses Sofer in *Teshuvot Hatam Sofer*, 2 *Even Ha-Ezer* 125.

75. In *Teshuvot Hatam Sofer*, 2 *Even Ha-Ezer* 125. Rabbi Sofer (1762-1839) lived in Hungary.

76. There is a dispute as to whether adopted children inherit from their adoptive parents; see *Lekutai Mair* 18:2. All agree, however, that such children do not inherit by operation of the intestacy rules of Jewish law. Those who argue that such children inherit do so based on the presumptive will of the parents. For more on this, see Rabbi Moshe Findling, "Adoption of Children," *Noam* 4 (1961): 65-93 (Hebrew).

77. *Iggrot Moshe*, 1 *Yoreh Deah* 162.

78. See *Beit Shmuel*, *Even Ha-Ezer* 13:1, who notes that this is a rabbinic fear and not grounded in Torah Law.

sibling. Indeed, a contemporary of Rabbi Feinstein, Rabbi Joseph Elijah Henkin, carries this view to its logical conclusion and posits that adoptive children should not call their parents by the term "mother" and "father" (since they are not, and using such titles would be deceptive) but should instead use the diminutive "aunt" and "uncle," which more commonly denote in our society a respectful (but more genetically distant) relationship.[79] Similar such views are posited by many other rabbinic decisors who have written on adoption, including Rabbi Gedalya Felder and Rabbi Mair Steinberg in their contemporary classic works, both of whom concur that adoptions in the Jewish tradition ought to be open adoptions.[80] Most authorities posit that closed adoptions are absolutely forbidden.[81] Rabbi Feinstein, however, is prepared to contemplate the possibility that if the identity of the biological parents cannot be determined, and yet one can ascertain that the children are Jewish, there may be no formal obligation to tell adopted children that they are adopted; it is merely a good idea.[82] Rabbi Solovietchik echoes this formulation when he states, "There is no need to withhold from the adopted child information concerning his or her natural parents."[83]

In those societies where secular law does not permit open adoption,

79. See Y. E. Henkin, *Kol Kitvai Hagaon Rav Yosef Eliahayu Henkin* 2:98 (1989). This letter is undated, but appears to be from the 1950s.

80. See Rabbi Gedalya Felder, *Nahalat Tzvi* 35-40 (2nd ed.), and Rabbi Mair Steinberg, *Lekutai Mair,* pp. 19-23. Both authorities posit that no less than seven distinctly different pieces of information should be shared. They are the following:

1. Is the mother Jewish and eligible to marry in the Jewish community?
2. Is the mother single or married?
3. Who is the father, and is he eligible to marry in the Jewish community?
4. Is the child eligible to marry in the Jewish community?
5. Is the child a Priest, Levite, or Israelite?
6. Does the mother or father have other children (potential siblings) placed for adoption?
7. Is this child Jewish? May she marry a Priest?

81. *Minhat Yitzhak* 4:49. See also Rabbi Menashe Klein, *Mishneh Halakhot* 4:49, who lists more than a dozen reasons why Jewish law directs that children who are adopted be told of that fact, and if their natural parents are known, that such information be shared with them.

82. Moses Feinstein, *Iggrot Moshe, Yoreh Deah* 161-62. Children who are converted to Judaism need to be told such, as minors who convert have the right of refusal (may renounce their Judaism) upon reaching adulthood and being informed of the fact that they are converts. See also *Yam Shel Shlomo, Ketubot* 1:35. A contrary view is provided by Rabbi Moshe Sternbuch, *Teshuvot veHanhagot* 2:678.

83. Soloveitchik, *Family Redeemed,* p. 61.

Jewish law posits that the relevant information needs to be kept in some form of a communal central registry that people have to check before they get married. Such registries were (and still are)[84] kept in many communities in the United Kingdom, where for many years adoptions were closed.[85]

Conclusion

The Jewish tradition has no legal institution called "adoption," even as it recognized that there would be cases where people other than natural parents would care for children. Indeed, Jewish law denied itself the legal authority to authorize the transfer of parental status from the natural parents to the "adoptive" ones. This is consistent with the general rules of status in Jewish family law, where personal status and private acts are beyond the jurisdiction of the legal system. The refusal of Jewish law to create the new legal fiction of an adoptive family stands in stark contrast to Roman and modern American law, both of which recognize the rights of the court system to recast parenthood to fit into the custodial arrangement. The divergence between these law codes on a policy level in fact reflects a fundamental difference between the American and Jewish legal systems in terms of the scope and reach of the law. Jewish law articulates the fundamental inability of a governing body to destroy essential parental relationships created at birth. American jurisprudence grants itself that power; the law can artificially create parental relationships in the best interest of the child. Jewish jurisprudence denies itself that power; families once naturally created cannot ever be destroyed. As Rabbi Soloveitchik observes, however, the relationship between children and their nonbiological custodial parents is one of greater moral, philosophical, and religious significance than a natural parental relationship, as the former is predicated on voluntary choice, which is the hallmark of all sacred covenantal relationships.

---

84. Meyer Steinberg, *Responsum on Problems of Adoption in Jewish Law*, ed. and trans. Maurice Rose (London: Office of the Chief Rabbi, 1969), pp. 11-12.

85. Although the issues of accidental brother/sister incest seem rare, such cases clearly do arise. Consider, for example, Bob Herbert, "A Family Tale," *New York Times*, 31 December 2001, sec. A, p. 11.

7. Adoption: A Roman Catholic Perspective

LISA SOWLE CAHILL

According to the late Pope John Paul II, the adoption of children whose birth families are unable to care for them is part of the mission of the Christian family as "domestic church":

> Christian families, recognizing with faith all human beings as children of the same heavenly Father, will respond generously to the children of other families, giving them support and love not as outsiders but as members of the one family of God's children. Christian parents will thus be able to spread their love beyond the bonds of flesh and blood, nourishing the links that are rooted in the spirit and develop through concrete service to the children of other families, who are often without even the barest necessities. . . . Rediscovering the warmth of affection of a family, these children will be able to experience God's living and provident fatherhood witnessed to by Christian parents, and they will thus be able to grow up with serenity and confidence in life.[1]

This chapter will set this relatively novel (and idealistic) Catholic view of adoption against older attitudes toward and reasons for adoption, and set Catholic views within the context of evolving adoption practices in the United States. It will note the influence of market forces on adoption, and the emergence of international adoption as an increasingly prevalent alterenative for would-be parents. Some ethical criticisms of adoption practices will be presented, especially criticisms for-

---

1. John Paul II, *On the Family (Familiaris consortio)*, 15 December 1981 (Washington, D.C.: United States Catholic Conference, 1982), p. 41.

mulated from a social justice perspective. Catholic social teaching provides a resource to address these criticisms. A distinctively Catholic approach to adoption will be compared to Christian approaches that stress biblical and religious themes such as *agape,* covenant, hospitality to the stranger, and self-sacrifice. Though certainly not inimical to such ideals, the Catholic approach stresses more strongly the adoption of children as a way of recognizing and participating in the common good of society, and of fulfilling one's own parental aspirations. While altruism may be an initial motivation, adoptive families cannot thrive without the strong bonds and mutual benefit that create healthy families by birth and marriage.

The grounding of Catholic ethics in "natural law" will be offered as an approach that can be useful in understanding the paradigmatic but not absolute role of biological kinship in establishing families and in evaluating adoption as an analogy to biological parent-child ties. Besides natural law, Catholic social ethics also focuses on the common good. While valuing the biological family, Catholic ethics provides a way to understand non-kin care for children in terms of the best interests of children and of communities, and opens the door to a vital role for local communities in setting ethical adoption practices.

Certain elements of the Catholic approach to adoption will receive a critical analysis as well. Catholicism has had a persistent tendency to justify adoption as an alternative to "evil" practices such as abortion and the use of reproductive technologies. It has also situated its defense of adoption within advocacy for the moral superiority of the "traditional" family structure. Therefore Catholic views of adoption have incorporated inadequate stances on the self-determination of women, especially birth mothers; of the ethics of adoption as involving more than an alternative reproductive "choice" for infertile couples; and of the need to balance protection of a particular normative family form with the best interests of children. Advocacy for adoption in its own right, with its own set of ethical challenges and problems, remains underdeveloped in Catholic tradition.

On the whole, however, it will be argued that Catholic social teaching offers a valuable resource for setting adoption within a broader social perspective. Catholic social teaching provides a framework for appreciating the moral importance and interdependence of adoptive families, birth families, and the social conditions that create both a demand for adoption and a source of adoptable children. A discussion of Holt International Children's Services, a Christian international adoption and child welfare agency,[2] will serve as a vehicle for the guiding thesis that, in light of the values of Catholic social teaching about justice and the common good, adoption ethics requires a more integrated approach to adoption as part of a total program of support for children, families, and communities under stress.

Catholicism and the History of Adoption

As other chapters in this volume attest, the Catholic church did not always look benignly on adoption. The stigmatization of illegitimacy was once seen as essential to the protection of procreation within marriage; only children by blood could be accepted as legitimate heirs.[3] "Both medieval canon law and early modern common law had firmly rejected the Roman and civil law of adoption," notes John Witte in this volume. "Classic common law had treated natural blood ties between parent and child as essential to the formation of a stable Christian family."[4] At the same time, explicit legal validation of adoption was not necessarily required to permit families informally to assume the care of children of living relatives and friends, as well as of orphans.[5] Sometimes these arrangements, the main purpose of which was usually to provide an heir, were given legal confirmation through contracts, special legislation, or the filing of a deed to the child.[6]

In the nineteenth century, the poverty and illness that trailed indus-

2. My own family includes two birth children and three boys adopted (at ages five, five, and eight) from a children's home in Bangkok, Thailand, through Holt International Children's Services and a Boston-area agency, Wide Horizons for Children. Our Thai sons are now twenty-one, twenty-one, and nineteen. We have returned with the children to Thailand several times, and continue to be closely involved with Holt. Thai social workers who worked with our children while they were in care have visited our home in Massachusetts. At this writing in 2004, my husband Larry Cahill is serving a two-year term as Chair of the Board of Directors of Holt. I had the opportunity to visit the Holt head offices in Eugene, Oregon, in April 2003. I am especially grateful to three Holt social workers, Lisa Vertulfo, Robin Mouny, and Carol Stiles, as well as to Holt Vice President Susan Cox, who generously met with me, shared adoption stories and concerns, and provided me with materials and angles for this essay. Some of the information for the essay, especially on Holt adoptions and international adoption, was obtained in conversation with these members of the Holt staff.

3. John Witte, "Ishmael's Bane: The Sin and Crime of Illegitimacy Reconsidered," this volume.

4. Witte, "Ishmael's Bane."

5. Stephen B. Presser, "Law, Christianity, and Adoption," this volume.

6. L. Anne Babb, *Ethics in American Adoption* (Westport, Conn.: Bergin and Garvey, 1999), p. 36.

trialization resulted in many displaced and orphaned children, often from immigrant parents. Destitute children were frequently kept off the streets by internment in almshouses, which one sociologist refers to as "catchall repositories for a variety of deviants — the indigent, the aged, the insane, minor criminals, and homeless juveniles."[7] Beginning in the 1820s, social reformers attempted to provide more specialized care for children. In the late nineteenth century, in the so-called Progressive Era, child-saving reforms increased. Activists hoped to establish and develop the role of private agencies in carrying out social welfare programs on behalf of and in cooperation with the state. Like modern Catholic social teaching, which was coming to expression in a series of papal encyclicals beginning in 1891 (Leo XIII's *Rerum novarum*), these reformers have been accused of trying to exert social control over immigration and other disruptive social trends, in order to bring them into conformity with white, middle-class, and in this case Protestant expectations.[8] The turn-of-the-century history of child welfare advocacy in the United States, however, especially Protestant-Catholic friction, can also be used to illustrate two important values of Catholic social teaching: the importance of the biological family as a social unit, and the importance of local decision-making about social issues, in coordination with state authority and resources.

In 1876, the National Conference of Charities and Correction passed a resolution advocating the removal of children from almshouses. By 1900, twelve states had adopted such legislation.[9] Humane societies and other private charitable foundations assumed care for many of these children. Charles Loring Brace, founder of the New York Children's Aid Society, organized "orphan trains" to carry unwanted urban slum children to new and supposedly more useful lives in the Midwest, where they were placed as workers with farm families. Many of these children had been born into urban, immigrant Irish Catholic families but were raised as Protestants after being resettled with foster families. This drew the accusation that Brace and his organization were motivated by the aim of proselytization and conversion.[10] The Catholic press portrayed the foster

---

7. John R. Sutton, "Bureaucrats and Entrepreneurs: Institutional Responses to Deviant Children in the United States, 1890-1920s," *American Journal of Sociology* 95, no. 6 (1990): 1375.

8. Sutton, "Bureaucrats and Entrepreneurs," pp. 1372, 1393.

9. Sutton, "Bureaucrats and Entrepreneurs," p. 1374.

10. Madelyn Freundlich, *The Role of Race, Culture, and National Origin in Adoption* (Washington, D.C.: Child Welfare League of America, 2000), p. 4. See also Sutton, "Bureaucrats and Entrepreneurs," p. 1375.

system as a virtual slave trade in which Irish youth were sold to the highest bidder at auctions in Midwestern towns.[11]

The Catholic community responded with its own child protection system, at first designed to separate Catholic children from the Protestants and to protect the faith of the former. L. Silliman Ives, a prominent Catholic New Yorker, denounced the orphan trains, and Catholics organized efforts to place Catholic children with Catholic families. This venture did not meet with success, since most urban Catholics were recent immigrants and hardly prepared to take on responsibility for additional children. Institutional care was preferred to Protestant foster families. Most of the Catholic children who remained under care in the nineteenth century were placed in training schools or children's homes.[12] The first institutions were built by the Irish, followed by German, Polish, and Italian immigrants, all of whom wanted to protect not only religious but ethnic identity. The Irish used their considerable voting power to pass legislation in New York and elsewhere ensuring that children could be placed only with organizations of their own faith. Catholic lay organizations such as the Catholic Union and the St. Vincent de Paul Society kept watch over the enforcement of these laws. Lay activists also began to advocate that custodial institutions be supplemented by foster care programs.[13] Catholic charity officials were important in forming organizational ties between the private sector and public agencies. When Thomas Mulry, a prominent Irish reformer, became president of the St. Vincent de Paul Society, he argued for the formation of a Catholic foster placement system, to enhance the professional standing of Catholic child welfare workers in the public eye. Mulry also gave voice to the long-standing Catholic position that children should be reunited with their natural families whenever possible, and insisted that locally based private agencies were best suited to this task, as well as to that of providing temporary institutional care when necessary. In 1899, the St. Vincent de Paul Society established the Catholic Home Bureau to administer the placement of children in New York. The Bureau was granted a charter as an official agency of the New York Department of Public Charities, which guaranteed access to state funds. Similar Catholic agencies were established in Baltimore, Washington, Detroit, and New Jersey.

The policies promoted by the St. Vincent de Paul Society were tre-

---

11. Sutton, "Bureaucrats and Entrepreneurs," p. 1375.
12. Freundlich, *Role of Race, Culture, and National Origin,* p. 6.
13. Sutton, "Bureaucrats and Entrepreneurs," pp. 1376, 1377.

mendously influential in determining the structure of Catholic charity efforts and in setting a model for cooperation between the public and private sectors. Even though most Catholic child-care institutions were run by religious orders, they successfully fought for access to public funds, while preserving their right of religious and institutional self-determination.[14] In 1910, the National Conference of Catholic Charities was founded. Key goals were family preservation and the reunification of separated children with their families.[15] Catholic Charities also gave Catholic child welfare efforts more professional credibility and public legitimacy. As Catholic Charities expanded its adoption services through the 1960s, its mission around adoption was primarily to place the infants of unwed mothers with childless Catholic couples, following cultural norms of secrecy about identities of parties to the adoption.

The first adoption laws in the United States had been enacted in 1851 in Massachusetts, but it was not until the middle of the next century that infant adoption increased significantly. Between 1945 and 1965, there were two hundred licensed maternity homes in the United States, two-thirds of which were sponsored by the Florence Crittendon Association, Catholic Charities, and the Salvation Army, and which provided for about twenty thousand adoptions annually. Obvious reasons for a dramatic drop in numbers of available infants since that time are the increased availability of contraception and abortion and a sexual revolution that brought pregnancy outside marriage into the open and made unmarried parenting more socially acceptable. About 80 percent of unmarried mothers gave up their children for adoption in 1970, compared to only 4 percent in 1983.[16]

International Adoption and Holt International Children's Services

Since World War II, North American (and European) couples have increasingly turned to international adoption as a way to build families. Catholic Charities and other Catholic organizations, along with Protestant and nondenominational adoption services, have been involved in placing foreign children in American homes. Catholic Charities Baltimore has in fact been a major partner of Holt Korea (see below) in placing chil-

14. Sutton, "Bureaucrats and Entrepreneurs," pp. 1375-79.
15. Babb, *Ethics in American Adoption*, pp. 38-39.
16. Babb, *Ethics in American Adoption*, p. 47.

dren from Korea in the United States. International adoption has not been a main focus of Catholic Charities, however, nor of its global social action counterparts, Caritas International and Catholic Relief Services. Rather, these and other international Catholic organizations concentrate on services to individuals, families, and communities under stress, and provide support for children primarily within their families, or through local service projects such as education and after-school centers, or, when necessary, group care (for example, for AIDS orphans in Africa,[17] or Sudanese refugee children in the United States[18]). The primary mission of Catholic Charities is to advance social relations in accord with Catholic social teaching, which since the 1960s has been increasingly concerned with just and participatory worldwide social institutions.[19]

Within this social justice mission, however, the Catholic approach to adoption (primarily domestic adoption) has shifted significantly in the past half century. Catholic Social Services of Green Bay, Wisconsin, is credited with being the first American agency to promote open adoption, in 1974. Responding to increased inquiries from adoptees about birth parents, adoption professionals there reasoned that more open communication between birth and adoptive parents might mitigate later frustration among adopted children.[20] In 1979, the director of pregnancy and adoption services at Catholic Charities, Chicago, reported that a support association for adoptive parents had been formed, and that the agency was implementing better programs of support for the "adoption triad," including assistance and counseling with regard to searches among birth parents and children.[21]

In 1985, *Social Thought*, the journal of Catholic Charities and the School of Social Service at Catholic University, gave an award to an article urging that adoption services provided to pregnant teenagers exemplify a social justice commitment. The author noted the numbers of teens

17. See, for example, efforts of Catholic Relief Services in South Africa to care for AIDS orphans by mobilizing community support and resources to provide education, health care, and counseling, including support for child-headed households (Catholic Relief Services website, www.catholicrelief.org/where_we_work/africa/south_africa. Accessed 22 April 2004).

18. Evelyn L. Kent, "Catholic Charities Resettles Sudan's 'Lost Boys,'" 3 October 2002, Catholic Charities website, www.catholiccharitiesinfo.org. Accessed 19 July 2004.

19. For more information on Catholic Charities, see their website, www.catholiccharitiesusa.org. Accessed 22 April 2004.

20. Babb, *Ethics in American Adoption*, p. 58.

21. Frances Cashman, "Origins: New Challenges for Adoption Agencies," *Social Thought* 5, no. 4 (1979): 15-23.

choosing abortion over adoption and raised the questions whether adoption services provided adequate respect for and sensitivity to the needs of the clients and whether Catholic providers were being aggressive enough in their resistance to discriminatory social institutions. "Charities must learn to question the legal structures, procedures, and assumptions which negatively affect their young clients. Charities must 'denounce' oppressive structures, and 'announce' its liberating truth," he claimed, citing the liberation theologian Gustavo Gutiérrez.[22] In 2003, Catholic Charities of Boston, specializing in placing "minority and older children," claimed to be the leader in special needs adoptions in Massachusetts, in cooperation with state and federal programs.[23]

Since Holt International Children's Services sees adoption as foundational and central to its identity, it will in this chapter serve as the primary example of a Christian organization that fulfills Catholic social principles and values as applied to adoption. The argument here is not, obviously, that such principles and values are uniquely Catholic or can be embodied only in social action under Catholic auspices. It is, rather, that certain approaches to adoption are mandated by the worldview and values represented in Catholic social tradition, and that Holt embodies in practice the values fostered by that outlook. In fact, it is a key premise of Catholic social teaching that its basic social values and commitments are not exclusively "Catholic," for the whole point of the social encyclicals is to develop social consensus and cooperation, among those of many faiths, around the notion of the common good that it promotes.

In the case of adoption, Holt International is a more useful illustration than Catholic Charities, because Holt was founded to promote international adoption, and adoption remains core to its identity and mission. Since the Holt example takes the ethics of adoption into the international arena, it also provides an occasion to pursue questions of justice in adoption in a larger context of social responsibility and transformation. This larger context is the major focus of Catholic social tradition, but international (and domestic) Catholic child welfare efforts are more focused on aid to poor families and single parents, and on caring for children locally, than on adoption. In the words of the Vice President for Social Policy of Catholic Charities USA, "Our best hope for securing a safe and happy fu-

22. Richard Voss, "A Sociological Analysis and Theological Reflection on Adoption Services in Catholic Charities Agencies," *Social Work* 11, no. 1 (1985): 42.

23. "Adoption," Catholic Charities of Boston website, www.ccab.org/adoption.htm. Accessed 22 April 2004.

ture for our children is to appropriate the resources necessary to heal and preserve broken families."[24] According to its website, Catholic Charities' legislative priorities for 2004 were to advocate for affordable housing, increase federal supports to children and families, improve access to health care, welcome refugees and immigrants, and implement more fair tax and labor policies. Clearly, all of these have an effect on the ability of parents and families to raise children, and on the availability of children for adoption. Holt, on the other hand, still devotes most of its attention and resources to adoption. Yet, as will be discussed, Holt is increasingly complementing adoption efforts with other child, family, and community services that reflect the holistic approach to justice for children that is implied and more explicitly stated by Catholic social teaching. The Catholic vision and the Holt example are complementary.

Since the emergence of international adoption as a major social phenomenon in the United States, altruistic and religious motives have been combined with the desires to parent, to seek out infants or toddlers, to escape dealing with birth mothers who select couples and establish conditions and costs of adoption, to avoid the damaging effects of the American foster care system on children, and sometimes to access a larger supply of Caucasian children (for example, from Eastern Europe since 1989). In 1998, Americans adopted nearly sixteen thousand children from abroad, more than ten thousand of whom came from Asia, Central and South America, Africa, and the Caribbean.[25] In 2003, about twenty thousand children from other countries were adopted by families in the United States.[26]

In some ways, American individualism has paid off for children. Always a racially mixed nation of immigrants, American society is more able than some more traditional societies, especially in Asia, to accept each child as a person in his or her own right with basic needs and untapped potential and to incorporate children unrelated by blood as equal members within a family structure. At the same time, endemic racism in the United States has deterred the adoption of African and African-American children and the full acceptance of racially "different" children, especially

24. Sharon Daly, "Testimony to the Subcommittee on Human Resources of the House Committee on Ways and Means," Hearing to Consider H.R. 5292, Flexible Funding for the Child Protection Act of 2000, 3 October 2000, Catholic Charities website, www.catholiccharitiesinfo.org. Accessed 19 July 2004.

25. Adam Pertman, *Adoption Nation: How the Adoption Revolution is Transforming America* (New York: Basic, 2000), p. 254.

26. Information provided by Holt staff; see note 2 above.

in more homogeneous communities. Adoption professionals and adoptive families are increasingly aware of the need for every child to retain connection with his or her biological, ethnic, and cultural roots, and the consequent need for those involved with adoption to respect these connections in making placements and most particularly to prevent family disruption from occurring in the first place. Despite efforts to enable family preservation or adoption within a child's culture of birth, children in need of families remain tragically plentiful around the globe. In addition to this fact, a consumer approach to children, also abetted by American individualism, has created "black" and "gray" markets for "desirable" adoptees (for example, infant Asian girls); adoption entrepreneurs negotiate significant personal profits by arranging adoptions, sometimes by obtaining children deceptively or coercively.[27]

Since World War II, the primary reason children have been available for adoption to the United States from other countries is civil strife and economic deprivation. Between 1948 and 1953, American couples adopted over eight thousand children from war-torn European countries and Japan.[28] After the Korean War, Congress enacted legislation establishing uniform adoption procedures of foreign children, specifically aimed at the adoption of children fathered by American servicemen. In 1954, a missionary visited the church of a rural Oregon farming couple, Harry and Bertha Holt, and presented a documentary about Amerasian children in Korea. Inspired by their Christian evangelical faith, the Holts, who had already raised six birth children, sold property in order to raise the funds to lobby Congress for the legal change. They adopted eight babies from Korea, placed others with friends, and established a children's home and services in Korea, including a facility for mentally and physically disabled children. The Holts are buried at this facility, Ilsan, now a residential center for 270 handicapped children and adults.[29]

The largest and oldest international adoption and child welfare agency in the United States, Holt International Children's Services has a $17 million annual budget and provides services to thirty thousand to forty thousand children annually.[30] In 2004 Holt worked in the United

27. See Madelyn Freundlich, *The Market Forces in Adoption* (Washington, D.C.: Child Welfare League of America, 2000).

28. Pertman, *Adoption Nation*, p. 54.

29. For information on the Holt history and organization, see the Holt International website, www.holtintl.org. Accessed 22 April 2004.

30. Susan Palmer, "Experienced Executive Takes Top Position at Holt," *The Register-Guard* (Eugene, OR), 7 July 2004, pp. A1, D4.

States and sixteen other countries (China, Bulgaria, Ecuador, Guatemala, Haiti, India, Mongolia, North Korea, Philippines, Romania, Russia, South Korea, Thailand, Uganda, Ukraine, and Vietnam). Of the approximately twenty thousand children placed annually for adoption in the United States from international sources, Holt provides homes for about 950.[31] The motto of Holt, in the words of its founder Harry Holt, is "Every child deserves a home of his own."[32] Its services, in order of priority, are family preservation, family reunification, adoption within a child's country of birth, and inter-country adoption placements.[33] Of the children Holt serves each year, about one third are maintained in or reunited with their birth families, one third placed with adoptive families in their country of origin, and one third placed with families abroad.[34] Holt International provides many post-adoption services to families and children, including "Holt Heritage Camps" for adopted children in their birth countries, family tours of these countries, support for birth family searches, and new placements for children in the rare cases in which a placement of a child in an adoptive family disrupts. Holt families are encouraged to experience the joys and benefits of being small interracial and intercultural communities and to make every effort to encourage experiences of their children's birth culture in their family life in the United States.

Holt also funds improved institutional care, foster families, and education for children in their birth countries. Fees from adoption are used in part to support family and children's services in the countries from which children are placed. Usually both children's services and adoption are combined within Holt's efforts in any given country. Exceptions, however, are child welfare services in Haiti, and a small pilot program just begun in Uganda in 2003. It is not anticipated that these programs will involve the adoption of significant numbers of children into the United States. In Haiti, Holt provides services for homeless children and children in orphanages, as well as children at risk of abuse as domestic workers. The Uganda program provides in-country services only, to AIDS orphans and children with AIDS, in partnership with a local effort, Action for Children, and in cooperation with the Ugandan government and other lo-

31. See note 2 above.

32. This motto has been presented on the Holt website (www.holtintl.org), stationery, and in other publicity. For several examples, see www.holtintl.org/search/ksearch.cgi?terms=%22Every+Child+Deserves+a+Home+of+His+Own%22&search2.x=30&search2.y=9. Accessed 19 July 2004.

33. Palmer, "Experienced Executive," pp. A1, D4.

34. See note 2 above.

cal groups. The Holt focus in Uganda is not adoption but care for children within their families and communities. This venture illustrates Holt's commitment to serve the best interests of children, not only to provide children for couples hoping to expand their families. Returning from a visit to the Uganda project, during which a Holt-funded community center was dedicated, board member Julie Banta remarked that Holt support is "a way to keep kids within the community," and "It's empowering the community to take care of its own."[35]

Holt-supported agencies in countries outside the United States operate with a relative degree of autonomy from the parent organization. Social workers and other professionals in the receiving countries staff the projects and make decisions about expenditures and child placements. The original Holt international venture, Holt Korea, eventually obtained legal recognition and economic support from the Korean Government. Since the 1970s it has operated in cooperation with Holt International in Eugene, Oregon, but with a separate (and much larger) budget and administrative structure. Although the reasons for this development were multiple, including political and economic issues in Korea, the independence and local ownership of Holt Korea represents a success story in terms of local self-determination and culture-specific oversight of the goals, limits, and contexts of adoption.

Lest Holt's success in fulfilling Christian ideals of social service and transformation seem unreal or utopian, it must be stressed that its administrators and staff are all too aware of the ethical problems that beset international adoption, and admittedly run afoul of these in some cases. Such problems include setting priorities for locations and services in a world of finite resources; working in a variety of cultures with different legal and ethical norms and levels of tolerance for extra-legal dealings; ensuring that adequate options are presented to birth mothers, often desperately poor, so that children are released under noncoercive circumstances; obtaining and presenting to adoptive families adequate medical and social histories of available children; and balancing the obligation to provide any possibly unfavorable information to the adoptive families with the need not to endanger an adoption by presenting information that may cause a negative overreaction on the part of the adopting family.

Holt has always cooperated respectfully with professional staff

35. Quoted in Ellen Schroeder, "Missions of Hope," *Star-Telegram* (Dallas-Fort Worth), 1 December 2003, Star-Telegram website, www.dfw.com/mld/dfw/news/local/states/texas/northeast. Accessed 1 December 2003.

around the world from other religious traditions, including Buddhists, Hindus, and Muslims. Holt has always worked on the assumption that it is best for children to remain in their own countries, with families of birth, no matter what their culture and religion. Yet because of Holt's evangelical roots and commitments, the integration of American staff and adoptive families from other Christian denominations and from non-Christian traditions has presented challenges. The board of directors is composed primarily of evangelical Protestant Christians, with occasional Roman Catholic membership, including one Roman Catholic chair. Similarly, the staff at Holt remains largely evangelical, but a few Catholic and non-Christian members are included in the organization. The biblical and faith dimensions of Holt remain key, however. Adoption is held up as a form of service "to the Lord," with unusual numbers of evangelical families, often with older birth children, adopting multiple children with multiple handicaps. Holt's recent decision to establish a policy limiting the number of children that one family is allowed to adopt both illustrates the power of a religious commitment to serve children and exemplifies the tension that can sometimes arise between Christian idealism and the need to maintain strong professional standards in ensuring that adoptive homes are adequately equipped to handle the special challenges they confront.

Adoption and Catholic Social Teaching

Catholic ethical and social teaching reinforces at least three major components of the Christian approach to adoption illustrated by Catholic agencies and especially by Holt, as an international agency that identifies adoption as central to its identity and mission but increasingly places adoption within a complex network of social problems and solutions. These "Catholic" components are Christian altruism and service, especially the preferential option for the poor; the importance of the natural law and of the common good as constituting a framework for understanding the rights and responsibilities of individuals, families, institutions, and communities; and the principle of subsidiarity, which highlights the importance of local efforts and local authority in addressing social problems. Again, these aspects of a social vision are not limited to Catholics, though the way in which they are advanced as the basis on which persons of various faiths can pursue common social aims has historically been more characteristic of Catholic social teaching than of Protestantism. The point is not that Catholicism has exclusive rights to such ideals, but that formation in the Catholic tradition should encourage attention to them. Yet a historically Protestant adoption agency, Holt, can help illustrate what they would look like in the context of international adoption.

Like Protestants, Catholics emphasize that care for children in need can be a vital expression of gospel values. John Paul II saw the Christian family as a "domestic church" in which spiritual formation and service to others are nourished. It is part of the mission of families to build up the church, and also to contribute to a more just society, especially by caring for those on the margins of society. The "apostolate of the family" requires works of material and social aid to other families, especially "those most in need of help and support," including "the poor, the sick," "orphans," "spouses that have been abandoned, unmarried mothers, and mothers-to-be in difficult situations."[36] Similarly, the *Catechism of the Catholic Church* advises childless couples "to give expression to their generosity by adopting abandoned children."[37]

On the third anniversary of the death of Mother Teresa (beatified in 2003), John Paul II commended the adoption work of her order, the Missionaries of Charity, to a group of adoptive families gathered in her honor. Despite its questionable historical accuracy, the assertion of the pope that Mother Teresa is to be credited with "the adoption movement" illustrated his conviction that adoption is a relationship that can be imbued with spiritual value. In the pope's view, the very existence of so many children without families "suggests adoption as a concrete way of love."[38] Adoptive families testify that "this is a possible and beautiful way, despite its difficulties; a way, moreover, which is even more feasible than in the past in this era of globalization which shortens all distances."[39] He recognized that there is "a form of 'procreation' which occurs through acceptance, concern and devotion. The resulting relationship is so intimate and enduring that it is in no way inferior to one based on a biological connection."[40]

Brenda Destro emphasizes the view that, from the perspective of Catholic theology, adoption is a covenant. In her view, covenant is a

36. John Paul II, *On the Family*, §71.

37. *Catechism of the Catholic Church*, English translation (London: Cassell, 1994), p. 510.

38. John Paul II, "Address to the Meeting of Adoptive Families Organized by the Missionaries of Charity," 5 September 2000, Official Vatican website, www.vatican.va/holy_ father/john_paul_ii/speeches/2000. Accessed 4 April 2004.

39. John Paul II, "Meeting of Adoptive Families."

40. John Paul II, "Meeting of Adoptive Families."

hermeneutical framework that allows the best interests of the child to be foremost, rather than the interests and preferences of parents or of those who might profit financially from adoption. Destro holds up the adoption of Moses by Pharaoh's daughter, and the adoption of Jesus by Joseph. "The first model of a Christian family is one that is bound more by covenant than by biology. . . . With faith and sacrifice, Mary and Joseph overcame their fears and made a covenant with God and each other to raise Jesus. . . . God entrusts parents with the duty to care for his children, just as Mary and Joseph cared for His Son."[41] Although Destro's essay is pastoral and homiletic rather than systematically theological and exegetical, it demonstrates the use of biblical and theological categories within Catholic tradition to advocate for child-centered adoption as an expression of religious identity.

More distinctive of Catholic approaches to adoption than of Protestant, perhaps, is the utilization of Catholic social categories to place the adoption relationship within a justice framework. This is not to say that Protestant or other religiously inspired adoption agencies lack concern for justice and the common good; it is to say, rather, that Catholicism has a well-developed philosophical and theological tradition that explicitly connects such concerns with Christian values. The modern papal social encyclicals in particular have provided concepts such as "natural law" and "the common good" that are useful in explaining and facilitating the cooperation of Catholic child welfare and adoption efforts with their non-Catholic and non-Christian counterparts, whether secular or sponsored by other faith traditions.

Since at least the writings of Thomas Aquinas in the thirteenth century, Catholicism has elaborated a vision of the social order based on common human moral experiences, values, and obligations; measured by a standard of justice; and knowable to all persons of goodwill who reflect reasonably on the nature of a good society. In the past century, philosophical postmodernism and economic globalization have made Catholics, along with the rest of the modern world, aware of huge difficulties that attend any attempts at intercultural understanding and collaboration. Yet Catholic social tradition persists optimistically in defending the possibility that religions and cultures can work together to improve the human

41. Brenda Destro, *Celebrating the Good Message of Adoption* (Washington D.C.: United States Conference of Catholic Bishops, 2003), p. 2; also published by the United States Conference of Catholic Bishops Secretariat for Pro-Life Activities on the USCCB website, www.usccb.org/prolife/programs. Accessed 10 October 2003.

lot. In Thomistic terms, "natural law" refers most basically to the idea that the Creator has endowed all persons and societies with the ability to reason out the essential requirements of a good human life and a good society and to act upon those requirements. For example, all cultures enact protections on human life and provide institutions to organize labor, education, marriage, and child-raising, although the specifics must vary locally and historically.[42]

At the end of the nineteenth century, in response to industrialization and the emerging "threat" of Marxist reforms, the Roman Catholic popes began a tradition of social encyclical letters that has continued to the present day. Originally moderately reformist, while still hierarchical and protective of the right to own private property, the social encyclicals have become increasingly critical of huge global disparities in wealth and human welfare and of the excesses of market capitalism. These more recent documents have called for more radical reforms centered on the social and political participation of all classes and peoples, and on a preferential option for the poor (to use a phrase characteristic of liberation theology). In the words of the Second Vatican Council's *Gaudium et spes* (Pastoral Constitution on the Church in the Modern World),

> Every day human interdependence grows more tightly drawn and spreads by degrees over the whole world. As a result the common good, that is, the sum of those conditions of social life which allow social groups and their individual members relatively thorough and ready access to their own fulfillment, today takes on an increasingly universal complexion and consequently involves rights and duties with respect to the whole human race. Every social group must take account of the needs and legitimate aspirations of other groups, and even of the general welfare of the entire human family.[43]

The concept of the common good assumed special significance during the pontificates of John XXIII and Paul VI; following their lead, John Paul II placed social issues within the perspective of the global and not merely national common good. Moreover, he defined the personal and social virtue of "solidarity" as an indispensable component of the actual at-

---

42. For general discussion, see Stephen J. Pope, "Natural Law and Christian Ethics," in *Cambridge Companion to Christian Ethics,* ed. Robin Gill (Cambridge: Cambridge University Press, 2001), pp. 77-95.

43. *Gaudium et spes,* §26, in *Catholic Social Thought: The Documentary Heritage,* ed. David J. O'Brien and Thomas A. Shannon (Maryknoll, N.Y.: Orbis, 1992), p. 181.

tainment of social justice, especially as including the "'preferential option for the poor.'"[44]

The virtue of solidarity is realized concretely in and for the common good only when all parts of society work independently. From the earliest social encyclicals onward, local and more inclusive forms of community and authority have been related according to a "principle of subsidiarity."[45] While Leo XIII and his successor Pius XI were more concerned about the autonomy of smaller groups, including the family, from socialist collectivism, popes since John XXIII have been at least equally adamant about the duty of the state or even a "world authority" to intervene when local autonomy results in power imbalances that harm the poor. On the whole, the principle of subsidiarity operates in Catholic social tradition critically to connect local and higher-order social authorities, policies, and laws, so that all levels of society are engaged (at least ideally) in defining social practices, and so that detriments to the common good that originate in one sphere are more susceptible to correction from counter-forces that emerge in another.

One of the most important spheres of society in Catholic tradition is the family — not just the modern, nuclear, public-private family, but the historically more dominant model of family as an intergenerational kinship network, linking different kin groups by marriage. Families provide the formation of personal identity and the human relationships that children need to thrive; they are also the most basic unit of social organization and supply the working material from which social constructions of kin, clan, tribe, ethnicity, race, and nationhood are built. Biological identity and connection are not unique to humans and do not determine in and of themselves humanity's highest interpersonal and spiritual relationships. Yet the Catholic natural law tradition recognizes that biological kinship is an extremely important factor in identity and in social organization, and is rightly a valued facet of all cultures everywhere.

Respecting the universal human importance of families and in light of the principle of subsidiarity, John Paul II called for "complementary functions" of family and society in fostering the common good and the good of all persons. "In the conviction that the good of the family is an indispensable and essential value of the civil community, the public author-

44. John Paul II, *Centesimus annus,* §11, in *Catholic Social Thought: The Documentary Heritage,* ed. David J. O'Brien and Thomas A. Shannon (Maryknoll, N.Y.: Orbis, 1992), p. 447.

45. For a discussion, see Charles E. Curran, *Catholic Social Teaching, 1891-Present: A Historical, Theological and Ethical Analysis* (Washington, D.C.: Georgetown University Press, 2002), pp. 141-44.

ities must do everything possible to ensure that families have all those aids — economic, social, educational, political and cultural assistance — that they need in order to face all their responsibilities in a human way."[46] Families themselves act as subsidiary social agents of the common good when they undertake "social service activities" in favor of the poor. Families provide "hospitality," "opening the door of one's home, and still more of one's heart, to the pleas of one's brothers and sisters."[47] While willing to welcome the stranger, Catholics should seek the common good, not just extra opportunities for charity. Thus Catholic families should urge those in positions of public authority to ensure that every family can enjoy its own home, "the natural environment that preserves it and makes it grow."[48] Such duties are more than individual options or local charity; they are to be supported and defended by "the laws and institutions of the state."[49]

Several implications for adoption ethics are at this point self-evident. First of all, Catholics and other Christians are motivated by identification with Jesus' care for the poor. The parable of judgment in Matthew 25 commends to every Christian the recognition of Christ in any person, no matter how disreputable or impaired, who lacks the necessities of food, shelter, clothing, or companionship. Second, Christians and others have membership in multiple interlocking societies whose good they share in common and for which all are responsible. First among these is the family. Families, usually based on biological kinship and marriage unions, have human and Christian value. Kin relationships, however, are not absolute. The Christian notion of family can incorporate "non-kin" members who are assimilated into the family structure by love. Because Catholic tradition values natural human bonds and loyalties, it tends not to see humanly fulfilling love and Christ-like sacrificial love as being in opposition to one another, as have some Protestant interpretations of discipleship. All parenthood entails sacrifice, and yet it can provide unparalleled fulfillment, bringing new relationships of intimacy and reciprocal connection.[50] This is as true of adoptive as of natural parent-child relationships.

46. John Paul II, *On the Family,* §45.
47. John Paul II, *On the Family,* §44.
48. John Paul II, *On the Family,* §44.
49. John Paul II, *On the Family,* §44.
50. See Christine Gudorf, "Parenting, Mutual Love, and Sacrifice," in *Women's Consciousness, Women's Conscience: A Reader in Feminist Ethics,* ed. Barbara Hilkert Andolsen, Christine E. Gudorf, and Mary D. Pellauer (San Francisco: Harper and Row, 1987), pp. 175-91.

While local, national, and global communities should make every effort to maintain the familial, kinship, ethnic, racial, and cultural connections for children at risk, adoption can also be a morally worthy and humanly fulfilling way of resolving the human problems that result in a family's inability to care for a child that is born to it. First of all, adoption serves children; second, it serves all family members who enter into loving and responsible relationships through adoptive arrangements; third, it serves communities by relieving social and economic stress in some, and by challenging others to expand their horizon of membership and belonging.

International adoption takes the early Catholic child welfare struggle for local self-determination within public-private partnerships to a new level and provides a test of the Catholic principle of subsidiarity. Catholic social ethics calls upon those with more resources to share power with those who have less, building respect and equality on the basis of a shared commitment to the best interests of children. Subsidiarity demands a participatory approach to adoption practices and policies. The coordination of international partners in adoption requires dialogue and aims at mutual understanding despite cultural differences about families, sexuality, maternity, appropriate child-care practices, and the symbolic significance of children in cultures and religions. The Holt experience shows both that local service providers can offer indispensable insight about family services and adoption placements and that central leadership on professionalism and transparency can help raise ethical performance. A bias toward local self-determination should be complemented by the knowledge that sometimes wisdom derived from adoption experience in several cultures can help guide traditionalist, xenophobic, or short-sighted policies in given social settings toward policies that are more adequate to the good of all the parties served, especially that of children.

Finally, adoption can never be separated from the larger contexts of relationships and responsibilities within which adoption occurs. Adoption is always a response to conditions of distress and disruption. The first moral obligation of all concerned with adoption is to alleviate its originating conditions insofar as possible by addressing the forms of structural inequality and injustice that cause some parents, families, and communities to be unable to care for all their children. These persons and communities are never isolated in their distress and despair. Other persons, groups, economic classes, and nations are participants in the conditions of common good — or harm — within which birth families become fragile and adoption appears as the best among difficult alternatives.

Therefore all who are involved in or concerned about adoption must be responsive to more comprehensive issues of social justice.

The ethics of adoption, from a Catholic perspective, includes working to reduce the need for adoption. It requires amelioration of the hurtful effects of separating birth parents and children and of removing children from their natural communities under duress. It demands an end to the commercialization of adoption services that results in unjust and illegal methods of obtaining and placing children outside their birth families.[51] It also urges us to understand adoption as a relationship that can be immensely fulfilling for parents and children alike, and that can have uniquely positive effects on families and communities. As Leslie Doty Hollingsworth asserts, "Children's rights to be raised in safe and healthy environments by their biological families and in their cultures of origin are primary and should be equally available to all children."[52] Nevertheless, at the same time and for the foreseeable future, "international adoption represents the only viable immediate solution to the suffering in the lives and well-being of children globally."[53]

Critique of the Catholic Approach to Adoption

The way the Catholic church has addressed adoption in three specific contexts has to some extent undermined the power of its social justice message on adoption. These three contexts are abortion, reproductive technologies, and same-sex marriage. Unfortunately, some representatives of official Catholic teaching have prioritized resistance to these three phenomena to such an extent that the character of its adoption advocacy has been distorted, especially at the higher levels of the pope, Vatican, and national bishops' conference.

Adoption is frequently presented as a plank in an anti-abortion platform. Describing the "apostolate of the family" as assistance to those in need, John Paul II in *Familiaris consortio* urged help for "unmarried mothers and mothers-to-be in difficult situations who are tempted to have re-

51. Ethical abuses in adoption practices are discussed extensively in this volume. For further treatment, see Babb, *Ethics in American Adoption;* Freundlich, *Market Forces in Adoption;* and Leslie Doty Hollingsworth, "International Adoption among Families in the United States: Considerations of Social Justice," *Social Work* 48, no. 2 (2003): 209-17.

52. Hollingsworth, "International Adoption," p. 216.

53. Hollingsworth, "International Adoption," p. 216.

54. John Paul II, *On the Family,* §71.

course to abortion. . . ."[54] In his speech honoring Mother Teresa, he cited her as having "said to mothers tempted by abortion: 'Give me your children.'"[55] Brenda Destro takes this line of thought quite a bit further in asserting that "most advocates of women's rights" do not support adoption and "seem uncomfortable with adoption's focus on 'the best interests of the child' and with the prospect of taking the pregnancy to term because they see pregnancy as a hardship. Such feminists may advocate for 'choice,' but not for those choices which require some sacrifice. Adoption — like most responsible choices — requires sacrifice."[56] This kind of analysis not only impugns the motives of women who choose abortion, sometimes because they believe it the best way to spare a child suffering, but also distances the adoption situation from advocacy for the rights of women. It contrasts unfavorably to the developing stance of many Catholic adoption agencies and of Holt International to support the human dignity and self-determination of birthmothers. More important, it militates against what the author calls her own "good message" that adoption is a rewarding and fulfilling experience for adoptive parents, and that birth parents and adopted children can both be well-served by the adoption experience. In the Catholic approach, adoption needs to be firmly and consistently connected to pregnant women's welfare, options, and rights.

A second "negative" context of Catholic adoption advocacy is the battle against use of the new reproductive technologies. Following the 1968 anti-birth-control encyclical of Paul VI, *Humanae vitae*, the Catholic church disallows any methods of conception or contraception that artificially separate sex from procreation and vice versa. The *Catechism of the Catholic Church* advises "spouses who still suffer from infertility after exhausting legitimate medical procedures" to "unite themselves with the Lord's Cross," and to adopt "abandoned children."[57] Adoption is supposedly an act of love, but such rhetoric heightens the idea that it is only under consideration because other more attractive or more effective remedies have been disapproved.

Richard Doerflinger, on behalf of the Committee for Pro-Life Activities of the U.S. bishops, gave testimony before Congress in which he argued that in vitro fertilization and other forbidden infertility therapies be outlawed. Doerflinger rightly called adoption a solution to infertility that

55. John Paul II, "Meeting of Adoptive Families."
56. Destro, *Celebrating the Good Message*, p. 1.
57. *Catechism*, §2379, pp. 509-10.

could benefit everyone, and called for more adequate funding and tax benefits.[58] This speech, however, along with Destro's essay, were among the few adoption resources provided on the web by the U.S. Catholic Conference. Adoption must be presented as more than a third-best alternative, after natural childbirth and childbearing by artificially assisted conception. Indeed, what should be the key reason for Catholics to object to reproductive technologies — disproportionate utilization of medical resources by the privileged — rarely if ever figures in official attacks. It is precisely this social justice framework that should be operative in recommending adoption.[59] A much more positive and empowering message about adoption needs to be communicated if couples who can or do have birth children are to be attracted to it and if infertile couples are to embrace it enthusiastically and in keeping with the best interests of children.

A third negative context for the presentation of adoption is created by increasingly strident Catholic opposition to the legal recognition of civil unions for gay couples. In 2000, participants in a congress convened at the Vatican by the Pontifical Council for the Family issued a statement asserting that "recent attempts to legalize adoptions by homosexual persons . . . must be strongly rejected."[60] They cite the view of the pope that the bond between persons of the same sex cannot constitute a real family or ground a claim to adopt children. They invoke the principle of the child's higher interests to rule out the possibility of adoption by same-sex couples.[61] In July 2003, responding to heightened attempts in the United States to pass legislation recognizing same-sex unions, the Congregation for the Doctrine of the Faith issued a vehement counterargument. It featured the unsubstantiated claim that, "as experience has shown, the absence of sexual complementarity in these [gay] unions creates obstacles in

---

58. Richard A. Doerflinger, "Alternative Reproductive Technologies: Implications for Children and Families," 21 May 1987, United States Conference of Catholic Bishops website, www.usccb.org.prolife/issues/ivf/ivftest52187. Accessed 22 April 2004.

59. Maura A. Ryan places adoption under the virtue of "hospitality" and within a social justice framework. She points out, however, that not only infertile couples have a responsibility to care for the welfare of children in need of families, and that adoption is not always a clear-cut solution to infertility (Maura A. Ryan, *The Ethics and Economics of Assisted Reproduction: The Cost of Longing* [Washington, D.C.: Georgetown University Press, 2001], pp. 56-60).

60. Pontifical Council for the Family, "Children: Springtime of the Family and Society," §II, Official Vatican website, www.vatican.va/roman_curia/pontifical_councils/family/documents/rc_pc_family_doc_20010329_jub-fam-conclusion_en.html. Accessed 4 April 2004.

61. Pontifical Council for the Family, "Children," §II.

the normal development of children. . . . Allowing children to be adopted by persons living in such unions would actually mean doing violence to these children."[62] The statement insisted further that adoption by gays "would be gravely immoral" and would contradict the "best interests of the child," as upheld by the United Nations Convention on the Rights of the Child.[63]

In fact, in such statements the best interests of children have become a casualty of the Vatican's overriding interest in protecting the normative moral and civil status of a particular family structure, the two-parent, heterosexual, nuclear, gender-unequal family. Even granting the preferability for children of a heterosexual married couple as parents, the best interests of children must be gauged by the other options available for particular children. Just as the general preferability of intact birth families does not invalidate the legitimacy of adoptive families in particular circumstances, the preferability of a male and a female parent does not invalidate the legitimacy of same-sex parents.

Gregory Maguire, a Catholic, a writer, and a member of a same-sex parenting couple with three children, is eloquent on this point. He refers to himself and his partner as "capable adults in need of loving children in a world where children are in need of capable loving adults."[64] While not rejecting the goodness of gender complementarity, he refuses to place it "above all other concerns." He continues,

> Same-sex parents who adopt children aren't in danger of significantly dwindling the stock of abandoned, destitute, or orphaned children. The supply well outpaces the demand. No married heterosexual couple that wants to adopt will go home empty-handed because we have adopted. Ought children to be left in the streets and minimally staffed orphanages because we worry about gender complementarity? To me, the moral question is one about the just application of resources and one's talents. We can provide a good home for otherwise "at risk" children.[65]

62. Congregation for the Doctrine of the Faith, "Considerations Regarding Proposals to Give Legal Recognition to Unions between Homosexual Persons," §7, available on the Official Vatican website, www.vatican.va/roman_curia/congregations/cfaith/documents/rc_con_cfaith_doc_20030731_homosexual-unions_en.html. Accessed 4 April 2004.

63. Congregation for the Doctrine of the Faith, "Unions between Homosexual Persons," §7.

64. Daria Donnelly, "A Gay Parent Looks at His Church: An Interview with Novelist Gregory Maguire," *Commonweal* 130, no. 18 (2003): 20-22.

65. Donnelly, "A Gay Parent," p. 21.

To be an ethical and effective advocate for adoption, the Catholic church does not necessarily have to back down on abortion, reproductive technologies, and gay unions, whatever the merits of its positions on these issues. It does, however, have to put its priority on children, and on the worth of adoption in its own right as an alternative form of family-building, when birth families are unable to remain together. Otherwise, politically motivated positions on issues bearing on adoption can and will undermine real and practical commitment to children and families, including adoptive families.

At the practical level, agencies such as Catholic Charities have a substantial track record in implementing Catholic social teaching in the area of adoption. In recent years, Catholic adoption services have increasingly emphasized respect for and obligations to children, birth parents, and adoptive families, and have enhanced their efforts to provide loving, stable families for special needs children. Internationally, Catholic agencies place more emphasis on serving children within their birth communities than in placing them with foreign families. Similarly, as has been noted, Holt International Children's Services is expanding its mission to family preservation and support for homeless children in the local community.

Together, Catholic agencies and Holt illustrate five "Catholic" principles for adoption ethics: (1) Adopting children can fulfill the gospel command to love one's neighbor, through a "preferential option for the poor." (2) Adopting children creates families that can fulfill the needs of all members for intimacy, love, and support, thus going beyond "sacrifice" to "fulfillment." (3) Adoptive relationships do not erase the importance and value of biological kinship, as well as of ethnic and racial identity, especially for adoptees. (4) Adoption is part of a larger social justice picture. It is ethically mandatory for all those involved in adoption to challenge social structures that disrupt families, exploit women and children, and create the necessity for families with resources to adopt the children of families unable to meet basic needs. (5) Adoption ethics requires the participation and decision-making authority of all participants, including birth families and adoptive families, as well as of service providers who can represent the needs and interests of communities that send children to families abroad through international adoption.

8. Adoption: A Protestant Agapic Perspective

STEPHEN G. POST

What is a Protestant to think of adoption? This is a complex question, if for no other reason than that it is seldom discussed in theological circles. Protestant thought strongly endorses a covenant of love in which birth parents become social parents as well. And yet such a view, which emerges from the requirements of love, opens a door for relinquishment and adoption as required by love in exceptional cases. Protestant and Catholic social thought differ on adoption insofar as covenant theology and natural law have somewhat different implications. Protestant thought is less willing to take a moral and social-parental "ought" from the "is" of birth parenting. This allows Protestantism more latitude in developing social practices around the background theology of Christianity, which is, after all, a religion in which salvation occurs through "adoption" as a child of God by virtue of faith in an adoptee messiah relinquished to Joseph by a heavenly father.

Protestant latitude, historically considered, has not been untainted by anti-Catholicism. In this volume ("Law, Christianity, and Adoption"), Stephen Presser underscores the remarkable development of adoption law and practice in Protestant America. Protestant efforts to save Catholic children from mid-nineteenth-century urban squalor and from Catholicism itself included sending them via "orphan trains" to such places as the Western Reserve of Ohio and Michigan, even against the wishes of biological parents. Needless to say, Protestant and Catholic attitudes differed toward the trains of the 1850s and 1860s. The policy was supported by Protestants.[1] The

1. See Jean Bethke Elshtain, "The Chosen Family," *The New Republic,* 14 and 21 Sept. 1998, p. 47.

Catholic church, in contrast, was unwilling to break up biological families; instead, it developed innumerable children's institutions to provide temporary church-sponsored relinquishment centers for Catholic parents.[2] Partly, of course, American Catholicism was defending its own demographic interests against Protestant assaults in the form of adoption. Yet there was also a broader historical Protestant acceptance of adoption as contrasted with Catholic natural law tradition, allowing us to surmise that the American Protestant embrace of adoption flowed in considerable part from earlier theological and legal underpinnings.

In this chapter, I reflect first on the wider theological context of adoption, and then turn to adoption in a remarkable but not uncommon practical context. I then ask if, in Protestant thought, adoption is inferior to, or merely secondary to, birth parents raising their children. Under a Barthian influence, I will suggest the latter. Before concluding with the ways in which adoptive love is resonant with *agape* in Protestant thought, I briefly take up evolutionary psychology as an example of a how a theory loosely akin to natural law in its procreative genetic essentialism might go too far in attempting to undermine the moral idealism that defines adoptive relinquishment and parenting. This choice of foci reflects no firm methodological orthodoxy; however, the chapter does raise what could, with some caveats, be considered essential questions around adoption and Protestant thinking. I refrain from discussing the highly significant issue of the experience of relinquishment of a child, which involves a number of ethical axes around the principles of both autonomy and justice, only because I have treated this matter elsewhere with due epistemological emphasis on the experience of women.[3]

The Theological Context of Adoption

While the above-mentioned Protestant-Catholic distinction is defensible, it should nevertheless be remembered that Christianity in general espouses hospitality to the stranger and Good Samaritanism, inclusive of the relinquished child. Contemporary Catholicism, for example, vividly endorses adoption as the moral alternative to abortion. Christianity in

---

2. Elizabeth McKeown, "Adopting Sources: A Response to Stephen Post," *Journal of Religious Ethics* 25, no. 1 (spring 1997): 169-75.

3. See Stephen G. Post, *More Lasting Unions: Christianity, the Family, and Society* (Grand Rapids: Eerdmans, 2000).

general challenges the assumption that the only real kinship is based on birth, biology, and blood. The ties of nature are important, but not absolute under the freedom of God. Families can be built as well as they can be begotten; every principle in action admits of some exception.

Yet Christian communities of faith must be reminded of this. My Episcopal *Book of Common Prayer,* in its current form, includes under the rubric "Thanksgiving for a Child" a celebration entitled "For an Adoption."[4] It reads, "As God has made us his children by adoption and grace, may you receive (Name) as your own son (daughter)." It continues, responsively, "May God, the Father of all, bless our child (Name), and us who have given to him our family name, that we may live together in love and affection; through Jesus Christ our Lord. Amen."[5] While not found in earlier versions of the *Book of Common Prayer,* which was limited to the celebration "For the Birth of a Child," here we have a creative and salutary set of passages endorsing adoption.

The idea of adoption was contributed to Christian tradition by St. Paul. Five of Paul's texts mention adoption as a means of obtaining permanent enjoyment of an improved status as legal heir and having old debts canceled. The Pauline appropriation of a theology of adoption is exceedingly technical and too complex for this discussion, but I should note that adoption in some broad sense is a part of his vision of Christian membership and salvation. Somewhat simplistically stated, human beings are *not* by nature the *fully* adopted children of God, although they are otherwise still within the range of divine love. Jesus, as the Christ, however, *is* the son of God, and God is prepared to fully adopt as children those who accept Christ. Adoption is thus at the very core of the Christian narrative of salvation by faith.

Adoption is also central to Christianity because Jesus of Nazareth was himself raised by a de facto adoptive father. According to orthodox theology, Jesus was conceived by the Holy Spirit — a prospect made more plausible against the background of our increasing scientific capacities to engage in nonprocreative reproduction. He was the son of God in a way that did not involve Joseph as a biological father. Indeed, Joseph might easily have rejected Jesus as illegitimate. But instead, Joseph became the social father of Jesus, thus protecting him from fatherlessness and from public scorn, and Mary from a desperate fate. So it is that in the Christian narrative, we are saved by the birth of a child who was also an adoptee.

4. *Book of Common Prayer* (New York: Church Publishing, 1979), p. 440.
5. *Book of Common Prayer,* pp. 440-41.

Early Christianity endorsed adoption theologically as metaphor for salvation; although more historical study is needed, adoption was also endorsed in practice as a necessary response to human contingencies. In ancient Rome, relinquishment occurred under a mythological canopy: a statue of a she-wolf suckling the foundlings Romulus and Remus stood over the forum in Rome from the third century B.C.E., conveying the potentially happy outcomes for abandoned children. The benefits of relinquishment were thus creatively ensconced in cultural symbol and ethos. With the development from Roman antiquity to Christianized Europe in the fourth and fifth centuries, a new sacred canopy captured the happy prospects of the relinquished infant and the acceptability of the birth mother's gift, which at that time took on deeper religious meaning. The self-perception of Christians was that they had been adopted by God to substitute spiritually for the biological lineage of Abraham. Given the centrality of this theology to the post-Constantinian formation of Western culture, Christian literature includes numerous examples of idealized images of adoption. Converts all believed that they were adopted into the faith, sometimes setting aside hostile biological families. They were provided with a "birth" through baptism — a kind of rescue from abandonment. The convert had "spiritual parents" who took special care in nurturing his or her faith; these parents "took up" a child, much as in adoption.

Yet Alan Donagan rightly points to the moral centrality of a principle he identifies with the Hebrew-Christian tradition: "It is impermissible for human beings voluntarily to become parents of a child, and yet refuse to rear it to a stage of development at which it can independently take part in social life."[6] This traditional view, argues Donagan, derives from the precept of parental responsibility. The child deserves a stable marital union and nurture by his or her natural parents. He acknowledges, however, that "For a child whose natural parents cannot assume this authority, for any reason from death to temperamental unfitness, other arrangements must be made, for example, adoption; but they are considered to be intrinsically inferior."[7] While it is significant that Donagan's summation of the tradition includes ample reference to the parent-child relationship, and while he is correct about the appropriate dominance of the expectation that "natural parents" will raise their children responsibly, I disagree

---

6. Alan Donagan, *The Theory of Morality* (Chicago: University of Chicago Press, 1977), p. 101.

7. Donagan, *Theory of Morality*, p. 102.

with his assertion that adoption is "considered to be intrinsically inferior." I will allow that adoption is a secondary, rather than a primary, aim that emerges in dire necessity. This does not, however, suggest the label "inferior."

Donagan, however, captures an essential parental and covenantal precept of Judaism and Christianity. Among theologians, this precept has been forcefully stated by Paul Ramsey. In his characteristic appeal to *agape* and creation ordinance, he summarizes Judeo-Christian thought as follows:

> Nevertheless, we procreate new beings like ourselves in the midst of our love for one another, and in this there is a trace of the original mystery by which God created the world because of His love. God created nothing apart from His love; and without divine love was not anything made that was made. Neither should there be among men and women (whose man-womanhood — and not their minds or wills only — is in the image of God) any love set out of the context of responsibility for procreation, any begetting apart from the sphere of love.[8]

Ramsey writes that God binds together "nurturing marital love and procreation," an "original mystery" of God's covenant with creation *in imagine Dei* (in the image of God). Not to rear is "a refusal of the image of God's creation in our own."[9] Without quarreling over Ramsey's presentation of Christian expectations concerning covenantal bonds, I am asking when the mysterious connection between procreation and parental love might be reluctantly set aside, consistent with *agape,* in the best interests of the child.

Among Roman Catholic thinkers, few have been more articulate in affirming the importance and mystery of parental love than Gabriel Marcel. Marcel adds another important point: "But reflection shows us none the less clearly, that adoption must always be exceptional, that a society in which it became very frequent would be in danger of devitalization, for it can only be a graft of the tree of life, sometimes marvelous and sometimes, alas, abortive."[10] Marcel's understanding here is consistent with the

---

8. Paul Ramsey, *Fabricated Man: The Ethics of Genetic Control* (New Haven: Yale University Press, 1970), p. 38.

9. Ramsey, *Fabricated Man,* p. 39.

10. Gabriel Marcel, "The Creative Vow As Essence of Fatherhood," in *Homo Viator: Introduction to a Metaphysic of Hope,* trans. Emma Craufurd (Gloucester, Mass.: Peter Smith, 1978), p. 124.

principle of creation; but while there is a social vitality in parental rearing by birth parents (I do not side with Plato's utopia of state child rearing), I nevertheless find the word "devitalization" to be unfair to those many adoptive parents without whom society would suffer. Like Donagan, Marcel does not include sufficient positive evidence of the full contribution of adoption to social life. On a biographical note, Marcel and his wife adopted two children after they discovered that Mme. Marcel was sterile.

Among the Protestant theologians, Karl Barth offers an elevation of adoption that is both influential and intriguing. While he rightly emphasizes that the idea that birth parents should rear their child is central to Christian thought, he goes farther than other Protestant thinkers of which I am aware in stressing that child rearing by birth parents should not be absolutized. There will be practical circumstances ("ought implies can") that make rearing impossible to fulfill for biological parents. And "under divine command parenthood will necessarily involve readiness for exceptional circumstances" when it may be disturbed through providential necessity by God's "extraordinary claims and constraints."[11] More important, Barth holds that parents must realize that *"it is not their relationship to their children which is divine but the will of God in which this relationship is rooted."*[12] The First Commandment precludes idolatry: God may require that one reluctantly set aside a parental relationship at great sacrifice when the clear best interests of the child, whom God also loves, are at stake. The authority of parents ensconced in the command to honor father and mother is based on a "spiritual mission."[13] While "biological fatherhood has a weight and honor," the mission of parenting can be fulfilled "even apart from physical parenthood."[14] In the last analysis, "no human father, but God alone, is properly, truly, and primarily Father."[15] Thus the biological parents are relativized under divine freedom.

The Christian tradition provides an impressive cultural umbrella for the principle of rearing the children one brings into the world. The fact that Christianity creates a sacred canopy for rearing one's birth children is important, since the stability of cultural life and the well-being of the vast majority of children are both secured by this moral imperative. Nevertheless, Christianity also provides a sacred canopy for the adoptive family, and this is equally important. Barth, in particular, is the relevant thinker

11. Karl Barth, *Church Dogmatics* (Edinburgh: T. & T. Clark, 1961), III/4:285.
12. Barth, *Church Dogmatics*, III/4:285 (italics mine).
13. Barth, *Church Dogmatics*, III/4:244.
14. Barth, *Church Dogmatics*, III/4:244.
15. Barth, *Church Dogmatics*, III/4:245.

in this context. It may be in some small part the Barthian influence on evangelical Protestant Christianity in the Unites States that has elevated adoption to the pinnacle of moral idealism, for in the final analysis the only "real" parent of any child is God. The Anglins, as described in the next section, are more Barthian than they know, for they see in adoption *agape* love and couple this with a special sense of vocation to the adoption of children with special needs.

Acres of Hope (and the Mayan Dude Ranch)

The Barthian tone of evangelical Protestant practice is exemplified by the story of Patty Anglin, the child of missionary parents.[16] In 1969, her father decided to bring the family back to the United States from Africa. After suffering through her own divorce as well as her parent's separation, Patty met and married Harold Anglin. Their child, Thomas James or "T.J.," joined Patty's two children from her previous marriage and Harold's previous four children. Already the Anglins were becoming a large family. One day, while T.J. was still a toddler, a social worker came to their family church and spoke about the growing need for foster parents. Harold and Patty were deeply moved by the social worker's message about children who needed a loving environment or else could develop emotional problems, as well as social or learning disorders. "We felt God telling us that there was room for other kids and we should help them by providing a loving Christian foster-care environment for them."[17] Therefore, Harold and Patty decided to care for special needs infants during the first months of their lives after parental rights had been terminated by the court. The Anglins' biological children were also involved in the infants' lives; "[t]hey all took it in stride and in the process each of them developed a sensitivity of their own for special-needs children."[18]

Eventually, the Anglins were ready to open their home in Michigan to foster children. The first child they took in was a three-year-old Hispanic boy named Pedro. Although Patty and Harold were not aware of Pedro's exact family background, they agreed to give him a home. The Anglins were quite surprised when they were confronted with a crazy little

16. Patty Anglin with Joe Musser, *Acres of Hope: The Miraculous Story of One Family's Gift of Love to Children without Hope* (Uhrichsville, Ohio: Promise, 1999).

17. Anglin, *Acres of Hope,* p. 48.

18. Anglin, *Acres of Hope,* p. 50.

kid who tried to hit and kick everyone in sight. Harold finally grabbed Pedro and held him down for hours, while Pedro struggled to get away. The next day, the Anglins received a call from the social worker, who told them that Pedro had been one of eleven children who had been physically abused by their father. "The months that followed were very trying. I had to constantly call upon God for His help. We had to deal with all kinds of physical and emotional problems that Pedro acquired in his brief little life in that dysfunctional family."[19]

After fostering many different children, it became traumatic for the Anglins to give them up. "The anguish of giving up these children that we had come to love was awful."[20] Luckily for them, Pedro's biological father gave up custody, and Pedro was theirs. The process of adoption took three years, but it was worth it. Pedro eventually grew up into a "creative, intelligent, sensitive, personable, and wonderful human being. It was all there inside him when he came to us that day. We only had to peel back the layers of hurt and resentment that he had built as a defense mechanism."[21] Pedro was the first of many children whom the Anglins would come to love.

The Anglins took in other children like Pedro, each with specific problems and histories. Many of them had traumatic experiences growing up, a teenage mother who could not support them, or some form of disability. After Pedro, the Anglins adopted Cierra, who had a thirteen-year-old mother, and Serina, Cierra's little sister. Before the Anglins could continue their mission to take in these children, however, the family needed a new home. They were already running out of room and wanted a bigger yard where the children could play. "Harold and I had talked and dreamed about the possibility of moving to the West, maybe Montana, and finding an old small ranch and living off the land," said Patty. "However, a dream was all it was. I could never see a way for us to act on it."[22]

Before they knew it, though, the Anglins had an opportunity to make their dream come true. Harold was offered an early retirement package as an incentive for him to quit his job as a teacher at the local high school. Thus the Anglins had the opportunity to earn more money to buy a new home. They didn't decide whether Harold should take the offer until Patty went to visit her sister in Wisconsin. While there, she noticed a

19. Anglin, *Acres of Hope*, p. 59.
20. Anglin, *Acres of Hope*, p. 60.
21. Anglin, *Acres of Hope*, p. 65.
22. Anglin, *Acres of Hope*, p. 155.

farm across from a school building and immediately fell in love with it. Patty's sister, however, told her that the farmer who lived there was *not* willing to sell. Patty persisted, and took a drive down the long driveway to the house. Luckily, Patty met the farmer who owned it and he offered to take her on a tour of the two-hundred-acre farm. Patty told the farmer her story and explained that her family would love his property. She tentatively asked if he would sell, and after just a moment's pause, he agreed! Furthermore, the farmer agreed to sell for a very low price. After Patty checked with Harold back in Michigan, the Anglins acquired the two hundred acres, a farmhouse, barn, buildings, timber, grassland, cropland, and a beaver pond. "I recall praying as we drove down the lane with our family for the first time. *Lord, this farm is going to be for our children. This place is a vision I have as a safe haven for children, a place of hope. Acres and acres of hope. Yes, that's it! That'll be the name of our farm, Acres of Hope.*"[23] And just like that, the Anglins' dream came true.

Harold and Patty acquired some animals, and Harold learned how to farm. Everyone had different chores to do, but there was plenty of playing to be done in the hills or in the woods. After the Anglins bought *Acres of Hope,* they adopted children, an Indian boy named Ari, and two brothers, Tirzah and Tyler, who had lived in six different foster homes in just eighteen months. Soon afterward, Patty and Harold also took in Levi, a boy who had been placed in a dumpster by his drunken mother in Cincinnati, Ohio. Finally, the Anglins saved the life of little Zachary, who was born to Nigerian parents vacationing in America. The parents wished to kill the child, as was their custom when a baby has retardation.

Patty and Harold ended up with a total of fifteen children. The Anglins were kept busy advocating for special needs children in many ways. "The overwhelming majority of foster parents are not in it for the money. Most could do better financially at other jobs, even flipping hamburgers at the local fast food chain at minimum wage."[24] It was, in fact, Patty's love of children and belief that it was her mission in life to help them that drove her desire to take care of so many, especially ones with disabilities.

Patty Anglin is now the chairperson of Children's Health Alliance of Wisconsin. She works with families and agencies in Wisconsin to solve child heath issues and lobby for better state involvement in providing health care for children. She is also regional coordinator for Adopt Amer-

23. Anglin, *Acres of Hope,* p. 164.
24. Anglin, *Acres of Hope,* p. 272.

ica Network, helping hundreds of families find children like her own to adopt. Finally, Patty speaks at churches and addresses her concerns about adopting special needs kids. After all, she believes that "Jesus told us to look after the children, widows, and orphans. We *all* need to take responsibility for the problem and be part of its solution."[25] Patty invites us to "reach out in love to a needy child and give that little boy or girl something valuable — *love* and *hope*."[26]

Acres of Hope is the name of the Anglins' farm and their nonprofit organization, which is dedicated to helping children and giving emotional support and financial assistance to families dealing with children who have emotional or physical challenges. "In addition, our mission is to promote greater community understanding, acceptance, and support for families involved in adopting special-needs children cross-racially and cross-culturally."[27]

Is there anything especially Protestant about the Anglin story? Probably not, because one could point to very similar stories among Catholics. Moving from Wisconsin to Texas, we migrate south to the Mayan Dude Ranch, where three generations of the Hicks clan have grown up on a 350-acre spread. Patriarch and matriarch Don, 70, and Judy, 66, married for fifty years, had ten children and adopted two more. The family has grown to fifty-four members, including thirty grandchildren, eight of whom are adopted. Many have gone out into the world or live in other corners of Texas. All are practicing Roman Catholics. They feel that with all that God has done for them, adoption is the way to repay a bit. Adoption has become a tradition for them all, and they feel collectively that God is always wanting to bring more unwanted children into their arms.[28]

The media these days is replete with such examples of cross-racial, cross-ethnic, and cross-national adoption by parents who believe that what they are doing is a small gain for a better world freed of the in-group/out-group hostilities that the evolutionary psychologists argue are the flip side of in-group altruism. How much should we idealize adoption? Is it an equally valid first option along with rearing one's birth children? Protestant thought would not go this far.

25. Anglin, *Acres of Hope,* p. 281.

26. Anglin, *Acres of Hope,* p. 282.

27. Anglin, *Acres of Hope,* p. 288.

28. "From the Heart: Generations of Caring — One Family's Circle of Adoption," *Family Circle* (18 June 2002): 76-80.

Is It Self-Deception? The Evolutionary Psychologist's Suspicion

A story like the Anglins', ensconced in Protestant theology, rightly strains natural law assumptions about "is" and "ought." There is something a tad "unnatural" about adoption when viewed from the deterministic perspective of the "selfish gene" which only tolerates behaviors that launch it into the next generational cohort. A story such as the Anglins' throws a wrench in the thought world of evolutionary biologists, who tend to dismiss adoption because it undermines their theory that all human altruism is determined by genetic interests. David P. Barash, for example, with no significant evidence to support his proposition, treats adopting parents as psychologically confused by impulses left over from our hunter-gatherer past. "Each of us," he writes, "is a genetic slingshot, a catapult that shoots genes into the future."[29] Barash acknowledges that we are unique in "being able to say no to various biological imperatives, breeding not the least."[30] But the fact that we are capable of saying no does not mean that "we typically do so, or that it always feels good."[31] Barash does not think that, on a certain psychological level, adopting parents can possibly feel content: "After all, to adopt is to expend time and resources on behalf of someone unrelated to the adoptee."[32] It may seem like adoption is "genuine altruism (that is, beneficence toward another without compensation of either kin selection or reciprocity)," but according to Barash this is not really true.[33] He offers as evidence the fact that adoption is not most people's first choice, in that they would rather have biological offspring. I must quickly interject, however, that while many parents adopt after they have tried unsuccessfully to procreate, there are also many parents with biological children who also adopt, and there are many who adopt children without making any prior effort to procreate. Such adopting parents may do so out of spiritual commitments to the ideal of *agape* or unlimited love.[34]

Yet Barash, who draws on none of the significant existing social scientific studies about the human experience of relinquishment and adop-

---

29. David P. Barash, *Revolutionary Biology: The New, Gene-Centered View of Life* (New Brunswick, N.J.: Transaction, 2001), p. 139.
30. Barash, *Revolutionary Biology*, p. 139.
31. Barash, *Revolutionary Biology*, p. 139.
32. Barash, *Revolutionary Biology*, p. 149.
33. Barash, *Revolutionary Biology*, p. 149.
34. Anglin, *Acres of Hope*.

tion, simply asserts that it can be only unsatisfactory because it flies in the face of his theoretical models. While adoption may satisfy the evolutionary desire to be a parent, he believes that it can never be ultimately fulfilling. Moreover, in a remarkable exhibition of undocumented assertions, Barash argues that when adoption evolved in small hunter-gatherer groups, the adopted child was likely to have been a genetic relative, satisfying the demands of kin altruism; in addition, it surely resulted in various forms of reciprocity from the group at large, satisfying the demands of Tit for Tat game theory. Adoption today, Barash concludes, is merely an evolutionary holdover. The problem with Barash's reasoning is that he knows nothing about the history and practice of adoption; if he did, he would realize that it does not fit his theoretical models.

Yet such reasoning contains a grain of truth. The genealogical family combines the bearing and rearing of the child in a manner that nature recommends. A married couple's wish to have their "own" child captures something fundamental and "good."[35] There is no question that the sciences of evolutionary biology and evolutionary psychology, grounded in the biological investment of parents in continuing their genotype into future generations, support the fundamental nature of the drive to raise a child of one's own making. A mother and father see themselves in the child; correlatively, the child benefits from identifying his or her biological lineage, although this is hardly essential for a child's thriving. The successful practice of adoption, however, is proof that parents do transcend the "selfish gene" of the early-school evolutionary biologists, and that children do prosper without the narrative of a biological lineage.

The importance of connecting bearing and rearing is reflected in the fact that the adoptive parent-child relationship has been described in law with the terms "as-if-begotten" and "as-if-genealogical."[36] The adopted child is granted a new birth certificate. The adopting parents are even sometimes matched with the child's basic physiological features, enabling the adopting parents to take on the characteristics of birth parents so the child will not "miss" a sense of biological ancestry. This mimicry, however, strikes me as biased against adoption, and is increasingly rare in adoption practice. Moreover, current practice is to inform the child of the adoption, which

35. William Werpehowski, "The Vocation of Parenthood: A Response to Stephen Post," *Journal of Religious Ethics* 25, no. 1 (spring 1997): 178.

36. Judith S. Modell, *Kinship with Strangers: Adoption and Interpretations of Kinship in American Culture* (Berkeley: University of California Press, 1994), p. 2.

makes mimicry futile.[37] The majority of adoptive parents inform the child early, generally around age five, although some wait longer.[38] This mimicry also has the unfortunate result of implying that the genealogical family is the "real" one, and creates the unfortunate perception of the adoptive family as inferior to the biological one. Adoption does not need mimicry. Instead, it should be exalted for the salutary love that it manifests.

Adoption is a vivid counter-gene practice; it puts the almighty gene in its place. The gene has been described as "a cultural icon, a symbol, almost a magical force" and as the secular equivalent of the soul: "Fundamental to identity, DNA seems to explain individual differences, moral order, and human fate."[39] Sociologist Marque-Luisa Mirangoff has defined genetic welfare as a distinctive worldview that insists on degrees of genetic perfection, somewhat to the detriment of the social welfare orientation that stresses environment and social intervention.[40] People begin to see the world differently. "The emergence of Genetic Welfare," writes Mirangoff, "unlike the 'passionate movements' of the past, is a quiet revolution insinuating itself into everyday life in incremental fashion."[41]

The impact of a religious system and culture on the practice of adoptive parenting suggests that human beings are not narrowly determined by their genes, and that parental love can transcend the biological parent-child axis in the practice of adoption. It transcends this kin axis in other, even wider ways as well. Insofar as natural law theory, despite is essential validity in this context, overlooks the plasticity of parental love as manifest in the "good" of adoption, it misses something important.

Some Concluding Reflections

Parental love is a complex phenomenon. It is not unlimited, because it sometimes grows weary, cold, overly controlling, and even vengeful. There

37. Mary Watkins and Susan Fisher, *Talking with Young Children about Adoption* (New Haven: Yale University Press, 1993).

38. Marshall D. Schecter and Doris Bertocci, "The Meaning of the Search," in *The Psychology of Adoption,* ed. David M. Brodzinsky and Marshall D. Schecter (New York: Oxford University Press, 1990), pp. 62-90.

39. D. Nelkin and M. S. Lindee, *The DNA Mystique: The Gene As a Cultural Icon* (New York: Freeman, 1995), p. 2.

40. Marque-Luisa Mirangoff, *The Social Costs of Genetic Welfare* (New Brunswick, N.J.: Rutgers University Press, 1991).

41. Mirangoff, *Social Costs,* p. 24.

are doubtless some elements in this love that might be described as proprietary and even solipsistic — "I love this child because he or she looks like me and, with luck, will pursue more or less the same success in life that I have pursued." Parental love may not appreciate the importance of differentiation in the life of the child, who must establish his or her own identity. Thus one can argue against reproductive cloning, in which even the differentiating substrate of genetic uniqueness is lost.

But there is no serious question that this imperfect human love, which may be more or less limited, is the basis for whatever capacities we have for deep universal compassion. Such love seems, judging from the dominance of the parental metaphor in both the Hebrew Bible and the New Testament, to represent the most orthodox and simultaneously the most suggestive heuristic key into what is the universe's greatest wonder and mystery.

Love implies an interest in and a concern for another that sets aside recalcitrant and adversarial impulses. We humans are mammals who nestle and cuddle our young, and we feel affection and compassion for them. Like many other mammalian species, a law of self-sacrifice emerges whereby parents invest in their offspring and even lay down their lives for their children. This parental quality of sacrifice is clearly one of the reasons why mammals, and humans in particular, have succeeded. Spirituality is in large part the endeavor to extend such loving affections to all humanity, including the weak and even one's enemies.

Of all loves, the most faithful is parental love. Parents usually take special interest in and responsibility for even the most imperiled newborns and debilitated children. They keep an open door for their children even when adolescence becomes difficult and opportunities are squandered. They try to sustain and enhance life. The Anglican thinker Dorothy L. Sayers summarized biblical images of the parenthood of God: "In books and sermons we express the relation between God and mankind in terms of human parenthood."[42] And she adds this: "When we use these expressions, we know perfectly well that they are metaphors and analogies; what is more, we know perfectly well where the metaphor begins and ends."[43] We know that God does not procreate in the same sense as humans do, and we are using the analogy with a kind and benevolent parent in mind rather than a careless, cruel, and injudicious one. The metaphor

42. Dorothy L. Sayers, *The Mind of the Maker* (San Francisco: Harper Collins, 1987), p. 25.

43. Sayers, *Mind of the Maker,* p. 25.

is limited to the best kinds of behavior on the part of parents, and nothing less. Even at this, we know that such metaphor is somewhat anthropomorphic, yet we measure God by our own experience because we have no other experience from which to measure. All our thinking about God is analogical, as Thomas Aquinas underscored. As Sayers wrote of this analogical theologizing, "We need not be surprised at this, still less suppose that because it is analogical it is therefore valueless or without any relation to truth. The fact is, that all language about everything is analogical; we think in a series of metaphors."[44]

Adoption is a remarkable, splendid, genetically unleashed expression of parental love which approximates *agape*. While the importance of parental love is not a new theological idea, it is always in need of articulation. John Fiske, the philosopher-theologian of Harvard, wrote an important and classic essay in 1899 entitled *Through Nature to God*.[45] In this work Fiske argued that the central fact in the evolution of *Homo sapiens* is prolonged infancy and its principle correlative, deepened parental love. Fiske, who was theologically reflective, stated that he found the then new word "altruism" unattractive, but useful for rapport with the social sciences. He too saw the beginnings of altruism in maternal care as "no doubt the earliest; it was the derivative source from which all other kinds were by slow degrees developed."[46] The instincts and emotions related to the preservation of offspring were favored and cultivated by natural selection as the alternative to extinction, and they achieved an apex in human parental love as "cherishing another life than one's own."[47] Furthermore, "the capacity for unselfish devotion called forth in that relation could afterward be utilized in the conduct of individuals not thus related to one another."[48] The section in which Fiske develops this thesis is entitled "The Cosmic Roots of Love and Self-Sacrifice," for he believed that the emergence of such cherishing love resulted from the ethical trend of the universe and represented the pinnacle of cosmic creativity. With the lengthening of human infancy, more powerful affective capacities for compassion and love evolved. Fiske thus provided an interpretation of Darwinian evolution that was contrary to Thomas Huxley and Herbert Spencer, whose writings in the 1890s captured only the brutal aspects of the survival of the fittest.

44. Sayers, *Mind of the Maker,* p. 23.
45. John Fiske, *Through Nature to God* (Boston: Houghton Mifflin, 1899).
46. Fiske, *Through Nature to God,* p. 121.
47. Fiske, *Through Nature to God,* p. 120.
48. Fiske, *Through Nature to God,* p. 121.

This chapter is intended to be suggestive, within a broadly Protestant perspective, of the ways in which the scope of parental love can be widened. Under the right cultural influences, such love is able to embrace the relinquished child in the practice of adoption, leaving aside all genetic concerns. It can be transposed into the higher key of love for all humanity through a theology of adoption, which is both Pauline and Barthian and, if I might coin a word, Josephian. Yet even untransposed, parental love is part of the divine economy in which each of us can experience the unique attentiveness and undivided concern of a mother and father, from which we are able to make analogical leaps in imagining what divine love must be like.

9. Suffering the Suffering Children: Christianity and the Rights and Wrongs of Adoption

TIMOTHY P. JACKSON

Suffer the little children to come unto me, and forbid them not: for of such is the kingdom of God.

MARK 10:14 KJV

Through much of recorded history . . . adoption by nonrelatives has been utilized more to meet the needs of adults than to help children.

ADAM PERTMAN[1]

We are fighting abortion with adoption.

MOTHER TERESA[2]

Introduction

Christians have compelling reasons to pay close attention to adoption practices. These reasons may occasion both pride and embarrassment. On the one hand, Christian charity has traditionally called on the faithful to care for the needy and vulnerable, especially children, and this virtue has made the church a supporter and facilitator of many admirable adop-

---

1. Adam Pertman, *Adoption Nation: How the Adoption Revolution Is Transforming America* (New York: Basic, 2000), p. 20.
2. Quoted in "Mother Teresa: A Film by Ann and Jeanette Petrie" (Petrie Productions, distributed by Dorason Corporation, 1986).

tions. Christianity itself grew out of God's "adoption" of the Gentiles, the gracious extension of a covenant to those not originally God's people. According to some accounts, Jesus himself was "adopted" either by Joseph or by God. Therefore, a positive attitude toward adoption is tied to the very identity of Christian belief and believers.

On the other hand, various Christian ideals have served to condemn certain adoptions as unnatural or vicious, thus making life miserable for all those involved in the adoptive relation. For example, conceptions of a divine separation of the races have led some Christians to reject interracial adoption as against God's will, even as conceptions of a divine endorsement of heterosexual monogamy have led other Christians to oppose single-parent and gay or lesbian adoption.

The issue is not simply whether Christian churches or individuals endorse or reject particular adoption practices; rather, it is *how* these practices are approached that makes a crucial difference. Even where adoption is championed, the method may be cruel or counter-productive. Shaming unwilling or vulnerable young mothers into surrendering their offspring, for instance, is itself a shameful practice, whether supposedly motivated by Christian *agape* or not. Facilitating a willing transfer of parental oversight for the sake of a better life for a child is, in contrast, to aid a Christ-like self-sacrifice.

This chapter aims to clarify Christianity's historical judgments of, and contributions to, adoption theory and practice — admittedly, a mixed picture. It has five sections. Section I examines how the Bible defines adoption, noting how a fundamental complexity here bears on Christian attitudes toward the practice. Section II looks at the rights that ground the moral and legal permissibility of adoption and how they relate to the Christian notion of sanctity. Section III investigates the ethics of single-parent and gay adoption as particularly pressing issues. Section IV looks briefly at the right of adoptees to know their biological identities and that of their birth parents. Finally, in Section V, I return to explicitly biblical themes and ask how views on christology affect basic perceptions of adoption.

My enduring assumption is unremarkable but worth stating: no mother or father should be intimidated, shamed, or coerced into surrendering her or his child for adoption, unless the parent is demonstrably negligent or abusive, but voluntary adoption is sometimes the most loving act *for* the child and *by* the birth parent. My specific theses are more substantive and controversial: (a) adoption is not merely the bestowal of a new (legally created) identity but also the acknowledgement of a pre-existing (divinely created) humanity; (b) the primary adoption right is that of orphaned, unwanted, destitute, or abused children to be adopted; (c) it is the sanctity of these children's lives, rather than their dignity, that gives them the positive right to be cared for by conscientious adults;[3] and (d) attention to the sanctity rights of adoptive children should move us to permit both single adults and same-sex couples to adopt.

Traditional conceptions of Joseph and Mary, Jesus and God, can both aid and hinder a proper appreciation of the morality of adoption, so Christian theologians ought to make it abundantly clear why adoption is (or should be) an act of love rather than a shameful secret. As with artificial contraception and assisted reproductive technology, this will require reevaluating the ancient Alexandrian principle that having sex without getting children and getting children without oneself having had sex are inherently illicit. The principle should be amended, I argue, but not merely set aside.

I. Biblical Definitions and a Key Complexity

There is no endorsement, or even explicit mention, of adoption as an ongoing practice in Old Testament law. There are, in effect, three references to *acts* of adoption — of Moses (Exod. 2:10), Genubath (1 Kings 11:20), and Esther (Esther 2:7, 15) — but, as is often noted, these all take place outside of Palestine and thus in contexts foreign to Jewish rule and custom.[4] Torah tradition as such simply does not admit that someone who is not one's biological child can be rendered one's son or daughter by legal act (see the essay in this volume by Michael Broyde). It was Saint Paul who first introduced the notion of adoption into Judeo-Christian theology.

The New Testament Greek word translated by the NRSV as "adoption" is *huiothesia,* from *huios* (meaning "son") and *tithemi* (meaning "to put or place"). The term appears five times in Paul's epistles (Rom. 8:15; 8:23; 9:4; Gal. 4:5; and Eph. 1:5), but not once in the Gospels. Construed literally, *huiothesia* is gendered and connotes a placing or taking in of someone as a male heir. The *International Standard Bible Encyclopedia* (ISBE) defines

---

3. A negative right is a claim not to be interfered with, not to have something taken from one, while a positive right is a claim to be actively assisted, to have something provided for one independently of personal effort or merit.

4. My colleague Hendrik Boers has pointed out to me that, although these adoption *locations* were outside of Jewish rule, the *stories* are not simply records of the incidents and do partly reflect Jewish custom.

the word, generally, as "the legal process by which a man might bring into his family, and endow with the status and privileges of a son, one who was not by nature his son or of his kindred."[5] One can readily see why Paul — that liminal figure at the dividing line between the historical Jesus and the Holy Spirit, Judaism and Christianity, Rome and barbarism — would have been attracted to adoption metaphors. In many ways, he knew himself to have been an outsider graciously allowed in: a man who never met the historical Jesus called nevertheless to be an apostle, a persecutor of the early Christian church converted into its greatest champion, as well as a Pharisaic Jew enabled to be a Roman citizen. It was definitive of Paul's genius that he saw in his personal experiences a model of God's way with the wider world and was able to translate this into a powerful message of gifted salvation: "when the fullness of time had come, God sent his Son, born of a woman, born under the law, in order to redeem those who were under the law, so that we might receive adoption as children" (Gal. 4:4-5 NRSV).

The ISBE's general definition of adoption captures Paul's central theological usage, but it also hides an important complexity. In the Greco-Roman culture against whose background Paul wrote, the "placing" associated with *huiothesia*[6] evidently involved either (1) the production of a new (legal) identity for someone who was not a natural son, or (2) the affirmation of a pre-existing (legal) identity of someone who was in fact a natural son.[7] "Adoption" entailed, that is, either the generation of an entirely novel filial status or the recognition and formal celebration of a filial status that was already real, though perhaps denied, occluded, or only partially realized. When a Roman boy came of legal age, for instance, he might be said to be "taken in" or "adopted" by his father as heir. Or when a prodigal son mended his ways and returned to his home and biological family, his father might welcome him and "place" him back into the domestic fold as again a son. The first case is a rite of passage in which a

---

5. T. Rees, entry for "Adoption," §IV, in *The International Standard Bible Encyclopedia*, ed. James Orr, Search God's Word website, http://www.searchgodsword.org/enc/isb/view.cgi?number=T221. Accessed 10 April 2004. This view is shared by *Easton's Bible Dictionary*, which defines "adoption" as "the giving to anyone the name and place and privileges of a son who is not a son by birth" ("Adoption," Bible Tools website, http://bibletools.org//index.cfm/fuseaction/Def.show/RTD/Easton/Topic/Adoption. Accessed 10 April 2004).

6. The Latin equivalent is *adoptio* or *arrogatio (adrogatio)*, depending on whether the son is or is not still under his birth father's legal authority *(patria potestas)*.

7. See W. E. Vine, Merrill F. Unger, and William White Jr., *Vine's Complete Expository Dictionary of Old and New Testament Words* (Nashville: Thomas Nelson, 1996), s.v. "adoption."

present identity is fulfilled, while the second case is a painful trial in which a proper identity is rediscovered. But both are very different from a transformation in which an altogether alien identity is conferred. Even if a biological son has, in some sense, publicly to grow into himself, this "adoptive" process is one of maturation in which intrinsic attributes are unfolded, rather than a whole-cloth change imported or imposed from without.

The pressing question asks itself: Is the "adoption" referred to by Paul in Ephesians, Romans, and elsewhere the production of a new identity or the affirmation of an old one? Is the adoptive operation an "artificial" contrivance engineered by God alone, or does it have an "ontological" basis in human nature? Putting the query yet a third way, do even elect human beings come short of being naturally God's children, such that Christ's agency changes their very essence, or does the Messiah's life, death, and resurrection reveal a filial relation with God the Father that is already (part of) humanity's birthright?

I can only sum up the studied ambivalence of the Christian tradition by answering "both/and." Many orthodox theologians have held that being made "in the image of God" (Gen. 1:27) is an empirical fact about humanity, and that this created identity constitutes a "resemblance to" or "consanguinity with" God, in some analogical sense.[8] We are by nature God's "children," rather than God's accidents, playthings, or victims, and even the fall into sin has not totally destroyed this "genetic" legacy. Even so, the infinite qualitative difference between creature and Creator remains. Only Christ, the second person of the Trinity, is of one substance with the Father; only Christ, the eternal Son, is begotten not made. Moreover, after the dawn of sin, Christ's redemptive act on the cross is an indispensable means of restoring right relation with God. The believer's adoption as son or daughter, his or her being filled with the Holy Spirit so as to address the Deity with "Abba" (Rom. 8:15-17), is not simply a recognition of a pre-existing reality but is also a "new creation" (2 Cor. 5:17). The new creation must have some continuity with the old — how else can I say that it is *I* who am saved? — but it is not enough to be reminded that we are images of God. We must be not merely edified, but ransomed, as a free man might purchase a slave out of captivity (cf. Rom. 7:14). All are in

---

8. Some theologians — e.g., Karl Barth, Helmut Thielicke, and Karen Lebacqz — prefer to see the *imago*, or what is sometimes referred to as the "dignity" of human life, as a relational phenomenon, a matter of God's grace rather than anything inherent in human beings. As understandable as this is as a safeguard against both pride and despair, however, it threatens the biblical doctrine of the goodness of creation.

bondage to the law and to sin (Rom. 3:9), and no amount of repentant introspection or just external action can liberate us. Still, God does not just annihilate the old order, God redeems it.

Indeed, Christ wins for the faithful even more than Adam lost in the fall. The elect are eventually sealed in permanent and loving communion with God beyond anything experienced by the innocent first parents in the Garden. The adoption made possible by the Redeemer builds on incarnate human nature, so to speak, but it is, most dramatically, an inbreaking of eternity into time. As such, our adoption is itself incomplete, both here and not yet. Through the practice of faith, hope, and love, human beings can have a foretaste of the new creation in history ("the first fruits of the Spirit"), but full adoption ("the redemption of our bodies") comes only in heaven and must be awaited with patience (Rom. 8:18-25).

In short, the distinction between sonship-created and sonship-recognized is not always clear-cut, in either Roman society or biblical theology.[9] Rather than lamenting this complexity, however, we can and should appreciate its implications for contemporary adoption. Even as the "sacred" adoption of individuals through Christ is partly God's recreation of them in the image of God's Son and partly God's affirmation of them as already made in God's image, so the "secular" adoption of individuals through the courts should be seen as having two sides or moments. On the one hand, secular adoption as currently practiced is the bestowing of a new legal identity on someone, male or female, who is not one's biological progeny. It is a matter of *invention* in the sense that filial rights and responsibilities now obtain by judicial fiat, where formerly there had been none. On the other hand, secular adoption is also the recognition of the shared humanity of the one adopted, his or her needs and potentials. In spite of loose talk about "adopting" a highway or a tree, the adoption that inaugurates a novel civic identity and familial relation is not purely arbitrary. Positive law does not generate human beings, or even legal heirs, *ex nihilo*. There are reasons why someone is or ought to be adopted, reasons stemming from our *discovery* of his or her indelible sanctity. Or so I will argue.

---

9. Even the possible senses in which Jesus was adopted, either by God or by Joseph, have been much debated by Christians. When, for example, God says of Jesus, "You are my Son, the Beloved; with you I am well pleased" (Mark 1:11 NRSV, at Jesus' baptism) or "This is my Son, the Beloved; listen to him" (Mark 9:7 NRSV, at Jesus' transfiguration), is this a statement that describes reality, a performative that alters it, or perhaps both? The question becomes particularly complicated when one compares parallel passages, such as Matthew 3:17 and 17:5. I will return to the question of Jesus' nature in Section V, but here I focus on humanity's "adoption as sons" (Gal. 4:5 RSV) and how it bears on civil adoption.

Let me now elaborate on the meaning of sanctity by first contrasting it with dignity and then relating both notions to the idea of rights.

II. Dignity, Sanctity, and Their Correlative Rights

"Dignity," as I define it, is a contingent achievement: a function of either the meritorious exercise of personal agency or, minimally, the bare possession of such agency. In either case, dignity inheres only in individuals sufficiently mature to be aware of themselves and their intentional plans across time. Dignity requires, that is, a robust sense of self. (The Latin term *dignitas* means "a being worthy" and originally applied to those few persons or political offices filled with grandeur and authority.[10]) Entailing an admirable or powerful display of self-governance, dignity, in turn, inspires respect in others. The dignity of persons, their rational autonomy, moved Immanuel Kant, for instance, to insist that they be treated as ends and not as means only.[11] Free agents are intrinsically valuable and not merely instruments to the maximization of others' utility.

Only persons, defined as autonomous subjects, have dignity. Insofar as fetuses and infants are not yet self-conscious agents, they lack dignity in the technical sense and thus are not the subjects of respect. They are pre-persons. Insofar as the profoundly retarded are not and never will be morally self-aware, they too are without dignity. They are nonpersons. And insofar as the permanently comatose and demented are no longer autonomous, they are nondignified post-persons.[12]

If "dignity" refers to contingent personal achievement, "sanctity," in contrast, refers to essential human nature. As I understand it, it is a function of universal human needs and potentials that do not presuppose self-awareness, self-control, or any other temporal attainment. (The Latin word *sanctitas* denotes "inviolability, sacredness" and was originally at home in a religious context.[13]) The relevant qualities include the need for

10. See Charlton T. Lewis and Charles Short, *A Latin Dictionary* (New York: Oxford University Press, 1987), s.v. *dignitas*.

11. Immanuel Kant, *The Critique of Practical Reason*, 5:87, in *The Cambridge Edition of the Works of Immanuel Kant: Practical Philosophy*, trans. Mary J. Gregor (Cambridge: Cambridge University Press, 1996), p. 210.

12. I do not mean to imply that Kant would conclude that fetuses, infants, the mentally handicapped, the comatose, and/or the demented may properly be treated as mere means to an end, but I do maintain that he gives us little or no basis on which to resist this conclusion.

13. Lewis and Short, *Latin Dictionary*, s.v. *sanctitas*.

food, shelter, clothing, and companionship, and/or the potential for growth, awareness, intelligence, emotion, and inspiration. If dignity calls forth respect, sanctity calls forth reverence; if dignity moves others not to thwart one's noumenal self, then sanctity calls on others to cultivate one's vulnerable soul. Shared human needs and potentials are not so much intrinsically valuable as the necessary conditions for value itself. On my reading of the Christian tradition, the most basic form of sanctity is the need or ability to give or receive agapic love. To give or receive such love is to know eternal life, to be a child of God.

And who, specifically, is a child of God? Even though fetuses, early infants, the retarded, and the demented are not dignified "persons" (i.e., not rational agents), they are nevertheless sacred human beings. If, to repeat, the measure of sanctity is the need or ability to give or receive agapic love, then the very young, the very old, and the very diminished "count." They all share our human needs and can profitably *receive* love, even if they cannot self-consciously give it.

The sanctity of human lives has a claim on us that is utterly unearned and entirely inalienable. I call this claim a "sanctity right," and it stems from human need and/or potential; it has nothing to do with past merit or demerit, present contract or breach of contract, or future status or lack of status. Moreover, the claim is not merely to inviolability, as in the case of dignity, but also to active assistance. Regardless of whether orphaned or unwanted children have been culpably injured by others, for example, it is the duty of those responsible for the common good (both church and state) to see to it that the children find a loving home. Tragic accident or natural calamity may be responsible for the fate of these children, but their "sanctity rights" to nurturance obtain in any case. They have, I maintain, a right to be adopted that precedes the interests and contingent choices of would-be parents.[14] Those in authority have a duty

---

14. There is precedent for the right I am defending. Section 28 of the South African Constitution, for example, specifies that "Every child has the right — . . . (b) to family or parental care, or to appropriate alternative care when removed from the family environment; . . [and] (d) to be protected from maltreatment, neglect, abuse or degradation" (quoted in Barbara Bennett Woodhouse, "The Constitutionalization of Children's Rights: Incorporating Emerging Human Rights into Constitutional Doctrine," *University of Pennsylvania Journal of Constitutional Law* 2, no. 1 [December 1999], University of Pennsylvania Law website, http://www.law.upenn.edu/journals/conlaw/issues/vol2/num1/woodhouse/node5_tf.html). The South African document is marred, I believe, by its attempt to ground children's rights in "dignity" rather than "sanctity," but the overall thrust of its case is clear and cogent. See also the United Nations' "Declaration of the Rights of the Child"

of charity to enlist and empower adoptive parents to care for needy children, rather than waiting for such parents to present themselves or for such children to seem appealing.[15]

In our late capitalist culture, it is hard not to assume that all things are either dignified persons or fungible property. It is hard, that is, to find the cultural space to recognize the sanctity of human life. If children are products with only use-value for their parents and/or the larger society, rather than human beings with sanctity in and of themselves, then the rights of would-be parents are consumer rights or property rights. If dignity rights are the only kind that are legally enforceable, as some have argued,[16] then being without dignity makes young children into mere commodities, at least for purposes of the law. How they are treated — indeed, whether they are suffered to live — is thus a matter of personal choice for others rather than of human decency for themselves. If, in contrast, even pre-linguistic children have a sanctity that is morally and legally significant, then the language of "free choice" and "consumer options" for adoptive (and biological) parents must give way to that of "human rights" and "loving care" for adopted children.[17]

I will eventually note the limits of the language of "rights" with respect to adoption, but the foregoing suggests an important clarification of that language. When talk of "rights" is used in adoption contexts, it is usually with reference to *the negative rights of would-be parents to adopt,* their right not to be legally restricted because of race, creed, gender, age, national origin, income level, marital status, or sexual orientation. This is a reflection of the fact that rights are normally attributed to autonomous adults, self-conscious agents who have "personal dignity."[18] Personal dignity rights are

---

(1959) and "Convention on the Rights of the Child" (1989), especially Articles 20 and 21 of the latter.

15. Thomas Aquinas is at best misleading when he writes that "man does not make him worthy whom he adopts; but rather in adopting him he chooses one who is already worthy" (Aquinas, *Summa Theologica,* trans. Fathers of the English Dominican Province, IIIa, q. 23, a. 1 [Westminster, Md.: Christian Classics, 1981], p. 2141). Like all sanctity rights, the right to be adopted does not depend on achieved worthiness but on intrinsic nature.

16. See, for instance, Ronald Dworkin, *Life's Dominion: An Argument about Abortion, Euthanasia, and Individual Freedom* (New York: Knopf, 1993), and Peter Singer, *Rethinking Life and Death: The Collapse of Our Traditional Ethics* (Oxford: Oxford University Press, 1995).

17. On the perverting influence of consumerist language on our understanding of adoption, see Rickie Solinger, *Beggars and Choosers: How the Politics of Choice Shapes Adoption, Abortion, and Welfare in the United States* (New York: Hill and Wang, 2001).

18. See my *The Priority of Love: Christian Charity and Social Justice* (Princeton, N.J.: Princeton University Press, 2003), especially ch. 5.

important, but they are not the only or even the most important variety of moral claim in adoption contexts. In fact, the impersonal interests of needy children are increasingly being placed center-stage in adoption debates. *The positive sanctity rights of children to be adopted* matter decisively.

Once the difference between dignity rights and sanctity rights is recognized, we can appreciate the possible conflict between personal claims by parents or society, on the one hand, and impersonal claims for adoptees, on the other. Does a woman who does not wish to carry a pregnancy to term have the right to kill the fetus or only to be free of the burden of its (late) gestation and (later) child care?[19] How do we balance her dignity with the sanctity of the life she is carrying, a life which may eventually be put up for adoption? Does an intermittently dysfunctional pair of birth parents have the right to retrieve their children from foster care over and over again, thus submitting the children to repeated traumas of dislocation? How do we weigh the claims of blood against the well-being of the brood? In cases of transracial or transnational adoption, do the adoptive parents have the right to choose the culture and/or religion in which their children will be raised, or should they feel obliged to learn about the race and native creed of their adoptive offspring and teach them about the same? How, in such cases, do we promote what much of the Christian tradition has taught should be a central concern of well-ordered sexuality: the care and education of children?[20] Do heterosexual couples have the exclusive right to adopt, when single parents or gay couples might provide a more caring home for the children? How do we substantiate or gainsay the traditional judgment that gay and lesbian relations are intrinsically disordered, "abominations" or "degrading passions" that are "unnatural" and "contrary to right reason"?[21]

We can only begin to adjudicate the "rights" and "wrongs" of adoption by placing primacy on the sanctity rights of needy children. What suffering children need most is a secure and loving environment, and the

19. Early on in pregnancy, the only way to escape the burden of gestation is an abortion that kills the embryo or fetus, but after about the twenty-third week, a C-section can often lead to "live birth" and thus to the possibility of adoption. Moreover, technology is pushing the survival date for "premies" further and further back. Although it strikes me as a Gnostic nightmare, we may eventually see MEG (mechanical external gestation) remove pregnancy from the female body altogether.

20. See, for example, Thomas Aquinas, *Summa Theologica*, "Supplement to Part 3," q. 49.

21. See, for example, Lev. 18:22; Rom. 1:26-27; and Aquinas, *Summa Theologica*, IIa IIae, q. 154, aa. 11 and 12.

best interests of these children dictate that they be placed in whatever situation best promises such ongoing support. Keeping biologically related families intact remains an important goal, but it does not trump all other factors. Rather than social service offices always struggling to return foster care infants to their birth parents, which often means shuttling the infants back and forth between volatile homes and multiple caretakers, the governing ideal is rightly stability and permanence.[22] The rights of the biological parents may be forfeited if they are repeatedly drug dependent, abusive, neglectful, or otherwise unwilling or unable to care consistently for their children. Conversely, some single, gay, disabled, and older parents are equally capable of attending to the needs and potentials of adoptive children as some married, heterosexual, healthy, and younger couples. In other words, *agape* can and does govern many "nontraditional" relations and households, even as it governs many traditional ones.

Once we acknowledge that "natural" family bonds can be severed from within, and that this severance licenses the state to intervene, then we must affirm a "political" right to be adopted or else we are simply whistling in the dark. If there is no right to be adopted, then it may actually be hurtful to hold up stability and permanence as child-care desiderata, since these will seem cruel illusions to many in distress. To insist on a needy child's right to be adopted is not, need I say, to imply that each individual in society has a personal duty to adopt. Quite specific circumstances may *occasionally* translate into a perfect duty to adopt, at least for a Christian, as when one's sibling and his or her spouse both die, leaving one's niece or nephew orphaned. But these cases are rare. I am maintaining, rather, that society as a whole has an imperfect duty to provide adequate adoption possibilities for its members.[23] In addition to the direct claim that sanctity has on us, the motive for this duty of beneficence may be found, in part, in a collective sense of gratitude for the unearned care that we ourselves have received — starting, if we are lucky, with our parents but including essential social services to which we have not antecedently contributed. The primary motive for Christians, however, is not intra-human indebtedness or reciprocity; it stems from the fact that we are loved first by God and are called on, in turn, to incarnate a holy will toward our neighbors (1 John 4:10-21). In spite of human powerlessness

22. Cf. Pertman, *Adoption Nation*, p. 215.

23. A perfect duty specifies precise details of obligatory action and often applies to a particular person, whereas an imperfect duty leaves more room to maneuver and often applies to a group.

and sin (Rom. 5:6-8), human needs and potentials are attended to by the God who is agapic love, and finite agents are commanded to do likewise.

In baptism, the whole congregation promises to help raise the child, so there is a theological model of the kind of communal responsibility I have in mind. Moreover, adoption services need not always be handled governmentally, through the state. Churches and other nonprofit organizations and communities can take on the responsibilities involved, with the state applauding and licensing, but not directly running, a host of faith-based or social-justice-based initiatives.[24] Such initiatives have the virtue of keeping family creation close to the parties most immediately involved, in accordance with the principle of subsidiarity.[25] Some worry that "independent" adoptions that work outside of governmental agencies are readily corrupted by financial incentives, and the so-called "gray market" in adoptable children does at times approximate baby selling. So even a proponent of subsidiarity, such as myself, must affirm the state's proper (if limited) place in regulating adoption procedures.

To flesh out and back up these claims, let me examine in more detail two forms of adoption called by some "abominable" and by others "liberating": single and homosexual adoption. These forms of adoption clearly challenge traditional conceptions of sex, marriage, and the family. But how should we understand them, morally, when focus is on the sanctity of the children involved, rather than the dignity of the would-be adoptive parents or the utility of the general society?

III. Abomination, Liberation, and Two Controversial Forms of Adoption

Nontraditional adoption crosses time-honored boundaries (for example, of race and ethnicity) and/or calls into question the meaning of gender in marriage (as in, for example, gay and lesbian unions). Sometimes the undermining of social divisions or the blurring of familial boundaries is deeply troubling and harmful. Most of us would agree, for instance, that the Bible rightly calls incest, child-sacrifice, and bestiality "abominations" (Lev. 18:6-30). The devastating effects of these practices are well-documented. At other times, however, past distinctions between groups or types of people are themselves destructive and in need of subversion.

24. I wish to thank Brent Waters, Mary Stewart Van Leeuwen, Stephen Presser, and John Witte for helping me to clarify the points made in this paragraph.

25. For more on this principle, see the essay by Lisa Cahill in this volume.

Few of us would now applaud the idea that it is an "abomination" for the Egyptians to eat with the Hebrews (Gen. 43:32) or an incitement to "prostitution" for ethnic groups to intermarry (Exod. 34:16).[26]

Is nontraditional adoption necessarily abominable, or might it actually be liberating for all concerned? The basic meaning of the word "abominable" is indicated by its etymology, which *The Oxford English Dictionary* notes is either *absit + omen* or *ab + homine*.[27] The former possibility, which I will call "the theological reading," is the older of the two and construes the abominable as what is without good omen or God's blessing, what offends the Fates or incurs God's wrath. The latter, "anthropological" reading entered the English language through John Wycliffe's 1382 translation of the Bible — he and his associates followed the French Medievals in spelling "abhominable" with an "h" — and sees the abominable as what departs from or destroys the essentially human.[28]

As with "abomination," two general readings of "liberation" are possible. The Latin root of the word "liberate" *(liber)* means "free";[29] but there are at least two possible elaborations of this freedom, elaborations as old as Augustine: mere freedom of choice *(liberum arbitrium)* or the more holistic notion of good disposition, candor, and personal integrity *(libertas)*. Bare freedom of choice (liberty of indifference) refers exclusively to the will and says nothing about the ends to which free choice is put, while *libertas* is a more normative notion in which the whole person (rather than just the will) flourishes. Liberation in the sense associated with *libertas* entails more than having an external encumbrance removed. We do speak of "liberating" a town, say, when we mean delivering it from foreign occupation; but the most robust sense of "liberation" involves internal empowerment, a revolution in the soul rather than in its circumstances, an immense heightening of crucial capacities.

If love is from God and God himself is love (1 John 4:7-8), and if the fundamental human need and capacity is to come into loving relation with God and other human beings (Matt. 22:36-40), then we have a basic definition of both "abomination" and "liberation." The abominable is

26. Old prejudices die hard, of course; Anwar Sadat was assassinated, in part, precisely for being civil to Menachem Begin.

27. *The Compact Edition of the Oxford English Dictionary*, vol. 1 (Oxford: Oxford University Press, 1984), s.v. "abomination."

28. This paragraph and the ones that immediately follow borrow extensively from my *Love Disconsoled: Meditations on Christian Charity* (Cambridge: Cambridge University Press, 1999), ch. 4.

29. *The Compact Edition of the Oxford English Dictionary*, s.v. "liberation."

what fundamentally thwarts or destroys the potential to love or be loved, while the liberating is what fundamentally expands or generates this potential. To be capable of loving care is to be capable of knowing and pleasing God and of furthering human beings as themselves of intrinsic worth, while to be in need of loving care is to need valuing by God and others. To care for human beings as such is to value their status as (real or potential) valuers, and to need care from other human beings is to require their valuation in order to acquire moral ends of one's own. Personal care is, in other words, self-conscious and other-regarding. Yet, more important, developing personhood, becoming ourselves, requires that others extend to us gratuitous attention before we are self-conscious agents. Because of their need and potential to give and receive love — what I have called their "sanctity" — the pre-personal lives of children have profound worth. Not until full personhood is actualized do our lives self-consciously matter to us: only then do we value ourselves as valuers. But the need and potential for agapic love, even in fetuses, is at the root of the possibility of an abominable thwarting or a liberating expansion of humanity.

Loving care is the great gift given in adoption, a favor that is usually returned once the adoptee is capable of personal response. The chief aim of adoption is to foster human beings who are themselves caring and cared for, in a context where attentive care is otherwise missing. However stunted institutionalized children may be, and however different they may be from their prospective adoptive parents, the need and capacity for loving care is a universal human trait, as ubiquitous as language competence among undamaged individuals. If it is not cultivated by other caring human beings, it atrophies and is never actualized. In denying the importance of and opportunity for loving care, we not only deprive others of care here and now but also render them (and us) unable to care or to be cared for in the future. The loss is ultimately of the potential for dignity, as well as of the reality of sanctity.

Just as abominations contract humanity's capacity to care or be cared for, thus making for bondage to bondage, so liberations expand that capacity, thus making for "freedom to be free" (in Arturo Paoli's phrase, echoing Galations 5:1).[30] To be liberated is not first of all to change our circumstances but to be changed ourselves. Unlike abominations, however, liberations undermine our prevailing social categories in highly beneficial ways — ways which allow for new and exponentially better forms of being and acting. Liberations make for a broader expanse of hu-

---

30. Arturo Paoli, *Freedom to Be Free* (Maryknoll, N.Y.: Orbis, 1973).

manity both individually and collectively as well as, for believers, a deeper communion with divinity. Blood ties between parents and children are among the most powerful human connections, but adoption transcends these to a large degree — even if adoptees and birth parents remain in contact — by placing custodial responsibility for raising children in the hands of persons not those children's biological parents. This empowerment augments the moral identity of the adoptive parents, making them more giving, but it most centrally augments the moral development of the adoptees, making them more stable, secure, and fulfilled. Adoption allows us to integrate as many loving individuals as completely into the moral community as possible. Thus "liberation leads to liberation."

Do single-parent and gay or lesbian adoptions undermine prevailing ideas of sex, marriage, and family in negative or positive ways? Are they "unnatural" in the sense of abominably destructive of the goodness of nature, "unnatural" in the sense of liberatingly broadening of that goodness, or perhaps neither? There are different kinds of single parents — never married, divorced, and widowed — and the households of each will tend to vary. But concerns over single parenting typically focus on three issues: (1) the economic stability of the household, (2) the psychological development of the children, and (3) the moral impact on the wider society. These worries are perhaps inevitable for a culture historically founded on heterosexual marriage. Looking at the relevant sociological data, however, I am increasingly convinced that a committed single person can give the type and amount of care that liberates all parties to an adoption to be better human beings.[31] Even if one maintains that single parenting is not ideal (see below), it ought not to be stigmatized as such, independently of context, motive, concrete actions taken, and social consequences achieved.[32] One's personal dignity does not depend on having a spouse, nor does one's ability to give love to a child. The possibility of good single parenting is implicitly recognized by the state when it does not automatically remove even minor children from the home of a widow or widower.

Similar things might be said about gays, lesbians, the elderly, and the physically impaired. The dignity of such individuals, so often denied *a priori*, is a function of their willingness and ability to embody love and jus-

---

31. For a review of the literature, see Nancy E. Dowd, *In Defense of Single-Parent Families* (New York: New York University Press, 1997).

32. As Dowd herself notes, "Removing the stigma against single-parent families should not, *must* not, keep us from recognizing the problems they confront. At the same time, recognition of the value of single-parent families is also crucial" (Dowd, *Single-Parent Families*, p. xviii).

tice, in parental contexts and elsewhere, even as any indignity stems from the opposite. Some gay, old, and handicapped folks behave abominably, but so do some who are straight, young, and able-bodied. There is no escaping the need to look at specifics rather than "types."

That said, as important as it is to recognize the dignity rights of a range of adults, adoption debates are best served, I believe, by looking carefully at the sanctity rights of needy children. Rather than focusing on the rights of marginalized would-be parents, we should accent the rights of suffering children to be adopted by the marginalized. This is dictated by the charitable principle of attending first to the most vulnerable — an idea as old as Jesus' identification with "the least of these" (Matt. 25:45) and as new as liberation theology's "preferential option for the poor." What is abominable — that is, what is against God's will, or stifling of humanity — is to deny a suffering child a loving home that he or she might otherwise have. Many singles and homosexuals could provide such a home to the hundreds of "unadoptables" trapped in foster care or warehoused in large institutions. It is not being raised in a nontraditional family that causes needless human suffering, but rather being uncared for, in utero or out. A child without a consistent adult caregiver often becomes all but incapable of love and trust, and thus the spiral of abuse and neglect perpetuates itself into the next generation.

Consider the legal implications of shifting focus from the right to adopt to the right to be adopted. There is no explicit constitutional right to adopt, so challenges to a state's ban on gay adoption, for example, must rely on general appeals to "due process and equal protection" (for both gay males and lesbians), as enunciated in the Fourteenth Amendment.[33] The problem, however, is that cases that do not involve explicitly protected classes or fundamental rights shift the burden of proof to plaintiffs — for instance, homosexual persons who wish to adopt. All the state need do is show a "rational basis" for precluding nontraditional adoption, such as the state's authority to regulate family law in accordance with local standards. A more plausible case can be made for the constitutional right to *be* adopted by available and willing parents. Amendment XIV, Section 1, of the United States Constitution reads,

> All persons born or naturalized in the United States, and subject to the jurisdiction thereof, are citizens of the United States and of the

33. See, for example, Laurie Cunningham, "Florida's Gay-Adoption Ban Goes to 11th Circuit," *Fulton County Daily Report,* 5 March 2003, pp. 1 and 6.

state wherein they reside. No state shall make or enforce any law which shall abridge the privileges or immunities of citizens of the United States; nor shall any state deprive any person of life, liberty, or property, without due process of law; nor deny to any person within its jurisdiction the equal protection of the laws.

To be denied adoptive parents that one might otherwise have — for example, a single person or a gay or lesbian couple — is closer to being deprived of "life, liberty, or property" in basic ways, as well as to being denied "the equal protection of the laws." An adult's life, liberty, and property are not fundamentally at risk if he or she does not adopt a child, but a needy child's life, liberty, and property may be so at risk if he or she is not adopted. The Fourteenth Amendment safeguards citizens from the unwarranted deprivation of life, liberty, and property, and this is traditionally interpreted as a negative right not to be interfered with. I have contended, however, that human sanctity entails some positive rights to be assisted. In this regard, the right to be adopted is analogous to the right to basic health care or to social security.

Children always do better with reliable, ongoing parental oversight. In addition, singles and homosexual couples often will embrace "special needs" children — the older, the impaired, the biracial, the ethnically alien — either because the would-be parents identify with these neglected souls or because these children are the only candidates that the system will consider handing over to a nontraditional household. All persons who are willing and able to provide a caring home should be allowed to adopt any available children; we must not imply that ostracized people can adopt marginalized children only because "ideal" couples do not want them. But, given present institutional realities, to deny a special needs child the possibility of a single father or mother or of homosexual parents may be to deny that child/citizen his or her only real chance at being loved.

Some worry that endorsing single-parent adoption will encourage women to get pregnant out of wedlock, and perhaps encourage men to impregnate them. If an unmarried adult, male or female, can properly raise a child, male or female, why should society continue to hold out a marital union of husband and wife as the most proper context for procreation? Won't countenancing single adoptive parents mean more "illegitimate" children, since the stigma of single parenthood will have been removed, including from the very young? This is a reasonable concern about unintended social consequences. It is important to distinguish, however, between adopting a child who already exists without supportive parents and purposely conceiving a child out of wedlock. For a father or mother intentionally to conceive a child out of wedlock does a disservice to the child. In spite of the increasing emotional, economic, and political independence of women from men, denying a child the benefit of two parents committed to each other increases the likelihood of juvenile and long-term difficulties for that child. The debate rages on concerning the extent to which family form, such as single parenthood, *causes* problems of poverty and other disadvantages for children and the extent to which it merely *correlates* with them.[34] Quoting V. Groze, Kathy S. Stolley writes that "it appears that 'marital status has little, if any, effect on adoption outcome as it relates to disrupted or intact adoptions.' Thus, a recommendation may be supported to actively recruit single adults as adoptive parents."[35] But Wade Horn avers,

> The empirical literature is quite clear . . . that children do, indeed, do best when they grow up in an intact, two-parent, married household. Even after controlling for differences in income, children who live with their married parents are two times less likely to fail at school, two to three times less likely to suffer an emotional or behavioral problem requiring psychiatric treatment, perhaps as much as 20 times less likely to suffer child abuse, and as adolescents they are less likely to get into trouble with the law, use illicit drugs, smoke cigarettes, abuse alcohol, or engage in early and promiscuous sexual activity. One is hard pressed to find a single indicator of child well-being which is not adversely impacted by divorce or being born out-of-wedlock.[36]

34. See Dowd, *Single-Parent Families,* esp. pp. 26-27. In sometimes suggesting that a family's form has little or nothing to do with how well its members fare, Dowd overstates her case, I believe. But in accenting the centrality of poverty, gender stereotyping, racial discrimination, and other variables not directly equatable with family structure, she nonetheless provides a helpful corrective to a narrow traditionalism that would vilify all single parents.

35. Kathy S. Stolley, "Statistics on Adoption in the United States," *Future of Children: Adoption* 3, no. 1 (spring 1993): 37.

36. Wade Horn, "Take a Vow to Promote Benefits of Marriage," *Washington Times,* 2 November 1999. The disadvantages of single-parent households are not due exclusively to the impact of divorce or illegitimacy, moreover. See, for example, Arthur J. Norton and Paul C. Glick, "One Parent Families: A Social and Economic Profile," *Family Relations* 35 (1986): 9-17. For more on the benefits of the "committed, intact, equal-regard, public-private family," see the essay by Don Browning in this volume. Browning and Nancy Dowd can be usefully read together. Despite their different accents and agendas, they both would affirm, I believe, Dowd's thesis that "Powerful incentives remain — and should remain — for raising children in two-parent families. Supporting single-parent families need not translate into destabilizing two- or multiple-parent families" (Dowd, *Single-parent Families,* p. xix).

One may grant the goodness of single-parent adoptions as (partial) remedies for the plight of homeless children — we must not make the perfect the enemy of the good — and one may also acknowledge the right of single birth parents to keep their offspring if they can provide for them. (Emphasis is typically on single birth *mothers,* thus the dignity and rights of single birth *fathers* are frequently overlooked.) Yet one may still affirm, as I do, that stable marriage is the ideal setting for raising children. The ideal abides not simply because two parents can be more efficient than one but also because two can more fully model, in their interpersonal relations, the give and take of love.

An extended family of grandparents, aunts, uncles, cousins, and others can, of course, provide a wide range of affection and support for the children of a single parent, as well as for the parent himself or herself. (The same can be said for an extended church of ministers, deacons, elders, lay leaders, and so on.) And I in no way mean to imply that single-parent households, per se, are faulty or undesirable.[37] In spite of a 50 percent divorce rate in the United States, however, the conjugal love of two people still promises dynamics of care and commitment — touching God, one another, and any children — that simply cannot be had in any other way. Indeed, it is for just this reason that I favor legalizing same-sex marriage. For gays and lesbians who wish to adopt, no less than for heterosexuals, stable marriage should be the primary familial context. That context stands the best chance to benefit, maximally, all three elements of the adoption triad: the child, the biological parents or family, and the adoptive parents or family.

In spite of the three issues identified above, single fathers and mothers, biological and adoptive, are ever more socially acceptable these days. But two major objections to homosexual adoptive parents are less easily overcome: (a) the fear that the same-sex couple will intentionally or unintentionally drive an adopted child into a gay or lesbian "lifestyle," and (b) the fear that one or both members of the couple will molest the child in their care, especially a child who is of the same sex as the couple. On the first score, states like Florida (and Utah and Mississippi) commonly maintain that adoptees need heterosexual role models to develop "normal" sexual identification.[38] A same-sex household frustrates healthy

---

37. A man contemplating becoming a single adoptive father can take encouragement from Barbara J. Risman's judgment, shared by an increasing number of experts, that "'mothering' is not an exclusively female skill" (Risman, "Can Men 'Mother'?: Life As a Single Father," *Family Relations* 35 [1986]: 95).

38. Cunningham, "Florida's Gay-Adoption Ban," p. 6.

child development, the argument runs, so even if the best interests of the child translate into the right to be adopted, the pool of potential parents should be limited to the heterosexual. On the second score, the ready association of homosexuality with pederasty still persists in our culture.[39] The recent scandal of numerous Catholic priests abusing children in their care, across decades and seemingly with impunity, has bolstered the tendency both to equate gayness with child molestation and to take public steps to stop the predation.

It is tempting to address the first fear, of same-sex couples pushing adopted children into homosexuality, by "biologizing" the issue. Some are comforted by the thought that sexual orientation seems largely a matter of genetic predisposition, as though having little or no choice in a mode of being is sufficient ground to affirm (or at least to tolerate) it.[40] Virtually all gays and lesbians come from traditional heterosexual families, which indeed suggests that their orientations are more a matter of nature than of nurture. Moreover, the sociological evidence does not appear to support the thesis that gay and lesbian parents are more likely to raise gay and lesbian children.[41] But to think that these data settle the *moral* question is to be guilty of the genetic fallacy. The issue is not whether sexual identity is biologically determined, individually chosen, or socially conditioned — it may well be a function of all three factors — but whether homosexual parents can be just and loving to their children. If they cannot, then the causal reasons why they are same-sex oriented matter very little: they should not

39. Take, for example, the statement by the Ramsey Colloquium on "The Homosexual Movement," *First Things* 41 (March 1994): 15-21. Though thoughtful and nuanced in many ways, the statement rather uncritically maintains that "public anxiety about homosexuality is preeminently [and legitimately] a concern about the vulnerabilities of the young," especially their vulnerability to "seduction and solicitation" (p. 20). We rightly worry about child abuse, but unless we observe that heterosexual seduction and solicitation of children is also anxiety provoking, the impression is left that gays and lesbians are especially prone, as such, to harm children.

40. For a detailed review of the literature on possible physiological bases of homosexuality, see Qazi Rahman and Glenn D. Wilson, "Born Gay? The Psychobiology of Human Sexual Orientation," *Personality and Individual Differences* 34, no. 8 (June 2003): 1335-1559. For the cautious suggestion that this study gives us ethical grounds on which to settle gay rights disputes, see Nicholas D. Kristof's editorial, "Gay at Birth?" *New York Times,* 25 October 2003.

41. See Ann Sullivan, ed., *Issues in Gay and Lesbian Adoption* (Annapolis Junction, Md.: Child Welfare League of America, 1995); Stephen Hicks and Janet McDermott, eds., *Lesbian and Gay Fostering and Adoption: Extraordinary Yet Ordinary* (London: Jessica Kingsley, 1998); and Frederick W. Bozett and Marvin B. Sussman, eds., *Homosexuality and Family Relations* (New York: Haworth, 1990).

be allowed to adopt. If, in contrast, they can be good parents, they should be permitted (even encouraged) to adopt. To have no freedom of choice with respect to an action or disposition may well be exculpating, but pathologies are to be checked regardless of whether they involve personal guilt. Even if alcoholism is understood as a disease, for instance, we still arrest people for DUI and eventually take away their drivers' licenses. The key question, to repeat, is not whether a particular sexual orientation is causally determined, but whether it is socially destructive.

The second fear, of homosexual child molestation, can be guarded against in the same fashion as heterosexual child molestation: with careful public oversight and strong legal sanctions. If a couple, gay or straight, has a history of child abuse, they are obviously not fit candidates for adoptive parenting. And if a couple, gay or straight, is convicted of child abuse, they should be severely punished with fines and imprisonment, as well as the loss of parental rights. Just as a loving straight father would be offended by the suggestion that he is sexually interested in his daughter, just as a loving straight mother would be offended by the suggestion that she is sexually interested in her son, so a gay or lesbian parent who loves his or her child will take umbrage at the innuendo of incest. Incest is indeed an abomination with devastating effects on young psyches,[42] but gay parents are just as capable of honoring the sanctity of their children's lives as are straight parents. (If this is not so, one wonders why even Florida permits homosexuals to be foster parents, even to care for the same foster child for a period of years.) The virtue and criterion that ought to govern all relations between adopters and adoptees is a charity that actively promotes the good of all parties, including the good of untroubled psychic individuation for children. Putting the key point cautiously, most studies with which I am familiar find no detrimental impact on children of parental homosexuality.[43]

A final word is in order about the linkage, for juveniles, between abomination and liberation. It is precisely the "unfinished" quality of

42. On the destructive psychological and social effects of incest, heterosexual and homosexual, see Jean Renvoize, *Incest: A Family Pattern* (New York: Routledge and Kegan Paul, 1982); Robin Fox, *The Red Lamp of Incest: An Enquiry into the Origins of Mind and Society* (Notre Dame, Ind.: University of Notre Dame Press, 1983); Diana E. H. Russell and Rebecca M. Bolen, *The Epidemic of Rape and Child Sexual Abuse in the United States* (Thousand Oaks, Calif.: Sage, 2000); and Susan Forward and Craig Buck, *Betrayal of Innocence: Incest and Its Devastation* (New York: Penguin, 1988).

43. See Julie Schwartz Gottman, "Children of Gay and Lesbian Parents," *Marriage and Family Review* 14, no. 3 (1989): 177-96, cited in Dowd, *Single-Parent Families*, p. 51.

children, their innocence and dependency, that makes them so readily both the victims of abomination and the beneficiaries of liberation. If children were not so undeveloped and un-self-aware, they could engineer their own care and not be so subject to adult cruelty or kindness. As it is, they can be radically stunted or enriched by their elders. We do not know why some adults are moved to solicitous wonder by the "mystery" of a child, to use Martin Marty's term,[44] while others are induced by that same "mystery" to take advantage of that same child. But to dismiss, prey upon, or otherwise despise the young and vulnerable is virtually definitive of inhuman and impious behavior.[45] To check such abomination, liberating adoption policy will put the best interests of the child ahead of adult rights. That done, new rights and old wrongs are brought to light for both children and adults.

IV. Identity, Dignity, and the Right to Know

Even as needy children, especially when younger, have a sanctity right to be adopted, including by single or homosexual parents, so adopted children, especially when older, have a dignity right[46] to know their biological identities, including who their birth parents and siblings are, if this knowledge is available.[47] Knowing one's genetic history can be indispensable to wise or timely health decisions, as in choosing between types of cancer treatment or searching for donor organs for transplant. Beyond this bio-medical benefit, however, there is a profound psycho-social good at stake. Knowing personal origins, genetic and cultural, is often crucial for forming a robust sense of self. (Dignity itself I have defined as requir-

44. See Martin Marty, "Mapping the Frontiers of the Study of Religion and Children: In Theology and Ethics," unpublished manuscript, pp. 16-18.

45. I follow an ancient exegetical tradition in holding, for instance, that Abraham is "Father of the Faith" not because he is willing to sacrifice Isaac but because he is willing to overturn the ritual burnt offering of the first-born son in favor of a more egalitarian and charitable view of father-child relations. See my *Love Disconsoled*, ch. 6 ("Is Isaac Our Neighbor?").

46. As noted, a central motive for adopting individuals, early and late, is reverence for their sanctity, but parents taking in older persons (e.g., troubled teenagers) may also look to the latter's dignity and what it takes to respect it. Need I say, all human lives possess sanctity, while some (the personal) have both sanctity and dignity.

47. In some instances, information on birth parents and/or siblings is unlikely to be available. For many Chinese adoptees, for example, there simply are no records with actual names. I thank Cindy Meyer for helping me to clarify this and related points.

ing self-awareness and/or self-control over time.) We are historical beings, and to appreciate one's relation to other people in the present, one must understand one's own genesis in the past. Here secrecy and shame are abominable, stunting of mature development, while openness and pride are liberating. As Rickie Solinger notes,

> In many ways, the idea of adoptees searching for their biological roots and claiming rights to information about themselves was, itself, shaped by liberation movements emerging in the 1960s. In the 1970s, through ALMA [the Adoptees' Liberty Movement Association] and other organizations, adoptees claimed the right to own the truth about their origins. Among the pioneers of "identity politics," adoptees fused liberation, the search for self-hood, and special group identity to define and assert a political cause.[48]

An adopted child may decline to exercise his or her right to know birth parents and any siblings, but having the option to know or not know is itself empowering, a recognition of the adopted child's dignity as a free agent. A birth mother who relinquished her child to adoption may decline to interact with that child in later life, but to conceive and deliver a child carries with it the obligation to allow that child to know who he or she is, his or her full selfhood in relation to others. The same goes, *mutatis mutandis,* for a birth father. Due to legal constraints or medical disabilities, birth parents may not always be free to fulfill the duty of disclosure I describe. But nondisclosure should be the exception rather than the rule. This becomes especially clear when one reads what Solinger calls "adoptees' heart-wrenching expressions of their need to find themselves by finding their lost parents."[49] This need seldom has anything to do with how kind or unkind adoptive parents have been. The desire to uncover the truth is usually a function of neither dissatisfaction with adoptive families nor morbid curiosity; it appears to be an innate and healthy drive toward self-awareness for many adoptees.[50] Jesus himself, considered by many to be history's most famous adopted child,[51] seems to have been driven by a passionate desire to know his lineage, even as Matthew and John take particular interest in his genealogy — Matthew biologically and John metaphysically.

48. Solinger, *Beggars and Choosers,* p. 81.
49. Solinger, *Beggars and Choosers,* p. 84.
50. Solinger, *Beggars and Choosers,* pp. 83-84.
51. Moses finishes a close second, I suppose, or is it a dead heat?

V. Jesus Christ As Adopted Son

Was Jesus Christ adopted, and if so by whom and for what purpose? Nestorians and other Adoptionists separate the human and divine natures of Christ, maintaining that he represents a dual sonship. "Christ as God is indeed the Son of God by generation and nature, but Christ as man is Son of God only by adoption and grace."[52] Jesus the historical figure, that is, is not coeternal with the Heavenly Father but rather is "adopted" by God at a particular moment in time (at his baptism, transfiguration, or resurrection). On this view, Mary is not *Theotokos* (Mother of God) but rather the birth mother of a human child. In turn, Jesus' unity with the divine will is a moral union, not a hypostatic one. For Nestorians, Jesus is not the divine *Logos* but the Son of God by way of trans-species adoption of the lower by the higher. God takes in Jesus, so to speak, to foster a redemptive providential plan, but Jesus is not an eternal person of the blessed Trinity.

Adoptionists typically hold that their position is required if the true humanity of Jesus is to be preserved and if normal human beings are to have any hope of following Jesus into heavenly salvation, as fellow adoptees of the Father.[53] Broadly Adoptionist views have genuine appeal precisely because they seem to allow a greater connection between actual people and the exemplary life and teaching of Jesus. The Bible nowhere calls Jesus the adopted Son of God, but Jesus himself calls people to become sons and daughters of God. "Love your enemies and pray for those who persecute you, so that you may be children of your Father in heaven," he declares in Matthew 5:44-45, ending with the injunction, "Be perfect, therefore, as your heavenly Father is perfect" (Matt. 5:48 NRSV). Becoming "children of the Most High" (Luke 6:35 NRSV) is open to all who love their enemies, do good, and lend without expecting return. And this process sounds very much like being adopted by a righteous and powerful Father. In fact, it resonates well with my emphasis on the right of needy children to be adopted by responsible adults.

In addition, to aver that Mary is the Virgin Mother of God and that Jesus of Nazareth is of one substance with the Father *(homoousion)* may suggest that ordinary sexual reproduction is dirty or shameful and that Jesus Christ is something like a clone of God miraculously placed inside

---

52. "Adoptionism," §1, in *New Advent Catholic Encyclopedia,* New Advent website, http://www.newadvent.org/cathen/01150a.htm. Accessed 10 April 2004.

53. See the discussion of Elipandus of Toledo and Felix of Urgel, both writing in the eighth century, in "Adoptionism in Spain," in *The Westminster Dictionary of Church History,* ed. Jerald C. Brauer (Philadelphia: Westminster, 1971), pp. 8-9.

of Mary's womb. Such a picture makes it difficult to take seriously imperatives to embody Christ-like love in this life. If Jesus Christ is superhuman and utterly *sui generis,* how can we take to heart his final commandment to love as he loves? An impossible model is arguably no model at all.

For all its power, however, there are a number of moral and theological problems with the Adoptionist scenario. First, it makes adoption by God depend on one's personal merit or achievement, when, as I have argued, it is the sanctity of human life that inspires the strong to take in the weak. Surely the point of Jesus' comments on becoming "children of God" is the existential one that we must become who and what we already are: made in God's image and called to holiness. According to Genesis, we are already God's sons and daughters, so our "adoption" is, at least in part, a recognition of an ongoing identity. Second, Adoptionism negates the powerful doctrine that the incarnation is God's kenotic act of self-humbling that *allows us to adopt God.* God takes on human form to show us both the need and the potential of a sacred child — and all children are sacred — and Joseph (and Mary?) rise to the occasion as "adoptive" parents. Joseph is frequently the forgotten man in traditional accounts of the nativity, but the generosity of his not putting away a pregnant Mary and of raising a son not his own is entirely lost on Adoptionists. Third, Adoptionism fails to take sin seriously as a blight on humanity in need of redemption. We cannot overcome sin, and thus love as we ought to love, without divine assistance. The fact that this assistance comes through acceptance of vulnerability, first in the manger and then on the cross, should not surprise us. This is God's characteristic way with the world. As First John observes, "In this is love, not that we loved God but that he loved us and sent his Son to be the atoning sacrifice for our sins" (1 John 4:10 NRSV). Once more, God's adoption of us also rescues us from a bondage that we ourselves cannot break.

There are good reasons, then, why the various brands of Adoptionism have been labeled problematic, indeed heretical, by the overwhelming majority of Christian denominations. Most Catholics and many Protestants insist that Mary is the Virgin Mother of God and that Jesus as human is the "natural" (i.e., supernatural) Son of God, not merely God's adoptive son. Mary's virginity and Jesus' sonship are affirmations of the sanctity of human life, not denials of its earthiness, since both doctrines highlight the redemptive presence of God with us in the flesh. If Jesus were merely the biological son of Mary and Joseph, his life, death, and resurrection would make his holiness an impossible ideal for the rest of us; even as, if Jesus were but the adopted Son of God, this would make filiation with God dependent on our own contingent achievement. There are moral justifications, in short, for declaring that Mary is *Theotokos,* and that in Jesus Christ there is but one nature, one person, fully divine and fully human. "Christ, Son of God, by His eternal generation, remains Son of God, even after the Word has assumed and substantially united to Himself the sacred Humanity; Incarnation detracts no more from the eternal sonship than it does from the eternal personality of the Word."[54] Jesus is adopted by Joseph, to repeat, but in insisting on knowing and living out his divine sonship, the Christ himself affirms the right of all adoptees to discover their full identity.

If Jesus was adopted by Joseph, and if Jesus nevertheless insisted on affirming his true identity, his supernatural "sonship," then we should not forbid suffering children from being adopted by those radically different from themselves or, where possible, from knowing their actual ancestry. On the contrary, adoptive children in "nontraditional families" have an especially privileged role in the *imitatio Christi.*

There is, of course, a more radical form of "adoptionism" that leaves God entirely out of the picture and sees Jesus as the bastard son of Mary and an anonymous human father, perhaps a Roman soldier who impregnated Mary while she was betrothed to Joseph. On this account, Mary is either an adulteress or a rape victim, and the cuckolded Joseph is supremely admirable for either forgiving her sin or overlooking her violation. For Joseph to consent to wed Mary and to raise Jesus as his own child makes him, not Jesus, the second Adam who undoes the poisonous male myth of Eve's transgression in the Garden. And it is Jesus' awareness that he is illegitimate that makes him intensely concerned with his own identity and gives him his deep empathy with those who are socially outcast. [55] This naturalistic view can teach us much about the courage of adoptive fathers and the right of birth mothers *not* to surrender their children to strangers; it can also help us reject the contempt for illegitimate children that has plagued Hebrew-Christian culture at least since Ishmael.[56] But with this secular story, we have left the fold of Christian faith altogether.

54. "Adoptionism," §1, *New Advent Catholic Encyclopedia.*

55. For a recent defense of this early Ebionite view, see Stephen Mitchell, *The Gospel According to Jesus* (New York: HarperCollins, 1991), esp. pp. 21-28 and 95-97.

56. On these subjects, see John Witte's essay in this volume.

TIMOTHY P. JACKSON

Conclusion: The Image of God and the (Un)Naturalness of Sex

If God is agapic love (1 John 4:16), then to be made in God's image must be to possess a love-related feature. We tend to think here of the *capacity to give love,* but divine blessing exists perhaps even more profoundly in the *need to receive love.* The need for love is itself a sublime part of love. Thus I equate the image of God with the essential need *or* ability to receive *or* give *agape,* a condition that includes fetuses (wanted and unwanted), children (legitimate and illegitimate), the handicapped, the senile, and, need I add, the single and the married, the gay and the straight. In God, goodness and power merge, but we must always remember that that power is made perfect in weakness (2 Cor. 12:9). Indeed, in children we see that we are fundamentally "mirror images" of God, not because children are demonic but because they need so palpably to receive love that they thereby reverse our typical understanding of God as pure might and sovereign independence. The mystery of both Yahweh and youth is its gifted yearning. God started out self-sufficient yet chose to create the world, an imponderable willingness to cease to be all-in-all. God then become incarnate in this world, in part to redeem creatures but also in part to receive their love in return. We, in contrast, start out entirely dependent on others and grow to, at most, a partial autonomy in which we can freely give of ourselves. To adopt a needy child is to participate in this holy dialectic of giving and receiving.

This account of the *imago Dei* might seem to settle things, but the issue of adoption cannot be separated from the backdrop of increasingly divergent religious and secular criteria for proper sexual and familial relations. Adoption practices both shape and are shaped by those criteria. At its best, adoption is motivated by the desire to care for and educate children, but it might seem to be a problematic case of acquiring offspring without having had sex. If the Roman Catholic Church forbids artificial means of conception, why does it permit adoption? Similarly, if traditional postnatal adoption is admirable, why not think of artificial insemination by donor as very early prenatal adoption? Why should parent-child consanguinity be essential to "reproduction" here? In spite of its historical commitments to forms of "natural law," Christianity ought to be wary of too readily identifying the "natural" with the normative. What is natural, as opposed to artificial, is often hard to specify. And Protestants, at any rate, are generally reluctant to take fallen human proclivities, much less nonhuman nature, as definitive of virtue. Nature is "red in tooth and claw," as Tennyson observed in "In Memoriam," and many instinctive human impulses are cruel or destructive. At the heart of Christianity, and thus of Christian views on adoption, stand two *super*-natural acts: the incarnation and the passion of Christ. These, not instinct or habit, provide the moral cues for how to live, as any sophisticated version of natural law theory recognizes.

It is not getting children without having had sex or having sex without getting children that is the issue, but rather whether the sex is loving and the children are loved. Christian sex (and adoption) is not finally defined by what is "natural" or "unnatural," but by what is Christ-like and thus perfecting of nature. Marriage and the fruit of children may have initially been confined to a procreative Adam and Eve in the Garden of Nature, but we now live east of Eden and, even without the fall, Christ represents a *donum superadditum* who wins for us (gay and straight) forms of community not "naturally" possible. If, by the grace of the incarnate Word, we are to love those who are strangers or enemies to us and to let them teach us virtue, then surely we can permit inspired singles and homosexuals to be parents. Better still, surely we can support them and even see in them part of the meaning of (God's) parenthood and family.

Jesus Christ was an iconoclast, associating with the poor and marginalized and putting the immediate needs of vulnerable human beings ahead of social conventions and religious traditions. His iconoclasm was liberating in the extreme. If Jesus was single, as the Gospels suggest, then Christians cannot idolize the married state; if children are among the most vulnerable, as surely they are, then Jesus' own example ought to move us to provide for them; and if Jesus was inspired by a quest to determine his true ancestry, as Peter appreciated (see Matthew 16:13-18), then we cannot deny contemporary adoptees the chance to discover who they are. If Jesus Christ is the supernatural and sinless Son of God whom the Father allows Joseph (and us) to adopt, in sum, then Christians have the best motive imaginable to endorse the rights of suffering children to be given loving homes and genetic histories. The language of "rights" and "duties," even "sanctity rights" and "duties of charity," may ultimately cede pride of place to talk of "faith, hope, and love." (Exclusive reference to "rights" and "duties" may imply an overly adversarial set of relations.) But both God and Joseph express their love across bloodlines and social divisions, and both are faithful to children gotten without benefit of "natural" sex. We as a society can only hope to do the same. Not only does adoption revere the sanctity of a human life; to the extent that we nurture "the least of these," we also care for Christ himself (cf. Matt. 25:45).

My overarching conclusion is straightforward: supporting the positive right of helpless or abused children to be adopted ought to be a fundamental Christian, and national, commitment. This is especially true if one holds, as I do, that elective abortions are immoral and should be illegal after the first trimester.[57] One cannot be pro-parent, advocating the negative rights of would-be adopters not to be interfered with, without first being pro-child, advocating the positive rights of adoptees to be cared for. And one cannot be anti-abortion, recognizing in fetuses the right-to-life, without also being pro-adoption, recognizing in infants the right-to-life-in-a-family. Being pro-adoption does not mean humiliating unwed or indigent birth parents, or denying them the right to care for their children if they are able and responsibly choose to do so, but it does mean putting the best interests of the children first. The interests of the adoptees should also be the primary factor in determining the extent of contact that birth parents might later have with their relinquished children.

My thesis that needy children have the right to be adopted invites the question of how, practically, to offer a remedy to these children. To stop excluding single people and same-sex couples from adopting is one concrete step, but even more important is the cultivation of a sense of corporate accountability for the problem. This is a matter not so much of legal policy as of lived charity.[58]

57. See my *Priority of Love*, ch. 5. Pertman notes that, sadly, there is still often more stigma associated with putting one's child up for adoption than with having an abortion (*Adoption Nation*, p. 12). Does any other social attitude better crystallize the conflict between the culture of death and the culture of life?

58. I wish to thank three groups for their helpful discussion of an earlier draft of this essay: the participants in the Adoption Roundtable at Emory Conference Center on March 30, 2003, many of whom are contributors to this volume; members of Emory University's Center for the Interdisciplinary Study of Religion, Project on the Child, especially our facilitators, Don Browning, Martin Marty, and John Witte; and those present at the Candler Faculty Research Lunch on February 16, 2004, especially the convener, Luther Smith, and my respondent, Jon Gunnemann.

III. Legal Perspectives

10. Law, Christianity, and Adoption

STEPHEN B. PRESSER

One day in the early 1880s, about half-past three in the afternoon, forty homeless children traveling on an "orphan train" from New York City arrived in Nobles County, Minnesota. They were taken directly from the train station to the county courthouse, where "a large crowd was gathered."[1]

The children, most if not all of whom had never been away from the streets of the metropolis, were introduced "one by one, before the [Midwestern] company," and "in a stentorian voice," an agent for the Children's Aid Society of New York "gave a brief account of each." According to one witness, "Applicants for children were then admitted in order behind the railing and rapidly made their selections." If the selected child "gave assent, the bargain was concluded on the spot." The witness continued, "It was a pathetic sight, not soon to be forgotten, to see those children and young people, weary, travel-stained, confused by the excitement and unwonted surroundings, peering into those strange faces, and trying to choose wisely for themselves." Still, "[i]t was surprising how many happy selections were made under such circumstances." In just a few hours, "nearly all of those forty children were disposed of."

Scenes like this one took place hundreds of times, in many places west of the Eastern seaboard, and, in this manner, many thousands of children from New York found homes in families away from the city.

---

1. Quotations in these three paragraphs are taken from the eyewitness account of Hastings H. Hart, quoted in Stephen O'Connor, *Orphan Trains: The Story of Charles Loring Brace and the Children He Saved and Failed* (Boston: Houghton Mifflin, 2001), p. 251.

Some research for this essay was supported by the Searle Fund, whose support is gratefully acknowledged.

While there were occasional individual misfortunes and exploitations, by and large this unprecedented child placement effort resulted in the felicitous augmentation of many rural families. Still, mechanisms were needed both to ensure the welfare of the children placed and to secure their legal rights as equal members of their new families. The piety of those who placed and eventually provided for these children more or less ensured the former, and the creation of an American law of adoption secured the latter. Accordingly, this chapter explores the historical development of American adoption law, and the role of religion in its implementation.

The American Law of Adoption

The American law of adoption furnishes a unique window into conceptions of law and society in general and the family in particular. As one recent historian of adoption law remarked, "Adoption and adoption policy 'implicate[] our most deeply held beliefs and values about family, community, and identity.'"[2] The first piece that I published, a paper done under the direction of legal historian Morton J. Horwitz, was a survey called "The Historical Background of the American Law of Adoption."[3] Horwitz, who was then engaged in writing his brilliant study, *The Transformation of American Law 1780-1860* (1977),[4] had noticed that unlike continental Europe, for most of their legal history England and America had no generally applicable legal mechanisms for adoption. The common law was hostile to the practice, and the common law maxim was that "only God can make an heir."[5] And yet, in the period running from about 1850 to

2. Amanda C. Pustilnik, "Private Ordering, Legal Ordering, and the Getting of Children: A Counterhistory of Adoption Law," *Yale Law and Policy Review* 20 (2002): 296. For some further rumination on the intersection between religion and the legal history of the family, see, for example, John Witte Jr., "God's Joust, God's Justice: An Illustration from the History of Marriage Law," in *Christian Perspectives on Legal Thought*, ed. Michael W. McConnell, Robert F. Cochran Jr., and Angela C. Carmella (New Haven: Yale University Press, 2001), pp. 406-25.

3. Stephen B. Presser, "The Historical Background of the American Law of Adoption," *Journal of Family Law* 11, no. 2 (1972): 443-516.

4. It was awarded the Bancroft prize, the highest accolade the history fraternity can bestow, in 1978.

5. The notion that only God could make an heir comes from the treatise commissioned by and bearing the name of Ranulf de Glanvill, the twelfth-century advisor to Henry II. It may well have been that before the Normans the common law (such as it was) was not hostile to adoption, and that the prohibition on adoption may have had more to

1880, virtually every American state[6] passed a statute providing that adopted children, if particular procedures were followed, would be treated as natural children if their adopted parents died intestate, and, indeed, would generally be so regarded by the law.[7] Horwitz wondered what led to this relatively sudden turnabout for American law, and urged me to try to find out.

There had been some work done on the history of adoption up until that time (1970), but not much. What there was seemed to suggest that there really had not been a great need for the law to get involved, since earlier child placement practices — placing orphans with relatives, or putting them into apprenticeship arrangements — seemed until the middle of the century to adequately handle child custody arrangements.[8] With the waves of immigration which began in the 1820s, however, and

---

do with resisting testamentary bequests and *inter vivos* gifts to nonrelated persons in an era when familial responsibilities in the feudal system predominated; or, conversely, hostility to adoption may have been explainable as a reaction to the Norman custom (immediately after the Conquest) of appointing successors to a military fief. It is also possible that since the practice was known to flourish on the continent, and there was generally hostility to non-English practices, "the common law's failure to incorporate adoption may be attributable to some extent to English xenophobia" (Presser, "Historical Background," p. 451). On these points see generally Presser, "Historical Background," pp. 448-52.

6. David Ray Papke, "Pondering Past Purposes: A Critical History of American Adoption Law," *West Virginia Law Review* 102 (1999): 462, observes that "[b]y 1876, twenty-four states had similar legislation [to the first general act, passed in Massachusetts in 1851], and by the turn of the century something resembling modern adoption was available in every state." The Massachusetts Act was the first to establish a requirement of judicial oversight for adoption. Earlier statutes in Mississippi and Texas had placed a legal imprimatur on previously completed adoptions, but Massachusetts established the new trend of requiring judicial approval based on findings made by courts. The Massachusetts statute "created a judicial safety-check of the private arrangement" (Pustilnik, "Private Ordering," p. 282).

7. As David Ray Papke has summarized this legislation, the statutes "required that living biological parents of the child give formal permission for adoption and that both the adopter and his spouse (if any) formally petition to adopt. A judge then made the adoption decision, asking in the process if the adoption petitioner or petitioners were 'of sufficient ability to bring up the child' and if the adoption was 'fit and proper.' 'The heart of the adoption transfer,' the historian Jamil Zainaldin has stated, 'became the judicially monitored transfer of rights with due regard for the welfare of the child and the parental qualifications of the adopters'" (Papke, "Pondering Past Purposes," pp. 461-62).

8. But see Yasuhide Kawashima, "Adoption in Early America," *Journal of Family Law* 20 (1982): 677-96, for the argument that the presence or absence of adoption does not have to do with the failure or inadequacy of other child custody institutions, as well as the claim that even before the statutes were passed in the middle and late nineteenth century, there were actual adoptions taking place through testamentary bequests.

with the concomitant rise of an urban proletariat in this country, there suddenly was greater pressure on traditional child placement institutions. There has since been important and significant work in the history of adoption from a variety of perspectives,[9] but thirty years ago the meager history of adoption law seemed to conclude that it was simply this pressure on traditional child placement institutions that led to a need to reform the law of adoption.[10]

Religious Motivation of Adoption Reformers and Their Opponents

What I discovered, as I looked into the issue, is that it was one thing to understand that immigration and other social forces led to a group of orphans or other displaced children who needed care,[11] but another thing to explain how adoption — a process that involves, in effect, taking a

---

9. For a sampling see, e.g., Jamil S. Zainaldin, "The Emergence of a Modern American Family Law: Child Custody, Adoption, and the Courts, 1796-1851," *Northwestern University Law Review* 73 (1979): 1038-89; Kawashima, "Adoption in Early America"; Michael Grossberg, *Governing the Hearth: Law and the Family in Nineteenth-Century America* (Chapel Hill, N.C.: University of North Carolina Press, 1985) (stressing the patriarchal nature of nineteenth-century family law); Papke, "Pondering Past Purposes" (a Marxist account); and Pustilnik, "Private Ordering" (from a feminist perspective).

10. The adoption of infants as a widespread practice appears to have come about a bit later. As one historian notes, "'the adoption of babies, let alone newborns, was exceedingly uncommon' until a confluence of factors, including the development of infant formula, the belief in the impact of environment, rather than heredity, on child development, and a decrease in birth rates during and after World War I, contributed to the rise of infant adoption" (Annette Ruth Appell, "Blending Families through Adoption: Implications for Collaborative Adoption Law and Practice," *Boston University Law Review* 75 [1995]: 1004 n. 29, quoting Burton Z. Sokoloff, "Antecedents of American Adoption," *Future of Children* [spring 1933]: 22).

11. As the issue was summarized by one very recent historian of adoption law:

There is no doubt that there was a "child question" in the 1800s. Urbanization and immigration brought vast numbers of people into the cities, particularly Manhattan. The "three great waves" of immigration, running from the early 1800s to 1914, brought over thirty-five million immigrants through New York City. By the mid-1800s, approximately one and a half million immigrants lived in poverty in Manhattan tenements; approximately three thousand children were abandoned and/or homeless.

The concentration of destitute children in New York and Boston caused these cities to become the first large-scale focus of child welfare efforts, including adoption. (Pustilnik, "Private Ordering," p. 283, footnotes omitted)

stranger into one's family and, as it were, artificially changing the family's composition — ended up being the means of choice for child placement. After all, other means, such as orphanages or work houses — institutions that were bourgeoning along with the general rise of the asylum in nineteenth-century America[12] — could have been used. What I found, the deeper I probed, was that religion, and, in particular, a form of simple evangelical Christianity that seemed to be sweeping the country at the time,[13] offered at least a partial explanation.[14]

Seminal figures such as Charles Loring Brace, who was instrumental in the placing of thousands of children in homes in the West through his work with the Children's Aid Society in New York, made clear that their motivation was a religious one.[15] For Brace (and others like him), to find a Christian family in which to place an orphan, to give that orphan the stability American farm life provided, was to exhibit the kind of Christian loving-kindness Jesus preached and was to do his work on earth. As Brace asked, "Will not, in the far-away dim Eternity, a day come in which a voice,

12. See generally David J. Rothman, *Discovery of the Asylum: Social Order and Disorder in the New Republic* (Boston: Little, Brown, 1971).

13. See, e.g., Jon Butler, Grant Wacker, and Randall Balmer, *Religion in American Life: A Short History* (New York: Oxford University Press, 2003), pp. 182-95, 292-98 (describing the rise of evangelism in the first half of the nineteenth century and the importance of simple biblical Christianity in the last decades of the nineteenth century); Edwin Gaustad and Leigh Schmidt, *The Religious History of America: The Heart of the American Story from Colonial Times to Today,* rev. ed. (San Francisco: HarperSanFrancisco, 2002), pp. 231-54 (describing the American "social gospel" of the second half of the nineteenth century).

14. The complex of factors appears to include also a change in the perception of childhood itself, from one in which the needs of the child are not perceived as differing significantly from the needs of the adult (so that all that is required is to provide for the child's training in a profession or calling) to one in which child welfare is seen as requiring nurturing in a warm environment isolated from the adult world; from an era in which all that was thought necessary was a narrow training in particular vocational skills to one in which general education was believed necessary for good republican citizenship; and from an era in which the state or the established church dictated one's status and constricted social mobility to one in which popular sovereignty was more important and social mobility was possible if not actually encouraged. For an exposition of this complex of factors, see generally Presser, "Historical Background," and Zainaldin, "Emergence of a Modern American Family Law."

15. Brace's efforts at placing orphans in adopted families were preceded by a Boston religious organization called the Children's Mission, which "began shipping homeless or destitute children by train to rural areas of the East Coast and Midwest" (Pustilnik, "Private Ordering," p. 284). While Brace's religious orientation was apparently Protestant, "The New York Sisters of Charity of St. Vincent de Paul, for example, established a similar service in 1869 exclusively for Catholic children" (Pustilnik, "Private Ordering," pp. 285-86).

sweeter than all earthly music, shall sound to the depth of your soul, bringing rich peace and joy, and saying 'Inasmuch as ye did it unto one of the least of these, ye did it unto me!'" In other words, as Brace stressed, by seeking to place children for adoption in Christian homes, one would be acting "for humanity, for Christ, for God."[16]

According to adoption historian David Ray Papke, Brace's "Society 'gathered up homeless children from the urban streets and sent them into the country — many to the Midwest — to work and build character on clean, honest, Protestant farms.' As of 1892, the Society had 'farmed out' an amazing 84,318 children."[17] The efforts of Brace's organization continued until 1927, "placing a total of about one hundred and fifty thousand children with rural families."[18] If one adds in the efforts of other societies inspired by Brace's work, then, by 1929, "roughly 250,000 city children had found foster homes through these programs."[19] Fully a third of Brace's charges were placed with families in New York, and Brace's work in plac-

---

16. Presser, "Historical Background," p. 482. "Men who feel for the poor, the helpless, the forsaken as their brethren; and who do not forget that in working for the least of these they are working for Christ," Brace explained, understood that "ONE has died for him, even as for the child of the rich" (Presser, "Historical Background," pp. 482-83 n. 155). Brace believed that it was a mistake to rear children in large groups, as was the practice in orphanages and asylums, because they bred bad habits. Better to place orphans in loving Christian families, where good habits could be inculcated. As he put it, "[W]e assert boldly, that a poor child taken in thus by the hand of Christian charity, and placed in a new world of love and of religion, is *more likely to be tempted to good,* than to tempt others to evil" (Presser, "Historical Background," p. 483 [emphasis in original]).

17. Papke, "Pondering Past Purposes," p. 465, quoting from Lawrence M. Friedman, *A History of American Law* (New York: Simon and Schuster, 1973), p. 433. Papke also notes, "For a complete study of the Children's Aid Society, see Miriam Z. Langsam, *Children West: A History of the Placing-out System of the New York Children's Aid Society, 1853-1890 (1964)*" (Papke, "Pondering Past Purposes," p. 465 n. 42). For more on Brace and the Children's Aid Society, see the more recent O'Connor, *Orphan Trains.* It should be noted that Papke (and O'Connor) take a somewhat more dyspeptic view of Brace's work, and that of the other "child-savers," than Brace himself did. Brace must have believed in good faith that his effort was a noble, charitable, and Christian one, but Papke observes that it may often have been cruel to rip some of the children placed in the West from their friends and occasionally their families in the East, and that even where the goal of adoption was achieved, it may not necessarily have been what was, in an ideal sense, best for the child. As Papke puts it, "Yet, when adoption did occur, it was in a sense the ideal end to the aggressive and often biased process of progressive 'child saving.' Now graced with a bourgeois, Americanized adoptive home, the [immigrant or lower class] child could develop the proper values and civic identities of the dominant classes" (Papke, "Pondering Past Purposes," p. 468).

18. Pustilnik, "Private Ordering," p. 284.

19. O'Connor, *Orphan Trains,* p. xvii.

ing thousands of children put pressure on the New York and other legislatures to put the law's imprimatur on these newly created or augmented families and to complete the Christian effort by giving adopted children the same legal rights as natural children.[20]

The efforts of Brace and those like him seemed of a piece with the endeavors of other evangelical, religiously inspired reformers who, believing in the perfectability of humankind,[21] set off in the early years of the nineteenth century to abolish slavery, encourage temperance, and provide for the rights of women. These were men and women who had rejected the Calvinist "New England teachings" with their self-centered "morbid reflection," and who had come to believe that their efforts were best expended in turning outward to "preach the gospel to the poor"; they felt that "[i]n the course of feeding and caring for the poor," they would inculcate "consciously or unconsciously, refinement, purity, self-sacrifice, and Christian obligation."[22] But if strands of Unitarian or evangelical religion encouraged this "ferment of reform," there seems to have been resistance to it from other religious traditions in America, which counseled hesitance in interfering with traditional family arrangements.[23] This perspec-

20. The efforts of Brace's society, and that of many others like it, had as their eventual goal the adoption of the children they placed in families. This goal was apparently not reached in all cases, with the percentage of successful adoptions being somewhere between 20 percent and 60 percent, which, considering all the factors involved, was a reasonably successful rate. See generally O'Connor, *Orphan Trains,* pp. 150-52.

21. As Brace's biographer O'Connor reports, "Brace was a proponent of a decidedly optimistic view of human nature. He saw human beings as fundamentally good, and evil as largely exterior to our essential character. Although Brace certainly acknowledged the role of biological inheritance in behavior, he believed that moral character was shaped primarily by the environment" (O'Connor, *Orphan Trains,* p. 155).

22. Presser, "Historical Background," p. 481. For the religious influences on Charles Loring Brace, see the recent biography by Stephen O'Connor, *Orphan Trains.* O'Connor explores the connections between Brace and the Beecher family (his father lived in Lyman Beecher's home, married Beecher's sister-in-law, and also taught Harriet Beecher Stowe). Brace was a committed abolitionist and was profoundly influenced, O'Connor explains, by Horace Bushnell, minister of Hartford's North Congregational Church, who was "regarded by many as the most important American religious thinker of the nineteenth century"; Bushnell "devoted his life to mediating between the vengeful God of the Puritan founders of his church and the Unitarian God of love who seemed to better express the spirit of his prosperous and increasingly easy era" (O'Connor, *Orphan Trains,* p. 18). "More than any single theologian," according to O'Connor, "Bushnell helped diminish American Calvinism's emphasis on infant damnation and depravity, largely by showing how one's religious identity — including one's readiness for salvation — could be shaped during the earliest years of life" (O'Connor, *Orphan Trains,* p. 18).

23. As child custody historian Jamil Zainaldin put it, English law did not permit

tive showed up in some court decisions on adoption laws that strictly construed the new legislation, on the theory that it was an innovation on the common law, and perhaps that it represented an interference with God's rightful monopoly on the making of families.[24]

Reformers like Brace and the evangelicals had a socially democratic conception of humankind, and for him and for them each person was a unique and valuable child of God. (A similar spirit animated some of the abolitionists.) For others, however, who quite possibly reflected an older American Calvinist tradition that suggested that some were "elect" and others were not, the questionable background of many of the children Brace and others were placing led them to wonder whether "adopted" children should really be accorded the same privileges as "natural" children.

One of the earliest historians of the law of adoption, William H. Whitmore, was of this view, and clearly indicated that the inferior genetic equipment of the subjects Brace and others were proposing for adoption ought to impose caution on anyone who might contemplate taking them into his or her family. Whitmore subscribed to a version of "biological determinism"[25] current in the late nineteenth century, a theory which led

---

adoption because "it denied the Christian canons of marriage and legitimacy. . . . Parental authority was viewed as absolute, proprietary and God-given, and consequently unalterable by man" (Zainaldin, "Modern American Family Law," pp. 1044-45).

24. For this position, see, e.g., *Ferguson v. Jones,* 17 Ore. 204, 20 Pac. 842, 3 L.R.A. 620 (1888), where the court observes, "The permanent transfer of the natural rights of a parent was against the policy of the common law. The right of adoption, as conferred by [an Oregon] statute, was unknown to it, and repugnant to its principles. Such right was of civil law origin, and derived its sanction from its code. The right of adoption, then, begun in derogation of common law, is a special power conferred by statute, and the rule is that such statutes must be strictly construed." This is true even if the harsh result to the adopted child contradicts "our views as to what constitutes natural rights, or justice or equity." For a discussion of this case, and others in which courts' high regard for blood bonds led them to deny arguments based on the welfare needs of the adopted child, see Presser, "Historical Background," pp. 492-99. As R. Alta Charo recently observed, "Since biological realities are often mistaken for a divine or natural blueprint of the social world, challenging what appears to be writ in physiology will often be received with outrage, humor, incredulity, or dismissiveness; rarely will it be received with comprehension and acceptance" (R. Alto Charo, "Biological Truths and Legal Fictions," *Journal of Health Care Law and Policy* 1 [1998]: 326-27).

25. On the nineteenth-century "biological determinism" that underlay conceptions of women's roles, as well as ideas about race, see Charo, "Biological Truths." Charo observes that "[b]y appealing to the apparent clarity and physical permanency of biological notions of life and death, male and female, mother and father, law constrains itself. Instead of asking what sort of social arrangements should constitute a 'family' for which 'family law' will apply, it begins by asking what sort of biological arrangements constitute a family" (Charo,

some to think that there were "born criminals,"[26] and others generally to disparage the lower classes. As Whitmore wrote in his 1876 treatise, *The Law of Adoption*, "Considering the fact that the subjects of adoption are so largely taken from the waifs of society, foundlings or children whose parents are depraved and worthless; considering also the growing belief that many traits of mind are hereditary and almost irradicable [*sic*]; it may be questioned whether the great laxity of the American rule [permitting adoption] is for the public benefit."[27] Whitmore thus supported strict construction of the adoption laws and seemed, actually, to sympathize with the common law's position that "only God can make an heir." To some extent, then, one's religious attitude, or at least one's attitude about society and the nature of humankind, determined one's advocacy of or dismay at the new American law of adoption.

Adoption As a Contemporary Legal and Cultural Battleground

Same-Sex Adoption and a "Counterhistory" of Adoption

Recently the involvement of religion in the history of adoption has been all but forgotten[28] as other social factors have assumed prominence, but

"Biological Truths," p. 303). Consistent with the perspective taken in this essay and in Presser, "Historical Background," Charo recognizes that "[a]doption, a statutory creation not existing at common law, though long taking place informally or with private legislation, is evidence of a strong social tradition that recognizes the purely social and psychological dimensions of parenting, even where these occur in the absence of biological ties" (Charo, "Biological Truths," pp. 306-7). For Charo's words "strong social tradition" we might substitute "a particular Christian set of beliefs."

26. On the notion of "born criminals," and the influence in the United States of its chief advocate, Cesare Lombroso, see generally Craig Haney, "Criminal Justice and the Nineteenth Century Paradigm: The Triumph of Psychological Individualism in the 'Formative Era,'" *Law and Human Behavior* 6 (1982): 191-235, particularly 209-18, 221-26, excerpted and discussed in Stephen B. Presser and Jamil S. Zainaldin, *Law and Jurisprudence in American History: Cases and Materials,* 4th ed. (St. Paul, Minn.: West, 2000), pp. 494-515.

27. William H. Whitmore, *The Law of Adoption* (Albany, N.Y.: J. Munsell, 1876), pp. 73-74, discussed in Presser, "Historical Background," pp. 466-70.

28. Which is not to say that religion is not still intimately involved with the administration of adoption statutes. According to one recent account, "Explicit and implicit discrimination in adoption statutes abounds. Adoption statutes in almost every state have discriminated on the basis of religion, prohibiting inter-religious adoptions; a significant minority of state statutes continue to incorporate some preference for religious matching" (Pustilnik, "Private Ordering," p. 289 [footnotes omitted]).

the battle over the wisdom and substance of the law of adoption is just as fierce as it was in the nineteenth century. In one case, there has been an attempt to write a "counterhistory" of adoption law, in order to legitimate a particular proposed development of the doctrine. This has happened in the case of adoptions by same-sex couples, which are barred by statute in some jurisdictions.[29] While most historians, according to Amanda C. Pustilnik, have seen the history of American adoption only in the passage of the adoption statutes in the nineteenth century and have stressed adoption's nonexistence at common law, she believes that it is more appropriate to see adoption as a practice growing out of private planning, as it existed both in the United States and in Europe before the wave of American statutes in the mid nineteenth century.[30] And there is no denying that recent research has shown that there were many instances in which family members "adopted" (without benefit of sanctioning legislation) the children of relatives or friends, or even orphans, and accomplished this "adoption" either through contractual arrangements or through wills.[31] Pustilnik's argument is that history shows that one doesn't need the state to dictate particular or particularly restrictive categories for bringing someone into one's family; it ought to be a matter for individuals to decide for themselves, and if such arrangements through contract or testamentary document have been upheld and encouraged in the past, they ought to be so upheld and encouraged now.[32]

The notion of same-sex adoption raises a particularly profound issue in adoption, and that is whose interests the adoption law ought to

29. Pustilnik, "Private Ordering," pp. 290-91. The continued validity of those statutes is probably cast into doubt by the recent United States Supreme Court decision forbidding Texas from criminalizing private acts of homosexual sex. See note 76 below.

30. Pustilnik, "Private Ordering."

31. See generally Kawashima, "Adoption in Early America," and other sources cited by Pustilnik, "Private Ordering."

32. As Pustilnik explains:

Recognizing that adoption practice and law have permitted diverse families to form according to the needs of their participants suggests that law should play a more limited role in defining the content of adoptive homes. The role of law should instead be that of evaluator and ratifier of the arrangements individuals come together to create. More immediately, the "counterhistory" of adoption may free certain decision-makers to expand their interpretation [of] restrictive or silent statutes to permit these family forms. Or, in stripping away the shield of strict construction as a justification for denial of a nontraditional adoption petition, this different history may force decision-makers to express their prejudices in an open, contentious idiom of discrimination — which may also help bring about reform. (Pustilnik, "Private Ordering," p. 296)

serve. In the case of same-sex couples who might seek to adopt, the argument seems to be that adoption law should not discriminate on the basis of the sexual orientation of proposed adoptive parents. The argument also necessitates not circumscribing the ambit of permitted adoptive parents based on a particular religious preference for traditional family structure or particular religious hostility to homosexual conduct. Those who would champion the purported right of same-sex couples to adopt seem most interested in the rights or interests of those couples, rather than the more traditional "best interests of the child" standard which has governed child custody proceedings, including adoption, for most of the years since the passage of the adoption statutes. Those who argue for equality of treatment for same-sex couples also seem to be reflecting the currently dominant individualistic secularism rather than the conservative Christianity of the nineteenth century, particularly the Calvinist strand of Christianity hostile to the law of adoption.

Independent Adoption

Whether same-sex couples may adopt may be one of the most challenging problems currently facing the law of adoption, but there are many others. For many parents, adoption is now much more difficult to achieve than formerly. Fewer children are available in this country as a result of advances in the technology of birth control, the acceptance of single parenthood, the removal of the stigma from "illegitimacy," and the legalization of abortion.[33] In particular, because of the relatively easy availability of abortion, there are fewer children resulting from unwanted pregnancy.[34] It was these children, in many instances, who ended up being placed in adoptive homes. Now it is not uncommon for American couples to adopt foreign children, or even to hire surrogate mothers for the express purpose of bearing them a child.[35] The demand for adopted children has also

33. Appell, "Blending Families," p. 1008.

34. "The number of American pregnancies is lower than at any point in the last two decades, and an estimated 22 percent of those pregnancies are terminated by abortions. This means that fewer domestic infants are available for adoption. . ." (Papke, "Pondering Past Purposes," p. 475).

35. See, e.g., Papke, "Pondering Past Purposes," p. 476. Papke observes that "[b]ecause of the declining number of healthy white babies, adoptions in the United States have already declined since the 1970s, but Americans instead are turning to artificial insemination, in vitro fertilization, and other varieties of technology-assisted reproduction. Surrogacy

spawned a relatively new practice, "independent" or "private" adoptions, where parties make their own arrangements to find and adopt children rather than using the services of state-supervised adoption agencies, such as orphanages or departments of children and family services.[36] "Of the approximately 130,000 legal, nonrelative adoptions in the United States annually, about eighty-five percent are [now] transacted privately; only about fifteen percent occur through state agencies or state-regulated agencies."[37]

In the case of agency adoptions, adoptive parents rarely know the provenance of the children they adopt, and the agency structure exists, in part, in order to maintain the anonymity of birth parents, particularly birth mothers. With independent adoptions, however, one or more of the birth parents and the adoptive parents may meet, and consideration, such as payment for hospital or other expenses, may even pass between them. In the case of surrogate mothers, of course, there may be explicit compensation for the undertaking. In some instances of independent adoption, this consideration either for birth parents or for fees to adoption arrangers such as lawyers can come perilously close to actually buying children for adoption,[38] and thus the practice is occasionally described as a "gray

---

will also become increasingly common, especially as the states fully legalize it" (Papke, "Pondering Past Purposes," p. 476).

36. For an introduction to the history of and the arguments for and against independent adoptions (e.g., independent adoptions can be faster and give more discretion and aid to the birth mother, but agency adoptions give more certain termination of parental rights and run less of a risk of "baby selling"), see, e.g., Susan A. Munson, "Comment, Independent Adoption: In Whose Best Interest?" *Seton Hall Law Review* 26 (1996): 803-31.

37. Pustilnik, "Private Ordering," p. 287. Pustilnik makes a convincing case that whether or not it occurred on the radar screen of the law, adoption ought to be regarded as primarily a creature of private contractual arrangements, and she believes the majority of adoptions have always been through this means. See generally her "Private Ordering." Independent adoptions are as much creatures of contract as statute.

38. As Papke has put it,

[I]n the midst of the twentieth century adoption boom, infants became the most wanted adoptive children. Would-be parents were willing to spend large amounts of money for babies, especially healthy, white babies. These babies constituted an economic drain on their parents' assets; the babies had no economic value. But still, in the context of what sociologist Viviana Zelizer calls the "sentimentalization of adoption," would-be adoptive parents become willing to expend large amounts of time and money on an infant, on "the priceless child." (Papke, "Pondering Past Purposes," p. 470)

Papke theorizes that private (independent) adoptions are growing as a percentage of adoptions and are "likely to dominate in the future," because "adoptions managed and directed

market" for children.[39] Selling children violates moral, religious, and social norms, to say nothing of the Thirteenth Amendment. The risk of such child selling and the possibility that the best interests of the child will not be paramount have led to a somewhat hostile attitude on the part of many states and jurists toward "independent adoption," with full state sanction of independent adoption coming only very recently in some of those states.[40]

Nevertheless, as the scarcity of adoptable children meeting the particular religious, racial, or ethnic preferences of adopting parents contin-

---

by a private attorney are most able to accommodate adoptive parents' preferences" (Papke, "Pondering Past Purposes," p. 471). He continues:

> This type of adoption is the most consumer-driven. While county welfare departments must balance the interests of struggling biological families, children who have been removed from their homes, and the preferences of those perhaps willing to adopt, private adoption attorneys can listen chiefly to their paying clients, i.e., the would-be adoptive parents. While non-profit adoption agencies are to some extent guided by religious beliefs or humanist philosophies, private adoption attorneys can abide by what the client wants.
>
> One might worry that private adoptions would slide into illegal or borderline baby sales, and there are indications that this does go on. But instead of calls to restrict private adoptions, there are louder calls to defer even more fully to consumer demands and market forces. (Papke, "Pondering Past Purposes," pp. 471-72)

39. The problem of the "gray market" and other factors have led one thoughtful commentator to argue against permitting any but "agency" adoptions:

> When one compares the sparsity of litigation arising from agency adoptions with the volume and length of litigation arising from independent adoptions, it is easy to draw the conclusion that independent adoptions are not in anyone's best interests. Finding solutions, however, is a much more difficult task. If adoption is viewed as a process through which childless parents can obtain a child, independent adoption has distinct advantages: shorter waiting periods; immediate placement of the child in the prospective adoptive home; no risk of discrimination by an agency; and a more open adoption. If, however, adoption is seen as the process through which society provides homes for parentless children, the independent adoption loses its appeal. The risks of lengthy litigation, great expense, and black or "grey" market babies cannot be in the best interests of any child. (Munson, "Independent Adoption," p. 830 [footnotes omitted])

40. For New Jersey's recent statutory acceptance and supervision of the process see, e.g., Munson, "Independent Adoption." New Jersey's earlier attitude was revealed in a statement by New Jersey's great twentieth-century chief justice, Arthur T. Vanderbilt, in *Lavigne v. Family and Children's Soc'y,* 11 N.J. 473, 482, 95 A.2d 6, 14-15 (1953), where he observed, "There are many advantages to society in having adoptions arranged through unselfish, experienced nonprofit associations rather than by private individuals who lack skill in this delicate work and who may have personal motives other than the best interest of the child."

ues, the practice of "independent adoptions" appears to be on the increase, and, as well as the moral and legal difficulties created by the consideration which passes from adoptive parents to birth parents and adoption facilitators, the mere fact that there is contact between the two sets of parents leads to other problems, such as competition for the affections of the adopted child, and the attendant possible divided or conflicted loyalties on the child's part. For Charles Loring Brace, and for other nineteenth-century evangelical Christian reformers who were instrumental in placing thousands of orphans in adoptive homes, the focus of their simple Christianity seemed to be to give these children the benefits of Christian family upbringing. Brace did seem to suggest that the efforts of the adoptive families in providing for the instruction and salvation of souls who might otherwise be lost in an urban netherworld would also redound to the benefit of the adoptive families themselves, because they would be doing Christ's work, and thus could presumably expect a reward in the next world. Brace's primary concern, though, seems to have been the welfare of the adopted children.

"Best Interests of the Child"? The Adoption Triad

More recent adoption advocacy, consistent perhaps with a more complex view of legal relationships, and also recognizing the prevalence of independent adoptions where there is at least indirect contact between birth and adoptive parents, has suggested that this "best interests of the child" exclusive focus misses the essence of modern adoption. Perhaps overstating it a bit, but nevertheless making an important point, one of the more cynical modern adoption historians has suggested that adoption has become simply a form of "consumption" for the adoptive parents, who "seek to obtain the child held out by advertising and general cultural imagery as central to the good, successful life."[41]

A more nuanced suggestion, from Annette Ruth Appell,[42] is that the modern adoption practice is best viewed as a "triadic" relationship or "triad," involving occasionally competing interests of birth parents, adoptive parents, and adopted child. Consistent with Appell's belief that the

---

41. Papke, "Pondering Past Purposes," p. 469. Papke goes on to observe, "'Family' in contemporary America is taken to include children or at least a single child. Adoption is a way to accomplish this goal" (Papke, "Pondering Past Purposes," p. 469).

42. Appell, "Blending Families," p. 997.

"best interests of the child" ought still to be the lodestar of adoption law, although she admits that that standard "is problematic, given its vacuousness and subjectivity,"[43] she believes that adoption ought to be conceptualized as "a way of providing security for and meeting the developmental needs of a child by legally transferring ongoing parental responsibilities for that child from the birth parents to the adoptive parents, and, in the process, creating a new kinship network that forever links the birth family and the adoptive family through the child who is shared by both."[44] For Appell, "If adoption is to become truly child-centered, those participating in it as professionals, advocates, parents, law makers, and adjudicators must resist defining the process as the creation of one family and the dissolution of another."[45] An adopted child herself, Appell argues that there is an inevitable desire, once an adopted child learns of his or her adoption, to find out more about his or her birth family,[46] and that the birth family (including, for example, the birth grandparents and the birth siblings) will still have an interest in the adopted child.

There is some suggestion in the empirical literature that keeping contact with the birth family, even when an adoption goes forward, is beneficial to both that birth family and the child, particularly in the case of older adopted children;[47] but there is also a problem of divided loyalties, and a risk that after years of building a family relationship with an adoptive family, an adopted child may conclude that he or she prefers his or her birth family, leading to emotional trauma inflicted on all parts of the

43. Appell, "Blending Families," p. 1052.
44. Appell, "Blending Families," p. 1061.
45. Appell, "Blending Families," p. 1060.
46. As Appell explains,

Although the adoptive family can provide the child with love, nurture, and security, it cannot provide the adoptee with the physical, genetic, or ethnic connection that the adoptee shares uniquely with the birth family. Thus adoptees, whether adopted as infants or as older children, frequently feel a deep and enduring need throughout childhood and adulthood to know or learn about their birth parents. In describing this need, one psychologist and former foster child stated that "the desire to know one's biological origins and parentage results from a deeply felt psychological and emotional need, a need for roots, for existential continuity, and for a sense of completeness." Adoptees experience significant challenges to their identity formation by virtue of these missing elements. This does not suggest, however, that adoption is a failure or that adoptees are inordinately susceptible to pathology. It does suggest that information about or from the birth family can assist adoptees in developing an image of self. (Appell, "Blending Families," pp. 999-1000 [footnotes omitted])

47. Appell, "Blending Families," pp. 1019-20.

triad. For that and for many other reasons, it appears, state welfare agencies handling adoptions have generally made it a practice to seal the records. As Appell explains, "This secretive arrangement purportedly serves each member of the triad by protecting him or her from the shame of pregnancy outside of marriage, the shame of 'illegitimacy,' or the shame of infertility. Another rationale for the secrecy is to facilitate the formation of the adoptive family by excluding the birth parents while the adoptive parents and adoptee begin to develop emotional and psychological bonds."[48] Appell believes that these risks ought to be balanced against the greater psychological and emotional benefits that can come from promoting the "triadic relationship"; increasing advocacy of this view perhaps explains the explosive growth in the number of states who are now willing to permit some kind of "open" adoption in order to permit adopted children to know more about their birth families and, if Appell is correct, to allow all parts of the "extended family," the adoption "triad," to flourish.

Judicial "Patriarchy"?

Finally, as "independent" and "open" adoptions have become more common, and as courts have grappled with the practices of surrogate parenting, there have been several well-publicized cases involving infants placed for adoption having their adoptions revoked, as courts have, as a result of their reading of the law, elevated the rights of birth parents over those of adoptive parents.

One example is the 1992 "Baby Jessica" case.[49] Jessica's purported birth parents had signed releases of their parental rights, but Jessica's birth mother later revealed that another man was the father; that actual birth father was permitted, by the Iowa Supreme Court, to gain custody of the child, even though the child's "best interests" might have been in remaining with her adoptive parents. Those adoptive parents had cared for "Baby Jessica" virtually from her birth, and were ordered to give her up when she was approximately nineteen months old. In moving and troubling language, and perhaps employing the kind of exclusive focus on statutes that "counter-historian" Pustilnik condemns,[50] the Court declared, "As tempt-

48. Appell, "Blending Families," p. 1007.
49. *In re B.G.C.,* 496 N.W.2d 239 (Iowa 1992). The case is discussed in Munson, "Independent Adoption," pp. 817-18.
50. Pustilnik, "Private Ordering."

ing as it is to resolve this highly emotional issue with one's heart, we do not have the unbridled discretion of a Solomon. Ours is a system of law, and adoptions are solely creatures of statute. As the district court noted, without established procedures to guide courts in such matters, they would 'be engaged in uncontrolled social engineering.' This is not permitted under our law; 'courts are not free to take children from parents simply by deciding another home appears more advantageous.'"[51] As one commentator on the case indicated, "The Supreme Court [of Iowa] explained in very certain terms . . . that the best interests of the child are not grounds for determining whether to terminate a birth parent's rights."[52]

The 1994 "Baby Richard" case[53] was, if anything, even more heart-rending than the "Baby Jessica" case. "Baby Richard" was three years old, and had spent virtually all of that time with his adoptive parents, when the Illinois Supreme Court directed that he be turned over to his birth father. Baby Richard's birth mother consented to the child's adoption when he was four days old, but concealed the name of his father. The birth mother told the birth father, from whom she was then estranged, that the child had died shortly after his birth. Fifty-seven days after Baby Richard was born, however, the birth father discovered that the child was alive, and the father sought to contest the pending adoption. An Illinois trial court terminated his parental rights, on the grounds that his consent to adoption was unnecessary because he had not shown any interest in the child during the first thirty days of its life, and this decision was affirmed by an Illinois court of appeals, based on Baby Richard's "best interests." The Illinois Supreme Court, however, held that the "best interests of the child" test could only be considered after the termination of the birth parents' rights, and that in the case before it the birth father's rights were wrongfully terminated. This was because the birth mother had deceitfully tried to deprive the birth father of his parental rights and the prospective adoptive parents had "failed to make the required good-faith effort to notify the birth father and should have relinquished custody of the baby

51. *B.G.C.,* 496 N.W.2d 241.

52. Munson, "Independent Adoption," p. 818. In pertinent part the court's language was, "We agree with the district court that under [Iowa's adoption statute] section 600.3(2) parental rights may not be terminated solely on consideration of the child's best interest but that specific grounds for termination under chapter 600A must also be established. [The birth father's] parental rights had not been terminated, and the adoption proceedings were therefore fatally flawed" (*B.G.C.,* 496 N.W.2d 245).

53. *In re Petition of Doe to Adopt Baby Boy Janikova,* 638 N.E.2d 181 (Ill.), cert. denied, 115 S. Ct. 499 (1994).

when the birth father asserted his parental rights."[54] The Illinois Supreme Court's key language was as follows:

> The finding that the father had not shown a reasonable degree of interest in the child is not supported by the evidence. In fact, he made various attempts to locate the child, all of which were either frustrated or blocked by the actions of the mother. Further, the mother was aided by the attorney for the adoptive parents, who failed to make any effort to ascertain the name or address of the father despite the fact that the mother indicated she knew who he was. Under the circumstances, the father had no opportunity to discharge any familial duty.
>
> In the opinion below, the Appellate court, wholly missing the threshold issue in this case, dwelt on the best interests of the child. Since, however, the father's parental interest was improperly terminated, there was no occasion to reach the factor of the child's best interests. That point should never have been reached and need never have been discussed.[55]

In somewhat defensive, but still poignant, language the Illinois Court concluded that the adoption statutes of Illinois "are designed to protect natural parents in their preemptive rights to their own children wholly apart from any consideration of the so-called best interests of the child." Driving its point home, the court stated, "If it were otherwise, few parents would be secure in the custody of their own children. If best interests of the child were a sufficient qualification to determine child custody, anyone with superior income, intelligence, education, etc., might challenge and deprive the parents of their right to their own children. The law is otherwise. . . ."[56]

In both the "Baby Jessica" and "Baby Richard" cases, then, courts focused on the provisions of the statutes, statutes that may have originally been passed to further "best interests" of adopted children,[57] and pro-

<hr>

54. The quoted language is from the analysis of the case in Munson, "Independent Adoption," p. 820.

55. *Petition of Doe*, 638 N.E.2d 182.

56. *Petition of Doe*, 638 N.E.2d 182-83.

57. Indeed, as a concurring opinion by Justice McMorrow in the Baby Richard case observed, quoting Illinois's statute, "To justify its conclusion, the Appellate court in the present case found it significant that the Illinois legislature has declared in the Adoption Act that the 'best interests and welfare of the person to be adopted shall be of paramount consideration in the construction and interpretation of this Act.' (750 ILCS 50/20a (West 1992).) [Nevertheless,] I do not believe that this broad policy statement justifies the Appellate court's holding" (*Petition of Doe*, 638 N.E.2d, 183 [McMorrow, J., concurring]). Clearly

ceeded to declare that parental rights trumped the interests of adopted children and any rights of adoptive parents.[58]

The nineteenth-century common law, in keeping with its generally patriarchal flavor, tended to preference the father's rights to the child, which were recognized more as property rights than nurturing obligations. The "Baby Jessica" and "Baby Richard" cases may indicate that this attitude lingers in the law. Still, in the course of the nineteenth century, in child custody disputes there was an increasing recognition that during a child's "tender years" it was more appropriate to place a child with its mother. Nevertheless, some have argued that as the "best interests of the child" standard took hold in the middle of the nineteenth century, the patriarchal rule of the common law preferencing the father was replaced by the administration of a "best interests" rule administered by a "patriarchal" judiciary. As Michael Grossberg, one of the most important historians of American family law, explains,

---

torn, however, Justice McMorrow dissented from the Supreme Court's decision to deny a rehearing in the case, apparently because he wanted to hear further argument that the "best interests of the child" ought to take precedence over strict construction of the statute. As he explained:

> Issues that form the basis of my vote to allow the petitions for rehearing include: the extent of the court's duty to protect children when that protection may conflict with parental rights established by law; the propriety of the court's disregarding laws designed to prevent the taking of a child from biological parents where the evidence of parental unfitness may be insufficient but where the best interests of the child call for such separation; whether the broad policy statement in the Adoption Act concerning the best interests of the child should be interpreted as predominant over the articulated requirements of the Act; and whether which, if any, of the courts involved in this case misapprehended, unduly emphasized, or attached inappropriate credibility to certain evidence presented at trial. Further argument on these matters would be helpful. (*Petition of Doe*, 638 N.E.2d, at 191 [McMorrow, J., dissenting from the denial of rehearing])

58. The statement in the text might fairly be read as oversimplifying the issue before the court in the Baby Richard case, or as engaging in unfair criticism of Chief Justice Heiple, who wrote the majority's opinion. Heiple *was* subjected to grossly unfair demagogic attacks by Chicago Tribune newspaper columnist Bob Greene and others. Heiple nicely summed up the difficult issues he faced with a turn of phrase that might please Professor Papke (see his "Pondering Past Purposes") and alarm Professor Appell (see her "Blending Families.") "This much is clear," Chief Justice Heiple wrote; "[a]doptive parents who comply with the law may feel secure in their adoptions. Natural parents may feel secure in their right to raise their own children. If there is a tragedy in this case, as has been suggested, then that tragedy is the wrongful breakup of a natural family and the keeping of a child by strangers without right. We must remember that the purpose of an adoption is to provide a home for a child, not a child for a home" (*Petition of Doe*, 638 N.E.2d, 190 [Opinion denying a rehearing]).

Over the course of the Nineteenth Century, trial and appellate judges became the primary domestic-relations agents of the expanding republican state. They assumed those powers in a special way. Judges were new kinds of patriarchs, ones invested with a power over some domestic relations that rivaled that of their [familial patriarchal] predecessors. They used the broad discretionary authority conferred on them by equity and common-law procedures, and conceded by legislative inertia, to rewrite the laws governing the allocation of resources, rights, and duties within the home and between family members and the state. As the major arbiters of Nineteenth Century family governance, judges took the lead in framing and applying the growing body of American domestic-relations law. Family law became their patriarchal domain.[59]

Grossberg explains that the discretion that nineteenth-century judges assumed over such matters as the rights of children and married women, child custody, divorce, and adoption "encouraged a conception of judges involved in family disputes as stern but just fathers."[60] What these judges did, Grossberg maintains, was to create a set of doctrines characterized by "gender biases, racial and ethnic animosities, domestic-relations individualism, child nurture beliefs, household economics, and idealized visions of the bourgeois family."[61] "The judicial acquisition of patriarchal powers," Grossberg asserts, "stemmed from the traditional assumption that married women lacked the economic and intellectual independence to act without male supervision (and thus needed special protection), combined with the new faith in separate and mutually exclusive spheres [of husband and wife] so central to the organization of the republican family."[62]

59. Grossberg, *Governing the Hearth,* p. 290. Grossberg suggests that those seeking a more general statement of this judicial patriarchy theme should consult his article "Who Gets the Child? Custody, Guardianship, and the Rise of Judicial Patriarchy in Nineteenth Century America," *Feminist Studies* 9 (1983): 235-60, and Janet Rifkind, "Toward a Theory of Law and Patriarchy," *Harvard Women's Law Journal* 3 (1980): 83-95. See also, for a statement that nineteenth-century child custody law partakes of "judicial patriarchy," Zainaldin, "Modern American Family Law."

60. Grossberg, *Governing the Hearth,* p. 293.

61. Grossberg, *Governing the Hearth,* pp. 293-94.

62. Grossberg, *Governing the Hearth,* p. 300. States Grossberg, "To a significant degree, the courts' power had its origins in Nineteenth Century gender alliances and castes, especially the rigid segregation of worldly males and home-bound females. The judicial patriarchy represented a refined and revised legal version of the distinction between the male authority to govern the home and the female responsibility to maintain it" (Grossberg, *Governing the Hearth,* p. 300).

Evidence supporting this "patriarchal" view of nineteenth-century family law can certainly be found in such infamous utterances as that of Supreme Court Associate Justice Joseph P. Bradley in *Bradwell v. Illinois* (1873), where he proclaimed, in the course of an opinion affirming Illinois's denial of Myra Bradwell's application to be admitted as a member of the bar:

> [T]he civil law, as well as nature herself, has always recognized a wide difference in the respective spheres and destinies of man and woman. Man is, or should be, woman's protector and defender. The natural and proper timidity and delicacy which belongs to the female sex evidently unfits it for many of the occupations of civil life. The constitution of the family organization, which is founded in the divine ordinance, as well as in the nature of things, indicates the domestic sphere as that which properly belongs to the domain and functions of womanhood.
>
> ... The paramount destiny and mission of woman are to fulfill the noble and benign offices of wife and mother. This is the law of the Creator. ...[63]

Evincing a similarly patriarchal and purportedly religious cast are the remarks of the highly regarded New York Justice Greene C. Bronson in an 1842 child custody case. In his opinion in the case, Justice Bronson strongly castigated a mother for refusing to leave New York to move with her Canadian husband and children to his native Nova Scotia:

> It is possible that our laws relating to the rights and duties of husband and wife have not kept pace with the progress of civilization. It may be best that the wife should be declared head of the family, and that she should be at liberty to desert her husband at pleasure and take the children of the marriage with her. But I will not enquire what the law ought to be. That prerogative belongs to others. I will however venture the remark, even at the hazard of being thought out of fashion, that human laws cannot be very far out of the way when they are in accordance with the law of God.[64]

Justice Bradley's and Justice Bronson's religious views, and their judicial patriarchy, seem of a piece with the hierarchical religious attitude of

63. *Bradwell v. Illinois,* 83 U.S. (16 Wall.) 130, 141, 21 L. Ed. 442 (1873) (Bradley, J., concurring).

64. *People ex rel. Barry v. Mercein,* 3 Hill. 399, 422-423 (Supreme Court of Judicature of New York, 1842) (concurring opinion of Justice Bronson).

William Whitmore, which led him to disparage the adoption statutory project itself. It is tempting to see the "Baby Jessica" and "Baby Richard" cases as errors by a patriarchal judiciary, or at least one, as Pustilnik argues, overly concerned with statutory provisions and insensitive to the actual history of adoption.

Feminist scholars critical of what they believe to be the law and society's generally patriarchal assumptions have made some powerful points,[65] but if even the administration of a "best interests of the child rule" implicates patriarchy, it is difficult to understand how we might leave patriarchy behind. We might argue that we might best replace a patriarchal rule with one that preferences women, but should we then favor the interests of the birth mother, or of the adoptive mother, or of female children? Indeed, whether or not one is a feminist and opposed to patriarchy, it remains unclear why any part or sub-part of the adoption triad should be preferenced above any other, and perhaps this is why even Appell, who favors "triadic" analysis, ends up advocating a "best interests of the child" standard.

Conclusion: Seeking to Resolve the Current Issues Influenced by Adoption's History

Is it then appropriate for the law to continue to give a preference to birth parents, or to birth mothers? Should the protection of the best interests of the child remain the standard for the courts? Is judicial review of adoption decisions inevitably patriarchal? Does anyone have a clear idea of what the "best interest" of a child is when there is a conflict between birth parents and adoptive parents? Is there any way in which the religious influence on the history of nineteenth-century adoption law might be of use in solving some of these current legal dilemmas?[66]

---

65. See, e.g., Grossberg, *Governing the Hearth*, and for an excellent and provocative short survey of family law from a feminist perspective, see Susan Frelich Appleton, "From the Lemma Barkeloo and Phoebe Couzins Era to the New Millennium: 130 Years of Family Law," *Washington University Journal of Law and Policy* 6 (2001): 189-203.

66. And if these problems are not knotty enough, consider family law historian Susan Frelich Appleton's recent observation:

Some of the greatest excitement in contemporary family law emerges from studying adoption law, first developed in the Nineteenth Century, side by side with modern alternatives to adoption, including in vitro fertilization and all variations of "surrogacy" arrangements. Medicine now permits so-called "technological adoptions" — with some

The challenge of taking a stranger into one's family is a profound one, the enterprise of raising a child is frequently difficult, and not one that is easily accomplished without the aid of others.[67] The evangelical Christianity of reformers such as Charles Loring Brace stressed the altruism that religion helps encourage, and the faith of those who took in the orphans he placed must have been indispensable to the success of their newly augmented families. The nineteenth-century "social gospel" of Brace and others embraced the concept of shared reciprocal responsibility in a democratic manner at odds with earlier hierarchical American Calvinist concepts. The older attitudes on the part of judges and other lawyers frustrated somewhat the ends of adoption reformers, and it might be said that something like that conflict still bedevils the law and practice of adoption today.

For the last few decades, the legal academy has predominantly acted under the impression that it is best to view American law, or at least American constitutional law, as having been conceived free from any religious influence; that we have, as one allegedly historical tract put it, "A Godless Constitution."[68] There is no doubt that all through American history there have been those who have been concerned about mixing church and state, and that among their number are to be found not only some of the most famous Americans, most notably Thomas Jefferson and James Madison, but also intriguing somewhat lesser figures such as Roger Williams and Isaac Backus. But there have been other Americans, including titans such as George Washington and Patrick Henry, and such lesser known figures (to the general public at least) as Supreme Court Justices Joseph Story and Samuel Chase, who have argued, as cogently as their challeng-

authorities opining that today a child might have five parents and other authorities concluding that such children might lack even a single "parent" whom the law recognizes. The news here is not all good: What happens to children awaiting adoptive homes once prospective parents can buy the eggs and sperm of their dreams? To what extent do new reproductive options send the message that women really have no choice but to have children? (Appleton, "From the Lemma Barkeloo," p. 202)

67. Hence the now well-worn aphorism that it takes a village to raise a child. See, e.g., Hillary Rodham Clinton, *It Takes a Village: And Other Lessons Children Teach Us* (New York: Simon and Schuster, 1996).

68. Isaac Kramnick and R. Laurence Moore, *The Godless Constitution: The Case against Religious Correctness* (New York: Norton, 1996). For criticism of "The Godless Constitution," see, e.g., Stephen B. Presser, "Some Realism about Atheism: Responses to 'The Godless Constitution,'" *Texas Review of Law and Policy* 1 (1997): 87-121, and *God and the Constitution: Towards a New Legal Theology* (London: Institute of United States Studies, University of London, 1998).

ers, that the rule of law itself depends on a firm religious foundation for the state.[69]

To paraphrase the creed of the Federalists, the group that governed the nation during its first decade under the Federal Constitution of 1789, there could be no order without law, no law without morality, and no morality without religion.[70] And the religion that proponents of this assertion contemplated was not one from which the state was to be completely divorced; rather, in the view of the Federalists, at least, one of the principal obligations of government was to support religion, thereby ensuring the stability and the prospering of the state. This was evident in the fact that eleven of the thirteen original states had some sort of religious qualifications for the franchise or for the holding of public office, and, at the time of the passage of the First Amendment, three states still had established churches. Indeed, while the First Amendment has been invoked in our own time as a means of ending mandatory prayer and Bible reading in the nation's public schools (to say nothing of the recent Ninth Circuit decision holding that the words "under God" in the Pledge of Allegiance are unconstitutional),[71] we are, nevertheless, slowly beginning to remember that the First Amendment itself was actually conceived not as a bar to all religious establishments, but merely to keep the federal government from interfering with the individual states' rights to determine for themselves how best to ensure the necessary religious foundation for good citizenship.[72]

One lesson from American history, then, is that our currently prevailing secular conceptions of local, state, and federal government were

69. See generally Stephen B. Presser, *Recapturing the Constitution: Race, Religion, and Abortion Reconsidered* (Washington, D.C.: Regnery, 1994). See also, on the linkage between Christianity and American liberty, M. Stanton Evans, *The Theme Is Freedom: Religion, Politics, and the American Tradition* (Washington, D.C.: Regnery, 1994). For Justice Story's declaration in 1844 that Christianity is a part of the common law, in that case the common law of Pennsylvania, see *Vidal v. Philadelphia*, 43 U.S. [2 How.] 127, 198 ("[W]e are compelled to admit that although Christianity be a part of the common law of the state, yet it is so in this qualified sense, that its divine origin and truth are admitted, and therefore it is not to be maliciously and openly reviled and blasphemed against, to the annoyance of believers or the injury of the public.").

70. See generally Presser, *Recapturing the Constitution*, pp. 86-97. For the notion that even John Marshall, the venerated titan of Federalist jurisprudence, evinced a piety that was a continual source of strength, see the fine new biography, R. Kent Newmyer, *John Marshall and the Heroic Age of the Supreme Court* (Baton Rouge: Louisiana State University Press, 2001).

71. *Newdow v. United States Congress*, 292 F.3d 597 (9th Cir. 2002), stay granted 2002 US App. LEXIS 12826 (9th Cir., 2002).

72. See, e.g., Steven D. Smith, *Foreordained Failure: The Quest for a Constitutional Principle of Religious Freedom* (New York: Oxford University Press, 1995), p. 49.

not necessarily shared by our framers, and that should give us some pause. We study history to learn from the mistakes of the past as well as to learn more about who we really are, and merely because we once had a different conception of law and religion doesn't, of course, mean that our current one is wrong. Still, in building a highly individualistic, secular, and largely amoral conception of the Constitution and our law, we've lost something vital, and many current social problems might be due, at least in part, to that loss.[73] It could be argued that George Washington and the Federalists got it right, and that unless we try to relearn what they knew, we're headed for rocky times. In any event, an understanding of the vital role religion once played in our jurisprudence and law does seem to illuminate some of the current dilemmas of the law of adoption.

Because of American law's current predominantly, aggressively secular and individualistic perspective, there seems to have been a recent tendency to conceive of adoption law as needing to make a choice between serving the "best interests" of the child or the "interests" of another member of the adoption triad. Thus the "Baby Richard" and "Baby Jessica" cases preferenced the birth father, and some courts or legislatures hesitate to allow same-sex adoption because they conceive of that practice as a subordination of the "best interests" of the child to the purportedly selfish preferences of the same-sex adopting couple. Without necessarily suggesting that we embrace the Christian religion of the nineteenth-century "social gospel," adoption reformers might still do well to borrow its understanding of American community and its exposure of the poverty of the concept of secular individualism. Analysts such as Appell, in their advocacy of viewing adoption as a triadic relationship and seeking to promote the participation in that relationship of all three elements of that triad, have revealed an understanding of adoption that is consistent with the religious motivation of individuals such as Brace.

One may not have to be a Christian to reach a position on adoption law that recognizes the essential shared humanity, individual worth and dignity, and reciprocal responsibility of those who, for whatever reasons, would seek to adopt or to place children for adoption. And one must avoid the trap of nineteenth-century patriarchal judges and commentators who preferenced a particular conservative vision of the family and

73. See generally, Presser, *Recapturing the Constitution*. This sense of what we have lost also seems to be the animating notion behind the recent critical biography of Oliver Wendell Holmes (the father of modern American legal secularism) by Albert W. Alschuler, *Law without Values: The Life, Work, and Legacy of Justice Holmes* (Chicago: University of Chicago Press, 2000).

justified that preference on the basis of a limited and exclusive version of Christianity. Perhaps all it takes is for adoption policy-makers to recognize the changed social, economic, political, intellectual, or cultural circumstances in the late twentieth and early twenty-first centuries, which have moved us somewhat away from the norm of the nuclear family which dominated nineteenth-century family law.

There is now "a decrease in the number of infants available for adoption, pressure by adult adoptees for information about their birth families, more fluid notions of what constitutes a family, and an increasing number of older children being raised in legally sanctioned substitute care."[74] As indicated in this chapter, these social and demographic factors are leading to legal reform of adoption, just as social and demographic factors led to the creation of general adoption statutes in the mid nineteenth century.

One avenue for that reform is to follow the insights of legal and constitutional secular individualism, to embrace the philosophy expressed, for example, in the famous "mystery passage" of *Planned Parenthood v. Casey*, that "[a]t the heart of liberty is the right to define one's own concept of existence, of the universe, and of the mystery of human life. Beliefs about these matters could not define the attributes of personhood were they formed under the compulsion of the state."[75] This would seem to lead one in the direction of abandoning state supervision of adoption, and perhaps deferring completely to private organization. But even if a majority of justices on the United States Supreme Court have so far failed to understand the limitations if not the absurdity of the mystery passage,[76] the mystery passage's view of human nature and liberty is, to say the least, deeply flawed, since meaning in life and happiness itself invariably involve relationships with others, if not with God.

Indeed, Appell's analysis of adoption as a "triad" reminds us that one can't resolve adoption problems in a manner that seeks to be concerned only with individuals. Appell, in the end, embraces the "best interests of the child" standard, but if Judeo-Christian beliefs teach us anything it is that there are interests we all share and that excessive focus on

---

74. Appell, "Blending Families," p. 1008.

75. *Planned Parenthood of Southeastern Pennsylvania v. Casey*, 505 U.S. 833, 851 (Plurality opinion, 1992).

76. The logic of the "mystery passage," described by Justice Scalia as the "sweet-mystery-of-life" passage, was recently reaffirmed, in the course of holding that private homosexual conduct is protected by the Fourteenth Amendment, in *Lawrence v. Texas*, 539 U.S. 558, 588 (Scalia, J., dissenting).

individuals is impoverishing; thus, the distinctions between the "best interests of the child" and the interests of all of those involved in the triad might be illusive or ephemeral, or, at some level, nonexistent. This is not the place to work out all the implications, but the simple awareness that the practice of adoption inevitably involves the rights and responsibilities of several parties should lead us away from the mystery passage, and back toward basic Judeo-Christian insights.[77] Just as was true for legal reform in the nineteenth century, such religious insight, toleration, and altruism may be required for the law of adoption and its challenges in the twenty-first century.[78]

77. See, to similar effect, Michael W. McConnell, Robert F. Cochran Jr., and Angela C. Carmella, introduction to *Christian Perspectives on Legal Thought*, ed. McConnell, Cochran, and Carmella, p. xix: "Whatever their differences, many thoughtful Americans of various religious and political stripes share a deep concern that modern life, including public life, has become dominated by selfish, shallow, materialistic, cruel and nihilistic values. Christianity, along with other faiths, may be an antidote to this great moral failing of our time."

78. Or for the law generally. See, e.g., Harold J. Berman, writing in the foreword to *Christian Perspectives on Legal Thought*, ed. McConnell, Cochran, and Carmella, p. xiii, where he observes that "from a Christian perspective, the purpose of our existing body of property law, criminal law, family law, tort law, and other branches of law is to create conditions in which sacrificial love of God and of neighbor, the kind of love personified by Jesus Christ, can take root in our society and grow."

11. Adoption Law and Controversies

ANN M. STANTON

Adoption is a legal institution that is adapting to evolving contemporary needs. Adoption is primarily a process for selecting fit parents for children, but it also serves society by finding children for prospective parents. As the number of infants who are relinquished for adoption by unwed mothers has declined in the past decades in the United States, Americans are adopting foreign-born children in increasing numbers. At the same time, there is pressure to encourage more people to become adoptive parents for the substantial number of children in foster care who are eligible for adoption.

This chapter will present the changing demographics of adoption in the United States and the basic process and legal requirements of adoption either through an agency or by independent placement. Several controversial issues in adoption law and practice will be addressed. First, an evolving issue is the legal means by which to protect the rights of unmarried fathers through notification of a pending adoption, or, in the alternative, to dispense with the need for consent. Second, there is considerable support for more openness in the adoption process and in opening sealed adoption records. Third, states are divided on the issue of whether gay and lesbian individuals or same-sex couples should be eligible to become adoptive parents. Finally, an ongoing controversy is the expectation that adoption is, and should remain, a gratuitous transfer even when it is acknowledged that substantial sums of money are exchanged.

Demographics

Only recently have authoritative statistics on the numbers of adoptions in the United States been collected. In Census 2000, for the first time, the category of "adopted son/daughter" was added as a category separate from "natural born son/daughter" and "stepson/stepdaughter."[1] There are 2.1 million adopted children in American households. Of these, 1.6 million adopted children were under the age of eighteen in the year 2000, making up 2.5 percent of all children under eighteen. Among the 1.7 million households with adopted children, 82 percent had just one adopted child, 15 percent had two adopted children, and 3 percent had three or more adopted children. The Census 2000 data do not distinguish whether an adoption was of a relative or a nonrelative or whether the child was adopted through a public agency, a private agency, or independently. Consequently, the Census does not distinguish among children who were adopted by their stepparents, children adopted by their grandparents or other relatives, and children adopted by other people to whom they are not biologically related.

Intra-family adoptions by relatives or stepparents have increased proportionately and in absolute numbers. Today, it is estimated that over half of all adoptions involve relatives by blood or marriage, including stepfamilies. The number of children adopted by relatives has been increasing since the late 1980s as a result of substantial increases in the number of children in foster care being placed in homes of relatives, and subsequently some of these placements becoming kinship adoptions. The increased number of stepparent adoptions reflects the increased number of children born to single parents who later marry, as well as the high incidence of divorce and remarriage of custodial parents. In these cases, if the divorced or never-married noncustodial birth parent objects to the adoption, the lack of consent prevents the adoption. The ongoing obligation on the part of a noncustodial parent to make child support payments can serve as an incentive for some noncustodial parents to consent to adoption, since adoption terminates the noncustodial parents' future support obligations.

There has been a decrease in the number of adoptions of infants by unrelated adults primarily as a result of the fact that there are fewer infants who are voluntarily relinquished for adoption. In contrast, in recent years

---

1. United States Census, *Adopted Children and Stepchildren, 2000* (Washington, D.C., August 2003). All statistics in this paragraph come from the Census 2000.

there has been an increase in the number of adoptions of older children. The adoption of children over the age of two years is usually handled by government agencies rather than privately. These older children generally have been made wards of the court and have spent time in and out of foster care while the public agency has made repeated attempts to reunify the family. Dependent children who are in foster care typically have been removed from the care of their birth parents for the children's own safety from child abuse, neglect, abandonment, or the parents' inability to care for them. There are additional cases in which birth parents relinquish their children to state agencies because of parental incapacity caused by mental or physical problems. When reunification fails, the agency may first seek voluntary consents for adoption from the parents before moving to sever the parents' rights in order to free the children for adoption. Sweeping changes in child welfare laws in 1997 under the federal Adoption and Safe Families Act have created increased numbers of "legal orphans," that is, children whose parents are alive but whose parental rights have been terminated. Under the federal initiative which has been adopted as state law, children who have spent at least fifteen out of the last twenty-two months in state care can be permanently taken away from their parents. Nationally, the number of parents whose rights are terminated has increased, and in 2000, approximately 51,000 children were adopted through state child welfare agencies.[2] Financial subsidies and assistance may be available to adoptive parents of foster children. Even the states can receive financial incentives if the number of adoptions from foster care increases. Many states struggle to find enough homes for the growing number of children in foster care who may be hard to place in adoptive homes because the children are older, children of color, children with physical, mental, or emotional problems, or children who are part of a sibling group.

Adoptions of children born in foreign countries have increased as the

2. U.S. Department of Health and Human Services, Administration for Children and Families, AFCARS website, http://www.acf.hhs.gov/programs/cb/publications/afcars/report7.pdf. Accessed 3 August 2004. The Adoption and Foster Care Analysis and Reporting System (AFCARS) is a source of information about adoption in the United States from the Children's Bureau of the Administration for Children and Families. States are required to collect data on all adopted children placed by the state child welfare agency and adopted children who are receiving assistance or services from the state agency directly or under contract with another agency. The National Adoption Information Clearinghouse (NAIC) provides a comprehensive resource on adoption, including adoption statistics, databases, and federal and state laws. See their website at http://naic.acf.hhs.gov. Accessed 3 August 2004.

number of healthy American infants eligible for adoption has decreased. The Census 2000 data show that 13 percent of adopted children in the United States of all ages are foreign-born. Of these, almost half were born in Asia, about one-third in Latin America, and about one-sixth in Europe. Korea is the source of about one-fifth of foreign-born adopted children of all ages. In recent years an increasing number of foreign-born children have come from China, with 28 percent of foreign-born adopted children under the age of six from China.[3] The current estimates are that children adopted from abroad account for one-fifth to one-sixth of all nonrelative adoptions in this country. The number of international adoptions grew from approximately seven thousand in 1990 to over twenty thousand in 2002.[4] The United States provides more than half of the adoptive homes for intercountry adoptions. International adoptions have been seen as a worthy humanitarian outreach to needy children, particularly since the Korean War when thousands of orphaned and abandoned children were available for adoption. There has, however, been some hostility to international adoption by those who view it as exploitation of poor foreign nations.[5] In recent years, political pressure and rising nationalism have changed the practice of international adoption. At present, prospective adoptive parents are looking to China, Eastern Europe, and Central and South America for children to adopt.

The availability of Native American children for adoption by non-Indians has been largely circumscribed by federal law. The Indian Child Welfare Act (ICWA) was passed in response to congressional findings that an alarmingly high percentage of Indian children were being separated from their families and tribes. ICWA contains placement preferences that bind state courts to give preference for adoption and foster care placement of an Indian child first to a member of the child's extended family, second to other members of the child's tribe, or third to other Indian families.[6] The number of Native American children being adopted by non-

3. United States Census, *Adopted Children and Stepchildren, 2000.*

4. "International Adoption," U.S. Department of State, Office of Children's Issues website, http://travel.state.gov/family/adoption_resources_02.html. Accessed 3 August 2004. This site is a source for information on international adoptions.

5. Elizabeth Bartholet, "International Adoption: Property, Prospects and Pragmatics," *Journal of American Academy of Matrimonial Lawyers* 13 (winter 1996): 181-210, and "International Adoption: Current Status and Future Prospects," *The Future of Children* 3 (spring 1993): 89-103. (Also available at http://www.futureofchildren.org/pubs-info2825/pubs-info.htm?doc_id=77427. Accessed 3 August 2004.)

6. Indian Child Welfare Act of 1978 (ICWA), 25 U.S.C. 1901 et seq.

Indians has declined dramatically since 1978, when the Indian Child Welfare Act went into effect.

American Adoption Law

Adoption is the legal creation of a parent-child relationship that is not based on biological parentage. The adoption process is governed by statutes in every state, since adoption was not recognized under common law. State adoption statutes were first enacted in the United States in the mid nineteenth century, and the law continues to evolve with variations among the states. Adoption is essentially a two-step procedure, although both steps may be accomplished in the same proceeding. The first step involves termination of all rights of the birth parents to the child. The second step is the creation of a new parent-child relationship with its attendant rights and responsibilities.

Termination of parental rights can occur voluntarily or involuntarily. Written consent to the adoption is generally required from the biological parents, unless there is an appropriate basis for dispensing with parental consent. Consent is not required from an individual whose parental rights have already been terminated. Some states have enacted statutes that dispense with the need for a father's consent to adoption of a child conceived through rape or incest. A state agency may seek the involuntary termination of parental rights in a judicial proceeding. In this latter situation, most states require a showing of parental unfitness based on abandonment, abuse, persistent neglect, or inability to care for the child.

An adoption proceeding is initiated by a petition filed by the prospective adoptive parents. After the petition is filed, the court generally refers the case to an agency of the court to conduct a home study and to issue a nonbinding report on the prospective adoption. The judicial adoption hearing is usually informal and uncontested. In many states, if the court approves the adoption, it may enter an interlocutory decree rather than a final decree. The prospective parents will be given custody of the child and in these states the child must live with the adoptive parents for a specified probationary time period, such as six months, before the adoption is finalized. In some other states, a final adoption decree can be entered at the conclusion of the initial hearing. Procedurally, stepparent adoptions have fewer legal regulations than stranger adoptions; for instance, the home study requirement may be waived and statutory waiting periods may be shortened. The procedural shortcuts for stepparent adoptions recognize that these individuals are already functioning as de facto parents before the adoption process is even begun. When an adoption is finalized, usually the original birth certificate is sealed in the court record and an amended birth certificate with the adoptive parents' names and the child's new name becomes the legal confirmation of the adoption. The effect of the adoption decree is to grant the adoptive parents all the rights and obligations of biological parents.

Since adoption law is governed by state law, there are variations among the states in the details of the adoption procedure and requirements. These inconsistencies among the states can be problematic for interstate adoptions. There have been several attempts to bring consistency to the process. The National Conference of Commissioners on Uniform State Law promulgated a Uniform Adoption Act in 1953, a revised version in 1969, and an amended version in 1971. In 1994, the Uniform Law Commissioners developed a new Uniform Adoption Act which addresses some of the current issues in adoption by creating a coherent framework for legitimizing and regulating both direct-placement and agency-supervised adoption.[7] Several states have enacted some provisions of these model acts, but state-to-state differences remain.

When children are transported across state boundaries to be adopted, there are additional legal requirements. All fifty states have passed the Interstate Compact on the Placement of Children, which requires an agreement between both participating states prior to the adoption placement of children transported interstate.[8] Under the Compact, the receiving state in which the prospective adoptive parents reside must make a study of the proposed placement and notify the sending state that the placement "does not appear to be contrary to the interests of the child." Subsequently, the child may be sent to the receiving state. While the law of the receiving state determines the appropriateness of an adoptive home, the law of the sending state determines the legality of the adoption. The Compact does not apply to adoptions by stepparents, relatives, or guardians when the child is sent or brought into another state by specified close relatives of the child. To avoid application of the Compact, and to simplify the process and eliminate delays in placement, an out-of-state mother may relocate to give birth in the receiving state. Failure to comply

---

7. Uniform Adoption Law (1994), Uniform Law Annotated, vol. 9.

8. Interstate Compact on the Placement of Children. See Ann M. Haralambie, *Handling Child Custody, Abuse and Adoption Cases,* second ed. (New York: McGraw-Hill, 1993), 2:95 and Appendix 14-1.

with the terms of the Compact, when it is applicable, constitutes a violation of the laws of both states and the adoption may be denied or set aside.

United States citizens seeking to adopt a child from a foreign country must satisfy three separate sets of legal requirements: the laws of the child's country of birth; United States immigration laws; and the laws of the state where the prospective parents are domiciled. Because of the possible problems in overseas adoptions, many potential adoptive parents work with an international adoption agency, but independent adoptions in which the adoptive parents deal directly with the foreign child placement agency are possible. Adoption procedures vary from country to country, but most require that a child who is placed for adoption be legally recognized as an orphan, or, if a parent is living, the child must be legally and irrevocably released for adoption according to local foreign law. Most countries require the full adoption of the child in the foreign court. Some foreign courts grant guardianship of the child to the prospective adoptive parent, which allows the prospective parent to take the child to the prospective parent's home country. The Child Citizenship Act of 2000, which amends the Immigration and Naturalization Act, has simplified the acquisition of U.S. citizenship for adopted children who are born abroad.[9] A certified copy of a final adoption decree can be submitted to obtain a certificate of citizenship.

There have been several attempts to achieve international uniformity in adoption law and reduce duplication of efforts, but they have not been successful. The most recent attempt at improving intercountry adoptions is the 1993 Hague Convention on Protection of Children and Cooperation in Respect of Intercountry Adoptions.[10] The Hague Convention does not seek standardized adoption laws or complete uniformity; rather, it would establish a minimum set of procedures to be followed in the sending and receiving states. The Convention requires that contracting states establish a central authority to oversee adoptions. The Convention seeks a reduction of redundancy in procedures in sending and receiving countries and the elimination of international trafficking in children for profit. Thus far, the Convention has been ratified by forty-seven countries and signed by another thirteen. The United States has signed but not

9. See "International Adoptions," §II, Bureau of Consular Affairs website, http://travel.state.gov/int'ladoption.html (U.S. Department of State summary of regulations of the international adoption process).

10. Hague Conference on International Law: Final Act of the 17th Session, Including the Convention on Protection of Children and Cooperation in Respect of Intercountry Adoption, 32 I.L.M. 1134 (1993).

yet ratified the Convention. The Convention is binding on an adoption only if both the sending and receiving countries have ratified it.

Controversial Issues in Adoption Law

Parental Consent or Appropriate Grounds for Waiver of Consent

The most significant legal requirement for a valid adoption is the consent of birth parents or a legitimate basis for dispensing with parental consent. A petition for adoption is not granted unless a court finds that the child's birth parents have executed consents to the adoption or the parents' rights have been terminated. The birth parents usually must be informed of the irrevocable nature of the consent, and it must be voluntary. A judgment of adoption can be held void if the birth parents did not give valid consent. The parental consent requirement is usually a straightforward matter with birth mothers. As a general rule, the woman who gives birth to a child is the child's legal parent and entitled to consent to or withhold consent to her child's adoption, although surrogate parenting and the new reproductive technologies now challenge this formerly simple concept. In many states, a birth mother cannot give a valid consent to adoption until seventy-two hours after the child's birth, so that any consent to relinquish an as yet unborn child would not be binding. In most states, if a birth mother changes her mind about her willingness to consent to adoption, revocation is not an option unless fraud, duress, or undue influence can be proved. Some states allow revocation within a certain limited period of time.

Generally, consent to adoption by the man who is the "presumed" father of a child is also required. A presumed father includes the mother's husband at the time of conception or birth, a man who has held himself out as the father, or a man whose name is on the birth certificate. A married father, even one without physical custody of a child, has legal custody rights and obligations. The rights of unmarried fathers traditionally did not include the right to notice of a proposed adoption. Until the early 1970s, fathers of children born out of wedlock generally were excluded from the category of parents whose consent to adoption was required. The United States Supreme Court has considered the status of unwed fathers in several cases.[11] The legal principle that has emerged from these

---

11. *Stanley v. Illinois,* 405 U.S. 45 (1972); *Quillain v. Wolcott,* 434 U.S. 24 (1978); *Caban v. Mohammed,* 441 U.S. 380 (1979); *Lehr v. Robertson,* 463 U.S. 248 (1983).

cases is that where the unmarried birth father fails to exercise his rights as a parent or express any interest in the child, the courts may treat him differently from the unmarried woman who is the mother of that child. As a result, the current practice is to require consent from a presumed father, and from a biological father who actively assumes a parental role with the child. The legal question is whether an unwed father meets statutory requirements in order to be entitled to notice of a pending adoption proceeding. Unmarried fathers who have lived with and cared for their children and who have legally established paternity have procedural and substantive rights so that their consent is required before an adoption can be granted. Unmarried fathers who have not asserted or established paternity, who have not lived with their children, or who have not made significant efforts to visit, support, or care for the children are not entitled to full parental rights with respect to adoption. The consent of an unmarried father may not be necessary if he has abandoned the child. Abandonment is usually interpreted to include any conduct of a parent which indicates an intention to forego all duties and to relinquish parental claims to the child.

The unwed father may also be an unnamed father. In some situations, the mother may not know the name of the father; in others, the mother knows who the father is but refuses to identify him. The mother may have chosen not to maintain contact with the father so that he does not know about the pregnancy or the birth of the child. If the mother declines to name the father, and no person claiming to be the child's father comes forward, it becomes necessary to terminate the rights of "John Doe, or any person claiming to be the father." Notice of the pending adoption by publication may be sufficient if the unnamed father does not have a relationship with the child and is not supporting the child.

Thirty-two states have developed "Putative Father Registry" programs for regulating the procedure for either obtaining consent or eliminating the need to obtain consent from unwed fathers.[12] Any time a man

12. Ala. Code §26-10c-1 (2001); Ariz. Rev. Stat. §8-106.01 (2001); Ark. Code Ann. §20-18-702 (Michie 2001); Colo. Rev. Stat. §190-5-105 (2001); Conn. Gen. Stat. §45A-716(B) (2001); Fla. Stat. Ch. 88.2011 (2001); Ga. Code Ann. §19-11-9 (2001); Haw Rev. Stat. §578-2(D) (5) (2000); Idaho Code §16-1513 (Michie 1999); 750 Ill. Comp. Stat. 50/12/1 (2001); Ind. Code. Ann. §31-19-5-12 (Michie 2001); Iowa Code §144.12A (2002); La. Rev. Stat. Ann. §9:400 (West 2002); Mass. Gen. Law ch 210, §4A (2002); Mich. Comp. Laws §710.33 (2001); Minn. Stat. §259.52 (2001); Mo. Rev. Stat. §192.016 (2001); Mont. Code Ann. §42-2-202 (2001); Neb. Rev. Stat. §43-104.01 (2001); N.H. Rev Stat. Ann. §170-B:5-a(I) (c) (2001); N.M. Stat. Ann §32A-5-20 (Michie 2001); N.Y. Soc. Serv. §372-C (2000); Ohio Rev. Code Ann. §3107.062 (Anderson

believes he may have contributed to the conception of a child out of wed-lock, he can register his name and the name of the woman with the appropriate state agency, along with the date of their sexual relations. Subsequently, if the woman bears a child that she relinquishes for adoption, the court will consult the confidential putative father registry to see if any man has identified himself as the putative father. If a man is identified, he is given legal notice of the impending adoption and notice that he has a limited time period, usually thirty days, to initiate a paternity hearing. If the man ignores the notice and does not seek to establish his paternity within the specified time period, he waives his right to establish paternity and his consent is not needed for the adoption to go forward. If he proceeds with a paternity action but genetic testing fails to establish his paternity, his consent to the adoption is not needed. If, on the other hand, he proceeds successfully to establish his paternity, he can object to the adoption and argue that he should have custody of the child. If the man who establishes his paternity does not obtain custody of the child, he will be held responsible for child support payments.

The putative father registry puts responsibility on the man to protect his own paternal rights. If he uses the registry, he has ensured that he will receive notice if a child who could be his is placed for adoption in the state. If he does not use the registry and is not identified as a potential father by the mother who is placing a child for adoption, he is foreclosed from bringing a paternity action after the child's adoption. From the court's perspective, the registry is the mechanism for providing notice of a pending adoption to the potential father, and if no man is identified, it obviates the need for a paternal consent. For adoptive parents, the court's reliance on the existence of the registry assures them that no man can subsequently challenge the adoption.

The existence of putative father registries reduces the uncertainty and delay for courts when the paternity of a child is unknown. It is problematic, however, in that most men are not aware that these registries exist. Another serious shortcoming is that the registries are state specific.[13] If a woman crosses state lines, and the man has no knowledge of this, she can give birth and place a child for adoption, and only the state registry

---

2001); Okla. Stat. tit. 10, §7506-1.1 (2000); Or. Rev. Stat. §109.096 (1999); 23 Pa. Cons. Stat. §5103(B) (2001); Tenn. Code Ann. §36-2-318 (2001); Tex. Fam. Code §160.256 (2002); Utah Code Ann. §78-30-4.14 (2001); Vt. Stat. Ann. tit. 15A, §1-110 (2001); Wis. Stat. §48.025 (2001); Wyo. Stat. Ann. §1-22-117 (Michie 2001).

13. Mary Beck, "Toward a National Putative Father Registry Database," *Harvard Journal of Law and Public Policy* 25, no. 3 (summer 2002): 1031.

where she has relocated will be consulted. The man who files with the registry in the original state will not receive notice. This problem could be overcome through interstate cooperation or by the use of a national putative father registry database.

Openness in the Adoption Process

A well-established trend in recent years has been a move away from the traditional doctrine that adoptive and biological parents should not know each other's identity. In private or independent adoptions, it has become common practice for birth parents, in particular birth mothers, to participate in the selection of the adoptive parents. There is an emerging consensus among the states that birth parents should be permitted to select adoptive parents.

Traditionally, confidentiality was an important factor in American adoptions. The judicial hearings concerning adoption are closed to the public, and adoption records are closed both to the public and to all the parties involved in the adoption: birth parents, adoptees, and adoptive parents. When an adoption is finalized, the original birth certificate is sealed in the court record of adoption and a new birth certificate is produced with the child's new name and the adoptive parents' names. The majority of states maintain sealed adoption records which can be opened only with a court order.

Today in most states, adoption agencies are required to compile comprehensive profiles of children and birth parents and to share the nonidentifying information with the adoptive parents at the time of placement. In the case of older adoption files, nonidentifying information is generally available to adult adoptees and to adoptive parents. Identifying information, however, is not available, except upon a judicial finding of "good cause." An adoptee's curiosity about his or her ancestry does not constitute "good cause" for disclosing the identity of the birth parents. A compelling need for medical or genetic information will usually meet the "good cause" standard for releasing information.

The trend has been to permit confidentiality and anonymity to be waived between members of adoptive families and the birth parents. Balancing the interests of all those concerned, including persons who were assured of anonymity when they relinquished a child for adoption, is a challenge. This issue will diminish in the future because most states now provide that birth parents be given an opportunity at the time of relinquishment, or later, to indicate whether or not they are willing to have their identities released. At present, more than forty states allow identifying information to be disclosed upon the mutual consent of all parties: nineteen states have mutual consent registries that allow access to confidential adoption records upon mutual consent; another six states permit identifying information to be released upon mutual consent without a formal registry, and seventeen states have established Confidential Intermediary Programs which permit adoptees, and usually also members of the birth family, to seek information through an intermediary.[14] If, for example, there is no waiver by a birth parent on file, an adoptee may request that an intermediary locate the birth parent to inquire whether the birth parent has interest in waiving confidentiality in order to be contacted by the adopted child. If the birth parent agrees to reveal his or her identity, the intermediary may be asked to facilitate a meeting with the adoptee. If, however, a biological parent prefers to remain anonymous, the adoptee is precluded from getting identifying information except through a judicial order based on "good cause."

In practice, most states permanently seal the court adoption records. Only a couple of states provide birth certificates to adult adoptees upon request.[15] Within the past decade several states have enacted statutes which differ in detail, but generally provide open records unless a birth parent has filed a disclosure veto. A few of these statutes operate only prospectively, applying to adoptions finalized after the effective dates of legislation.[16] The established trend which permits openness based on mutual consent is gradually replacing the tradition of secrecy and confidentiality.

---

14. States with mutual consent registries:

Ark. Stat. Ann. §§9-9-501 to -5098; Cal. Civil Code §§229.40-.70 (eff. July 1991); Fla. Stat. Ann §§63.162, 63, 165, 382.51; Idaho Code §39-259A; Ind. Code Ann. §§31-3-1-5, -4-26, -4-27; La. Rev. Stat. Ann. §§40:91 et seq; Me. Rev. Stat. Ann. Title 22 §2706-A; Md. Fam. Law. Code Ann. §§5-4A-01 et seq; Mich. Comp. Laws Ann. §710.68; Miss. Stat. Ann. §453.121; N.H. Rev. Stat. Ann. §170-B:19; N.Y. Pub. Health Law §4138-b, -c, -d; N.Y. Soc. Serv. Laws §§372, 373-a; Ohio Rev. Code Ann. §§3107.39-.41; Or. Rev. Stat. §§109.425 et seq; S.C. Code Regs. §20-7-1780; S.D. Codified Laws Ann. §§25-6-15.2, -15.3; Tex. Hum. Res. Code Ann. §§49.001 et seq; Utah Code Ann. §78-30-18; W.Va. Code §48-4A-1 et seq.

15. Alaska Stat. 18.50.500 (Michie 2000); Kan. Stat. Ann. 65-2423 (Supp. 1998).

16. Del. Code Ann. tit.13, 923 (Supp. 1998); Ind. Code Ann. 31-19-25-1 to -3 (West 1998); Md. Code Ann. Fam. Law 5-3A-01 to -05 (1999); Minn. Stat. Ann. 259.89 (b) (West 1998); Tenn. Code Ann. 36. 36-1-141; Vt. Stat. Ann., tit. 15A. 6-105 (b)(2) (Supp. 1998); Wash. Rev. Code 26.33f.345 (1997).

Suitable Adoptive Parents

The prospective adopters must be suitable parents, because adoptions are always intended to serve the best interests of the child. There is considerable disagreement over how this requirement is satisfied. Agencies attempt to place children with "fit" and caring parents and consider factors such as age, income, race, religion, and marital status. States typically require that all persons who seek to adopt must have a favorable assessment of their suitability and be certified as eligible to become adoptive parents before a child is placed in their home. Usually another favorable evaluation of the placement is required during a probationary period before the entry of a final adoption decree.

There is a lack of consensus on what criteria are appropriate. All except five states permit birth parents to make direct placements of children. Independent adoptions are unconstrained by agency regulations but ultimately require judicial approval.

Traditionally only married couples were thought to be appropriate as adoptive parents. Agencies also have discretion to "match" children with prospective adopters, and in many states, the agencies are required or permitted "when practicable" to match on the basis of religion, racial background, and cultural and ethnic heritage of the child. Transracial placements, particularly of black children with white adoptive parents, have been particularly controversial. The incidence of transracial adoption decreased after the National Association of Black Social Workers passed a resolution in 1972 opposing transracial adoption.[17] A federal law now prohibits a person or government agency involved in adoption from delaying or denying the placement of a child for adoption on the basis of the race, color, or national origin of the adoptive parent or the child involved.[18] The practice of honoring the birth mother's preference as to the religious affiliation of the adoptive parents has also been criticized when it delays the adoption placement.

All fifty states now allow single-parent adoptions. At present, however, two states, Florida and Mississippi, explicitly forbid lesbian or gay in-

17. See, e.g., National Association of Black Social Workers, *Preserving Black Families: Research and Action Beyond the Rhetoric* (New York: National Association of Black Social Workers, 1986); National Association of Black Social Workers, Position Paper, April 1972, in Rita James Simon and Howard Alstein, *Transracial Adoption* (New York: Wiley, 1977), pp. 50-52; Sandra Patton, *BirthMarks: Transracial Adoption in Contemporary America* (New York: New York University Press, 2000).

18. Adoption and Safe Families Act of 1997, Publ.L.No. 105-89, 111 Stat. 2115.

dividuals to adopt.[19] Judicial opinions in a few other states have denied homosexuals and bisexuals the right to adopt. Many states do not allow couples, whether heterosexual or homosexual, who are not married to adopt. For example, Utah bars the adoption of children by unmarried, co-habiting couples.[20] There are some exceptions. In Vermont, where same-sex couples can enter civil unions, they have the same opportunity to adopt as married couples.[21] New Jersey prohibits discrimination with respect to unmarried heterosexual or homosexual individuals or couples seeking to jointly adopt children.[22] Two states expressly permit "second-parent" or "co-parent" adoptions, and courts in more than twenty states have authorized second-parent adoptions.[23] In a second-parent adoption, one adult is usually the biological parent of a child and the second adult seeks to adopt the child and become the child's second legal parent. The increased numbers of children with special needs in foster care who are available for adoption has created pressure to find more prospective adoptive parents. Foster parents, single adults, and same-sex couples are increasingly seen as potential adoptive parents.

Adoption As a Gratuitous Transfer

Trafficking in children for adoption is an international concern. Independent adoptions are sometimes referred to as "gray market" adoptions because they fall somewhere between the highly regulated agency adoptions and the illegal baby-selling of "black market" adoptions. In independent adoptions by a stranger, it is not uncommon for the adoptive parents to pay the mother's pregnancy and birth-related medical and living expenses and adoption-related expenses, including legal and counseling fees. This arrangement is legal in most states so long as neither the mother nor an intermediary makes a profit and the court approves the expenditures.

The majority of states permit private placement and have sought to prevent profiteering in adoption placements by enacting laws that limit

19. Fla. Stat. Ch. 63.042(3); Miss. Code Ann. §93-17-3.

20. Utah Code Ann. §78-30-1.

21. Vt. Stat. Ann. tit. 15A §1-102 (b) (Supp. 1999).

22. See *Holden v. New Jersey,* No. C-203-97 (N.J. Super.Ct.Ch.Div. Dec. 17, 1997) (consent decree stating that New Jersey Division of Family Services would no longer enforce policy against joint adoptions by unmarried couples).

23. See Sandra Z. Paik, "Adoption and Foster Parenting," *Georgetown Journal of Gender and the Law* 2, no. 2 (spring 2001): 375; Michael T. Morley et al., "Developments in Law and Policy: Emerging Issues in Family Law," *Yale Law and Policy Review* 21, no. 1 (winter 2003): 169.

the compensation paid to intermediaries who arrange adoption placement. The concern is that if an intermediary who arranges an independent adoption were permitted to profit from the transaction, there would be a financial incentive to place children with adoptive parents who would pay the highest price. Consequently, some states prohibit the payment of a fee for adoptive placement; other states require itemization and court approval of fees and expenses. Excessive charges may result in forfeiture of the fee or even disallowance of the adoption.

Although the distaste for adoption to generate any kind of financial gain is strong, adoption is fundamentally a transaction in which a child is transferred from a birth parent in exchange for a promise by adoptive parents to support and care for the child; the birth parent, in turn, is relieved of these duties. Adoptions by stepparents, for example, often involve agreements to forgive the child support arrears of a noncustodial parent in exchange for the noncustodial parent's consent to the adoption. To facilitate the adoption of children with special needs, who are considered less "marketable," state and federal programs provide financial assistance, medical care, and other support services, as well as tax incentives. Federal law requires agencies receiving federal funds to make diligent efforts to recruit parents for these children.

Some commentators have concluded that a baby-selling market in adoptions exists but that it is distorted by state regulation.[24] A debate continues about how extensively adoption should be regulated. The preference to regard adoption as a gratuitous transfer, rather than a commercial or financial transaction, remains dominant.

Conclusion

American adoption law continues to evolve in response to societal pressures. While there are currently fewer healthy newborns in the United States who are available for adoption than there are prospective adoptive parents, there is an oversupply of older children with special needs in foster care who are available for adoption. The current public stance is to promote the permanent placement of children in families to enhance the

---

24. Richard A. Posner, "The Regulation of the Market in Adoptions," *Boston University Law Review* 67 (1987): 59-72; Ronald A. Cass, "Coping with Life, Law, and Markets: A Comment on Posner and the Law-and-Economics Debate," *Boston University Law Review* 67 (1987): 73-98; Melinda Lucas, "Adoption: Distinguishing between Gray Market and Black Market Activities," *Family Law Quarterly* 34 (fall 2000): 553-64.

children's opportunities for healthy development. The U.S. State Department website[25] is a source for information on international adoptions.

The challenge of obtaining parental consent for adoption from unwed fathers or an appropriate ground for waiver of parental consent is being addressed by the use of putative father registries that permit pre-birth registration and guarantee notice of a pending adoption to a man who files. The creation of a national database would eliminate interstate evasion of the registry notice mechanism. The existence and purpose of the registries should be publicized to increase awareness of their use in providing notice of a pending adoption and the opportunity to establish paternity.

The traditional legal insistence on the anonymity of the parties and confidentiality to create a complete substitution of the adoptive parents for the birth parents is diminishing. The greater openness in adoption practice appears to serve the interests of all the parties. The increased use of private placement supports the birth parents' desire to assess the suitability of potential adoptive parents. The adoptive parents have an interest in having the medical and social histories of their adopted children. The adoptees' interest in their ancestry is served by opening adoption records. The growing use of "open" adoptions and the availability of mutual access when there is mutual consent through the use of registries and confidential intermediaries illustrate the movement.

The recognition that beneficial permanent adoptive placements are not limited to traditional two-parent households has taken root. Single-parent adoptions currently account for many of the adoptions of hard-to-place children with special needs. The acknowledgment that parent-child bonds can develop and flourish in nontraditional households will increase the number of potential adoptive parents available and contribute to meeting the need for adoptive placements for special needs children who now languish in foster care.

The perception that adoption is a gratuitous transfer is contradicted by the recognition that some birth-related and legal expenses should be compensable. The financial and support incentives that are available from the government for the adoption of children with special needs reinforce the fact that money and services are needed to facilitate some adoptions.

25. U.S. Department of State, Office of Children's Issues, Adoption Resource website, http://travel.state.gov/family/adoption_resources. Accessed 3 August 2004.

12. Legal and Ethical Challenges of Embryonic Adoption

JOHN C. MAYOUE

The greatest challenge to the notion of human embryo adoption stems from fundamental disagreement and uncertainty as to the legal and ethical status of an embryo. Is it a form of life or a mere incident of property? These viewpoints are contrasted in two newspaper editions. In the classified section of the *Arizona Republic* on June 27, 1999, an advertisement ran between "Can't collect on a judgment?" and a notice seeking witnesses to a car accident; the ad read, "If you feel you have embryos or sperms stored with Arizona Institute for Reproductive Medicine, please contact us immediately. All unclaimed specimens will be destroyed as of July 15, 1999." In contrast, a cartoon appeared August 19, 2001, in the *Atlanta Journal Constitution* that showed a man explaining to his fellow poker players that the cooler sitting next to him didn't contain beer. Rather, it was "[his] weekend for visitation with the frozen embryos. . . ."

Nearly 500,000 embryos are cryopreserved (frozen) at some 430 assisted reproductive technology (ART) clinics in the United States.[1] The vast majority of these embryos were created during the in vitro fertilization (IVF) process, which often produces more embryos than are actually transferred to a woman's uterus.[2] Intense debate rages over the disposi-

1. David I. Hoffman et al., "Cryopreserved Embryos in the United States and Their Availability for Research," *Fertility and Sterility* 79 (May 2003): 1066; American Society for Reproductive Medicine, "Vast Majority of Cryopreserved Embryos Slated for Future Family Building," *ASRM Bulletin* 5, no. 30 (May 2003); Rick Weiss, "400,000 Human Embryos Frozen in U.S.: Number at Fertility Clinics is Far Greater Than Previous Estimates, Survey Finds," 8 May 2003, *Washington Post*, sec. A, p. 10.

2. American Society for Reproductive Medicine, "Vast Majority of Cryopreserved Embryos."

tion of these frozen embryos, which, for many, is a question of profound ethical, moral, and religious consequence.[3] Science, it seems, has greatly outpaced all other disciplines, and legal scholars, politicians, theologians, and medical ethicists alike are caught in a game of "catch up."[4] Legislatures and the courts are struggling to sort through the vexing questions raised by the cryopreservation of embryos, but the debate is occurring somewhat after the fact as hundreds of thousands of frozen embryos already languish in fertility clinics and research laboratories worldwide.

As a pragmatic matter, one area of universal agreement is that the inchoate status of frozen embryos creates the need for some decision-maker to select among five dispositions: (1) use by the progenitors of the embryo for their own reproductive goals, (2) donation of the embryo for approved research, (3) destruction of the embryo by allowing it to thaw and thus disintegrate, (4) maintenance of the embryo in a frozen state, or (5) donation of the embryo to an infertile individual or couple who cannot otherwise conceive.[5] Within the confines of a rapidly developing legal framework, participants in the IVF procedure retain great decisional authority in declaring the fate of the embryos containing their genetic material.[6] It is the fifth option — donation to infertile couples who want to conceive a child — which has resulted in the concept of "embryo adoption," a term first coined in 1998 by the Center for Human Reproduction.[7] Such an "adoption" occurs when an infertile individual or couple receives a frozen embryo that was created by progenitors who either affirmatively decided to donate the embryo or who abandoned the embryo, thus leaving another decision-maker — a clinic physician — to "dispose"[8] of it.[9]

---

3. Paul McKeague, "Proposed Law Would Allow Adoption of Human Embryos," *The Ottawa Citizen,* May 1999, Articles on Adoption website, http://www.cuckoografik.org/trained_tales/orp_pages/news/news7.html. Accessed 13 August 2003; Jeffrey P. Kahn, "'Adoption' of Frozen Embryos a Loaded Term," 17 September 2002, CNN website, http://www3.cnn.com/2002/HEALTH/09/17/ethics.matters. Accessed 13 August 2003; Lauri Gray Eaton, "Extra Embryos, What Is Their Future?" *San Antonio Medical Gazette,* 15 December 2000, cover.

4. Amy S. Jaeger, *Adoption Law and Practice* (New York: Matthew Bender, 2000), §§14-8-14-10, 14-15.

5. Jaeger, *Adoption Law and Practice,* §§14-26.

6. See discussion of case law below.

7. "Embryo Donation for 'Embryo Adoption,'" *CHR Voice* (spring 2003): 1.

8. The term "disposition" of human frozen embryos, while widely used, is considered pejorative by persons who consider human embryos to be a form of life.

9. Jaeger, *Adoption Law and Practice,* §§14-26.

Two programs that facilitate embryo adoption are the Snowflakes Embryo Adoption Program, administered by Nightlife Christian Adoptions, and the Embryo Adoption Program, created by the Center for Human Reproduction (CHR). The ultimate goal of each is to transfer unwanted frozen embryos to infertile individuals or couples who wish to use them to procreate. The Snowflakes program declares as its goal that "every embryo would be adopted and no new 'extra' embryos would be created"[10]; the CHR appears to be secular, focusing on avoidance of the "vexing ethical problems" created by a surplus of cryopreserved embryos.[11]

It is important to understand embryo adoption in the context of the process that has resulted in the global surplus of frozen embryos. As noted, the vast majority of embryos that are cryopreserved were created during the IVF process, which is the most common ART method used in the United States, and thus were created to assist infertile couples with their efforts to procreate.[12] The IVF procedure begins with a woman taking fertility drugs that induce her ovaries to produce a higher than usual number of eggs. The mature eggs are removed from the ovaries and placed in a solution. After incubation in a laboratory, the eggs are inseminated (mixed with sperm). Fertilization and early embryo development occur in a dish and both are confirmed after approximately twenty-four hours. Two to three days after retrieval from the incubator, the desired number of embryos is transferred to a woman's uterus, with the hope of implantation and development of the fetus to term.[13] Because the IVF process often produces more embryos than are necessary for transfer to the uterus,[14] surplus embryos can be preserved indefinitely at sub-zero temperatures by placing them in liquid nitrogen.[15] Freezing surplus embryos for later use greatly reduces both the monetary cost and the significant physical discomfort to the woman caused by repeated egg retrieval.[16]

10. "Snowflakes Embryo Adoption Program," Snowflakes website, http://www.snowflakes.org/. Accessed 13 August 2003.

11. Deroy Murdock, "The Adoption Option," *National Review Online,* 27 August 2001, National Review Online website, http://www.nationalreview.com/murdock/murdock082701.shtml. Accessed 29 July 2004; "Embryo Donation."

12. Hoffman et al., "Cryopreserved Embryos," p. 1063; "In Vitro Fertilization," Mayo Clinic website, http://www.mayoclinic.org/ivf-sct. Accessed 29 July 2003.

13. "The IVF Process," Mayo Clinic website, http://www.mayoclinic.org/ivf-sct/process.html. Accessed 29 July 2003; "In Vitro Fertilization."

14. Hoffman et al., "Cryopreserved Embryos," p. 1063; "The IVF Process."

15. David L. Theyssen, "Balancing Interests in Frozen Embryo Disputes: Is Adoption Really a Reasonable Alternative?" *Indiana Law Journal* 74 (1999): 714.

16. Theyssen, "Balancing Interests," p. 715.

Frozen embryos, while indefinitely preserved, may become nonviable for certain purposes given the passage of time.

Frozen embryo technology creates a time lapse between fertilization of the egg(s) and transfer into the womb. This time lapse is critical because it allows contingencies to intervene, such as divorce, a decision not to procreate, or an election to pursue traditional adoption.[17] Events such as these often render frozen embryos unwanted by their progenitors and lead to an alternate disposition or, in the worst-case scenario, abandonment.

Whatever the true current number of potentially "adoptable" embryos, advances in assisted reproductive technology may affect both the number of embryos frozen in the future and the desirability for adoption of those embryos. For example, a technique called "MicroSort" can separate Y-chromosome-bearing sperm (which produce males) and X-chromosome-bearing sperm (which produce females), allowing IVF patients to choose the sex of the embryos they create. Another advance involves piercing or "drilling" the egg and inserting sperm to increase the chances of fertilization.[18] Pre-implantation genetic diagnosis (PGD) is another major breakthrough, one that allows doctors to perform genetic "diagnoses" of individual embryos and to screen out those that are abnormal. This technology has profound implications for families with known risks for genetic disorders or women who have had multiple miscarriages.[19]

The sheer success rate of IVF could also encourage the creation of embryos. It has been reported that the average probability of a couple achieving birth of a child after one cycle of IVF is one in five, the same chances of a healthy couple conceiving each menstrual cycle. This amazing figure represents a doubling of the IVF success rate.[20]

Such advances beg the question — if technology can determine the sex of an embryo and screen it for genetic defects, and the IVF success rate is similar to that of natural conception, then what, other than monetary cost or social desirability, renders natural conception preferable? Will the prospect of a genetically screened, gender-determined baby be too much

17. Theyssen, "Balancing Interests," p. 715.

18. Daniel A. Potter, "MicroSort: Technology Separates the Boys from the Girls," MicroSort website, http://www.havingbabies.com/news/42_972_3897.CFM. Accessed 13 August 2003.

19. Sharyn Rosenbaum, "Treatment Advances Help Couples Overcome Infertility," *Scripps News,* 1 July 2003, Scripps website, http://www.scrippshealth.org/90_1532.asp. Accessed 13 August 2003; "Embryo Donation for 'Embryo Adoption.'"

20. "In Vitro Success Rate Doubles," 24 July 2003, CBS News website, http://www.cbsnews.com/stories/2003/07/24/tech/main565014.shtml. Accessed 13 August 2003.

to resist for those with financial means, even if they *could* conceive naturally? And what of their unwanted embryos? Surely people seeking to "adopt" an embryo would prefer those which have passed genetic muster and are of a known sex. Would this create a class of less desirable, abandoned embryos with a correspondingly lesser prospect of adoption? And what parallels are there between those less desirable embryos and living infants with some quality that makes them less desirable for adoption?

In addition to affecting the sheer number of frozen embryos, scientific advances such as genetic screening also create the possibility of "designer embryos," adding another dynamic to the embryo adoption landscape.[21] Although current embryo adoption programs already work with infertile people to "match" them to an embryo with a "wish list" of desirable characteristics,[22] the effect of genetic screening has the potential of taking such matching processes to new heights by creating two distinct classes of embryos — those that have and those that have not been screened.

Some medical officials have described embryonic genetic screening as a "non–first line treatment," in that it is only indicated when there are known risks for genetic disorders.[23] As seems to be a recurring theme, however, such limiting statements did not hold true for long. The BBC reported that a forty-three-year-old mother gave birth to a child who was genetically screened as an embryo even though there was *no* family history of genetic disorders. A British physician dubbed genetic screening "the future of IVF" because of its potential to increase the IVF success rate from 22 percent to 60-80 percent. Detractors of genetic screening, however, have called the technique "one more step toward designing a baby."[24]

Although conventional wisdom would indicate that any advance in IVF technology will make the procedure more attractive to infertile couples and thus result in the cryogenic preservation of still more embryos, one may also argue that technology such as genetic screening that increases the success rate of IVF may actually decrease the need for "spare embryos," which are typically frozen for use in the event that any given implantation attempt fails. Advancing technology, however, does not affect the number of embryos currently awaiting disposition.

21. "First Embryo Screening Birth," 4 August 2003, BBC website, http://news.bbc .co.uk/go/pr/fr/-/2/hi/health/3123633.stm. Accessed 13 August 2003.
22. "Embryo Donation for 'Embryo Adoption.'"
23. Rosenbaum, "Treatment Advances Help Couples."
24. "Designer Baby Born to UK Couple," 19 June 2003, BBC website, http:// news.bbc.co.uk/go/pr/fr/-/2/hi/health/3002610.stm. Accessed 13 August 2003.

A May 2003 study by a group of scientists and medical doctors in association with the Society for Assisted Reproductive Technology found that, of the nearly 400,000 cryopreserved embryos in the United States, 87 percent are being held for patient infertility treatment, less than 3 percent are awaiting donation to research, just over 2 percent are awaiting destruction per patient request, and approximately 2 percent, or 9,104 embryos, are awaiting donation to another patient. This 2 percent statistic might seem comforting, but an equally significant number appears to be the nearly 4 percent of embryos, or 13,878, found by the study to be in storage "for other reasons," which include lost contact with the patient, divorce, awaiting transport to long-term storage, and pending final decision as to disposition.[25]

These figures must, of course, be considered in light of the indisputable fact that any of the embryos currently labeled with a designation could become members of the "awaiting donation" or the "other" category in the event of a change in the circumstances or desires of their progenitors, as illustrated by current, but limited, case law.

Deciding how frozen embryos can be used and which alternatives for their ultimate disposition should be sanctioned requires us to define them beyond mere biological terms. There are three theories regarding the nature of cryopreserved embryos: (1) the human life theory views them as legally cognizable beings possessing all the rights and deserving all the protections accorded to living human beings; (2) the property theory considers them mere property of the parties who contributed the sperm and egg — property that, like all property, can be transferred, bequeathed, or otherwise disposed of according to the wishes of their owner(s); and (3) the special respect theory views them as something more than property, but less than human life itself. According to the third theory the embryos are, therefore, entitled to "special respect" in their treatment and disposition.[26]

The stakes are high as progress in the development of fertility and reproductive technology has occurred even faster than many scientists expected. State legislatures have begun to respond with statutory and regulatory schemes that create broad mandates and proscriptions, but only a handful of states have enacted legislation that deals directly with embryos.

25. Hoffman et al., "Cryopreserved Embryos," p. 1066.
26. American Fertility Society, "Ethical Considerations of the New Reproductive Technologies," *Journal of the American Fertility Society* 53, no. 6 (June 1990): 34S-35S.

Statutory Law

Louisiana's Civil Code provides that a frozen embryo is a "juridical person" which can neither be owned nor destroyed and therefore must either be used by its progenitors for reproduction, donated for "adoptive implantation," or kept in a cryopreserved state.[27] Thus couples in Louisiana who are unwilling to donate their "leftover" embryos to others must either forego IVF treatment altogether or seek treatment in another state. This statutory approach seems to comport with the human life theory in that it affords embryos certain protections typically accorded to living human beings. In contrast, Kansas law (in the statutory section that provides for the right to use birth control) expressly provides that frozen embryos *can* be destroyed either by allowing them to thaw or through use in scientific research.[28]

The California penal code criminalizes any use of an embryo, including implantation into a third party, without the written consent of the "embryo provider." These criminal provisions resulted from allegations that fertility clinics permitted use of embryos in research or implantation in other women without the consent or knowledge of the donors.[29] California law thus appears to permit any disposition of frozen embryos as long as that disposition is approved by the embryo's provider.

Kentucky law provides that public funds may not be used to pay for IVF procedures but that public medical facilities can be used for researching and conducting IVF as long as the procedures "do not result in the intentional destruction of a human embryo."[30] Therefore, like Louisiana's statute, Kentucky law appears to permit only two options for frozen embryos: implant them for reproductive purposes or keep them frozen indefinitely.

Florida law gives the donors of the embryo total decision-making authority regarding its disposition and requires that the donors "preordain" the embryos' fate by entering "a written agreement that provides for the disposition of the . . . preembryos in the event of a divorce, the death of a spouse, or any other unforeseen circumstance."[31] Absent a writ-

27. La. Rev. Stat. Ann. §§129-130 (West 2003).
28. Kan. Stat. Ann. §§65-6702 (West 2003).
29. Ca. Penal Code §367g (West 2003).
30. Ky. Rev. Stat. Ann. §311.725 (Baldwin 2003).
31. "Preembryo — A fertilized ovum up to 14 days old, before it becomes implanted in the uterus" (*The American Heritage Dictionary of the English Language,* fourth ed., s.v. "preembryo").

ten agreement, however, "decision-making authority regarding disposition of preembryos resides *jointly* with the commissioning couple."[32] Because the state does not expressly place any limits on donors or physicians, presumably the parties are free to agree to any use or disposition of their frozen embryos.

Pennsylvania law does not directly address the disposition of embryos. It is, however, unlawful in Pennsylvania to perform "any type of nontherapeutic experimentation or nontherapeutic medical procedure . . upon any unborn child."[33] Nontherapeutic is then defined as any act that is "not intended to preserve the life or health of the child upon whom it is performed."[34] The obvious question is whether an embryo (frozen or otherwise) constitutes an "unborn child." IVF is expressly condoned, but does that include disposition of the unused embryos? The statute addresses tests performed on an unborn child in utero, but what of an unborn child in vitro? If a frozen human embryo does not qualify as an unborn child, is it a "fetal tissue or organ"?

Legislation regarding embryos seems to be an attempt to articulate local public policy. Disputes about embryos, however, arise in fact-specific contexts. It is the courts that have traditionally decided what rights exist, to whom they belong, and whose rights are superior in the event of conflict.

Despite the over-twenty-year history of successful IVF treatment, case law dealing with frozen embryos is surprisingly limited. Only five cases have made their way to the states' highest courts. Given the relative lack of state law on the subject, these decisions have not been heavily steeped in legislative policy or intent, but are focused instead on broader notions of constitutional rights (in particular, the right to privacy under the Fourteenth Amendment) and public policy considerations. As legislation continues to lag behind developments in science and medicine, the courts may well be the primary source to determine the legal consequences of the startling advances in reproductive technology.

A critical first step in the analysis is to determine what is the legal status of the frozen embryos themselves — are they mere property, or a form of life, or do they exist somewhere along the continuum between those two extremes? What protections, if any, does the law currently afford them, and in whom does the law vest decision-making authority re-

32. Fla. Stat. Ann. §742.17 (West 2003).
33. Except for abortions, which are provided for elsewhere in the Tennessee statutes.
34. Pa. Stat. Ann. Tit. 18, §3216.

garding their fate? If they are mere property, is their disposition the exclusive province of their "owners"? And if they are "human life," how much protection will they be granted? These are questions of the greatest moral and legal order that must be answered if society is to decide if frozen embryos have a place in the traditional paradigm of adoption.

Case Law

Davis v. Davis,[35] a 1992 case before the Tennessee Supreme Court, was the first major decision to offer an analysis of the legal issues relative to the disposition of frozen embryos. Mary Sue and Junior Davis, a married couple, neither discussed nor agreed upon a disposition of their embryos in the event of a divorce.[36] Approximately two months after their preembryos[37] were frozen, Junior filed for divorce and Mary Sue requested control of the preembryos so that she could transfer them to her uterus after the divorce. Junior requested that they remain frozen until he determined whether he wanted to become a parent outside of marriage.[38]

The trial court stated that "human life begins at the moment of conception," declared the entities at issue "children in vitro," invoked the doctrine of *parens patriae* (state as protector of those who cannot protect themselves), held that it was in the best interest of the "children" to be born rather than destroyed, and granted custody of the "children" to Mary Sue.[39]

Junior appealed and the appellate court reversed the trial court, holding that Junior had a "constitutionally protected" right not to beget a child when no pregnancy had occurred and that the state did not have a compelling interest in ordering implantation that was against the will of either party. The appellate court declared that the preembryos were "not persons" and awarded the then divorced Davises joint control.[40]

---

35. *Davis v. Davis,* 842 S.W.2d 588 (Tenn. 1992).

36. *Davis,* 842 S.W.2d 592.

37. The *Davis* Court uses the term "preembryo" rather than "embryo" to describe the frozen entities at issue. Absent an alternative designation used by a court or statute discussed herein, this chapter will refer to the fertilized ovum as an "embryo." For a discussion of the difference between a "preembryo" and an "embryo," see John A. Robertson, "In the Beginning: The Legal Status of Early Embryos," *Virginia Law Review* 76 (1990): 437-517.

38. *Davis,* 842 S.W.2d 589.

39. *Davis,* 842 S.W.2d 589.

40. *Davis,* 842 S.W.2d 589.

Junior then appealed the issue to the Tennessee Supreme Court. It is illustrative of the dynamic nature of this issue that, by the time the case reached Tennessee's highest court, both of the Davises had remarried. Mary Sue no longer wished to use the preembryos herself, but instead wanted to donate them to a childless couple, and Junior wanted the preembryos to be destroyed. The Court discussed what it called the "Person vs. Property Dichotomy," and stated that the preembryos could not be considered "persons" under Tennessee law. The Court further relied on the benchmark United States Supreme Court case *Roe v. Wade,* which held that (under federal law) "the unborn have never been recognized in the law as persons in the whole sense."[41]

Thus the Court held that the "person" status granted to the embryos by the trial court could not stand, but also expressed concern that the appellate court's holding may have been too close to declaring them property.[42] In its effort further to define the status of preembryos on the person/property continuum, the Court looked to the three major ethical positions identified by the American Fertility Society:

1. After fertilization, the preembryo is a "human subject" and possesses the rights of a "person."
2. The preembryo is like any other human tissue, and therefore no limits should be placed on the discretion of those with "decision making-authority" as to the disposition of preembryos.
3. The preembryo should be given greater respect than other human tissue but should not be treated as a person.[43]

Ultimately, the Court adopted a version of the intermediate view in concluding that preembryos are neither "persons" nor "property," but rather have an interim status which "entitles them to special respect because of their potential for human life." Based on this view, the Court then held that the Davises' interest in the preembryos was not a "true property interest" but rather an interest "in the nature of ownership to the extent that they have decision-making authority."[44]

Lacking the benefit of a preexisting agreement among the parties and faced with the joint control arrangement granted by the appellate

41. *Davis,* 842 S.W.2d 594-95.
42. *Davis,* 842 S.W.2d 594-95.
43. *Davis,* 842 S.W.2d 596.
44. *Davis,* 842 S.W.2d 597.

court, however, the Court balanced the procreational rights of Junior and Mary Sue and held that Junior's interest in avoiding parenthood out-weighed Mary Sue's interest in donating the preembryos.[45]

In concluding its analysis, the Court established a three-step process to be applied when the disposition of frozen embryos is in dispute. First, look to the current preferences of the progenitors. Second, in the absence of an agreed upon preference, enforce any prior agreement between the genetic donors. Third, in the absence of any prior agreement, the relative interests of the parties in using or not using the preembryos should be weighed, with the party wishing not to procreate typically prevailing, as-suming the other party has some reasonable opportunity to become a parent. In a situation like the case at hand, the party wishing not to pro-create would always prevail over a party that merely wishes to donate the preembryos.[46]

As with many judicial decisions, *Davis* answers some questions but in doing so raises others. For example, the Court expressed dissatisfaction with declaring embryos either persons or property, but did it succeed in recognizing a middle ground between those two ethical approaches? The opinion makes absolutely clear that agreements concerning the disposi-tion of preembryos should be enforced. This approach acknowledges that the progenitors have an interest in the embryos that is "in the nature of ownership"; thus the Court's first approach to disposition disputes is to apply basic principles of contract law. But is such a property ownership approach consistent with the Court's conclusion that the embryos are *more* than mere property and deserve special respect? Is it possible for one to have an "ownership" interest in anything other than property? Are preembryos treated as anything more than property when the Court pre-serves the progenitors' rights contractually to guarantee that the preembryos will be destroyed?

Further, having established the parties' interest in deciding the fate of preembryos, at what point does this interest cease to exist? After con-cluding that an agreement to destroy unused embryos *would* be enforce-able between the parties, the Court then notes that agreements regarding abortion are *not* enforceable, because of the woman's right to privacy and autonomy. According to the Court, once the preembryo is transferred, all decision-making authority rests with the woman. But considering that mere transfer of the preembryo does not guarantee pregnancy, should

45. *Davis*, 842 S.W.2d 604.
46. *Davis*, 842 S.W.2d 604.

the male donor's "decision-making authority" cease immediately upon transfer?

Another question raised by a woman's right to abortion is the preembryo's legal status upon transfer. Prior to transfer, the preembryo is neither property nor person, but deserves "special respect." After transfer, however, under Tennessee law the woman has (at least during the first trimester) "an absolute right" to abort any resulting pregnancy. Doesn't this have the effect of giving the preembryo a lower legal status after implantation? Is that not counterintuitive to the possibility that implantation actually fosters growth *toward* individualization and humanity? Does it make sense that a preembryo, frozen outside the womb, should be treated with more deference than one developing in utero?

In its conclusion, the Court gives great deference to a "prior agreement concerning disposition," yet in the body of the decision states that such agreements may be later modified by agreement.[47] If prior agreements may be modified, then is their "contract-like" quality not diminished in favor of deference to the parties' current will?

Finally, the Court indicates that the party asserting the right not to procreate should prevail unless the other party has no reasonable opportunity to become a parent.[48] But as long as adoption is seen as a "reasonable" opportunity at parenthood, it would seem the party wishing not to procreate would prevail in virtually every case. And when that party prevails, the practical result is that the preembryos remain unused, and thus frozen until they degrade into nonviability. Is this nonfeasance good public policy?

York v. Jones,[49] the Virginia case cited by the appellate court in *Davis*, illustrates the inconsistency with which the courts have treated the frozen embryo issue. The *York* plaintiffs sued an IVF institute seeking to have their frozen embryo transferred to a clinic in another state. Prior to undergoing IVF treatment, the plaintiffs signed a "cryopreservation agreement" which limited the options for "disposing" of their embryos to donation to another couple, donation to research, or simply allowing the embryos to thaw. In refusing to transfer the embryos to another state, the defendant clinic successfully argued that the transfer of the embryos was not an option provided for by agreement. The court determined that the embryos were the subject of a bailment relationship, similar to the legal standing of an auto-

---

47. *Davis*, 842 S.W.2d 597.
48. *Davis*, 842 S.W.2d 604.
49. *York v. Jones*, 717 F. Supp. 421 (E.D. Va. 1989).

mobile left with a parking lot attendant. In contrast with the conclusion in *Davis,* the *York* court makes no attempt to classify frozen embryos[50] as anything more than mere property, and therefore its decision is based exclusively on an application of basic contract law.[51] Entirely absent from the opinion, however, is any explanation of why the court chose to treat the embryo at issue as mere property, an ethical position which comports with the view presented (but not adopted) in *Davis* that embryos are like any other human tissue and thus are to be treated as jointly held personal property. To a large extent, this silence reflects the limits of the judicial function — neither party argued that the embryo was anything more than property and, in effect, both sides simply wanted their contract enforced.[52] But should the court have gone further? It is well established that courts will not enforce contracts that are unconscionable or against public policy. Should the court, of its own volition, have considered whether it was against public policy for the state to treat embryos as property?

Further, would the court have been willing to enforce the contract between the Yorks and the clinic if it contained provisions of a more provocative nature, such as donation to a research center should the Yorks become delinquent in a storage payment? Such a forfeiture is common in contracts for the storage of inanimate personal property, but in the case of a frozen embryo, would the court have invoked a *Davis*-like "special respect" approach in order to avoid such a harsh result?

Kass v. Kass,[53] a New York state decision, presents another case in which a court enforced a prior written agreement in the face of a present disagreement as to the disposition of frozen embryos.[54] Before cryopreservation of surplus embryos produced by the IVF process, then-married Maureen and Steven Kass signed an agreement which stated that, should the parties no longer want to initiate a pregnancy or become unable to make a decision as to the disposition of the stored pre-zygotes, they would be "disposed of by the IVF program for approved research investigation."[55] Only three weeks later, the couple signed an uncontested divorce that stated the preembryos should be disposed of according to the

50. The *York* Court uses the term "pre-zygotes" to describe the frozen entities at issue.
51. *York,* 717 F. Supp. 427.
52. *York,* 717 F. Supp. 424-425.
53. *Kass v. Kass,* 91 N.Y.2d 554 (N.Y. 1998).
54. *Kass,* 91 N.Y. 2d 557.
55. *Kass,* 91 N.Y.2d 559-60; the Court adopted the term "pre-zygotes," used by the parties to the action and defined in the record as "eggs which have been penetrated by sperm but have not yet joined genetic material" (*Kass,* fn. 1).

terms of the consent agreement. Within weeks, however, Maureen sent a letter to the IVF clinic expressing her opposition to the destruction of the pre-zygotes and later filed suit requesting sole custody. Steven counterclaimed to have the consent agreement enforced and the pre-zygotes used for research purposes.[56]

The trial court granted Maureen custody of the pre-zygotes and directed her to implant them within a "medically reasonable time" based on its reasoning that "a female participant in the IVF procedure has exclusive decisional authority over the fertilized eggs created through that process, just as a pregnant woman has exclusive decisional authority over a nonviable fetus. . . ."[57] New York's highest court held that disposition of the pre-zygotes did not involve a woman's right of privacy or bodily integrity in the context of reproductive choice prior to implantation of the pre-zygote and, citing *Roe v. Wade*, held that pre-zygotes do not have the status of "persons" for constitutional purposes. Based upon that declaration, the Court narrowed its inquiry to the terms of the parties' agreement to determine who had dispositional authority.[58]

After strongly encouraging progenitors to enter carefully considered agreements,[59] the court held that the parties intended the pre-zygotes to be donated for research in the circumstances presented and enforced the agreement among them in derogation of Maureen's then-present wishes.[60]

Although the *Kass* court refused even to entertain the notion presented by *Davis* that the pre-zygotes should be afforded "special respect," the holdings of *Davis, York,* and *Kass* agree in their declaration that *prior* agreements between progenitors should be enforced. In enforcing the parties' agreement made prior to cryopreservation, the *Kass* court noted that agreements violative of public policy will not be enforced. A Massachusetts state court decision provides an example of the limiting effect of this doctrine.

A.Z. v. B.Z.[61] involved a divorced couple who successfully had children through the IVF procedure, and whose agreement was that in the event of separation any remaining preembryos[62] would be returned to the

---

56. *Kass*, 91 N.Y. 2d 560.

57. *Kass*, 91 N.Y. 2d 561.

58. *Kass*, 91 N.Y. 2d 564-65.

59. *Kass*, 91 N.Y. 2d 566-57.

60. *Kass*, 91 N.Y. 2d 569.

61. *A.Z. v. B.Z.*, 431 Mass. 150 (2000).

62. The Court used the term "preembryo" to refer to the "four-to-eight cell stage of a developing fertilized egg" (*A.Z.*, fn. 1).

woman for implantation.[63] Prior to the couple's separation and without the husband's knowledge, the wife attempted (without success) to conceive by thawing and implanting one of the preembryos frozen prior to the agreement. Concurrent with filing for divorce, the husband filed for a permanent injunction to prohibit the wife from using the remaining frozen preembryos.[64]

The Massachusetts Supreme Court held that, absent an enforceable agreement (as in *Davis*), the husband's interest in avoiding procreation outweighed the wife's interest in having more children.[65] This holding was based on the Court's declaration that the agreement was unenforceable because "forced procreation is not an area amenable to judicial enforcement," and thus violative of public policy.[66]

The Court clearly stated that it was expressing no view as to the enforceability of an agreement that provided for "destruction or donation of preembryos either for research or implantation into a surrogate."[67] But, though the Court emphatically declared that it would not force an individual to procreate, would not an agreement requiring that embryos be donated for implantation in a surrogate still compel one donor to become a parent against his or her will? Particularly in a divorce situation, is the father any less a parent if the embryo is implanted in a surrogate rather than in his former wife? As with the other cases described, the Court was not forced by the facts of this case to answer that question.

These cases, although often inconsistent in their reasoning, do present some common themes that directly affect embryo adoption. None of the cases examined bars progenitors from agreeing to donate embryos to third parties for reproductive use if that is their mutual present intent. But what about a prior contract between them which contravenes one of the party's present desires? The *Kass* court enforced a contract which disposed of embryos for research purposes even though one party desired custody. But had the contract stated that the embryos would be disposed of via donation to an infertile couple, it would seem that the "right not to procreate" would intervene and the contract would not be enforced. It was a far easier matter for the *Kass* court to enforce a contract that would lead to the embryos' destruction than to enforce one that would impose parenthood on one of the parties.

63. A.Z., 431 Mass. 155.
64. A.Z., 431 Mass. 153.
65. A.Z., 431 Mass. 160.
66. A.Z., 431 Mass. 161.
67. A.Z., 431 Mass. fn. 22.

It would appear that, based on the right not to procreate, a prior agreement to donate an embryo to a third party for implantation would not be enforced if it conflicted with a party's present desire *not* to procreate. It seems likely then, in the context of donation to third parties, that the developing case law will favor a party's interest in not procreating over another party's interest in donating to a third party. Such was the case in *Davis*. The *Davis* Court declared that a closer decision would have resulted had the woman wished to use the embryos *herself*, but, like the *Kass* court, offered adoption as an alternative, repeatedly emphasizing the man's right *not* to procreate.

The effect this has on embryo adoption is that, absent a *present* mutual agreement to donate embryos to a third party, the desire of one party not to procreate will outweigh the other party's desire to donate, thus preventing potential embryo donees from relying on a prior agreement among the progenitors. We have no case law which states that a court would enforce a prior agreement to donate when one of the parties has a present desire to avoid procreation. Although the *Kass* court enforced a prior agreement in the face of present disagreement, such enforcement did not result in the embryo's donation to a third party.

The issue of progenitors' agreements to donate embryos is of fundamental importance, but what of embryos that have been abandoned by their progenitors? How does their placement on the property/person continuum effect their transfer to donees? According to a personhood approach, as was adopted by the trial court in *Davis,* the law would address abandoned embryos in much the same way it treats abandoned children; but this approach was ultimately rejected by all of the cases reviewed.

A property/contract view might declare that abandoned embryos become the property of the clinic in which they are stored, an issue prompting one Florida physician to draft a presentation in which he declares, "From a legal perspective, the abandoned embryos probably belong to the practice. Because the couples have failed to maintain contact as well as meet their legal and financial responsibilities, it is quite possible that they have breached their original contract."[68] This statement clearly takes a property approach to abandonment of embryos, treating them as abandoned property rather than abandoned persons. The doctor, however, also states, "if embryos were simple cells, destroying them would not be

---

68. Craig A. Sweet, draft of presentation "Abandoned Life: What Should Be Done with Abandoned Frozen Embryos?" p. 8, DreamABaby website, http://www.dreamababy.com/download_files/Abandoned%20Embryos%20Presentation.pdf. Accessed 13 August 2003.

difficult. My personal view is that they should be treated with far greater respect than simple cells, but less respect than a living/breathing human being."[69]

It is axiomatic that the legal status of an embryo as a person or property is critical to use and disposition of the embryo. If property, then clinics holding embryos abandoned by their progenitors may look to the state-specific laws regarding abandoned property in combination with state law, if any, which guides what one can and cannot do with an embryo. In Louisiana, for example, the Florida physician would not have the option of destroying the embryos, as that is expressly forbidden by statute. In Kansas, however, the physician or clinic would be free to destroy the embryos, or donate them for either implantation or research. If an embryo is indeed human life, the terms "use" and "disposition" are fundamentally repugnant and certainly degrade its status.

Unanswered Questions

The concept of adoption can be traced to ancient times. Historically, laws regulating adoption have followed the Roman principle of law *adoptio naturam imitator* — adoption imitates nature.[70] Thus the law declares that an adopted child becomes the "natural" child of the adoptive parents, with the many attendant legal rights thereof. Adoption in the United States is strictly a statutory creation largely governed by state law, the purpose of which is to place children in a secure, permanent, and stable environment.[71] In doing so, adoption laws endeavor to prohibit adoption by unfit persons, to prevent natural parents from making hasty or ill-conceived decisions regarding adoption of their children, to provide adoptive parents with the information about the potential adoptive child and his or her background, and to protect adoptive parents from future interference by the natural parents.[72]

These laws reflect traditional, normative definitions of a "standard" family. Because judges are gatekeepers in the statutory scheme of adop-

69. Sweet, "Abandoned Life," p. 8.

70. Mitchell Waldmann, *American Jurisprudence Adoption,* second ed. (St. Paul, Minn.: West, 2003), vol. 2, §8.

71. Waldmann, *American Jurisprudence Adoption,* vol. 2, §9.

72. Waldmann, *American Jurisprudence Adoption,* vol. 2, §9; Amanda C. Pustilnik, "Private Ordering, Legal Ordering, and the Getting of Children: A Counterhistory of Adoption Law," *Yale Law and Policy Review* 20 (2002): 263.

tion, their individual views influence the way in which they interpret these statutes in the context of nontraditional adoptive families.[73] "Private adoptions," unless authorized by statute, are void as against public policy.[74]

Who may be adopted is also a matter of state law. The Uniform Partnership Act, adopted by at least five states, states that any "individual" may be adopted, and state laws typically state that only a "living person" may be adopted. Although the intent of this "living person" language is to prevent adoption after death,[75] it is plausible that in the context of frozen embryos courts could refuse formal adoption proceedings to a party (or parties) wishing to "adopt" an embryo by declaring it not a living person. This could be true of other statutes that use the term "child" or "person." For example, Arizona law defines a child as a "person" under eighteen years of age.[76]

In reviewing the questions which surround human embryos, one is struck with the fundamental lack of relationship between embryonic adoption, as proposed and as practiced, and the long-standing legal concept of adoption of born children. Certainly there are parallels, but it seems a broad and perhaps ill-conceived leap to use the term "adoption" in reference to an entity not yet classified as either a human being or a child.[77]

Adaptation of traditional principles of adoption to frozen embryos is problematic and fraught with conceptual difficulty. By way of example, many states require that the adoptee be a party to the proceedings.[78] In one such circumstance, an appellate court allowed a motion to dismiss an adoption proceeding where "the child was never before the court or in the court's control. . . ."[79] A compelling case could be made for the appointment of a guardian in embryonic adoption.[80] Questions would naturally

73. Pustilnik, "Private Ordering," p. 290.

74. Waldmann, *American Jurisprudence Adoption,* vol. 2, §7.

75. Waldmann, *American Jurisprudence Adoption,* vol. 2, §20.

76. Ga. Code. Ann. §19-8-13 (West 2003); Fla. Stat. Ann. §39.01 (West 2003); Ariz. Rev. Stat. Ann. §8-101 (West 2003); Waldman, *American Jurisprudence Adoption,* vol. 2, §1; Sara L. Johnson, *American Law Reports,* fourth ed. (St. Paul, Minn.: Lawyers Co-operative Publishing Company, 1986), vol. 48, §4, p. 860.

77. Other than under the statutory scheme of the State of Louisiana, discussed previously.

78. Johnson, *American Law Reports,* vol. 48, §4.

79. *Wathan v. Ugast,* 143 F.2d 160 (1944).

80. An interesting inquiry is whether the guardian is of a person or property, or both, in embryonic adoption.

arise regarding the investigative role of the guardian or the court. Do they undertake a traditional "fitness" investigation? If so, of whom? Is the investigation pre-implantation or at some other logical stage in the proceedings? What is the extent of the investigation? Does it include analysis of the "origin" of the embryo, its status among "related" embryos? Is there an investigation as to whether this is a "bartered" transaction and, if so, which payments are deemed legally or socially acceptable under the circumstances of the embryonic adoption?

Does the "best interests" standard fit embryonic adoption? If so, whose interests are considered paramount and how are they determined?

Who would be parties to such proceedings? Potential parties would include the donor and donee, a surrogate parent, the IVF storage facility or clinic, and perhaps the person or entity who cloned or created the embryo, in addition to the prospective adoptive parties. Third party interveners, such as grandparents, siblings, and other persons who make up the blended twenty-first-century family might also have standing.

May the donor of the embryo revoke consent? If so, under what circumstances and at what time? Of course, there could be more than one donor and multiple embryos adopted. Are confidentiality concerns less significant than in traditional adoption? Would the embryonic adoptee have the right to know his or her donative parents or "siblings"?

One might suggest that traditional notions of adoption must be tempered with a view that there are no "natural" parents in the in vitro creation of an embryo. After all, this is not natural procreation but "artificial" technology which creates the embryo. As such, who is considered the child's "birth mother"? Should the distinctions between genetic, birth, and adoptive parents be important to the process?

Many states require that there be at least a ten-year age difference between the adoptee and the adoptive parents. Embryonic adoption, however, could conceivably create a difference of sixty years between the adoptive parent and the embryo. Should embryonic adoption have a maximum age limit?

Adaptation of the adoption concept also must consider issues of posthumous conception. Do these children have rights of inheritance, survivor benefits, and the like?

The role of an IVF clinic or storage facility is important to embryonic adoption, more so if embryos are considered a life-form. Does the concept of embryonic adoption elevate an IVF clinic or storage facility to an orphanage-like institution, with concomitant duties, rights, and obligations?

In addition to the adaptation required, the very concept of embryonic adoption may run afoul of *Roe v. Wade*.[81] Does not encouragement of adoption of a human embryo elevate it to a constitutionally impermissible status? The great anomaly, of course, is that an embryo, consisting of as few as six cells, may have a higher pre-implantation legal status than a first-trimester fetus containing millions of cells. These positions are not easily reconciled.

Embryonic adoption, furthermore, raises profound questions regarding "greater good" societal goals. Given the relative ease with which embryos can be created, their potential for unlimited stem cell research that could possibly cure the maladies of millions, and the percentage of embryos that actually become fetuses, there is an overwhelming practical temptation to urge scientific donation of all unused or discarded embryos. Must we exclude valuable and perhaps lifesaving scientific uses of unwanted embryos if they are classified as entities capable of being adopted? Can embryonic adoption somehow be reconciled with the need to fuel scientific advances, particularly those related to aiding the afflicted or potentially afflicted? Do we increase the tension between science and religion by restricting embryonic research in favor of embryonic adoption or the classification of embryos as a form of life? Can the concepts be reconciled or coexist?

The concept of embryonic adoption is particularly troubling when viewed in the context of existing, needy children. Undeniably there are millions of children in this world with immediate, quantifiable, and direct needs such as food, clothing, and shelter, in addition to the intangible nurturing that traditional adoption encompasses. Can we justify the adoption of the discarded or unused embryos of persons with means to afford ART to the exclusion of currently disadvantaged children?

Advocating embryonic adoption is further complicated by pre-implantation genetic screening. Is it socially desirable that the "better" embryos are adopted first? If so, what becomes of the "inferior" embryos? Is their destruction any less of a societal problem because they have inferior genetic traits? Can one legitimately argue against screening for recognized diseases or defects, and does it make humanitarian sense to select for adoption the embryos less likely to become ill or, in the old parlance, a ward of the state? Can one logically draw a thoughtful and reasoned line between acceptable and unacceptable characteristics of screening?

Embryonic adoption to some is a mere continuation of the dramatic

---

81. *Roe v. Wade*, 410 U.S. 113 (1973).

changes in the twenty-first-century family, now heavily populated by single parents, stepparents, grandparents who are raising children, same-sex parents, and, now, children born through artificial reproduction technology. Unfortunately, increases in technology have whetted the insatiable appetite of today's genetic consumer. One must assume that at least some motivation for embryonic adoption is either to create or to adopt the "better" child, a concept which may be anathema to the traditional concept of societal adoption. Embryonic adoption, therefore, may to some extent represent the pursuit of human perfection through science.

In his 1843 short story "The Birthmark," novelist Nathaniel Hawthorne told the story of Aylmer, a scientist and man of "natural philosophy" who was fixated on the removal of a small crimson-colored birthmark on the cheek of his beloved wife. Aylmer's potion caused the blemish to disappear from his wife's face, but also directly caused her untimely death. As she lay dying, Aylmer's wife remarked that he had rejected the best earth could offer. "Yet, had Aylmer reached a profounder wisdom, he need not thus have flung away the happiness which would have woven his mortal life of the selfsame texture with the celestial. The momentary circumstance was too strong for him; he failed to look beyond the shadowy scope of time, and, living once for all in eternity, to find the perfect future in the present."[82]

---

82. Nathaniel Hawthorne, *Mosses from an Old Manse* (Pennsylvania: Orange Street Press, 1999), p. 61.

Ishmael's Bane: The Sin and Crime of Illegitimacy Reconsidered

JOHN WITTE, JR.

Introduction

Sex has long excited an intimate union between law and religion in the Christian West. Western churches and states have long collaborated in setting private laws to define and facilitate licit sex: rules and procedures for sexual etiquette, courtship, and betrothal, for marital formation, maintenance, and dissolution, for conjugal duties, debts, and desires, for parental roles, rights, and responsibilities, and much more. Western churches and states have also long collaborated in setting criminal laws to police and punish illicit sex. For many centuries, these two powers kept overlapping rolls of sexual sin and crime — adultery and fornication, sodomy and buggery, incest and bestiality, bigamy and polygamy, prostitution and pornography, abortion and contraception, and more. They also operated interlocking tribunals to enforce these rules on sex. The church guarded the internal forum through its canons, confessionals, and consistory courts. The state guarded the external forum through its policing, prosecution, and punishment of sexual crimes. To be sure, church and state officials clashed frequently over sexual jurisdiction. And their respective private and criminal laws related to sex did change a great deal — dramatically in the fourth, twelfth, and sixteenth centuries.

A preliminary version of this text was presented at the conference on "Religion and Criminal Law" at Arizona State University College of Law, February 7-8, 2002, and published in *Punishment and Responsibility* 5 (July 2003): 327-46. I wish to thank Patrick M. Brennan, Don S. Browning, Michael J. Broyde, Eliza Ellison, Timothy P. Jackson, and Ann M. Stanton for edifying conversations about this essay and related topics on sex, crime, and religion.

But for all this rivalry and change, Christianity, and the Hebrew, Greek, and Roman sources on which it drew, had a formative influence on Western laws about sex.

Most of these classic laws have now been eclipsed in America by the dramatic rise of new public laws and popular customs of sexual liberty. Courtship, cohabitation, betrothal, and marriage are now mostly private sexual contracts with few roles for church and state to play and few restrictions on freedoms of entrance, exercise, and exit. Classic criminal bans on contraception and abortion have been found to violate Fourteenth Amendment liberties. Classic prohibitions on adultery and fornication have become dead or discarded letters on most statute books. Free speech laws protect all manner of sexual expression, short of outrageous obscenity. Constitutional privacy laws protect all manner of sexual conduct, short of exploitation of children or abuse of others. Only the classic prohibitions on incest, polygamy, and homosexuality remain on most law books — now the subjects of bitter constitutional battles and culture wars.

One tender sexual subject has hovered perennially on the margins of law and religion scholarship and on the boundaries of criminal, private, and public law. That is the subject of illegitimacy — or, to be less politically correct but more historically accurate, bastardy. In the Western tradition, the bastard was defined as a child born out of lawful wedlock — a product of fornication, adultery, concubinage, incest, or other sexual crime and sin. A bastard was at once a child of no one (*filius nullius*) and a child of everyone (*filius populi*) — born without name and without home, the perennial object of both pity and scorn, charity and abuse, romance and ribaldry. Absent successful legitimation, bastards bore the permanent stigma of their sinful and criminal conception, signaled on certificates of baptism, confirmation, marriage, and death. They lived in a sort of legal limbo — with some claims to charity and support but with sometimes severely truncated rights to inherit or devise property, to hold high clerical, political, or military office, to sue or testify in certain courts, and more. These formal legal disabilities on bastards were often compounded by chronic poverty, neglect, and abuse — assuming that they escaped the not uncommon historical practice of being secretly smothered or exposed upon birth, or put out to nurse or lease with modest odds of survival.[1]

---

1. Mark Jackson, *New-Born Child Murder: Women, Illegitimacy, and the Courts in Eighteenth-Century England* (Manchester: Manchester University Press, 1996), pp. 29-48; T. E. James, "The Illegitimate and Deprived Child: Legitimation and Adoption," in *A Century of Family Law: 1857-1957*, ed. R. H. Graveson and F. R. Crane (London: Sweet and Maxwell, 1957),

Illegitimacy doctrine has been a common feature of most legal and religious traditions of the world. It has long been part of a common effort to regulate the scope of the paterfamilias's power and responsibility within the household, and to regularize inheritance of property, title, lineage, and (in some cultures) control of the household religion or the family's ancestral rites.[2]

In the Western tradition, the stigmatization of illegitimacy was given special support by Christian theology. Illegitimacy doctrine was a natural concomitant of the church's attempts to shore up marriage as the only licit forum for sex and procreation. Illegitimacy doctrine was also viewed as an apt illustration and application of the biblical adage that "the sins of the fathers [and mothers] shall be visited upon their children" (cf. Exod. 20:5, 34:7; Num. 14:18; Deut. 5:9). The Bible itself seemed to condone this reading in its story of Ishmael, the illegitimate son of Abraham, who was condemned already in the womb as a "wild man" and was ultimately cast out of his home with minimal prospects of survival. Later biblical laws banned bastards and their seed from the house of the Lord if not from the community altogether. The New Testament equated bastards with those stubborn souls who refused to accept the life and liberty of the gospel. Christian theologians and jurists alike found in these biblical passages ample new legitimacy for the doctrine of illegitimacy. The doctrine found a prominent place in the canon law and common law alike from the twelfth to the twentieth centuries.

Illegitimacy doctrine, however, runs counter to a number of standard criminal law doctrines that Christian theology also helped to cultivate.[3] Illegitimacy is an unusual kind of status offense that, by definition, forgoes required proof of actus reus, mens rea, and causation. Illegitimacy doctrine is an unusual form of deterrence that threatens harm to an innocent third party in order to dissuade a couple from committing various

---

pp. 39-55; Lionel Rose, *The Massacre of the Innocents: Infanticide in Britain 1800-1939* (London: Routledge and Kegan Paul, 1986); Mason P. Thomas, "Child Abuse and Neglect. Part I: Historical Overview, Legal Matrix, and Social Perspectives," *North Carolina Law Review* 50 (1972): 293-349.

2. John C. Ayer Jr., "Legitimacy and Marriage," *Harvard Law Review* 16 (1902): 22-42; Shirley Hartley, *Illegitimacy* (Berkeley: University of California Press, 1975); Peter Laslett et al., eds., *Bastardy and Its Comparative History: Studies in the History of Illegitimacy and Marital Non-Conformism in Britain, France, Germany, Sweden, North America, Jamaica, and Japan* (Cambridge, Mass.: Harvard University Press, 1980); Bronislaw Malinowski, *Sex, Culture, and Myth* (New York: Harcourt, Brace and World, 1962).

3. Patrick M. Brennan, "On What Sin (and Grace) Can Teach Crime," *Punishment and Society* 5 (2002): 347-65.

sexual crimes. And illegitimacy is a peculiar species of vicarious liability, a sort of *respondeat inferior* doctrine that imposes upon innocent children some of the costs of their parents' extramarital experimentation.

To be sure, a good deal of the classic law of illegitimacy is now falling aside in the United States. Most states have removed the most chronic disabilities on the illegitimate's rights to property, support, and standing. Several remaining legal disabilities on illegitimates have been struck down since 1968 as violations of the equal protection clause of the Fourteenth Amendment.

But what the Fourteenth Amendment gives with one clause it takes back with another. The Fourteenth Amendment equal protection clause does spare illegitimates from vicarious liability for their parents' extramarital experimentation. But the Fourteenth Amendment due process clause spares sexually active adults criminal liability for engaging in extramarital experimentation. With the legal stigma of both illegitimacy and promiscuity removed, it is perhaps no accident that illegitimacy rates in this country have soared. While illegitimate children no longer suffer many formal legal disabilities, they continue to suffer ample social disabilities in the form of higher rates of poverty and poor education, deprivation and child abuse, juvenile delinquency and criminal conduct. Moreover, I shall argue, a new species of in utero illegitimates has emerged in the past three decades, condemned even more severely by the very same Fourteenth Amendment that protects the rights of their mothers.

This essay offers some preliminary research and reflection on the theology and law of illegitimacy. Part I sketches a bit of the biblical context and sanction for this doctrine. Part II summarizes the classic canon law and common law on the subject, and some of the recent legal reforms in the United States. Part III offers some critical theological reflections on the doctrine of illegitimacy, and suggests a few historically informed remedies that might be applied to better the plight of the illegitimate today. Adoption is one obvious such remedy.

I. Biblical Sources and Sanctions of Illegitimacy

The Christian doctrine of illegitimacy was born in the biblical story of Ishmael, the bastard son of the great patriarch Abraham. The facts, as recorded in the first book of the Hebrew Bible, are these: At seventy-five years old, Abraham, a rich and powerful man, grew concerned about his lineage and legacy. He complained to God that he and his wife Sarah were without child. God promised him an heir and countless descendents (Gen. 15:1-6). But for ten years thereafter, he had no children (Gen. 16:3, 16). A concerned Sarah urged Abraham to take her slave maid Hagar as a concubine, and have children by her. Abraham obliged. Hagar conceived. Newly pregnant, Hagar "looked with contempt" upon Sarah, her barren mistress (Gen. 16:4).[4] Sarah was livid. She dealt harshly with Hagar, who fled.

An angel enjoined Hagar to return. The angel promised that her child would survive and indeed have many descendents. But the angel also spoke ominously of the bane that would befall her bastard child: "Behold, you are with child, and shall bear a son; you shall call his name Ishmael [meaning "God hears"]; because the Lord has given heed to your affliction. [But] [h]e shall be a wild ass of a man, his hand against every man and every man's hand against him; and he shall dwell over against all his kinsmen" (Gen. 16:11-12).

Ishmael was born and raised in Abraham's household. Abraham embraced him as his firstborn son, and circumcised him to signify him as one of God's own (Gen. 17:23). Almost fifteen years later, however, Abraham and Sarah were miraculously blessed with the birth of their own son Isaac (Gen. 17:1; 21:5). Sarah grew jealous of the adolescent Ishmael playing with her newly weaned son Isaac. She grew concerned about Isaac's claims to Abraham's vast wealth. "Cast out this slave woman with her son," she enjoined Abraham; "for the son of this slave woman shall not be heir with my son Isaac" (Gen. 21:8-10). After anguished reflection and prayer, Abraham obliged Sarah, contrary to his own affection for Ishmael and to the custom of the day that a master care for his slaves and their children, however conceived.

Abraham sent Hagar and Ishmael away into the desert, meagerly armed with food and water. Their provisions ran out. Ishmael grew weak. His mother cast him under a bush, walked away, and sat with her back to him, not wishing to hear or see him die. Ishmael cried. The angel returned to Hagar, his mother, and proclaimed: "Fear not; for God has heard the voice of the lad where he is. Arise, lift up the lad, and hold him fast with your hand; for I will make him a great nation" (Gen. 21:17-18). Miraculously, Hagar found a water well and saved Ishmael. Ishmael grew up to be a skilled huntsman and warrior. His mother later found him a wife from

4. All biblical quotations in this essay are taken from the Revised Standard Version of the Bible (*Harper Study Bible*, ed. Harold Lindsell, second ed. [Grand Rapids: Zondervan, 1972]).

among her kin. Ishmael fathered twelve (legitimate) sons who became princes of the tribes of the ancient Middle East (Gen. 25:12-18; cf. Gal. 4:24-25). He received no inheritance, but joined his half-brother Isaac in burying their father Abraham (Gen. 25:9). Ishmael lived a full life and died at 137 years (Gen. 25:17). Thus far the facts as reported in the Book of Genesis.

The ambiguous moral lessons of this story of Ishmael are echoed later in the rest of the Bible and in the Apocrypha. On the one hand, both the Old and New Testaments describe God as one who hears the cries and tends the needs of the "poor" and "fatherless," just as God heard and tended Ishmael. God's people are repeatedly enjoined to do likewise for the bastards and orphans in their midst (Job 29:12; Isa. 1:17; Jer. 5:28; James 1:27). These quiet biblical refrains on charity, however, are almost drowned out by the robust biblical orchestrations denouncing bastards and bastardy. The Mosaic law precluded illegitimates and their progeny from the priesthood, if not from corporate worship altogether: "No bastard [*mamzer*] shall enter the assembly of the LORD," Deuteronomy provides; "even to the tenth generation none of his descendents shall enter the assembly of the LORD" (Deut. 23:2). The prophet Hosea condemned the children of the adulteress: "Upon her children also I will have no pity, because they are children of harlotry. For their mother has played the harlot; she that conceived them has acted shamefully" (Hos. 2:4-5). The Book of Ecclesiasticus imposed on the children of the adulteress vicarious liability for the sins of their mother: "She herself will be brought before the assembly, and punishment will fall on her children. Her children will not take root, and her branches will not bear fruit. She will leave her memory for a curse, and her disgrace will not be blotted out" (Sir. 23:24-26). The Wisdom of Solomon struck an even more threatening tone for illegitimates: "[C]hildren of adulterers will not come to maturity, and the offspring of an unlawful union will perish. Even if they live long they will be held of no account, and finally their old age will be without honor. . . . For children born of unlawful unions are witnesses of evil against their parents when God examines them" (Wisd. Sol. 3:16-17; 4:6).

The New Testament went further and labeled as bastards *(nothos)* all those who reject the gospel's promise of Christian freedom from the law and sin. The legitimate children of Abraham are those who accept the gospel. The illegitimate children of Abraham are those who stubbornly cling to the law, notably the Jews (John 8:31-59; Heb. 12:8). Legitimates are free Christians whose lives are filled with promise. Bastards are enslaved non-Christians whose lives are without hope — and who accordingly live as the "wild man" Ishmael and need to be curtailed if not cast out. St. Paul captured this new variation on the Ishmael story in a jarring message to the new Christians in Galatia who insisted on continued adherence to the Mosaic law:

> Tell me, you who desire to be under law, do you not hear the law? For it is written that Abraham had two sons, one by a slave [Hagar] and one by a free woman [Sarah]. But the son of the slave was born according to the flesh, the son of the free woman through promise. Now this is an allegory: these women are two covenants. One is from Mount Sinai, bearing children for slavery; she is Hagar. Now Hagar is Mount Sinai in Arabia; she corresponds to the present Jerusalem, for she is in slavery with her children. But the Jerusalem above is free. . . . Now we, brethren, like Isaac, are children of promise. But as at that time he who was born according to the flesh persecuted him who was born according to the Spirit, so it is now. But what does the Scripture say? "Cast out the slave and her son; for the son of the slave shall not inherit with the son of the free woman." So, brethren, we are not children of the slave but of the free woman. (Gal. 4:21-31)

This passage would become a *locus classicus* for all manner of later Christian theories and practices concerning illegitimacy, as well as anti-Semitism.

II. A Primer on the Western Law of Illegitimacy

While the Western Christian doctrine of illegitimacy was born in the Bible, it was raised in Christian theology and jurisprudence. The juxtaposed biblical passages on illegitimacy have inspired nearly two millennia of biblical commentaries, and these conflicting moral judgments have passed into the canon law of the church, the civil law of the Continent, and the common law of England and America.

Classic Canon Law

On the one hand, Christian theologians and jurists have long sought to heed the cries of the Ishmaels of the world and to offer them comfort, charity, and kindness.[5] For example, the early church fathers and church

---

5. See John Boswell, *The Kindness of Strangers: The Abandonment of Children in Western Europe from Late Antiquity to the Renaissance* (New York: Pantheon, 1988), pp. 58-59, 72-73, 145, 150-53.

councils condemned the classic Roman law that gave the paterfamilias the power of life and death over his offspring, and that paid little heed to the smothering and abandonment of bastards born in his household — practices which later Christian emperors outlawed, at least with respect to children of wives and concubines. By the fifth century, the church's canon law grouped bastards with widows, orphans, and the poor as those *personae miserabiles* who deserved special care and charity from the church.[6] By the twelfth century, bastards were given special standing in church courts to sue for paternal support from indifferent or recalcitrant fathers.[7] Bastards were also common oblates in medieval Catholic monasteries, ecclesiastical guilds, foundling houses, and cathedral schools.[8] From the sixteenth century onward, they were also among those especially eligible for gratis matriculation in Protestant schools and guilds, where they received room, board, education, and vocational training.[9]

On the other hand, Christian theologians and moralists treated illegitimacy as a particularly good case for effectuating the biblical maxim that "the sins of the fathers [and mothers] shall be visited upon their children." The sins of Abraham and Hagar were adultery and concubinage. The sins of Sarah were contempt for God's promises and complicity in Abraham's adultery, as well as jealousy, cruelty, and greed. Ishmael bore vicarious liability for both sets of sins. There were many sins like those of Abraham and Sarah that should be treated comparably when they produced illegitimate fruit, medieval writers insisted. These included: (1) bodily sins, such as fornication, concubinage, prostitution, and incest; (2) faithless sins, such as breaches of vows of abstinence, chastity, betrothal, or marriage; and (3) spiritual sins of marrying one outside the faith or in violation of the church's rules for marital formation. Children born of all such sins were presumptively the new Ishmaels of the world, and presumptively subject to the same stigma and disabilities imposed on the Ishmael of old.[10]

---

6. Brian Tierney, *Medieval Poor Law: A Sketch of Canonical Theory and Its Application in England* (Berkeley: University of California Press, 1959); Gilles Couvreur, *Les pauvres ont-ils des droits?* (Rome: Libraria editrice dell'Universita Gregoriana, 1961), pp. 37-39.

7. R. H. Helmholz, "Bastardy Litigation in Medieval England," *American Journal of Legal History* 13 (1969): 360-83, and "Support Orders, Church Courts, and the Rule of *Filius Nullius*: A Reassessment of the Common Law," *Virginia Law Review* 63 (1977): 431-48.

8. Boswell, *Kindness of Strangers*, pp. 222-23, 302, 304.

9. John Witte Jr., *Law and Protestantism: The Legal Teachings of the Lutheran Reformation* (Cambridge: Cambridge University Press, 2002), pp. 257-92.

10. Ludwig Schmugge et al., eds., *Illegitimität im Spätmittelalter* (Munich: R. Oldenbourg Verlag, 1994).

The church refined its law of bastardy as it refined its law of marriage. The formative era was the twelfth through fifteenth centuries, when the church reached the height of its political and legal power. The church developed a complex system of new laws, called canon laws, which were enforced by church courts and other officials throughout Western christendom.[11] In this formative period, the canon law came to treat marriage systematically as at once a natural, contractual, and spiritual institution, created by God to produce children, to foster faithfulness among spouses, and to sanctify the couple, their children, and the broader Christian community. As a natural association, marriage was created by God to enable man and woman to "be fruitful and multiply" and to raise children together in the service and love of God. With the fall into sin, this natural association also became a remedy for lust, a channel to direct one's natural passion to proper service. As a contract, marriage was a binding contractual unit, formed by the mutual consent of the parties. This contract prescribed for couples a life-long relation of love, service, and devotion to each other and to their natural children. As a sacrament, marriage symbolized the eternal union between Christ and his church. Participation in this sacrament conferred sanctifying grace upon the couple and their children. Christian couples could perform this sacrament privately, provided they were capable of marriage and complied with the rules for marriage formation. Once properly formed, a Christian marital union was indissoluble, as much as Christ's bond to his church remains indissoluble. Children born of such Christian unions were the saints of the next generation, to be baptized, catechized, and confirmed in the Christian church, and nurtured, educated, and socialized in the Christian home.[12]

The canon law of illegitimacy was grounded in this understanding of marriage. Marriage was the proper and licit place for a Christian to pursue sex and procreation. Sexual intercourse outside of marriage was a serious crime and sin. The natural father and mother were best suited by nature to care for their own children, and in turn to be cared for by their children when they grew old and weak. The medieval canonists and moralists believed that relations between parents and "unnatural" children often would not endure or produce the enduring mutual care that was essential to stable domestic welfare. Blood ties between parents and children were an essential natural foundation for an enduring Christian family.

---

11. James A. Brundage, *Law, Sex, and Christian Society in Medieval Europe* (Chicago: University of Chicago Press, 1987); Theodor Mackin, *Marriage in the Catholic Church: What Is Marriage?* (New York: Paulist, 1982).

From these premises, the canon lawyers created a hierarchy of illegitimate children.[13] The first and least stigmatized class consisted of "natural illegitimates" born of concubinage or prenuptial sex between fiancées, or, somewhat worse, born of fornication or prostitution by their parents. These children could be legitimated by the subsequent marriage of their parents — though their parents could face severe sanctions for their sexual sin, particularly if they were recidivists.

The second class was those "unnatural illegitimates" born of the innocent sexual crimes of their parents. These were usually children born of a Christian couple who had married in good faith, then had sex and children, but later discovered a blood or family tie between them that rendered their marriage incestuous. Such children could be legitimated if the impediment to their parents' marriage was dispensed by the pope or other authorized church official.

The third and worst off class was "unnatural" illegitimates born to parents who had knowingly committed incest or adultery. Such children were permanently condemned to illegitimacy because they were born "not only against the positive law, but against the express natural law."[14] Their parents could never marry, given the continued ties of incest between them or the prior indissoluble marriage that their adultery had betrayed. Also irredeemable from bastardy were children born of bigamy or breached oaths of chastity or celibacy. In each of these cases, one or both parents had precontracted to another marriage or to a life of chastity. Such parents, too, could never be married and thereby legitimate their now illegitimate children. For, having made one set of unbreakable vows, they could not make another in a new marriage. Their children were permanently condemned as bastards.

At canon law, bastards were generally barred from the church's higher religious orders and offices, in emulation of the Deuteronomic law. In firmer decades and dioceses, bastards were also barred from sexual and marital relations, so that their dishonorable seed would die out as Ecclesiasticus and Wisdom had foretold. Canon law did allow for a child's legitimation through papal dispensation, but this was a rare

12. See John Witte Jr., *From Sacrament to Contract: Marriage, Religion, and Law in the Western Tradition* (Louisville, Ky.: Westminster/John Knox, 1997).

13. Robert Génestal, *Histoire de la légitimation des infantes naturales en droit canonique* (Paris: E. Lourex, 1905); Helmholz, "Bastardy Litigation"; Schmugge et al., eds., *Illegitimität im Spätmittelalter.*

14. Thomas Aquinas, *Summa Theologica*, trans. Fathers of the English Dominican Province, vol. 5 (Allen, Tex.: Christian Classics, 1948), q. 68.

prize reserved principally for well-heeled and well-connected royals and aristocrats.[15]

Classic Common Law

A parallel law of illegitimacy emerged in English common law. The canon law dealt with spiritual sanctions for the sexual sin of the parents and the pastoral care and control of their illegitimate child. The common law dealt with criminal punishment of the parents' sexual crime and the civil status and sanctions of their illegitimate child. Before the sixteenth century, these two laws of illegitimacy remained separate — jealously so in cases involving paternity and paternal property disputes. After the sixteenth-century Anglican Reformation, the two laws of illegitimacy began to merge slowly in England. Much of the canon law on the subject was ultimately absorbed into the early modern common law. It was the merged system taught by the English common lawyers that came to prevail in the American colonies and the young American states, albeit often amply adapted to local conditions and customs.

At classic common law, a child was considered illegitimate if "born out of lawful wedlock." Illegitimate were children born where there was no wedlock altogether — products of the crimes of fornication *(filii)*, concubinage *(spurii)*, prostitution *(mamzeres)*, or adultery *(nothi)*.[16] Illegitimate, too, were children born of putative marriages that were subsequently found to be unlawful and were annulled by reason of innocent or knowing bigamy or intentional incest.[17] Both English and American common law dropped the category of illegitimates born of breached vows of chastity or celibacy. American common law added a category of illegitimates born of miscegenation.

The common law, like the canon law, devised endless subclassifications among these illegitimate children. The most important distinctions turned on the severity of the sexual crime of the parents. Children born of adultery, intentional incest, or bigamy (and, in America before 1865, miscegenation) were the worst off, for these children were products of serious

---

15. Brundage, *Law, Sex, and Christian Society;* Schmugge et al., eds., *Illegitimität im Spätmittelalter.*

16. John Brydall, *Lex Spuriorum, or the Law Relating to Bastardy* (London: Atkins, 1703), pp. 4-14.

17. Matthew Bacon, *A New Abridgement of the Law,* fifth ed., 7 vols. (London: A. Strathan, 1798), s.v. "Bastardy"; Richard Adair, *Courtship, Illegitimacy and Marriage in Early Modern England* (Manchester: Manchester University Press, 1996).

felonies. They faced the most stringent treatment, and their parents faced criminal sanctions of fine, imprisonment, banishment, and, in serious cases of recidivism, execution. The common law rejected the civil law of adoption as a means of legitimating one's own or another's illegitimate children.[18] At the same time, the common law made escape from bastardy nearly impossible, save through procurement of a private act of Parliament or, in America, of the state legislature.

The common law diverged from the canon law at two crucial points, however, both to the further detriment of the bastard. First, at canon law, the post hoc marriage of the parents of a "natural illegitimate" child automatically legitimated the child, rendering it subject to its father's support, protection, authority, education, and inheritance.[19] At common law, no such legitimation could occur. A child born before his or her parents married remained illegitimate even if the parents subsequently married.[20] "Shotgun" weddings between conception and birth legitimated the child, but post-birth weddings were of no avail.

Second, at canon law, illegitimate children could sue in church courts for the support of their mothers and fathers, particularly if the parents were well-heeled. At common law, illegitimate children had no right to their parents' support, and their parents had no duty to deliver the same.[21] This harsh common law rule was slowly changed by the new English poor law of 1576 that empowered local justices of the peace to compel parents to support their illegitimate children who lived in the local parish and were dependent upon the parish church's charity.[22] But this English poor law reform was of no use for religious dissenters in England, or for those who lacked knowledge or means of access to the justice of the peace. And this poor law reform had no place in America; indeed, the harsh common law of no parental support for bastards persisted in some American states until well into the twentieth century.

Illegitimate children faced several other disabilities at both English and American common law. Lacking the honor of legitimate birth, they

18. James, "Illegitimate and Deprived Child"; Jamil S. Zainaldin, "The Emergence of a Modern American Family Law: Child Custody, Adoption, and the Courts, 1796-1851," *Northwestern Law Review* 73 (1979): 1038-89.

19. Helmholz, "Bastardy Litigation," pp. 362-65; Bacon, *Abridgement of the Law.*

20. William Blackstone, *Commentaries on the Law of England,* third rev. ed., ed. Thomas H. Cooley (Chicago: Callaghan, 1884), book 1, chap. 16.3.

21. James Kent, *Commentaries on American Law,* 2 vols. (New York: O. Halsted, 1827); Richard Burn, *Ecclesiastical Law,* sixth ed., 4 vols. (London: A. Strathan, 1797), 1:242-50.

22. Helmholz, "Support Orders," pp. 446-48.

were formally precluded from various honorable positions, particularly high political, military, admiralty, and judicial offices, as well as from service as coroners, jurors, prison wardens, church wardens, parish vestryman, or comparable positions of social visibility and responsibility. However well-propertied they became, bastards were also often denied access to local polls, clubs, schools, learned societies, and licensed professions. However well-qualified they might be, they were also formally precluded from ordination in the established Church of England.[23]

While most of these social disabilities had fallen into desuetude by the turn of the nineteenth century, various testamentary disabilities persisted firmly at common law. As a "child of everyone" *(filius populi)*, the bastard could receive alms and other forms of public charity. But as a "child of no one" *(filius nullius)*, the bastard had no inheritable and devisable blood that the common law would recognize. Bastards could thus inherit nothing from parents, siblings, or anyone else — whether name, property, title, honor, business, license, charter, or other devisable private or public claim or good.[24] American state laws extended this disability specifically to prohibit bastards from claiming wrongful death damages in tort, life or residual disability insurance proceeds, social security benefits, military benefits, and other such proceeds that were earmarked generically for the children of a deceased or disabled parent. Several states further prohibited or taxed private *inter vivos* gifts to bastards, and denied or impeded their standing in probate courts to sue for legacies from their intestate natural parents.[25]

Illegitimate children, in turn, were limited in their capacities to alienate or devise their own property. The estates of childless bastards, or of those who died intestate or with defective wills, were seized by officials. Even those illegitimates who donated or devised their property to surviving spouses or children by proper instruments were sometimes subject to special gift and inheritance taxes imposed by authorities on both sides of the Atlantic.[26]

These common law disabilities on illegitimates were considered necessary to protect licit marriage and to deter illicit sex. It was a commonplace of Anglo-American common law until the twentieth century that traditional marriage was, as the United States Supreme Court put it, a "godly

---

23. Brydall, *Lex Spuriorum*, pp. 15-34; Burn, *Ecclesiastical Law*; John Godolphin, *Reportorium Canonicum*, third ed. (London: Assigns of R. and E. Atkins, 1687), pp. 86-87, 279-80.

24. Blackstone, *Commentaries*; Kent, *Commentaries*.

25. Homer H. Clark, *The Law of Domestic Relations in the United States*, second ed. (St. Paul, Minn.: West, 1988).

26. Bacon, *Abridgement of the Law*; Clark, *Law of Domestic Relations*.

ordinance," "a sacred obligation," "a public institution of universal concern," "the very basis of the whole fabric of civilized society."[27] It was an equal commonplace that Christianity — including the Bible's commandments not to commit adultery, fornication, prostitution, incest, and other sexual sins and crimes — was a part of the common law. Illegitimacy doctrine was part and product of these Christian common law beliefs — a way for the law to symbolize proper family values and to scapegoat sexual sin at once. An Ohio judge put it thus in a 1961 case: "It might perhaps be mentioned that the Decalog, which is the basis of our moral code, specifically states that the sins of the father may be visited upon the children unto the third and fourth generation, so that the argument against making the children suffer for the mother's wrong can be attacked on ethical grounds."[28] Another authority defended the formal legal disabilities on illegitimates with these words in 1939: "The bastard, like the prostitute, thief, and beggar, belongs to that motley crowd of disreputable social types which society has generally resented, always endured. He is a living symbol of social irregularity, and undeniable evidence of contramoral forces."[29]

Modern American Reforms

Neither moral stigmatization nor legal disability, however, proved effective enough to deter the conception of illegitimate children. Illegitimacy rates in Europe and America — while subjects of endless debate among demographers — have, by all accounts, risen steadily since the first systematic records were kept in the sixteenth century. Illegitimacy rates stood at 2 to 5 percent in the sixteenth and seventeenth centuries in Europe. There was little discernible difference in the illegitimate rates in Catholic and Protestant polities, and surprisingly little demonstrable increase when polities raised the minimum age of marriage or tightened marriage formation rules.[30] With growing liberalization, urbanization, and emigration in the eighteenth and nineteenth centuries, illegitimacy rose to median levels of 5 to 10 percent in Europe and America, often well over 10 percent in some of the larger cities.[31]

---

27. See sources and cases quoted in Witte, *Sacrament to Contract,* p. 194.

28. Quoted in Harry D. Krause, *Illegitimacy: Law and Social Policy* (Indianapolis, Ind.: Bobbs-Merrill, 1971), p. 9.

29. Quoted in Krause, *Illegitimacy,* p. 1.

30. Laslett et al., *Bastardy and Its Comparative History,* pp. 102ff.; Peter Laslett, *The Family and Illicit Love in Early Generations* (Cambridge: Cambridge University Press, 1977).

31. Laslett, *Family and Illicit Love,* pp. 48-64; Crane Brinton, *The French Revolutionary Legislation on Illegitimacy* (Cambridge, Mass.: Harvard University Press, 1936), pp. 10-12, 72-76.

These rates gradually moved up a percentage point or two from around 1850 to 1950, with larger cities and more liberal communities sometimes reaching rates over 15 percent.

Both the growing numbers of illegitimates and the growing visibility of their poverty and exploitation in cities at the turn of the twentieth century led to a growing campaign to ameliorate their plight.[32] Especially during and after the New Deal, many American states reformed their criminal laws and private laws to give new protection to illegitimate (and legitimate) children. Firm new laws against assault and abuse of children offered substantive and procedural protections, particularly for those who suffered under intemperate parents and guardians. New criminal laws punished more firmly abortion and infanticide. Ample new federal and state tax appropriations were made available to support orphanages and other children's charities, and to establish new children's aid and social welfare societies. Child labor, particularly the cruel industrial exploitation of illegitimate children in factories and workhouses, was firmly outlawed by both federal and state laws. Educational opportunities for children were substantially enhanced through the expansion of public schools. The modern welfare state came increasingly to stand *in loco parentis* for needy children, offering them care, protection, and nurture, regardless of the legitimacy of their birth.[33]

Modern states also facilitated the legitimation of children. Abandoning a seven-hundred-year-old common law rule, many states in the first half of the twentieth century began to allow for legitimation of children through the subsequent marriage of their natural mother and natural father. More recently, most states extended this to allow for legitimation upon marriage of the natural mother to any man, not necessarily the father of the illegitimate children.

Modern states further facilitated legitimation of children by adopting the ancient doctrine of adoption. The common law had firmly rejected the Roman and civil law of adoption. Classic common law had treated natural blood ties between parent and child as essential to the formation of a stable Christian family, and an absolute condition for vesting the father's right and duty to control and support the child and to transfer family property to him or her. This left "unnatural" illegitimates without much prospect for legitimation. It also left childless couples without much hope

---

32. Gail Reekie, *Measuring Immorality: Social Inquiry and the Problem of Legitimacy* (Cambridge: Cambridge University Press, 1998), pp. 22-36.

33. Thomas, "Child Abuse and Neglect"; Krause, *Illegitimacy.*

for perpetuating their name and legacy, unless they could legitimate a child through a private act of Parliament or of the state legislature.

Massachusetts was the first common law jurisdiction to adopt adoption. An 1851 statute allowed for the permanent transfer of parental power to a third-party adopting adult who was biologically unrelated to the child. And, in turn, it automatically legitimated the adopted child as the adopting parent's own, providing the child with a name, support, and all the rights and privileges of a legitimate child during and after the adopting parent's lifetime.[34] A century later this was the norm throughout the United States, as well as in England.[35]

Even where children were not or could not be legitimated, modern states removed a good number of the common law disabilities against them. Most important, illegitimate children gained firmer standing in courts and surer footing through agencies to file paternity suits, and to sue their father for support during his lifetime. The growing presumption now in most states is that a father owes a duty of support to his natural children and can be subject to mandatory paternity tests in suspicious cases and to criminal sanctions in cases for failure to furnish mandated child support. Moreover, a good number of the traditional prohibitions against gifts and devises to illegitimates have fallen aside. In all states, mothers are entirely free to give their illegitimate children property by gift or testament. Illegitimate children, in turn, are freely entitled to receive property from mothers who have died testate or intestate. In most states, this same rule applies to inheritance between fathers and illegitimate children, though several states still impose restrictions on receipt of such paternal legacies, particularly in cases of the father's intestacy. Several states also give priority to legitimate children in cases of inheriting from grandparents or claiming reversionary or remainder property interests,[36] though these traditional preferences, too, are falling aside rapidly.

The plight of illegitimate children has been still further relieved through recent United States Supreme Court interpretations of the equal protection clause of the Fourteenth Amendment (and, in federal cases, the equal protection reading of the Fifth Amendment due process clause). In some two dozen cases since 1968, the Court has slowly drawn much of the remaining sting and stigma from illegitimacy — though the formal le-

34. See essay by Stephen Presser in this volume; Zainaldin, "Modern American Family Law."

35. Clark, *Law of Domestic Relations;* James, "Illegitimate and Deprived Child."

36. Clark, *Law of Domestic Relations;* Douglas E. Abrams and Sarah H. Ramsey, *Children and the Law: Doctrine, Policy, and Practice* (St. Paul, Minn.: West, 2000).

gal category of illegitimacy still remains licit under the equal protection clause. Illegitimate children are now equally entitled with legitimate children to recover tort damages or workman's compensation benefits for the wrongful death of their parents. They are equally entitled to make claims on the properties and estates of their parents. They are equally entitled to draw residual social security benefits, residual disability benefits, and life insurance proceeds from their deceased parents.[37]

There is ample irony in the protection afforded by the Fourteenth Amendment, however. The Fourteenth Amendment equal protection clause does remove much of the legal stigma from illegitimate birth. But the Fourteenth Amendment due process clause removes most of the legal sanction from extramarital sex. With the ill legal consequences of both illegitimacy and promiscuity largely removed, the number of illegitimates has exploded. In the past two decades, nearly one-third of all American children — and more than one-half of all African-American children — were born illegitimate.[38] While many of these children thrive in single, blended, and adoptive households, a good number more do not. Illegitimate children still suffer roughly three times the rates of poverty and penury, poor education and health care, juvenile delinquency and truancy, and criminal conduct and conviction when compared to their legitimate peers. Illegitimate children and their mothers also draw considerably more heavily upon federal and state welfare programs, with all the stigmatizing by self and others that such dependence often induces.[39] While the legal and moral stigma of illegitimacy may no longer sting much, the social and psychological burdens of illegitimacy remain rather heavy.

There is an even greater irony to the protection afforded by the Fourteenth Amendment. The extension of its guarantee of sexual liberty to include the right of abortion has sanctioned a whole new class of "illegitimates" in the past three decades. These new illegitimates are not those unwanted innocents who are born out of wedlock, but those un-

37. Clark, *Law of Domestic Relations;* Abrams and Ramsey, *Children and the Law;* Martha T. Zingo and Kevin E. Early, *Nameless Persons: Legal Discrimination against Non-Marital Children in the United States* (Westport, Conn.: Praeger, 1994).

38. Mark Abrahamson, *Out of Wedlock Birth: The United States in Comparative Perspective* (Westport, Conn.: Praeger, 1998); David Popenoe and Barbara DaFoe Whitehead, *The State of Our Unions* (Rutgers, N.J.: National Marriage Project, 1998-2000); David Blankenhorn, *Fatherless America: Confronting Our Most Urgent Social Problem* (New York: Basic, 1995).

39. Blankenhorn, *Fatherless America;* Reekie, *Measuring Immorality;* Zingo and Early, *Nameless Persons;* Lewellyn Hendrix, *Illegitimacy and Social Structures* (Westport, Conn.: Bergin and Garvey, 1996).

wanted innocents who are aborted before their birth. These unwanted innocents pay not with a sort of a civil death as in the past, but with an actual physical death without hope of a future.

This is not to suggest that children conceived out of wedlock are the only or even the majority of those being aborted. Nor is it to say that we must return to a system of criminalizing abortion and thus exposing unwanted innocents and their mothers to more desperate and dangerous measures. But I dare say that it is worth pondering the analogies between the current plight of the innocent being in utero (or even in vitro[40]) and the historical plight of the innocent youngster in limbo. Indeed, if the historical doctrine of illegitimacy was a Christian theology of original sin pressed to untutored extremes (as I shall argue below), this new form of illegitimacy is a constitutional theory of sexual liberty pressed to equally untoward extremes.

III. Theological and Legal Reflections

Given the shaping historical influence of Christian theology on the Western law of illegitimacy, perhaps it would be useful in conclusion to inquire a bit about what contemporary theology can still say about this doctrine and about its further reform.

It must be remembered that, despite all the recent changes in American law and culture, many religious communities, within and beyond the Abrahamic tradition, continue to maintain a theological doctrine of illegitimacy today. Some of these religious communities continue to predicate this doctrine on explicit theological and moral grounds of deterring extramarital sex, maintaining marital sanctity, and supporting the natural nuclear family. Illegitimate children born in these religious communities sometimes still continue to bear severe sanctions and disabilities imposed on them by internal religious law: indeed, "honor killings" of bastards and their mothers have recently risen in some firmer Muslim communities around the world.[41]

The First Amendment lawyer in me cannot resist saying a few words about this. The free exercise clause mandates that religious communities

---

40. See essay by John C. Mayoue in this volume, on the relative moral status of the fetus in the womb and the frozen embryo.

41. Abdullahi Ahmed An-Na'im, ed., *Islamic Family Law in a Changing World: A Global Resource Book* (London: Zed, 2002).

in this country be left free to preach and practice their theology and law of illegitimacy, without undue interference from the state. This corporate free exercise right does not license religious communities to threaten or harm the life and limb of any of their members, whether legitimate or illegitimate. Honor killings or anything remotely resembling the same have no place or protection. Nor does the free exercise clause license the community to impede any party's right to leave that religious community if the party finds its preaching and practice on illegitimacy unacceptable. But the free exercise clause should protect the religious community's right to preach and practice peaceably against illegitimacy, and to sanction and shun its illegitimates. Neither the voluntary members of that religious community nor anyone else should have recourse to state legislatures or courts to enjoin or punish the same. Both popular and unpopular religious beliefs and practices deserve constitutional protection. That is the price we pay for religious freedom for all.

Theological Critique

The theologian in me, however, cannot resist saying a few more words to challenge the traditional Christian doctrine of illegitimacy, which many conservative Christian churches still teach today. In my view, the Christian theological doctrine of illegitimacy is theologically illegitimate. It is a misreading of basic biblical texts. It is a misunderstanding of the doctrine of original sin. It is a missed insight into the true meaning and possibility of Christian families.

The biblical story of Abraham and Ishmael is just that — a story, which must be read as part of the full biblical *nomos* and narrative. It is a powerful, troubling, and sobering tale. It is, to my mind, best seen as an injunction to faithfulness and patience, a warning against concubinage and adultery, a testament to divine mercy and miracle, all of which lessons are underscored many times over later in the Bible. But Abraham's harsh treatment of Ishmael is no more to be emulated and implemented today than the later story of Abraham carrying his legitimate son Isaac to the top of a mountain to sacrifice him on an altar (Gen. 22:1-14).

Illegitimacy doctrine can find no firm anchorage in the familiar biblical adage that "the sins of the fathers shall be visited upon their children." Four times that passage recurs in the Bible. Twice, it appears in the Decalogue as a gloss on the Commandment prohibiting idol worship. "You shall not make for yourself a graven image . . . you shall not bow down to them or serve them; for I the LORD your God am a jealous God, visiting the iniquity of the fathers upon the children to the third and the fourth generation of those who hate me, but showing steadfast love to thousands of those who love me and keep my commandments" (Exod. 20:4-6; cf. Deut. 5:8-10). The sin at issue is idolatry, not adultery. And nothing is said here to distinguish among legitimate or illegitimate children of the next generations. The threat of vicarious liability is clear for any subsequent generations of children who continue to "hate God" or perpetuate idol worship. But "steadfast love" is promised to those who love God and keep God's commandments. Exactly the same promise is repeated in the other two passages that repeat this phrase of "visiting iniquity upon children." Legitimate or illegitimate children of sinners who perpetuate their parents' sin are condemned. But those children of sinners who are righteous receive God's steadfast love (Exod. 34:7; Num. 14:18). These passages do not teach a doctrine of double original sin for illegitimates. They preach the need for all to repent and be righteous.

Later biblical passages support this reading. In Deuteronomy, for example, Moses lays out various laws of crime and tort, and then explicitly rejects the law of vicarious liability within the family: "The fathers shall not be put to death for the children, nor shall the children be put to death for the fathers; every man shall be put to death for his own sin" (Deut. 24:16). In the next verse he adds: "You shall not pervert the justice due to the sojourner or to the fatherless" (Deut. 24:17; see also Deut. 27:19; Ps. 94:6; Isa. 9:17; Lam. 5:3). The prophet Ezekiel says clearly that in a community dedicated to "godly justice," children should not bear vicarious liability for their parents' sin:

> "You say, 'Why should not the son suffer for the iniquity of the father?' [I say:] When the son has done what is lawful and right, and has been careful to observe all my statutes, he shall surely live. The soul that sins shall die. The son shall not suffer for the iniquity of the father, nor the father suffer for the iniquity of the son; the righteousness of the righteous shall be upon himself, and the wickedness of the wicked shall be upon himself." (Ezek. 18:19-20; cf. Isa. 3:10-11)

This biblical teaching of individual accountability and liability is further underscored by New Testament teaching. If Christ's atonement for sin means anything for Christians, it means that no one, not least an unborn or newborn child, need be a scapegoat for the sins of his or her parents. In Christian theology, one Scapegoat for others' sins was enough. The New Testament says repeatedly that each individual soul will stand directly before the judgment seat of God to answer for what he or she has done in this life, and to receive final divine judgment and mercy (see esp. Matt. 25:31-46). Before the judgment seat of God, there will be no class actions, and no joint or vicarious liability for which the individual soul must answer.

Equally exaggerated, in my view, is the conventional theological teaching that blood ties are a sine qua non of faithful and stable family life and love. Kin altruism, of course, is an ancient classical insight, which came most famously into Christian theology via Thomas Aquinas's appropriation of Aristotle.[42] There is something fundamentally sound and sensible in the notion that a parent, particularly a father, will be naturally inclined to invest in the care of a child who carries his blood and name, who looks and acts like him, and who needs him in those tender years to survive.

But it is easy to press this naturalist argument for kin altruism too far. After all, the same Christian theology that insists on blood ties between parent and child insists on no blood ties between husband and wife. Indeed, to marry within the prohibited degrees of consanguinity is to commit the crime of incest, a serious offense if it is done with intent. But why should the legitimacy of parental love turn essentially on the presence of blood ties, but the legitimacy of marital love turn essentially on the absence of blood ties? The sacrificial love and charity demanded of a parent and of spouse are not the same, but they are certainly very comparable, and they must be discharged concurrently. Why is a blood tie so essential to one and not to the other relationship? This strikes me as a peculiar form of "social transubstantiation" doctrine — the same kind of strange fixation on blood that is revealed in traditional arguments about whether the wine is "transubstantiated" into blood during the sacrament of the Eucharist.

This is not to argue, as some do today, that the crime of incest must be dropped and that siblings and blood relatives must be left free to marry. It is instead to argue that natural blood ties between parent and child are not essential to stable families. Parental love, like marital love, is in its essence not only an instinct but also a virtue, not only a bodily inclination but also a spiritual intuition.[43] Blood ties between parents and

---

42. See Don S. Browning et al., *From Culture Wars to Common Ground: Religion and the American Family Debate* (Louisville, Ky.: Westminster/John Knox, 1997).

43. Timothy P. Jackson, *Love Disconsoled: Meditations on Christian Charity* (Cambridge: Cambridge University Press, 1999).

children should not be easily severed. But parental ties to children should not be predicated on blood ties alone. Real family kinship goes beyond "birth, biology, and blood."[44] Adoption of children is an option that must always be considered by some and applauded by all.

Adoption still remains a theologically tender topic today. Until a few generations ago, it was still forbidden or at least severely frowned on in many Christian quarters.[45] But adoption is one of the deepest forms and examples of Christian charity. A Christian need only look so far as the example of the first Christian family: Joseph, after all, adopted Jesus, the purportedly illegitimate child of Mary, and raised him in a stable family despite the absence of a blood tie to him.[46] A Christian might further look at how the New Testament describes God's mechanism for dispensing grace: Christians are adopted as heirs of salvation, despite the sins that they inherit (Rom. 8:15, 23; 9:4; Gal. 4:5; Eph. 1:5). That is the real point of Paul's jarring passage to the Galatians that we saw earlier. Adoption by grace is the theological means by which God removes the stigma of sin and the punishment it deserves.

Legal Implications

To castigate the traditional doctrine of illegitimacy, however, does nothing to ameliorate the current plight of outcast children. If theology no longer should support a doctrine of illegitimacy, and the law no longer should stigmatize the incidence of illegitimacy, what can be done about the current problem of so many children born out of wedlock, with all the predictions of social pathos and problems, dependency and delinquency that await them? The ancient angel's description of Ishmael's bane still seems altogether too apt a prediction of the plight of the modern illegitimate: "He shall be a wild ass of a man, his hand against every man and every man's hand against him; and he shall dwell over against all his kinsmen."

One obvious legal measure is to assign further responsibility where it is due: on both the mother and the father of the illegitimate child. Historically, adulterers, fornicators, and other sexual criminals paid dearly for their crimes — by fine, prison, or banishment, even by execution in extreme cases. But this remedy often only exacerbated the plight of the ille-

---

44. Stephen G. Post, *More Lasting Unions: Christianity, the Family, and Society* (Grand Rapids: Eerdmans, 2000), p. 124.

45. Post, *More Lasting Unions.*

46. Jane Schaberg, *The Illegitimacy of Jesus: A Feminist Theological Interpretation of the Infancy Narratives* (San Francisco: Harper and Row, 1987).

gitimate child, who in extreme cases was often left with no or little natural network of family resources and support. Today, adulterers and fornicators pay little if at all for their sexual behavior — protected in part by new cultural mores and constitutional laws of sexual privacy. Even if one wanted to pursue a neo-Puritan path — I, for one, do not! — it is highly unlikely that a new criminalization of adultery or fornication could pass constitutional or cultural muster.

But the elimination of criminal punishment for promiscuity should, to my mind, be coupled with a much firmer imposition of ongoing civil responsibility for the care and support of an innocent child born of such conduct. After all, the same constitutional text that exonerates promiscuity also licenses contraception, which is widely and cheaply available now, indeed free in many quarters. Those who choose to have children out of wedlock notwithstanding these options need to pay dearly for their children's support. I am no fan of shotgun marriages or forced cohabitation of a couple suddenly confronted with the prospect of a new child. But I am a fan of aggressive paternity and maternity suits, now amply aided by the growing availability of cheap genetic technology. I am also a fan of firm laws that compel stiff payments of child support for noncustodial parents, and that garnish the wages, put liens on the properties, and seek reformation of insurance contracts and testamentary instruments of those parents who choose to ignore their dependent minor children. I am equally a fan of tort suits by illegitimate children who can seek compensatory and punitive damages from their parents or their parents' estates in instances where these children have been cavalierly abandoned or notoriously abused. These and a good number of comparable provisions are happily becoming increasingly common in many American states today, with several federal laws providing interstate support and enforcement, and criminal law standing ready with sanctions when civil orders are chronically breached.

A second obvious legal measure is a much more robust engagement of the doctrine of adoption. For all the pro- and anti-abortion lobbying and litigation that has emerged in the post-*Roe v. Wade* era, there has been relatively little attention paid to the alternative of adoption. Historically, adoption legitimated illegitimate children, removing the cultural stigma and civil shadow that attended their birth. Today, adoption provides not only this protection but also one of the best hopes and remedies to the new illegitimates who are condemned in utero. Adoption should be much more aggressively advocated and actively facilitated — and amply celebrated and rewarded when a natural mother chooses to make this heroic sacrifice.

As several other chapters in this volume make clear, the law of adoption has improved somewhat in recent years, and both state and federal laws and appropriations have made it easier and cheaper than in past decades. But adoption is still a clumsy and expensive procedure to pursue in this country, which often makes it difficult for any but the well-to-do to adopt. The situation is made worse by the continued insistence of many states that natural fathers and mothers have an effective veto over adoptions — however irresponsible the parents may have been in conceiving the child and however notorious they may have been in neglecting or abusing the child in utero or upon birth. It is too easy to say that blood ties should mean nothing and that children should be placed only with the fittest parents. That is a dangerous step along the way to the bleak anonymous pattern of parenting contemplated coldly in Plato's *Republic* and B. F. Skinner's *Walden Two*. But a more generously funded, administered, and applied law of adoption would do much to alleviate the plight of the modern illegitimates.

Bastards, like the poor, will doubtless always be with us — subjects of pity and scorn, romance and ribaldry at once. Bastards may now have passed largely beyond the province of religion and criminal law. But they live on in our language and literature, with all the ambivalences of the first story of Ishmael. Contrast the sound still today (in movies or street talk) of the pitying phrase, "Oh, you poor bastard," with the angry retort, "You Damned Bastard!!" Read still today of the checkered career of the illegitimate love child in Hawthorne's *The Scarlet Letter* or Shakespeare's plays. Shakespeare's *King Lear* perhaps puts the puzzlement and protest over the illegitimate's plight best in the words of Edmund, the scheming bastard, who nonetheless could speak to the injustice of his status:

> Thou, Nature, art my goddess; to thy law
> My services are bound. Wherefore should I
> Stand in the plague of custom, and permit
> The curiosity of nations to deprive me,
> For that I am some twelve or fourteen moonshines
> Lag of a brother? Why bastard? Wherefore base,
> When my dimensions are as well compact,
> My mind as generous, my shape as true,
> As honest madam's issue? Why brand they us
> With base? with baseness? Bastardy base? Base?
> Who, in the lusty stealth of nature, take
> More composition and fierce quality

Than doth within a dull, stale, tired bed,
Go to th' creating a whole tribe of fops
Got 'tween asleep and wake? Well then,
Legitimate Edgar, I must have your land.
Our father's love is to the bastard Edmund
As to the legitimate. Fine word, "legitimate."
Well, my legitimate, if this letter speed,
And my invention thrive, Edmund the base
Shall top the legitimate. I grow. I prosper.
Now, gods, stand up for bastards.

(1.2.1-22)

Bibliography

Abrahamson, Mark. *Out of Wedlock Birth: The United States in Comparative Perspective.* Westport, Conn.: Praeger, 1998.

Abrams, Douglas E., and Sarah H. Ramsey. *Children and the Law: Doctrine, Policy, and Practice.* St. Paul, Minn.: West, 2000.

Adair, Richard. *Courtship, Illegitimacy and Marriage in Early Modern England.* Manchester: Manchester University Press, 1996.

"Adoption." Bible Tools website, http://bibletools.org//index.cfm/fuseaction/Def.show/RTD/Easton/Topic/Adoption.

"Adoption." Catholic Charities of Boston website, www.ccab.org/adoption.htm.

"Adoptionism." In *New Advent Catholic Encyclopedia.* New Advent website, http://www.newadvent.org/cathen/01150a.htm.

"Adoptionism in Spain." In *The Westminster Dictionary of Church History,* edited by Jerald C. Brauer, pp. 8-9. Philadelphia: Westminster, 1971.

Al-Ghazali. *Book on the Etiquette of Marriage.* In *Marriage and Sexuality in Islam,* edited by Madelin Farah, pp. 48-126. Salt Lake City: University of Utah Press, 1984.

Alexander, Richard. *The Biology of Moral Systems.* Hawthorne, N.Y.: Aldine de Gruyter, 1987.

Alschuler, Albert W. *Law without Values: The Life, Work, and Legacy of Justice Holmes.* Chicago: University of Chicago Press, 2000.

Amadio, Carol, and Stewart Deutsch. "Open Adoption: Allowing Adopted Children to 'Stay in Touch' with Blood Relatives." *Journal of Family Law* 22 (1983): 59-93.

Amato, Paul, and Alan Booth. *A Generation at Risk.* Cambridge, Mass.: Harvard University Press, 1997.

American Fertility Society. "Ethical Considerations of the New Reproductive Technologies." *Journal of the American Fertility Society* 53, no. 6 (June 1990).

American Society for Reproductive Medicine. "Vast Majority of Cryopreserved

Embryos Slated for Future Family Building." *ASRM Bulletin* 5, no. 30 (May 2003).

An-Na'im, Abdullahi Ahmed, ed. *Islamic Family Law in a Changing World: A Global Resource Book*. London: Zed, 2002.

Andolsen, Barbara. "Agape in Feminist Ethics." *Journal of Religious Ethics* 9 (spring 1981): 69-81.

Anglin, Patty, with Joe Musser. *Acres of Hope: The Miraculous Story of One Family's Gift of Love to Children without Hope*. Uhrichsville, Ohio: Promise, 1999.

Anson, Ofra, Arieh Levenson, and Dan Y. Bonneh. "Gender and Health on the Kibbutz." *Sex Roles* 22 (1990): 213-33.

Anzaldua, Gloria. *Borderlands/La Frontera: The New Mestiza*. San Francisco: Spinsters/Aunt Lute, 1987.

Appell, Annette Ruth. "Blending Families through Adoption: Implications for Collaborative Adoption Law and Practice." *Boston University Law Review* 75 (1995): 997-1061.

Appleton, Susan Frelich. "From the Lemma Barkeloo and Phoebe Couzins Era to the New Millennium: 130 Years of Family Law." *Washington University Journal of Law and Policy* 6 (2001): 189-203.

Ayer, John C., Jr. "Legitimacy and Marriage." *Harvard Law Review* 16 (1902): 22-42.

Babb, L. Anne. *Ethics in American Adoption*. Westport, Conn.: Bergin and Garvey, 1999.

Bacon, Matthew. *A New Abridgement of the Law*. Fifth ed. 7 vols. London: A. Strathan, 1798.

Baran, Annette, and Ruben Pannor. "Open Adoption." In *The Psychology of Adoption*, edited by David M. Brodzinsky and Marshall D. Schechter, pp. 316-31. New York: Oxford University Press, 1990.

Barash, David P. *Revolutionary Biology: The New, Gene-Centered View of Life*. New Brunswick, N.J.: Transaction, 2001.

Barth, Karl. *Church Dogmatics*. Vol. 3, part 4. Edinburgh: T. & T. Clark, 1961.

Bartholet, Elizabeth. *Family Bonds: Adoption and the Politics of Parenting*. New York: Houghton Mifflin, 1993.

————. "International Adoption: Current Status and Future Prospects." *Future of Children* 3 (spring 1993): 89-103.

————. "International Adoption: Property, Prospects and Pragmatics." *Journal of American Academy of Matrimonial Lawyers* 13 (winter 1996): 181-210.

Beck, Mary. "Toward a National Putative Father Registry Database." *Harvard Journal of Law and Public Policy* 25, no. 3 (summer 2002): 1031-93.

Becker, Gary. *Treatise on the Family*. Cambridge, Mass.: Harvard University Press, 1991.

Bellah, Robert, Richard Madsen, William Sullivan, Ann Swidler, and Steven Tipton. *Habits of the Heart*. New York: Harper and Row, 1986.

Benson, Peter, Anu Sharma, and E. Roehlkepartain. *Growing Up Adopted: A Portrait of Adolescents and Their Families*. Minneapolis: Search Institute, 1994.

Berger, Peter. *The Sacred Canopy: Elements of a Sociological Theory of Religion.* Garden City, N.Y.: Doubleday, 1967.

Berkman, John. "Adopting Embryos in America: A Case Study." *Scottish Journal of Theology* 55, no. 4 (2002): 438-60.

Berman, Harold J. Foreword to *Christian Perspectives on Legal Thought,* edited by Michael W. McConnell, Robert F. Cochran Jr., and Angela C. Carmella. New Haven: Yale University Press, 2001.

Berzon, Israel. "Contemporary Issues in the Laws of Yichud." *Journal of Halacha and Contemporary Society* 13 (1986): 77-112.

Bjork, Daniel W. *B. F. Skinner: A Life.* Washington, D.C.: American Psychological Association, 1997.

Blackstone, William. *Commentaries on the Law of England.* Third rev. ed. Edited by Thomas H. Cooley. Chicago: Callaghan, 1884.

Blair, D. Marianne Brower. "The Impact of Family Paradigms, Domestic Constitutions, and International Conventions on Disclosure of an Adopted Person's Identities and Heritage: A Comparative Examination." *Michigan Journal of International Law* 22 (2001): 587-671.

Blankenhorn, David. *Fatherless America: Confronting Our Most Urgent Social Problem.* New York: Basic, 1995.

Blum, Deborah. *Love at Goon Park: Harry Harlow and the Science of Affection.* Cambridge, Mass.: Perseus, 2002.

————. *The Monkey Wars.* New York: Oxford University Press, 1994.

Boswell, John. *The Kindness of Strangers: The Abandonment of Children in Western Europe from Late Antiquity to the Renaissance.* New York: Pantheon, 1988.

Bouchard, Thomas J., Jr. "Longitudinal Studies of Personality and Intelligence: A Behavior Genetic and Evolutionary Psychology Perspective." In *International Handbook of Personality and Intelligence,* edited by D. H. Saklofske and M. Zeidner, pp. 81-106. New York: Plenum, 1995.

Bowlby, John. *Attachment and Loss.* Vol. 1. New York: Basic, 1969.

Bozett, Frederick W., and Marvin B. Sussman, eds. *Homosexuality and Family Relations.* New York: Haworth, 1990.

Brennan, Patrick M. "On What Sin (and Grace) Can Teach Crime." *Punishment and Society* 5 (2002): 347-65.

Brinich, Paul M. "Adoption from the Inside Out: A Psychoanalytic Perspective." In *The Psychology of Adoption,* edited by David M. Brodzinsky and Marshall D. Schechter, pp. 42-61. New York: Oxford University Press, 1990.

Brinton, Crane. *The French Revolutionary Legislation on Illegitimacy.* Cambridge, Mass.: Harvard University Press, 1936.

Brodzinsky, David M. "Adjustment to Adoption: A Psychosocial Perspective." *Clinical Psychology Review* 7 (1987): 25-47.

Brodzinsky, David M., and Loreen Huffman. "Transition to Adoptive Parenthood." *Marriage and Family Review* 12 (1988): 267-86.

Brodzinsky, David M., and Ellen Pinderhughes. "Parenting and Child Development in Adoptive Families." In vol. 1 of *Handbook of Parenting*, edited by Marc Bornstein, pp. 279-311. Hillsdale, N.J.: Erlbaum, 2002.

Brodzinsky, D. M., M. D. Schechter, and R. M. Henig. *Being Adopted: The Lifelong Search for Self.* New York: Anchor, 1992.

Brodzinsky, David M., Leslie Singer, and Anne Braff. "Children's Understanding of Adoption." *Child Development* 55 (1984): 869-78.

Brodzinsky, David M., Daniel W. Smith, and Anne B. Brodzinsky. *Children's Adjustment to Adoption: Developmental and Clinical Issues.* Thousand Oaks, Calif.: Sage, 1998.

Brosnan, John Francis. "The Law of Adoption." *Columbia Law Review* 22 (1922): 332-42.

Browning, Don. *Atonement and Psychotherapy.* Philadelphia: Westminster, 1966.

—————. *Marriage and Modernization.* Grand Rapids: Eerdmans, 2003.

—————. *Religious Thought and the Modern Psychologies.* Minneapolis: Fortress, 1987.

—————. "Ricoeur and Practical Theology." In *Paul Ricoeur and Contemporary Moral Thought,* edited by John Wall, William Schweiker, and David Hall, pp. 251-63. New York: Routledge, 2002.

Browning, Don S., Bonnie Miller-McLemore, Pam Couture, Bernie Lyon, and Robert Franklin. *From Culture Wars to Common Ground: Religion and the American Family Debate.* Louisville, Ky.: Westminster/John Knox, 1997, 2000.

Browning, Don, and Gloria Rodriguez. *Reweaving the Social Tapestry: Toward a Public Philosophy and Policy of Families.* New York: Norton, 2001.

Broyde, Michael. "Cloning People: A Jewish View." *Connecticut Law Review* 30 (1998): 503-35.

—————. "The Establishment of Maternity and Paternity in Jewish and American Law." *National Jewish Law Review* 3 (1988): 117-52.

—————. *Marriage, Divorce and the Abandoned Wife in Jewish Law: A Conceptual Approach to the Agunah Problems in America.* Hoboken, N.J.: KTAV, 2001.

Brundage, James A. *Law, Sex, and Christian Society in Medieval Europe.* Chicago: University of Chicago Press, 1987.

Brydall, John. *Lex Spuriorum, or the Law Relating to Bastardy.* London: Atkins, 1703.

Burn, Richard. *Ecclesiastical Law.* Sixth ed. 4 vols. London: A. Strathan, 1797.

Buss, David. *The Evolution of Desire: Strategies of Human Mating.* New York: Basic, 1994.

Butler, Jon, Grant Wacker, and Randall Balmer. *Religion in American Life: A Short History.* New York: Oxford University Press, 2003.

Cahill, Lisa Sowle. *Family: A Christian Social Perspective.* Minneapolis: Fortress, 2000.

—————. *Sex, Gender, and Christian Ethics.* Cambridge: Cambridge University Press, 1996.

Cashman, Frances. "Origins: New Challenges for Adoption Agencies." *Social Thought* 5, no. 4 (1979): 15-23.

Cass, Ronald A. "Coping with Life, Law and Markets: A Comment on Posner and the Law-and-Economics Debate." *Boston University Law Review* 67 (1987): 73-98.

Catechism of the Catholic Church. English translation. London: Cassell, 1994.

Caughey, John L. *Imaginary Social Worlds.* Lincoln: University of Nebraska Press, 1984.

Charo, R. Alto. "Biological Truths and Legal Fictions." *Journal of Health Care Law and Policy* 1 (1998): 301-28.

Christian, Cinda, Ruth G. McRoy, Harold D. Grotevant, and Chalandra Bryant. "Grief Resolution of Birthmothers in Confidential, Time-Limited Mediated, Ongoing Mediated, and Fully Disclosed Adoptions." *Adoption Quarterly* 1, no. 2 (1997): 35-58.

Clapp, Rodney. *Families at the Crossroads: Beyond Traditional and Modern Options.* Downers Grove, Ill.: InterVarsity, 1993.

Clark, Homer H. *The Law of Domestic Relations in the United States.* Second ed. St. Paul, Minn: West, 1988.

Clinton, Hillary Rodham. *It Takes a Village: And Other Lessons Children Teach Us.* New York: Simon and Schuster, 1996.

Cohen, David. *J. B. Watson: The Founder of Behaviorism.* London: Routledge and Kegan Paul, 1979.

Congregation for the Doctrine of the Faith. "Considerations Regarding Proposals to Give Legal Recognition to Unions Between Homosexual Persons." Official Vatican website, www.vatican.va/roman_curia/congregations/cfaith/documents/rc_con_cfaith_doc_20030731_homosexual-unions_en.html.

Couvreur, Gilles. *Les pauvres ont-ils des droits?* Rome: Libraria editrice dell'Universita Gregoriana, 1961.

Cross, William E. *Shades of Black: Diversity in African-American Identity.* Philadelphia: Temple University Press, 1991.

Cunningham, Laurie. "Florida's Gay-Adoption Ban Goes to 11th Circuit." *Fulton County Daily Report,* 5 March 2003, pp. 1 and 6.

Curran, Charles E. *Catholic Social Teaching, 1891-Present: A Historical, Theological and Ethical Analysis.* Washington, D.C.: Georgetown University Press, 2002.

Cushman, Philip. *Constructing the Self, Constructing America: A Cultural History of Psychotherapy.* Cambridge, Mass.: Perseus, 1995.

Daly, Martin, and Margo Wilson. *Sex, Evolution, and Behavior.* Belmont, Calif.: Wadsworth, 1983.

Daly, Sharon. "Testimony to the Subcommittee on Human Resources of the House Committee on Ways and Means." Hearing to Consider H.R. 5292, Flexible Funding for the Child Protection Act of 2000, 3 October 2000. Catholic Charities website, www.catholiccharitiesinfo.org.

Daniel, G. Reginald. "Black and White Identity in the New Millennium: Unsevering the Ties That Bind." In *The Multiracial Experience: Racial Borders As the New Frontier,* ed. Maria P. P. Root. Thousand Oaks, Calif.: Sage, 1996.

Dawkins, Richard. *The Selfish Gene.* New York: Oxford University Press, 1989.

Destro, Brenda. *Celebrating the Good Message of Adoption.* Washington, D.C.: United States Conference of Catholic Bishops, 2003.

Doerflinger, Richard A. "Alternative Reproductive Technologies: Implications for Children and Families," 21 May 1987. United States Conference of Catholic Bishops website, www.usccb.org.prolife/issues/ivf/ivftest52187.

Donagan, Alan. *The Theory of Morality.* Chicago: University of Chicago Press, 1977.

Donnelly, Daria. "A Gay Parent Looks at His Church: An Interview with Novelist Gregory Maguire." *Commonweal* 130, no. 18 (2003): 20-22.

Dowd, Nancy E. *In Defense of Single-Parent Families.* New York: New York University Press, 1997.

Du Bois, W. E. B. *The Souls of Black Folk.* New York: Penguin, 1903.

Dunbar, Nora, and Harold D. Grotevant. "Adoption Narratives: The Construction of Adoptive Identity during Adolescence." In *Family Stories and the Life Course: Across Time and Generations,* edited by M. W. Pratt and B. H. Fiese. Mahwah, N.J.: Earlbaum, 2004.

Dworkin, Ronald. *Life's Dominion: An Argument about Abortion, Euthanasia, and Individual Freedom.* New York: Knopf, 1993.

Eaton, Lauri Gray. "Extra Embryos, What Is Their Future?" *San Antonio Medical Gazette,* 15 December 2000, cover.

Elshtain, Jean Bethke. "The Chosen Family." *The New Republic,* 14 and 21 September 1998, pp. 45-54.

"Embryo Donation for 'Embryo Adoption.'" *CHR Voice* (spring 2003): 1.

Evans, M. Stanton. *The Theme Is Freedom: Religion, Politics, and the American Tradition.* Washington, D.C.: Regnery, 1994.

Fanon, Frantz. *Black Skin, White Masks.* Trans. Charles Lam Markmann. New York: Grove, 1967.

Findling, Moshe. "Adoption of Children." *Noam* 4 (1961): 65-93.

Fishman, Aryei. *Judaism and the Collective Life: Self and Community in the Religious Kibbutz.* New York: Routledge, 2002.

Fiske, John. *Through Nature to God.* Boston: Houghton, Mifflin, 1899.

Fogg-Davis, Hawley. *The Ethics of Transracial Adoption.* Ithaca, N.Y.: Cornell University Press, 2002.

Forward, Susan, and Craig Buck. *Betrayal of Innocence: Incest and Its Devastation.* New York: Penguin, 1988.

Fox, Robin. *The Red Lamp of Incest: An Enquiry into the Origins of Mind and Society.* Notre Dame, Ind.: University of Notre Dame Press, 1983.

Frankena, William. *Ethics.* Englewood Cliffs, N.J.: Prentice-Hall, 1973.

Freundlich, Madelyn. *The Market Forces in Adoption.* Washington, D.C.: Child Welfare League of America, 2000.

————. *The Role of Race, Culture, and National Origin in Adoption.* Washington, D.C.: Child Welfare League of America, 2000.

"From the Heart: Generations of Caring — One Family's Circle of Adoption." *Family Circle,* 18 June 2002, pp. 76-80.

Funderburg, Lise. *Black, White, Other: Biracial Americans Talk about Race and Identity.* New York: William Morrow, 1994.

Gadamer, Hans-Georg. *Truth and Method.* New York: Crossroad, 1982.

Gaudium et spes. In *Catholic Social Thought: The Documentary Heritage,* edited by David J. O'Brien and Thomas A. Shannon, pp. 166-237. Maryknoll, N.Y.: Orbis, 1992.

Gaulin, Steven J. C., and Donald H. McBurney. *Psychology: An Evolutionary Approach.* Upper Saddle River, N.J.: Prentice-Hall, 2001.

Gaustad, Edwin, and Leigh Schmidt. *The Religious History of America: The Heart of the American Story from Colonial Times to Today.* Rev. ed. San Francisco: HarperSanFrancisco, 2002.

Généstal, Robert. *Histoire de la légitimation des infantes naturales en droit canonique.* Paris: E. Lourex, 1905.

Godolphin, John. *Reportorium Canonicum.* Third ed. London: Assigns of R. and E. Atkins, 1687.

Gold, Michael. "Adoption: The Jewish View." *Adoption Quarterly* 3, no. 1 (1999): 3-13.

Goodenough, Ward H. *Culture, Language, and Society.* Second ed. Menlo Park, Calif.: Benjamin/Cummings, 1981.

Gooding-Williams, Robert. "Look a Negro!" In *Reading Rodney King/Reading Urban Uprising,* ed. Robert Gooding-Williams. New York: Routledge, 1993.

Gottman, Julie Schwartz. "Children of Gay and Lesbian Parents." *Marriage and Family Review* 14, no. 3 (1989): 177-96.

Grisez, Germain. *Living a Christian Life.* Vol. 2 of *The Way of the Lord Jesus.* Quincy, Ill.: Franciscan Press, 1993.

Grossberg, Michael. *Governing the Hearth: Law and the Family in Nineteenth-Century America.* Chapel Hill, N.C.: University of North Carolina Press, 1985.

―――. "Who Gets the Child? Custody, Guardianship, and the Rise of Judicial Patriarchy in Nineteenth Century America." *Feminist Studies* 9 (1983): 235-60.

Grotevant, Harold D. "Adolescent Development in Family Contexts." In *Handbook of Child Psychology,* Volume 3: *Social, Emotional, and Personality Development,* edited by Nancy Eisenberg, pp. 1097-1149. New York: John Wiley and Sons, 1996.

―――. "Coming to Terms with Adoption: The Construction of Identity from Adolescence into Adulthood." *Adoption Quarterly* 1, no. 1 (1997): 3-27.

―――. "Openness in Adoption: Research with the Kinship Network." *Adoption Quarterly* 4, no. 1 (2000): 45-65.

Grotevant, Harold D., Nora Dunbar, Julie K. Kohler, and Amy Lash Esau. "Adoptive Identity: How Contexts within and beyond the Family Shape Developmental Pathways." *Family Relations* 49 (2000): 379-87.

Grotevant, Harold D., and Julie K. Kohler. "Adoptive Families." In *Parenting and Child Development in Nontraditional Families,* edited by M. E. Lamb, pp. 161-90. Mahwah, N.J.: Erlbaum, 1999.

Grotevant, Harold D., and Ruth G. McRoy. *Openness in Adoption: Exploring Family Connections.* Thousand Oaks, Calif.: Sage, 1998.

Grotevant, Harold D., Ruth G. McRoy, Carol Elde, and Deborah Lewis Fravel. "Adoptive Family System Dynamics: Variations by Level of Openness in the Adoption." *Family Process* 33 (1994): 125-46.

Grotevant, Harold D., Nicole Ross, Marianne Marchel, and Ruth G. McRoy. "Adaptive Behavior in Adopted Children: Predictors from Early Risk, Collaboration in Relationships within the Adoptive Kinship Network, and Openness Arrangements." *Journal of Adolescent Research* 14 (1999): 231-47.

Grotevant, Harold D., Gretchen Miller Wrobel, Manfred H. Van Dulman, and Ruth G. McRoy. "The Emergence of Psychosocial Engagement in Adopted Adolescents: The Family As Context Over Time." *Journal of Adolescent Research* 16 (2001): 469-90.

Gudorf, Christine. "Parenting, Mutual Love, and Sacrifice." In *Women's Consciousness, Women's Conscience: A Reader in Feminist Ethics,* edited by Barbara Hilkert Andolsen, Christine E. Gudorf, and Mary D. Pellauer, pp. 175-91. New York: Winston, 1985; San Francisco: Harper and Row, 1987.

Gustafson, James M. *Ethics and Theology.* Vol. 2 of *Ethics from a Theocentric Perspective.* Chicago: University of Chicago Press, 1984.

Habermas, Jürgen. *The Theory of Communicative Action.* Vol. 2. Boston: Beacon, 1987.

Haizlip, Shirlee Taylor. *The Sweeter the Juice: A Family Memoir in Black and White.* New York: Simon and Schuster, 1994.

Hamilton, William D. "The Genetical Evolution of Social Behavior," parts I and II. *Journal of Theoretical Biology* 7 (1964): 1-16 and 17-52.

Haney, Craig. "Criminal Justice and the Nineteenth Century Paradigm: The Triumph of Psychological Individualism in the 'Formative Era.'" *Law and Human Behavior* 6 (1982): 191-235.

Haralambie, Ann M. *Handling Child Custody, Abuse and Adoption Cases.* Second ed. New York: McGraw-Hill, 1993.

Hartley, Shirley. *Illegitimacy.* Berkeley: University of California Press, 1975.

Hawthorne, Nathaniel. *Mosses from an Old Manse.* Pennsylvania: Orange Street Press, 1999.

Helmholz, R. H. "Bastardy Litigation in Medieval England." *American Journal of Legal History* 13 (1969): 360-83.

———. "Support Orders, Church Courts, and the Rule of *Filius Nullius:* A Reassessment of the Common Law." *Virginia Law Review* 63 (1977): 431-48.

Helms, Janet E. *Black and White Racial Identity: Theory, Research, and Practice.* New York: Greenwood, 1990.

Hendrix, Lewellyn. *Illegitimacy and Social Structures.* Westport, Conn.: Bergin and Garvey, 1996.

Henkin, Yehuda Herzl. "The Significant Role of Habituation in Halakha." *Tradition* 34 (2000): 3-40.

Henney, Susan, Steven Onken, Ruth G. McRoy, and Harold D. Grotevant.

"Changing Adoption Practices Toward Openness." *Adoption Quarterly* 1, no. 3 (1998): 45-76.

Hetherington, E. Mavis, and John Kelly. *For Better or for Worse.* New York: Norton, 2002.

Hicks, Stephen, and Janet McDermott, eds. *Lesbian and Gay Fostering and Adoption: Extraordinary Yet Ordinary.* London: Jessica Kingsley, 1998.

Hoffman, David I., Gail L. Zellman, C. Christine Fair, Jacob F. Mayer, Joyce G. Zeitz, William E. Gibbons, and Thomas G. Turner Jr. "Cryopreserved Embryos in the United States and Their Availability for Research." *Fertility and Sterility* 79 (May 2003): 1063-69.

Hollingsworth, Leslie Doty. "International Adoption among Families in the United States: Considerations of Social Justice." *Social Work* 48, no. 2 (2003): 209-17.

hooks, bell. *Killing Rage: Ending Racism.* New York: Henry Holt, 1995.

Horn, Wade. "Take a Vow to Promote Benefits of Marriage." *Washington Times,* 2 November 1999.

Howe, Ruth Arlene W. "Adoption Practice, Issues and Law, 1958-1983." *Family Law Quarterly* 17 (1983): 123-97.

Howes, Carollee. "Attachment Relationships in the Context of Multiple Caregivers." In *Handbook of Attachment: Theory, Research, and Clinical Applications,* edited by J. Cassidy and P. Shaver, pp. 671-87. New York: Guilford, 1999.

Huard, Leo Albert. "The Law of Adoption: Ancient and Modern." *Vanderbilt Law Review* 9 (1956): 743-63.

"International Adoption." U.S. Department of State, Office of Children's Issues website, http://travel.state.gov/family/adoption_resources_02.html.

"International Adoptions." Bureau of Consular Affairs website, http://travel.state.gov/int'ladoption.html.

"In Vitro Fertilization." Mayo Clinic website, http://www.mayoclinic.org/ivf-sct.

"The IVF Process." Mayo Clinic website, http://www.mayoclinic.org/ivf-sct/process.html.

Jackson, James S., Wayne R. McCullough, and Gerald Gurin. "Family, Socialization Environment, and Identity Development in Black Americans." In *Black Families,* ed. Harriette Pipes McAdoo, second ed. Newbury Park, Calif.: Sage, 1988.

Jackson, Mark. *New-Born Child Murder: Women, Illegitimacy, and the Courts in Eighteenth-Century England.* Manchester: Manchester University Press, 1996.

Jackson, Timothy P. *Love Disconsoled: Meditations on Christian Charity.* Cambridge: Cambridge University Press, 1999.

———. *The Priority of Love: Christian Charity and Social Justice.* Princeton, N.J.: Princeton University Press, 2003.

———. "To Bedlam and Part Way Back: John Rawls and Christian Justice." *Faith and Philosophy* 8, no. 4 (October 1991): 423-47.

Jaeger, Amy S. *Adoption Law and Practice.* New York: Matthew Bender, 2000.

James, T. E. "The Illegitimate and Deprived Child: Legitimation and Adoption." In *A Century of Family Law: 1857-1957,* edited by R. H. Graveson and F. R. Crane, pp. 39-55. London: Sweet and Maxwell, 1957.

Janssens, Louis. "Norms and Priorities of a Love Ethics." *Louvain Studies* 6 (spring 1977): 209-37.

John Paul II. "Address to the Meeting of Adoptive Families Organized by the Missionaries of Charity," 5 September 2000. Official Vatican website, www.vatican.va/holy_ father/john_paul_ii/speeches/2000.

————. *Centesimus annus.* In *Catholic Social Thought: The Documentary Heritage,* edited by David J. O'Brien and Thomas A. Shannon, pp. 439-88. Maryknoll, N.Y.: Orbis, 1992.

————. *Familiaris consortio.* Official Vatican website, http://www.vatican.va/holy_father/john_paul_ii/apost_exhortations/documents/hf_jp-ii_exh_19811122_familiaris-consortio_en.html.

————. *On the Family.* Washington, D.C.: United States Catholic Conference, 1982.

Johnson, Daniel, and Edith Fein. "The Concept of Attachment: Applications to Adoption." *Children and Youth Services Review* 13 (1991): 397-412.

Johnson, Sara L. *American Law Reports.* Fourth ed. Vol. 48. St. Paul, Minn.: Lawyers Co-operative Publishing Company, 1986.

Jordan, Mark D. *The Ethics of Sex.* Oxford: Blackwell, 2002.

————. *The Invention of Sodomy in Christian Theology.* Chicago: University of Chicago Press, 1997.

————. *The Silence of Sodom: Homosexuality in Modern Catholicism.* Chicago: University of Chicago Press, 2000.

Kahn, Jeffrey P. "'Adoption' of Frozen Embryos a Loaded Term," 17 September 2002. CNN website, http://www3.cnn.com/2002/HEALTH/09/17/ethics.matters.

Kant, Immanuel. *The Critique of Practical Reason.* In Immanuel Kant, *The Cambridge Edition of the Works of Immanuel Kant: Practical Philosophy,* translated by Mary J. Gregor, pp. 133-271. Cambridge: Cambridge University Press, 1996.

————. *Foundations of the Metaphysics of Morals.* Indianapolis: Bobbs-Merrill, 1959.

Kasher, Menachem Mendel. "Artificial Insemination." *Noam* 1 (1957): 125-28.

Katz, Sanford N. "Re-Writing the Adoption Story." *Family Advocate* 5 (1982): 9-10.

Kawashima, Yasuhide. "Adoption in Early America." *Journal of Family Law* 20 (1982): 677-96.

Kent, Evelyn L. "Catholic Charities Resettles Sudan's 'Lost Boys,'" 3 October 2002. Catholic Charities website, www.catholiccharitiesinfo.org.

Kent, James. *Commentaries on American Law.* 2 vols. New York: O. Halsted, 1827.

Kinkade, Kathleen. *Is It Utopia Yet? An Insider's View of Twin Oaks Community in Its Twenty-Sixth Year.* Louisa, Va.: Twin Oaks, 1994.

————. *A Walden Two Experiment: The First Five Years of Twin Oaks Community.* New York: Wm. Morrow, 1973.

Kirk, H. David. *Shared Fate: A Theory of Adoption and Mental Health.* New York: Free Press, 1964.

Kohler, Julie K., Harold D. Grotevant, and Ruth G. McRoy. "Adopted Adolescents' Preoccupation with Adoption: The Impact on Adoptive Family Relationships." *Journal of Marriage and Family* 64 (2002): 93-104.

Kramnick, Isaac, and R. Laurence Moore. *The Godless Constitution: The Case against Religious Correctness.* New York: Norton, 1996.

Krause, Harry D. *Illegitimacy: Law and Social Policy.* Indianapolis: Bobbs-Merrill, 1971.

Kristof, Nicholas D. "Gay at Birth?" *New York Times,* 25 October 2003.

Laslett, Peter. *The Family and Illicit Love in Early Generations.* Cambridge: Cambridge University Press, 1977.

Laslett, Peter, Karla Oosterveen, and Richard M. Smith, eds. *Bastardy and Its Comparative History: Studies in the History of Illegitimacy and Marital Non-Conformism in Britain, France, Germany, Sweden, North America, Jamaica, and Japan.* Cambridge, Mass.: Harvard University Press, 1980.

Leo XIII. *Rerum Novarum.* In *Proclaiming Justice and Peace: Papal Documents from Rerum Novarum through Centesimus Annus,* edited by Michael Welsh and Brian Davies, pp. 3-39. Mystic, Conn.: Thirty-Third Publications, 1981.

Levinthal, Israel Herbert. *The Jewish Law of Agency, with Special Reference to the Roman and Common Law.* New York: (printed at the Conat Press, Philadelphia), 1923.

Lifton, Betty Jean. *Twice Born: Memories of an Adopted Daughter.* New York: Penguin, 1977.

Lubiano, Wahneema. "Black Ladies, Welfare Queens, and State Minstrels: Ideological War by Narrative Means." In *Racing Justice, Engendering Power: Essays on Anita Hill, Clarence Thomas, and the Construction of Social Reality,* ed. Toni Morrison. New York: Pantheon, 1992.

Lucas, Melinda. "Adoption: Distinguishing between Gray Market and Black Market Activities." *Family Law Quarterly* 34 (fall 2000): 553-64.

Mackin, Theodor. *Marriage in the Catholic Church: What Is Marriage?* New York: Paulist, 1982.

Maimonides. *The Code of Maimonides, Book Four: The Book of Women.* In *The Book of Marriage: The Wisest Answers to the Toughest Questions,* edited by Dana Mack and David Blankenhorn, pp. 500-509. Grand Rapids: Eerdmans, 2001.

Malinowski, Bronislaw. *Sex, Culture, and Myth.* New York: Harcourt, Brace and World, 1962.

Marcel, Gabriel. "The Creative Vow As Essence of Fatherhood." In *Homo Viator: Introduction to a Metaphysic of Hope,* by Gabriel Marcel, translated by Emma Craufurd, pp. 98-124. Gloucester, Mass.: Peter Smith, 1978.

March, Karen. "Perception of Adopting As Social Stigma: Motivation for Search and Reunion." *Journal of Marriage and the Family* 57 (1995): 653-60.

Mason, Mary M. *Designing Rituals of Adoption for the Religious and Secular Community.* Minneapolis: Resources for Adoptive Parents, 1995.

McBride, James. *The Color of Water: A Black Man's Tribute to His White Mother.* New York: Riverhead, 1996.

McConnell, Michael W., Robert F. Cochran Jr., and Angela C. Carmella. Introduction to *Christian Perspectives on Legal Thought,* edited by Michael W. McConnell, Robert F. Cochran Jr., and Angela C. Carmella. New Haven: Yale University Press, 2001.

McGough, Lucy S., and Annette Peltier Falahahwazi. "Secrets and Lies: A Model Statute for Cooperative Adoption." *Louisiana Law Review* 60 (1999): 13-90.

McKeown, Elizabeth. "Adopting Sources: A Response to Stephen Post." *Journal of Religious Ethics* 25, no. 1 (spring 1997): 169-75.

McLanahan, Sarah, and Gary Sandefur. *Growing Up with a Single Mother.* Cambridge, Mass.: Harvard University Press, 1994.

McLauliff, C. M. A. "The First English Adoption Law and Its American Precursors." *Seton Hall Law Review* 16 (1986): 656-77.

McNeill, John. "Natural Law in the Teaching of the Reformers." *Journal of Religion* 26, no. 3 (1962): 168-82.

McRoy, Ruth G., Harold D. Grotevant, Susan Ayers-Lopez, and A. Furuta. "Adoption Revelation and Communication Issues: Implications for Practice." *Families in Society: The Journal of Contemporary Human Services* 50 (1990): 550-57.

McRoy, Ruth G., Louis A. Zurcher, Michael L. Lauderdale, and Rosalie N. Anderson. "The Identity of Transracial Adoptees." *Social Casework: The Journal of Contemporary Social Work* 65, no. 1 (January 1984): 34-39.

———. "Self-Esteem and Racial Identity in Transracial and Intraracial Adoptees." *Social Work* 27 (November 1982): 522-26.

Meilaender, Gilbert C. *Bioethics: A Primer for Christians.* Second ed. Grand Rapids: Eerdmans, 2005.

———. *Body, Soul, and Bioethics.* Notre Dame, Ind.: University of Notre Dame Press, 1995.

———. *The Limits of Love.* University Park, Pa.: Pennsylvania State University Press, 1987.

———. *Things That Count: Essays Moral and Theological.* Wilmington, Del.: ISI, 2000.

Mendenhall, Tai J., Harold D. Grotevant, and Ruth G. McRoy. "Adoptive Couples: Communication and Changes Made in Openness Levels." *Family Relations* 45 (1996): 223-29.

Miall, Charlene. "The Stigma of Adoptive Parent Status: Perceptions of Community Attitudes toward Adoption and the Experience of Informal Social Sanctioning." *Family Relations* 36 (1987): 34-39.

Midgley, Mary. *Beast and Man.* Ithaca, N.Y.: Cornell University Press, 1978.

Minerbrook, Scott. *Divided to the Vein: A Journey into Race and Family.* New York: Harcourt Brace, 1996.

Mirangoff, Marque-Luisa. *The Social Costs of Genetic Welfare*. New Brunswick, N.J.: Rutgers University Press, 1991.

Mitchell, Stephen. *The Gospel According to Jesus*. New York: HarperCollins, 1991.

Modell, Judith S. *Kinship with Strangers: Adoption and Interpretations of Kinship in American Culture*. Berkeley: University of California Press, 1994.

Moore, David. *The Dependent Gene: The Fallacy of "Nature vs. Nurture."* New York: W. H. Freeman, 2001.

Morley, Michael T., Richard Albert, Jennie L. Kneedler, and Chrystiane Pereira. "Developments in Law and Policy: Emerging Issues in Family Law." *Yale Law and Policy Review* 21, no. 1 (winter 2003): 169-220.

Mother Teresa: A Film by Ann and Jeanette Petrie. Petrie Productions, distributed by Dorason Corporation, 1986.

Munson, Susan A. "Comment, Independent Adoption: In Whose Best Interest?" *Seton Hall Law Review* 26 (1996): 803-31.

Murdock, Deroy. "The Adoption Option." *National Review Online*, 27 August 2001. National Review Online website, http://www.nationalreview.com/murdock/murdock082701.shtml.

National Association of Black Social Workers. Position Paper, April 1972. In *Transracial Adoption*, by Rita James Simon and Howard Alstein, pp. 50-52. New York: Wiley, 1977.

————. *Preserving Black Families: Research and Action Beyond the Rhetoric*. New York: National Association of Black Social Workers, 1986.

Neil, Elsbeth. "Contact After Adoption: The Role of Agencies in Making and Supporting Plans." *Adoption and Fostering* 26 (2002): 25-38.

Nelkin, D., and M. S. Lindee. *The DNA Mystique: The Gene As a Cultural Icon*. New York: Freeman, 1995.

Newmyer, R. Kent. *John Marshall and the Heroic Age of the Supreme Court*. Baton Rouge: Louisiana State University Press, 2001.

Norton, Arthur J., and Paul C. Glick. "One Parent Families: A Social and Economic Profile." *Family Relations* 35 (1986): 9-17.

Nygren, Anders. *Agape and Eros*. Philadelphia: Westminster, 1953.

Obama, Barack. *Dreams from My Father: A Story of Race and Inheritance*. New York: Times Books, 1995.

O'Connor, Stephen. *Orphan Trains: The Story of Charles Loring Brace and the Children He Saved and Failed*. Boston: Houghton Mifflin, 2001.

O'Donovan, Oliver. *Begotten or Made?* Oxford: Clarendon, 1984.

————. *Marriage and Permanence*. Bramcote, U.K.: Grove, 1978.

————. *Resurrection and Moral Order: An Outline for Evangelical Ethics*. Grand Rapids: Eerdmans, 1986.

Outka, Gene. *Agape: An Ethical Analysis*. New Haven: Yale University Press, 1972.

Paik, Sandra Z. "Adoption and Foster Parenting." *Georgetown Journal of Gender and the Law* 2, no. 2 (spring 2001): 369-79.

Paoli, Arturo. *Freedom to Be Free*. Maryknoll, N.Y.: Orbis, 1973.

Papke, David Ray. "Pondering Past Purposes: A Critical History of American Adoption Law." *West Virginia Law Review* 102 (1999): 459-76.

Parham, T. A. "Cycles of Psychological Nigrescence." *The Counseling Psychologist* 17, no. 2 (1989): 187-226.

Parks, Mary. "Are Married Parents Really Better for Children?" Center for Law and Social Policy: Policy Brief, May 2003, no. 3.

Patton, Sandra. *BirthMarks: Transracial Adoption in Contemporary America.* New York: New York University Press, 2000.

Peters, Marie Ferguson. "Parenting in Black Families with Young Children: A Historical Perspective." In *Black Families,* ed. Harriette Pipes McAdoo, second ed. Newbury Park, Calif.: Sage, 1988.

Paul VI. *Humanae vitae.* Official Vatican website, http://www.vatican.va/holy_father/paul_vi/encyclicals/documents/hf_p-vi_enc_25071968_humanae-vitae_en.html.

Pertman, Adam. *Adoption Nation: How the Adoption Revolution Is Transforming America.* New York: Basic, 2000.

Peters, Ted. *For the Love of Children: Genetic Technology and the Future of the Family.* Louisville, Ky.: Westminster/John Knox, 1996.

Pinker, Steven. *How the Mind Works.* New York: Norton, 1997.

Pius XI. *Casti Connubii.* In *The Papal Encyclicals,* edited by Claudia Carlen, pp. 391-414. Wilmington, N.C.: McGrath, 1981.

Pohl, Christine. *Making Room: Recovering Hospitality As a Christian Tradition.* Grand Rapids: Eerdmans, 1999.

Pontifical Council for the Family. "Children: Springtime of the Family and Society." Official Vatican website, www.vatican.va/roman_curia/pontifical_councils/family/documents/rc_pc_family_doc_20010329_jub-fam-conclusion_en.html.

Pope, Stephen J. *The Evolution of Altruism and the Ordering of Love.* Washington, D.C.: Georgetown University Press, 1994.

————. "Natural Law and Christian Ethics." In *Cambridge Companion to Christian Ethics,* edited by Robin Gill, pp. 77-95. Cambridge: Cambridge University Press, 2001.

Popenoe, David. *Life without Father.* New York: Free Press, 1996.

Popenoe, David, and Barbara DaFoe Whitehead. *The State of Our Unions.* Rutgers, N.J.: National Marriage Project, 1998-2000.

Portello, Jacqueline. "The Mother-Infant Attachment Process in Adoptive Families." *Canadian Journal of Counseling* 27 (1993): 177-90.

Posner, Richard A. "The Regulation of the Market in Adoptions." *Boston University Law Review* 67 (1987): 59-72.

Post, Stephen G. *More Lasting Unions: Christianity, the Family, and Society.* Grand Rapids: Eerdmans, 2000.

————. *Spheres of Love: Toward a New Ethics of the Family.* Dallas: Southern Methodist University Press, 1994.

————. *A Theory of Agape: On the Meaning of Christian Love.* Lewisburg, Pa.: Bucknell University Press, 1990.

Poster, Mark. "Foucault and the Problem of Self-Constitution." In *Foucault and the Critique of Institutions,* ed. John Caputo and Mark Yount. University Park, Pa.: Pennsylvania State University Press, 1993.

Potter, Daniel A. "MicroSort: Technology Separates the Boys from the Girls." MicroSort website, http://www.havingbabies.com/news/42_972_3897.CFM.

Presser, Stephen. *God and the Constitution: Towards a New Legal Theology.* London: Institute of United States Studies, University of London, 1998.

————. "The Historical Background of the American Law of Adoption." *Journal of Family Law* 11, no. 2 (1972): 443-516.

————. *Recapturing the Constitution: Race, Religion, and Abortion Reconsidered.* Washington, D.C.: Regnery, 1994.

————. "Some Realism about Atheism: Responses to 'The Godless Constitution.'" *Texas Review of Law and Policy* 1 (1997): 87-121.

Presser, Stephen B., and Jamil S. Zainaldin. *Law and Jurisprudence in American History: Cases and Materials.* Fourth ed. St. Paul, Minn.: West, 2000.

Pustilnik, Amanda C. "Private Ordering, Legal Ordering, and the Getting of Children: A Counterhistory of Adoption Law." *Yale Law and Policy Review* 20 (2002): 263-96.

Rahman, Qazi, and Glenn D. Wilson. "Born Gay? The Psychobiology of Human Sexual Orientation." *Personality and Individual Differences* 34, no. 8 (June 2003): 1335-1559.

Ramsey Colloquium. "The Homosexual Movement." *First Things* 41 (March 1994): 15-21.

Ramsey, Paul. *Fabricated Man: The Ethics of Genetic Control.* New Haven: Yale University Press, 1970.

————. *One Flesh: A Christian View of Sex within, outside and before Marriage.* Bramcote, U.K.: Grove, 1975.

Rawls, John. *Collected Papers.* Edited by Samuel Freedman. Cambridge, Mass.: Harvard University Press, 1999.

————. *Political Liberalism.* Paperback ed. New York: Columbia University Press, 1996.

————. *A Theory of Justice.* Cambridge, Mass.: Harvard University Press, 1971.

Reddy, Maureen T. *Crossing the Color Line: Race, Parenting, and Culture.* New Brunswick, N.J.: Rutgers University Press, 1994.

Reekie, Gail. *Measuring Immorality: Social Inquiry and the Problem of Legitimacy.* Cambridge: Cambridge University Press, 1998.

Rees, T. Entry for "Adoption." In *The International Standard Bible Encyclopedia,* edited by James Orr. Search God's Word website, http://www.searchgodsword.org/enc/isb/view.cgi?number=T221.

Reitz, Miriam, and Kenneth W. Watson. *Adoption and the Family System.* New York: Guilford, 1992.

Renvoize, Jean. *Incest: A Family Pattern.* New York: Routledge and Kegan Paul, 1982.

Richardson, Frank C., Blaine J. Fowers, and Charles B. Guignon. *Re-envisioning Psychology: Moral Dimensions of Theory and Practice.* San Francisco: Jossey-Bass, 1999.

Ricoeur, Paul. *Freud and Philosophy.* New Haven: Yale University Press, 1970.

———. "The Teleological and Deontological Structures of Action: Aristotle and/or Kant?" In *Contemporary French Philosophy,* edited by A. Phillips Griffiths, pp. 99-112. Cambridge: Cambridge University Press, 1987.

Ridley, Matt. *The Origins of Virtue: Human Instincts and the Evolution of Cooperation.* Harmondsworth, U.K.: Penguin, 1996.

Rifkind, Janet. "Toward a Theory of Law and Patriarchy." *Harvard Women's Law Journal* 3 (1980): 83-95.

Risman, Barbara J. "Can Men 'Mother'?: Life As a Single Father." *Family Relations* 35 (1986): 95-102.

Robertson, John A. *Children of Choice: Freedom and the New Reproductive Technologies.* Princeton, N.J.: Princeton University Press, 1994.

———. "In the Beginning: The Legal Status of Early Embryos." *Virginia Law Review* 76 (1990): 437-517.

Rogers, Carl. *Client-Centered Therapy.* Boston: Houghton Mifflin, 1951.

———. "A Theory of Therapy, Personality, and Interpersonal Relationships." In vol. 3 of *Psychology: A Study of a Science,* edited by Sigmund Koch, pp. 184-256. New York: McGraw-Hill, 1959.

Rogers, Eugene F., Jr. *Sexuality and the Christian Body: Their Way into the Triune God.* Oxford: Blackwell, 1999.

Root, Maria P. P. "The Multiracial Experience: Racial Borders As a Significant Frontier in Race Relations." In *The Multiracial Experience: Racial Borders As the New Frontier,* ed. Maria P. P. Root. Thousand Oaks, Calif.: Sage, 1996.

———, ed. *Racially Mixed People in America.* Newbury Park, Calif.: Sage, 1992.

Rorty, Richard. *Philosophy and the Mirror of Nature.* Princeton, N.J.: Princeton University Press, 1979.

———. "Religion As a Conversation-Stopper." In *Philosophy and Social Hope,* by Richard Rorty, pp. 168-74. London: Penguin, 1999.

———. "Religion in the Public Square: A Reconsideration." *Journal of Religious Ethics* 31, no. 1 (spring 2003): 141-49.

Rosaldo, Renato. *Culture and Truth: The Remaking of Social Analysis.* Second ed. Boston: Beacon, 1993.

Rose, Lionel. *The Massacre of the Innocents: Infanticide in Britain 1800-1939.* London: Routledge and Kegan Paul, 1986.

Rosenbaum, Sharyn. "Treatment Advances Help Couples Overcome Infertility." *Scripps News,* 1 July 2003. Scripps website, http://www.scrippshealth.org/90_1532.asp.

Rosenberg, Elinor B. *The Adoption Life Cycle: The Children and Their Families through the Years.* New York: Free Press, 1992.

Rosner, F., and M. Tendler. *Practical Medical Halacha.* New York: Rephael Society, Medical-Dental Section of the Association of Orthodox Jewish Scientists, 1980.

Rothman, David J. *Discovery of the Asylum: Social Order and Disorder in the New Republic.* Boston: Little, Brown, 1971.

Russell, Diana E. H., and Rebecca M. Bolen. *The Epidemic of Rape and Child Sexual Abuse in the United States.* Thousand Oaks, Calif.: Sage, 2000.

Ryan, Maura A. *The Ethics and Economics of Assisted Reproduction: The Cost of Longing.* Washington, D.C.: Georgetown University Press, 2001.

Sayers, Dorothy L. *The Mind of the Maker.* San Francisco: Harper Collins, 1987.

Scales-Trent, Judy. *Notes of a White Black Woman: Race, Color, Community.* University Park, Pa.: University of Pennsylvania Press, 1995.

Schaberg, Jane. *The Illegitimacy of Jesus: A Feminist Theological Interpretation of the Infancy Narratives.* San Francisco: Harper and Row, 1987.

Schacter, Melech. "Various Aspects of Adoption." *Journal of Halacha and Contemporary Society* 4 (1982): 93-110.

Schaeffer, Sylvan. "Child Custody: Halacha and the Secular Approach." *Journal of Halacha and Contemporary Society* 6 (1983): 33-39.

Schecter, Marshall D., and Doris Bertocci. "The Meaning of the Search." In *The Psychology of Adoption,* edited by David M. Brodzinsky and Marshall D. Schecter, pp. 62-90. New York: Oxford University Press, 1990.

Schmugge, Ludwig, and Béatrice Wiggenhauser, eds. *Illegitimität im Spätmittelalter.* Munich: R. Oldenbourg Verlag, 1994.

Shapiro, Yoram. "Artificial Insemination." *Noam* 1 (1957): 138-42.

Shochatman, Eliav. "The Essence of the Principles Used in Child Custody in Jewish Law." *Shenaton LeMishpat HaIvri* 5 (5738): 285-301.

Shulhan Arukh. Vilna: Ha-Almanah veha-Ahim Rom, 1896.

Silk, Joan. "Human Adoption in Evolutionary Perspective." *Human Nature* 1 (1990): 25-52.

Simon, Rita J., Howard Altstein, and Marygold S. Melli. *The Case for Transracial Adoption.* Washington, D.C.: American University Press, 1994.

Singer, Peter. *Rethinking Life and Death: The Collapse of Our Traditional Ethics.* Oxford: Oxford University Press, 1995.

Skinner, B. F. *Walden Two.* New York: MacMillan, 1948.

Smedes, Lewis. *Sex for Christians.* Grand Rapids: Eerdmans, 1976.

Smith, Steven D. *Foreordained Failure: The Quest for a Constitutional Principle of Religious Freedom.* New York: Oxford University Press, 1995.

"Snowflakes Embryo Adoption Program." Snowflakes website, http://www.snowflakes.org/.

Sober, Elliott, and David Sloane Wilson. *Unto Others: The Evolution and Psychology of Unselfish Behavior.* Cambridge, Mass.: Harvard University Press, 1998.

Solinger, Rickie. *Beggars and Choosers: How the Politics of Choice Shapes Adoption, Abortion, and Welfare in the United States.* New York: Hill and Wang, 2001.

Soloveitchik, Joseph B. *Family Redeemed: Essays on Family Relationships.* Edited by David Shatz and Joel Wolowelsky. New York: Meorot Harav Foundation, 2002.

Steinberg, Meyer. *Responsum on Problems of Adoption in Jewish Law.* Edited and translated by Maurice Rose. London: Office of the Chief Rabbi, 1969.

Steinberg, Moshe. "Change of Sex in Pseudo-hermaphroditism." *Assia* 1 (1976): 142-53.

Stolley, Kathy S. "Statistics on Adoption in the United States." *Future of Children: ADOPTION* 3, no. 1 (spring 1993): 26-42.

Stout, Jeffrey. *Democracy and Tradition.* Princeton, N.J.: Princeton University Press, 2004.

————. "How Charity Transcends the Culture Wars: Eugene Rogers and Others on Same-Sex Marriage." *Journal of Religious Ethics* 31, no. 2 (summer 2003): 169-80.

Sullivan, Ann, ed. *Issues in Gay and Lesbian Adoption.* Washington, D.C.: Child Welfare League of America, 1995.

Sutton, John R. "Bureaucrats and Entrepreneurs: Institutional Responses to Deviant Children in the United States, 1890-1920s." *American Journal of Sociology* 95, no. 6 (1990): 1367-1400.

Sweet, Craig A. Draft of presentation, "Abandoned Life: What Should Be Done with Abandoned Frozen Embryos?" DreamABaby website, http://www.dreamababy.com/download_files/Abandoned%20Embryos%20Presentation.pdf.

Theyssen, David L. "Balancing Interests in Frozen Embryo Disputes: Is Adoption Really a Reasonable Alternative?" *Indiana Law Journal* 74 (1999): 711-38.

Thomas, Mason P. "Child Abuse and Neglect. Part I: Historical Overview, Legal Matrix, and Social Perspectives." *North Carolina Law Review* 50 (1972): 293-349.

Thompson, Becky, and Santeega Tyagi, eds. *Names We Call Home: Autobiography on Racial Identity.* New York: Routledge: 1996.

Thompson, Ross A. "Sensitive Periods in Attachment?" In *Critical Thinking about Critical Periods,* edited by Donald Bail, pp. 83-106. Baltimore: Paul H. Brooks, 2001.

Tierney, Brian. *Medieval Poor Law: A Sketch of Canonical Theory and Its Application in England.* Berkeley: University of California Press, 1959.

Tillich, Paul. "The Impact of Pastoral Psychology on Theological Thought." *Pastoral Psychology* 2, no. 101 (February 1960): 17-23.

Trivers, Robert. "The Evolution of Reciprocal Altruism." *Quarterly Review of Biology* 46 (1971): 35-57.

United States Census. *Adopted Children and Stepchildren, 2000.* Washington, D.C., August 2003.

Voss, Richard. "A Sociological Analysis and Theological Reflection on Adoption Services in Catholic Charities Agencies." *Social Work* 11, no. 1 (1985): 32-43.

Waal, Frans de. *Good Natured: The Origins of Right and Wrong in Humans and Other Animals.* Cambridge, Mass.: Harvard University Press, 1996.

Waldenberg, E. "Test Tube Infertilization." *Sefer Asya* 5 (1986): 84-92.

Waldmann, Mitchell. *American Jurisprudence Adoption.* Second ed. Vol. 2. St. Paul, Minn.: West, 2003.

Wallerstein, Judith, Julia Lewis, and Sandra Blakeslee. *The Unexpected Legacy of Divorce.* New York: Hyperion, 2000.

Walton, Frederick Parker. *Historical Introduction to the Roman Law.* Fourth ed. Rev. Edinburgh: W. Green and Son, 1920.

Warburg, Ronald. "Child Custody: A Comparative Analysis." *Israel Law Review* 14 (1978): 480-503.

Waters, Brent. "Does the Human Embryo Have a Moral Status?" In *God and the Embryo: Religious Perspectives on the Debate over Stem Cells and Cloning,* edited by Brent Waters and Ronald Cole-Turner. Washington, D.C.: Georgetown University Press, 2003.

————. *Reproductive Technology: Toward a Theology of Procreative Stewardship.* Cleveland: Pilgrim, 2001.

————. "Welcoming Children into Our Homes: A Theological Reflection on Adoption." *Scottish Journal of Theology* 55, no. 4 (2002): 424-37.

Watkins, Mary, and Susan Fisher. *Talking with Young Children about Adoption.* New Haven: Yale University Press, 1993.

Watson, John Broadus. "What the Nursery Has to Say about Instincts." In *Psychologies of 1925,* edited by Carl Murchison, pp. 1-34. Worcester, Mass.: Clark University Press, 1926.

Watson, John Broadus, and Rosalie Raynor Watson. *The Psychological Care of the Infant and Child.* New York: Norton, 1928.

Watson, Kenneth W. "Bonding and Attachment in Adoption: Towards Better Understanding and Useful Definitions." *Marriage and Family Review* 24 (1997): 159-73.

Weber, Max. *The Protestant Ethic and the Spirit of Capitalism.* New York: Charles Scribner's Sons, 1958.

Werpehowski, William. "The Vocation of Parenthood: A Response to Stephen Post." *Journal of Religious Ethics* 25, no. 1 (spring 1997): 177-82.

Whitmore, William H. *The Law of Adoption.* Albany, N.Y.: J. Munsell, 1876.

Williams, Gregory Howard. *Life on the Color Line: The True Story of a White Boy Who Discovered He Was Black.* New York: Dutton, 1995.

Wilson, Edward O. *On Human Nature.* Cambridge, Mass.: Harvard University Press, 1978.

Wilson, James Q. *The Moral Sense.* New York: Free Press, 1993.

Winant, Howard. *Racial Conditions: Politics, Theory, Comparisons.* Minneapolis: University of Minnesota Press, 1994.

Winkler, Robin C., Dirck W. Brown, Margaret van Keppel, and Amy Blanchard. *Clinical Practice in Adoption.* New York: Pergamon, 1988.

Witte, John, Jr. *From Sacrament to Contract: Marriage, Religion, and Law in the Western Tradition.* Louisville, Ky.: Westminster/John Knox, 1997.

———. "God's Joust, God's Justice: An Illustration from the History of Marriage Law." In *Christian Perspectives on Legal Thought,* edited by Michael W. McConnell, Robert F. Cochran Jr., and Angela C. Carmella, pp. 406-25. New Haven: Yale University Press, 2001.

———. *Law and Protestantism: The Legal Teachings of the Lutheran Reformation.* Cambridge: Cambridge University Press, 2002.

Wolterstorff, Nicholas. "The Role of Religion in Decision and Discussion of Political Issues." In *Religion in the Public Square: The Place of Religious Convictions in Political Debate,* by Robert Audi and Nicholas Wolterstorff, pp. 67-120. Lanham, Md.: Rowman and Littlefield, 1997.

Woodhouse, Barbara Bennett. "The Constitutionalization of Children's Rights: Incorporating Emerging Human Rights into Constitutional Doctrine." *University of Pennsylvania Journal of Constitutional Law* 2, no. 1 (December 1999). University of Pennsylvania Law website, http://www.law.upenn.edu/journals/conlaw/issues/vol2/num1/woodhouse/node5_tf.html.

Wong, Sau-ling C. "Diverted Mothering: Representations of Caregivers of Color in the Age of 'Multiculturalism'." In *Mothering: Ideology, Experience, and Agency,* ed. Evelyn Nakano Glenn, Grace Change, and Linda Rennie Forcey. New York: Routledge, 1994.

Wright, Richard. *Black Boy (American Hunger): A Record of Childhood and Youth.* New York: Harper Perennial Classics, 1998.

Wright, Robert. *The Moral Animal.* New York: Pantheon, 1994.

Wrobel, Gretchen Miller, Susan Ayers-Lopez, Harold D. Grotevant, Ruth G. McRoy, and Meredith Friedrick. "Openness in Adoption and the Level of Child Participation." *Child Development* 67 (1996): 2358-74.

Wrobel, Gretchen Miller, and Harold D. Grotevant. "Adoption." In *Children's Needs II: Development, Problems, and Alternatives,* edited by George G. Bear, Kathleen M. Minke, and Alex Thomas, pp. 287-98. Bethesda, Md.: National Association of School Psychologists, 1997.

Wrobel, Gretchen M., Harold D. Grotevant, Jerica Berge, Tai Mendenhall, and Ruth G. McRoy. "Contact in Adoption: The Experience of American Adoptive Families." *Adoption and Fostering* 27 (2003): 57-67.

Wrobel, Gretchen Miller, Harold D. Grotevant, and Ruth G. McRoy. "Adolescent Search for Birthparents: Who Moves Forward?" *Journal of Adolescent Research* 19 (2004): 132-51.

Wrobel, Gretchen Miller, Julie K. Kohler, Harold D. Grotevant, and Ruth G. McRoy. "The Family Adoption Communication Model (FAC): Identifying Pathways of Adoption-Related Communication," *Adoption Quarterly* 7, no. 2 (2003): 53-84.

Zack, Naomi, ed. *American Mixed Race: The Culture of Microdiveristy.* Lanham, Md.: Rowman and Littlefield, 1995.

Zainaldin, Jamil S. "The Emergence of a Modern American Family Law: Child Custody, Adoption, and the Courts, 1796-1851." *Northwestern University Law Review* 73 (1979): 1038-89.

Zingo, Martha T., and Kevin E. Early. *Nameless Persons: Legal Discrimination against Non-Marital Children in the United States.* Westport, Conn.: Praeger, 1994.

Contributors

Don S. Browning is Alexander Campbell Professor of Religious Ethics and the Social Sciences, Divinity School, University of Chicago, Emeritus. From 1991 to 2003, he directed the Religion, Culture, and Family Project at the University of Chicago. His numerous publications include *From Culture Wars to Common Ground: Religion and the American Family Debate,* which he co-authored, and *Marriage and Modernization: How Globalization Threatens Marriage and What to Do about It.*

Michael J. Broyde is professor of law at Emory University and the academic director of the Law and Religion program. He has published numerous articles and books on matters of Jewish law, including *The Pursuit of Justice: A Jewish Perspective on Practicing Law* and *Marriage and Family in Judaism: The Past, Present and Future.*

Lisa Sowle Cahill is the J. Donald Monan Professor of Theology at Boston College. She is the author of *Family: A Christian Social Perspective, Sex, Gender, and Christian Ethics,* and *Theological Bioethics: Participation, Justice, and Change,* as well as other books and articles. She and her husband, Larry Cahill, are the parents of five young-adult children, three of whom were adopted from Thailand.

Marcie Jackson will graduate from Rice University in 2006 with a B.A. in English and a teaching certificate. Her family has cared for foster children since she was five years old, and Marcie looks forward to becoming a foster parent herself some day. She composed her contribution to this project when she was sixteen, inspired by her foster sister, Destiny Marie.

Timothy P. Jackson is Associate Professor of Christian Ethics at the Candler School of Theology at Emory University in Atlanta, Georgia. He is also a Senior Fellow at the Center for the Interdisciplinary Study of Religion at Emory. He is the author of *The Priority of Love: Christian Charity and Social Justice* and *Love Disconsoled: Meditations on Christian Charity*.

Gilbert Meilaender holds the Phyllis and Richard Duesenberg Chair in Christian Ethics at Valparaiso University. Among his books are *Body, Soul, and Bioethics* and *Working: Its Meaning and Its Limits*.

John C. Mayoue is a graduate of Emory University Law School and practices in complex family law matters in Atlanta, Georgia. He is listed in *Best Lawyers in America,* is a Fellow in the American Academy of Matrimonial Lawyers, and is a member of the International Network of Boutique Law Firms. He is the author of *Balancing Competing Interests in Family Law* and *Southern Divorce,* as well as of numerous nationally published articles on family law.

Sandra Patton-Imani is Assistant Professor of American Studies in the Department for the Study of Culture and Society at Drake University. She is the author of *BirthMarks: Transracial Adoption in Contemporary America* and has published numerous essays on adoption, race, gender, family, and welfare. She is currently working on her next book, *Ghosts in the Tree: Adoption and the Specter of Choice,* an interdisciplinary ethnographic study of searches and reunions among adoptees and birthmothers.

Stephen G. Post is the President of the Institute for Research on Unlimited Love, which is supported by the John Templeton Foundation. He is also a professor in the Department of Bioethics, School of Medicine, Case Western Reserve University. His many books include *More Lasting Unions: Christianity, the Family, and Society* and *Spheres of Love: Toward a New Ethics of the Family*.

Stephen B. Presser is the Raoul Berger Professor of Legal History at Northwestern University School of Law. He is a legal historian and expert on shareholder liability for corporate debts. He holds a joint appointment with Northwestern's J. L. Kellogg Graduate School of Management and also teaches in Northwestern's history department. His books include *Recapturing the Constitution, Law and Jurisprudence in American History* (with Jamil S. Zainaldin), and *An Introduction to the Law of Business Organizations*.

Ann M. Stanton is a professor at the Arizona State University College of Law. She has served on the Arizona Judicial Council Committee on Child Support and Family Law, Arizona's Task Force on Juvenile Corrections, the Arizona State Board of Behavioral Health Examiners, the American Psychological Association's Committee on Legal Issues, and as chair of the Arizona Commission on Child Support Enforcement. Among her books are *When Mothers Go to Jail* and *Family Law: Cases, Text, Problems* (with Ira Mark Ellman and Paul M. Kurtz).

Jeffrey Stout is professor of religion at Princeton University. His books include *Democracy and Tradition* and *Ethics after Babel: The Languages of Morals and Their Discontents.* He will serve as president of the American Academy of Religion in 2007.

Mary Stewart Van Leeuwen is professor of psychology and philosophy at Eastern University in St. Davids, Pennsylvania. Her recent books include *My Brother's Keeper: What the Social Sciences Do (and Don't) Tell Us about Masculinity* and a volume edited with Don Browning and David Blankenhorn entitled *Does Christianity Teach Male Headship?*

Brent Waters is Director of the Jerre L. and Mary Joy Stead Center for Ethics and Values, and Associate Professor of Christian Social Ethics at Garrett-Evangelical Theological Seminary, Evanston, Illinois. He is the author of a number of books, including *From Human to Posthuman: Christian Theology and Technology in a Postmodern World* and *Reproductive Technology: Towards a Theology of Procreative Stewardship,* and he has written numerous articles and lectured extensively on the relationship among theology, ethics, and technology.

John Witte, Jr., is Jonas Robitscher Professor of Law and Director of the Center for the Study of Law and Religion at Emory University. A specialist in legal history, religious liberty, and marriage and family, he has published 120 articles and sixteen books, including *From Sacrament to Contract: Marriage, Religion and Law in the Western Tradition* and *Law and Protestantism: The Legal Teachings of the Lutheran Reformation.*

Gretchen Miller Wrobel is professor of psychology at Bethel University in St. Paul, Minnesota. Dr. Wrobel has published on issues related to children's adjustment to adoption and adoptive family communication, and has been a presenter on those issues at national and international professional conferences. Her research interests include child and adolescent adjustment to adoption, birth and adoptive family connections, and communication about adoption in families. Dr. Wrobel serves as editor of the journal *Adoption Quarterly*.

Index